# CAMBRIDGE GREEK AND LATIN CLASSICS

GENERAL EDITORS

E. J. KENNEY
*Fellow of Peterhouse, Cambridge*

AND

MRS P. E. EASTERLING
*Fellow of Newnham College, Cambridge*

# SOPHOCLES

# ELECTRA

EDITED BY

## J. H. KELLS

*Reader in Greek and Latin*
*University College London*

The right of the
University of Cambridge
to print and sell
all manner of books
was granted by
Henry VIII in 1534.
The University has printed
and published continuously
since 1584.

## CAMBRIDGE UNIVERSITY PRESS

CAMBRIDGE

NEW YORK    PORT CHESTER

MELBOURNE    SYDNEY

Published by the Press Syndicate of the University of Cambridge
The Pitt Building, Trumpington Street, Cambridge CB2 1RP
40 West 20th Street, New York, NY 10011, USA
10 Stamford Road, Oakleigh, Melbourne 3166, Australia

First published 1973
Reprinted 1985, 1987, 1989

Printed in Great Britain at the
University Press, Cambridge

Library of Congress catalogue card number: 73–182028

ISBN 0 521 08461 x hard covers
ISBN 0 521 09796 7  paperback

# CONTENTS

It is not prudent to oppose perfidy to perfidy – the most efficient weapon with which men can encounter falsehood is truth.          MACAULAY

# PREFACE

I differ at a good many points in this edition of Sophocles' *Electra* from many, and at times all, of my predecessors. Let me say, then, to begin with, how much I am sensible of owing to them (particularly to Jebb) and how much my admiration for them has grown as I proceeded. I have learnt from them to correct several sheer misconceptions with which I started out. Where I have disagreed, it is because reflection has not led me to alter my opinion.

Coming to contemporaries, I gratefully acknowledge the help I have received from the following: Professor T. B. L. Webster, who first suggested that I should edit the *Electra* in this series, and who placed at my disposal a number of papers of his wife's and other scholars'; Professors E. W. Handley, O. Skutsch, and E. G. Turner, who all generously encouraged me and helped in various ways to limit or arrange my teaching schedule so that I could give sufficient time to the *Electra*; all my friends and colleagues (including all the above, and also Miss M. L. Cunningham and Professor R. P. Winnington-Ingram), who helped me by discussion to clarify my views on the play; Miss Margaret Packer of the London Institute of Classical Studies, and Miss Frances Mills, Secretary to the Greek Department of University College London, who between them shared the task of typing and re-typing my manuscript. For the final form I am greatly indebted to the two general editors. To Mrs P. E. Easterling I cannot begin to express my gratitude. She read through the original version with devoted care and attention, corrected mistakes, made many constructive suggestions, and relieved me of much of the tedious detail of editorship; Mr E. J. Kenney as second reader also helped me greatly. So did Dr Jeremy Mynott, who showed me how to compress and reduce a script which in the end proved too long for the uses for which it was intended. Needless to say, none of those mentioned is responsible for the views I have expressed. I have also to thank the Henry Brown Fund for a substantial grant towards the publication.

I am grateful to the Oxford University Press for permission to adopt the standard Oxford Text of A. C. Pearson, with some modifications. A list of passages in which this edition differs from Pearson's text will be found on page 255. Where the first person is used in the *apparatus criticus*, it refers to Pearson, not to myself.

A word finally on my translations of certain passages of the Greek: I am aware that an Anglo-Irish idiom is apparent in them. This is deliberate, particularly in the more emotional passages, where I believe that Anglo-Irish is more faithful to the tone of the Greek.

Since writing the above I have to acknowledge a further considerable debt – to the University Printing House reader.

*December 1971*

J. H. KELLS

# INTRODUCTION

## 1. THE PLAY

Sophocles' *Electra* is undoubtedly one of the world's greatest plays. Even in the context of the other two remarkable tragedies written on the same subject by the two other great dramatists of the fifth century, it stands out with a peculiar excellence. From beginning to end it moves with a sense of inevitability, characteristic of Sophocles' best work and particularly his later work. Not a line, not a word is misplaced or (apart from stylistic ornament) superfluous. It is the work, not merely of a great artist, but of an inspired artist. The inspiration shows itself in the strong feeling which the play in places arouses in reader or audience, feeling whose origin or nature may be obscure to the percipient. The recognition-scene between Electra and Orestes (lines 1098–1231) is one of the most moving in literature, and cannot be read by a sensitive person or performed by accomplished actors without arousing the strongest emotion.

Yet this play has caused the greatest difficulty to critics. How are we to understand the stealthy killing of a mother[1] and (less important, perhaps) her lover and accomplice by the woman's son and daughter? We should remember here that the other two great tragedians had already (according to the usual view of the relative dates of the three plays)[2]

---

[1] It should be noted that, besides the *Electra*, Sophocles wrote at least two other tragedies concerned with an act of matricide (namely, the killing of Amphiaraus' wife, Eriphyle, by her son Alcmeon in revenge for her betrayal of his father into joining the fatal expedition of the Seven against Thebes). These were the *Epigoni* and the *Alcmeon*. They have not survived except in the shape of a few tantalising fragments. This much of the story is clear: that Alcmeon, after and consequent upon the matricide, was pursued and driven mad by the Furies; that *even after ritual purification* he continued to suffer bouts of madness; that he died a violent death in the course of the chain of intrigue which followed the matricide. These facts scarcely lend support to either of the two conventional views of the *Electra* described below, which assert that Sophocles *in it* either condoned or justified the killing of Clytaemnestra.

[2] The *Choephori* was produced (as the second part of the *Oresteia* trilogy) in 458 B.C. Euripides' *Electra* is generally thought to be prior to Sophocles' and

implied contradictory views of the rights and wrongs of the ancient story. Aeschylus in the *Choephori* had justified the matricide, but only in a certain context – only as a link in a chain (typically Aeschylean) of grim events leading to the evolution of civilised institutions. Euripides, on the contrary, denounced it, making his Orestes reproach Apollo, who commanded the matricide, 'Apollo, it was a mighty piece of ignorance that you oracled' (ὦ Φοῖβε, πολλήν γ' ἀμαθίαν ἐθέσπισας, Eur. *El.* 971), and Apollo's fellow-divinities, the Dioscuri, support this judgment in the epilogue to the play, 'wise though he is, it was not wise advice he offered you' (σοφὸς δ' ὢν οὐκ ἔχρησέ σοι σοφά, 1246). Compared with these other two dramatists, whose drift is manifest, Sophocles has in a curious but characteristic way withdrawn his meaning from open scrutiny. And thus he has made it possible for different scholars to come to quite opposite views as to the play's meaning, and the tone in which it is to be read or acted. There are also certain features which are peculiar to the Sophoclean play and set it aside from the other two. Why, for instance, is the pronouncement of Apollo's oracle at Delphi sanctioning (or appearing to sanction) the matricide, the pronouncement which is so central to both the other plays[1] and (one must assume) to the traditional story, dealt with so swiftly and almost cursorily at the very opening of the play? Why in this play alone does Orestes not *hesitate* before proceeding to the killing of his mother? Why has Sophocles *reversed the order* of the killings (Aegisthus being killed before Clytaemnestra in both the other plays, but Clytaemnestra before Aegisthus in Sophocles)? Finally and most strikingly, what has happened in Sophocles to the Furies, who traditionally pursued and persecuted Orestes for the killing of his mother? These are prominent both in Aeschylus and Euripides. Sophocles' play not merely omits them, but it ends with a note of apparent finality which seems to preclude them from any imagined sequel.

Broadly, three different types of answer have been given to these questions. The first (which we may call the 'amoral' theory) is that

---

is now usually dated about 418: see T. B. L. Webster *The tragedies of Euripides* (1967) 2f. and 143f., A. M. Dale, ed. of Euripides' *Helen* (1967) xxivff. Miss Dale argues (*ib.* note to 1050ff.) that Sophocles' *Electra* was written almost immediately before Euripides' *Helen*, i.e. about 413 (see the note to lines 59f. of this play).     [1] Cf. Aesch. *Cho.* 269ff.; Eur. *El.* 87 and 973.

Sophocles was simply not interested in the ethical or legalistic aspects of the story. His aim was to produce a brilliant, extrovert narrative, in the Homeric manner, of the events of Orestes' home-coming. Hence he has omitted all the ambiguities and dubieties of the traditional story, all the heart-searchings, all the *dark* side of Orestes' act, and above all the haunting Furies. His version is a thrilling piece of epic saga, with a striking centrepiece in the Paedagogus' report of the fictitious chariot-race in which Orestes is reported to have lost his life (Homeric in style, and indeed clearly related closely to the account of the chariot-race in *Iliad* 23. 287ff.). This is the theory that Jebb, for example, and J. D. Denniston mainly relied upon (cf. the Introduction to D.'s edition of Euripides' *Electra*). But it is noticeable that neither of these two fine scholars was altogether happy with it. Thus Jebb (Introduction xli) points out that Orestes would, according to Greek ideas then current with regard to homicide, be *polluted* by his mother's murder, and that the audience would have expected the Furies to appear *as the visible sign* of this pollution.

The second theory (which we may call the 'justificatory') argues that the play, so far from avoiding the moral issue of the matricide, actually makes it a central issue, and expresses downright approval of it. Having perhaps seen Euripides' play in the theatre with its attack on Apollo for having commanded the matricide, Sophocles, a staunch supporter of established religion and conventional morality, reacted by composing a work which would defend Apollo against Euripides' impious attack, re-assert the Aeschylean version, and show that the killing of Clytaemnestra and Aegisthus was both necessary and fully justified.[1] Accordingly, his Clytaemnestra is even more villainous and unredeemed than the Clytaemnestra of the other versions. His Orestes does not hesitate before killing her, because (quite simply) there is nothing for an honest son to hesitate about. And the Furies are omitted, boldly, for the same reason: why have Furies when no crime demanding punishment has been committed? But Sophocles has cleverly switched the order of the killings, in order to forestall the expectations of the audience (reared on the traditional tale). Had Clytaemnestra been killed at the end of the play, there would have been an inconvenient pause during which the audience

---

[1] Cf. T. B. L. Webster, *The tragedies of Euripides* 15, *Sophocles²* 195. Webster is probably the most insistent modern defender of the justificatory theory.

would have had time to expect the onset of the Furies. As it is, after Clytaemnestra's murder, our attention is immediately distracted by the approaching Aegisthus, and then after Aegisthus' death there is no occasion for the Furies.[1]

Most modern critics, with occasional doubts or reservations, have followed one or other of the above theories, or some variety or admixture of them. But there is a third theory, which may be called the 'ironic', and which is only to be found fully and explicitly expressed in an article by J. T. Sheppard (*C.R.* 41 (1927) 2–9). Sheppard thought that Sophocles no more approved or condoned the cold-blooded act of matricide than did Euripides, and that it was a travesty of the play to interpret it in either of these senses. Accordingly, he called his article '*In defence* of Sophocles' (my italics). Ranging Sophocles with Euripides as a *critic* of the matricide, he claimed his approach was in fact more subtle and less direct than Euripides': it is by ironic innuendo, by reading between the lines, that we see the act to be as odious as it is. It would of course be contrary to all we know of Sophocles to make him critical also of Apollo, whose authorisation of the matricide was a cardinal factor in the traditional story and has perhaps most influenced modern critics who see the matricide as justified. But Sheppard suggested that Apollo's response in Sophocles is not a true authorisation – because of the peculiar way in which Orestes framed his question: Orestes asked '*How* should I be avenged?' not '*Should* I be avenged?' (*El.* 37). In other words, he approached the oracle with his mind already made up on the basic issue, 'Should I kill my mother?' In such circumstances, Sheppard argued, the impious (if impious it was) intent already existed in the mind of the consultant; and it was the part of the oracle not merely not to try to dissuade him from it, but actually to encourage him to pursue it – in order that he might the sooner complete his own destruction! Sheppard cites a number of cases of similarly deceptive replies by Delphi in answer to leading questions.

Having thus cast suspicion upon Orestes' oracular mandate, Sheppard pointed to several passages which suggest difficulties and even disaster, not glory, for Orestes. Thus, when he comes out of the palace (1422 ff.), his sword dripping with his mother's blood, and

---

[1] I suggest a quite different reason for the divergence in my note to lines 1368f. of the play.

Electra asks him and Pylades, 'How are things with you?', he replies, 'Things in the house are well – *if Apollo oracled well*.' The question, thus poised dramatically, seems both to suggest a doubt in the speaker's mind and to create one in the audience's. If Sophocles was quite sure, and meant his audience to be quite sure, that the matricide was just and proper, why does he *propose* an 'if' at this critical stage? Was that not to weaken the case? Again, as Aegisthus is led into the palace to his death (a specially vindictive killing, be it noted, cf. 1504), he asks Orestes why, if the deed is καλόν ('good' or 'honourable'), he *needs the dark* in which to do it (1493f.). Orestes has no answer, except to express his intention that Aegisthus shall die 'in the same place' as Agamemnon. Aegisthus further alludes to 'this day's griefs of Pelops' clan – *and tomorrow's*' (1498). Again, Orestes is given no sufficient answer by the playwright.

Sheppard's reading of the play has been almost universally dismissed or ignored by modern critics. The reasons given by those who dismiss it are mainly two: first, that it is 'too subtle' (cf. H. J. Rose, *Greek mythology*, ch. 4, n. 36); second, that it would not have been clear to the audience, who would have expected the 'ordinary' version of the story: if Sophocles had meant to convey anything of the kind suggested by Sheppard, he would have had to express it in a much more explicit way.[1]

Perhaps the first duty of an editor introducing so controversial a play is to point out that there is (in the very nature of the case) no final answer to such questions. A work of art must speak for itself. And each person who experiences it must form his own views, assess his own reactions. Such works of art have a kind of built-in ambiguity, being not so much imitations of life as sources of life, producing fresh intimations in each new reader.

This said, I may also express my own belief that Sheppard's reading of the play has been very improperly neglected. The 'answers' which have been given to it are both trivial and ambivalent. It is illogical to say that an ancient tragedian could not depart from the 'ordinary' version of a story, when *ex hypothesi* that very same playwright has already departed from it greatly by omitting a large part of that story, namely the Furies. And is it not presumptuous to legislate on permis-

---

[1] Cf. C. M. Bowra, *Sophoclean tragedy* (1944) 216f.; H. Friis Johansen in 'Die Elektra des Sophokles', *Classica et Mediaevalia* 25 (1964) 9.

sible degrees of subtlety in an *ancient Greek* play, particularly when the
playwright is one so famous for his subtlety that he could (in the words
of the anonymous ancient *Life of Sophocles* 21) 'depict a whole character
from a single half-line or phrase'? Orestes' reference to the oracle is
fleeting (too fleeting). But the fleeting words are clear enough indica-
tion that Orestes did ask the wrong question of the oracle. And did
that not matter to Sophocles (Sophocles the pious, the punctilious),
whereas it mattered to Socrates (cf. Xen. *Anab.* 3. 2)? A fragment of a
lost play of Sophocles, 'and I am well aware that the god is such: to
wise men ever a riddler in oracles; to *fools* a blunt, direct instructor'
(καὶ τὸν θεὸν τοιοῦτον ἐξεπίσταμαι, | σοφοῖς μὲν αἰνικτῆρα θεσφάτων
ἀεί, | σκαιοῖς δὲ φαῦλον κἄν βραχεῖ διδάσκαλον, fr. 771), makes it clear
that Sophocles was well aware of the point of principle involved.
Sophocles' Orestes thought the oracle could be dealt with bluntly; he
regarded it as φαῦλος κἄν βραχεῖ διδάσκαλος. Therefore he is not
'wise', but (to that extent) a fool. But there is more characterisation
of Orestes to follow. Outlining to the Paedagogus the stratagem by
which he must introduce himself into the palace and tell a lying tale
of his (Orestes') death, and evidently feeling some uneasiness at this
proceeding, he reassures himself, 'I imagine that nothing that you *say*,
provided that it brings advantage, is objectionable' (61). It is an extra-
ordinary statement, and yet it has passed practically unnoticed by
commentators.[1] It is so unprincipled. And the unscrupulousness is of
a familiar kind, expressed in standard terms. Again and again, in
Greek literature of the age of Sophocles, when κέρδος ('gain' or
'profit') is juxtaposed with a moral value (ἀγαθόν, καλόν, δίκαιον,
and so on), it is, practically proverbially, represented as a sign of
*baseness* to prefer κέρδος to what is in principle good and honourable.
See, for example, the words of the time-serving Odysseus in Sophocles,
*Philoctetes* (111): ὅταν τι δρᾷς ἐς κέρδος, οὐκ ὀκνεῖν πρέπει ('whenever
one does something which leads to profit, one should not hesitate',
ὀκνεῖν of moral scruple): these words of Odysseus, of whose principles
the *Philoctetes* amounts to a rebuttal, are a mere variation on Orestes'.[2]

[1] Of the whole speech C. H. Whitman (*Sophocles* (1951) 155) says, 'In a
few lines Orestes is depicted, chivalrous and noble, *with no problem and
no special dramatic interest*' (my italics).
[2] See also Aesch. *Ag.* 342, Soph. *Aj.* 1349, *Ant.* 310ff., *O.T.* 594f., 889.
Compare Soph. fr. 28 τοιαῦτά τοί σοι πρὸς χάριν τε κοὐ βίᾳ | λέγω· σὺ δ'

However, the wording of the oracular consultation and the preliminary characterisation of Orestes are by no means the essential reason for disagreeing with those who believe that the *Electra* either justifies or condones the matricide. I believe that these things are crucial, but only as the earliest of a series of subtle but forceful dramatic touches which all add up to the same effect: and that effect, if I am not mistaken, amounts to a kind of suspended abhorrence of the act itself, of sustained tragic pity that it should have been necessary or have come about.

To me, the very centre of the play is the moment when Clytaemnestra, having heard the report of her son's death in glory at the Pythian Games, suddenly goes back on everything she has so far stood for, and bursts out 'O god! What am I to say of these things? Am I to call them fortunate, or...terrible but beneficial? I am in a sad state if I have to save my life by the sufferings of my own flesh and blood!' (766–8), and again 'It is a queer thing to be a mother. Even when you suffer despite at their hands, you cannot hate those you bore' (770–1). It seems astonishing to me that editors and critics have almost all failed to appreciate the tragic import of these lines, the enormous reversal that they constitute in the stage-action, with its far-reaching significance for the play's total meaning. What the critics almost all do is to recognise that Clytaemnestra exhibits 'some maternal feeling' for Orestes; but they then proceed to discount it by arguing that there is *too little of it*, and that, after all, she resumes her original attitude at 773ff. Here again (as with Orestes' consultation of the oracle) the fallacy lies in the statistical character of the approach. Clytaemnestra expresses her maternal grief in not many lines. Therefore it does not matter much! Also, she goes back upon it: but no one points out that the long speech in which she does so is poetry of so intense and tragic a quality that it makes her, inevitably, a *commanding and tragic figure*. Why did Sophocles put such words into her mouth, if he meant her to be a repellent, minor figure? In fact, he

αὐτὸς ὥσπερ οἱ σοφοὶ τὰ μὲν | δίκαι᾿ ἐπαίνει, τοῦ δὲ κερδαίνειν ἔχου 'Pay lip-service to Justice, but actually cling to Gain!' (notice that Orestes immediately refers to οἱ σοφοί (62)); fr. 833 τὸ κέρδος ἡδύ, κἄν ἀπὸ ψευδῶν ἴῃ (Pearson remarks on the 'discreditable sentiment' and quotes *Electra* 61 (along with other parallels), but without drawing any inference about Orestes); fr. 834 οὐκ ἐξάγουσι καρπὸν οἱ ψευδεῖς λόγοι.

didn't. And in this scene he subtly transfers our sympathy to her. It is a kind of reversal which is not infrequent in Sophocles as well as Euripides,[1] and it illustrates the fact that the dramatist who knows his job is not a moralist with a thesis, but an artist who lays bare the realities of the human heart overlaid as they may be by the accidents of time and circumstance.

Yet a thesis may help in the understanding of a work of art. Let me now put the following hypothesis before the reader. Let us suppose that Sophocles set out to write his play with the following ideas in mind:

'I live in a society which makes vengeance and vindictiveness a guiding principle of conduct.[2] Euripides has written many fine plays which turn, at their most critical moments, on the application of this ethic.[3] I myself have represented it in my *Ajax* and *Antigone* in that form in which it concerns the denial of burial to the dead enemy (that being merely a prolongation of hatred into death itself – "to kill the dead twice over", τὸν θανόντ' ἐπικτανεῖν, as Teiresias describes it (*Ant.* 1030)). I have made my finest heroine,

[1] Cf. (for Sophocles) the treatment of Polynices in the *Oedipus Coloneus*: denounced as a worthless rascal by Oedipus, he is shown independently, in the farewell-scene with Antigone, as going bravely to a doom which he knows is inevitable, and as feeling disinterested love for his sisters (*O.C.* 1399ff.). (It is as if the dramatist were trying deliberately to correct the impression which his own character-creation, Oedipus, has given.) And (for Euripides) cf. the ending of the *Hecuba*: the villain Polymestor turns on his captors (Agamemnon and Hecuba) and foretells (with prophetic insight) *their* deaths (*Hec.* 1257ff.). We are made to feel that the tables are suddenly and surprisingly turned; that they will in turn pay for the act of revenge that they have perpetrated on him.

[2] From the earliest historical times Greeks (like many peoples today) were taught popularly and proverbially to 'love and aid their friends and *hate and injure their enemies*': cf. Solon fr. 1. 5; Theognis 363–4; Pindar *Pyth.* 2.83f.; Plato *Meno* 71e; *Crito* 49b. In Plato's *Republic* 'doing harm to one's enemies' is offered as a definition of 'Justice' (*Rep.* 1.332b), and this conception is there for the first time analysed and shown to be philosophically untenable (*ib.* 334b ff.).

[3] The classical instance is Euripides' Medea. She would not have killed her children but for her desire to appear βαρεῖαν ἐχθροῖς καὶ φίλοισιν εὐμενῆ (*Med.* 807ff.). Cf. also Aeschylus *Ag.* 1377f., *Cho.* 122f.; Sophocles *Ant.* 641ff. (it can scarcely be held that the speaker, Creon, is right!), *O.C.* 1189f. (the ethic contradicted); Euripides *Andr.* 437f., *Hipp.* 48ff., *Tro.* 64ff., *Bacch.* 877ff., etc.

Antigone, deny the ethic of hatred in favour of that of love, "It is not in my nature to side with enmity, but only with friendliness", οὔτοι συνέχθειν, ἀλλὰ συμφιλεῖν ἔφυν (*Ant.* 523) – in answer to Creon's "Never can one's enemy be a friend, even when he is dead", οὔτοι ποθ' οὑχθρός, οὐδ' ὅταν θάνῃ, φίλος. I see now, as the long and terrible war against the Peloponnesians drags on, the ethics of reprisal become more embittered and more pervasive.[1] I will write a tragedy about the classical revenge-situation, in which Electra and Orestes kill their mother, in recompense for their father's death. It is a situation in which tradition on the whole regards Electra and Orestes as justified. Clytaemnestra had herself killed Agamemnon in revenge for the sacrifice of her daughter, Iphigenia. I will not try to whitewash her. Indeed I shall show her living ignobly on the proceeds of her crime along with her partner in it, Aegisthus, treating her daughter badly and spitefully, and even praying for her son's death. But I shall, in one swift dramatic instant, make her go back on it. I shall show her natural love for her absent son emerging against all appearances and overcoming her unnatural hostility towards him. By this I shall show that "nature" (φύσις, in this case the instinctive, ineradicable love of the mother for her child) is a stronger and deeper force than "law" (νόμος, not the civilising law of states, but the primitive, automatic law of vengeance: "life for life, eye for eye, tooth for tooth").

'As for Orestes and Electra, I shall handle them with continuing irony. I shall not make the traditional Furies haunt them: that would be too crude, too outward a phenomenon for my conception. I shall show their minds working inevitably (under revenge-

---

[1] The spirit in which the war was fought was conditioned by the fact that the Greeks had long become accustomed to identify the word for 'public enemy' (πολέμιος) with that for a private one (ἐχθρός) – a fact which is not generally understood, but which emerges *passim*, for example, from Thucydides (the Corinthians, for instance, in their speech urging Sparta to go to war with Athens, continually speak of the Athenians as ἐχθροί: Thuc. 1. 68ff.). Since the public enemy was ἐχθρός, the ethic of 'hate and harm your enemy' could be applied to him. It goes without saying that the same ethic could also be used to support that half-way house between public and private belligerence known as *stasis*. (As is pointed out in the Introduction to Headlam's posthumous *Agamemnon* (ed. Pearson, 1910, 23) the 'enterprise of Aegisthus' against Agamemnon is treated by Aeschylus as a case of *stasis*: the same applies to Orestes' venture in Sophocles.)

motivation) so that they advance further and further in infatuation, grow further and further *away from reality*.[1] Thus Orestes will mishandle the oracle. And having elicited his (imputed) oracular mandate, he will proceed to the deed of matricide (the most horrible act humanly conceivable) almost jauntily, with no religious motivation but a very materialistic one.[2] He will callously forgo the opportunity to reveal himself to his sister *before* announcing himself as dead (thus throwing her into shocked despair, when she, as well as Clytaemnestra, has to listen to the news and believe it). He will kill his mother, knowing nothing of her state of mind (that she feels love and grief for him, that her assumed hatred has been the product of fear: for him she will simply be "bad" (κακή, 1289) – only whites and blacks, no greys, no subtleties, no surprises for this militaristic, unsubtle man).

'But the play shall above all be Electra's tragedy. She shall be my familiar, impetuous, idealistic, aristocratic, *noblesse oblige* heroine (a latter-day Antigone), but this time committed to the proposition that nobility expresses itself in joining in hatred, not in love. And, given her dedication to a single purpose, her intransigence, and her lack of realistic commonsense (σωφροσύνη), we shall see how relentless association with the revenge-principle ruins her mentally and morally. Herself childless, she shall fail to comprehend her mother's maternality, mistaking the psychology of fear for that of pride. Distraught by Orestes' cruel deceit in representing himself to her as dead (as well as by her own too insistent pursuit of vengeance), she shall betray growing signs of madness as the play proceeds. Her fevered imagination will feed on the picture of herself and her sister basking in triumphant acclaim among the townspeople as the slayers of Aegisthus and Clytaemnestra (973 ff.). Only in the

---

[1] It seems to be a trait of Sophocles to show his characters 'growing away from reality'. The classical instance is the growth in Oedipus' mind of the delusion that he is the object of a palace-plot to drive him out of Thebes (*O.T.* 345ff.).

[2] Mme Ronnet (*Sophocle poète tragique* (1969) 232f.), though she presents on the whole an amoral view of the *Electra*, observes acutely that religion surprisingly plays a minimal part in Orestes' and Electra's words and actions: 'L'initiative vient des hommes, d'Oreste, qui agit autant par intérêt (pour retrouver son patrimoine) que par devoir filial, et par-delà Oreste, de celle qui l'a fait élever en vue de la vengeance.'

Recognition-scene with Orestes (for whom she feels like a mother, 1145-6 and 1232) will she reveal (like Clytaemnestra after the narrative of the chariot-race) the reverse side of her nature: that she also is a creature born to join in loving, not in hating. But the cool Orestes and the sinister Paedagogus will change all that. Orestes will suppress her emotion and subdue it to his calculating purposes (1232ff.). The Paedagogus, as the spirit of vengeance incarnate, will further clamp the grim execution of their mother on the pair. Electra will delay the action strangely, while her delirium causes her to see in the Paedagogus the image *of her dead father*, risen from the grave to walk the earth again, while she abases herself before the person of the Paedagogus (1357f.) "O dearest hands, and you who have the dearest feet to do your bidding" – Who cares about the Paedagogus' hands and feet? He himself is embarrassed by Electra's attentions (1364ff.). But soon she will lend herself to the deed of matricide, hovering, herself a Fury, at the palace-gates, straining to catch her mother's dying cries, hissing in her venom (1410 f.), gloating in hideous triumph, and urging her brother to "strike, if you have the strength, a second blow!"

'Luring on Aegisthus to his destruction she will *deny him the right to speak in his own defence* (1483ff.), and the right to *burial* (1487ff.).[1] And in all this she will seek, not justice or piety, but satisfaction for her wounded feelings, her wrongs (1489f.).'

This is the only kind of formula which seems to me to fit the play. It shows the instrument of vengeance wryly turning, in the hands of those who use it, to strike at their own sanity and their deepest humanity. The play is a continuous exercise in dramatic irony. It contains pity for Clytaemnestra, for Electra herself, and even for the upstart Aegisthus. But no approval or encouragement for Orestes or his mentor, the Paedagogus. It is such men that can complacently

---

[1] To speak in one's own defence, as well as to be tried at law, are rights which the Greeks claimed almost instinctively. When these are proposed and *denied*, it is matter for remark: cf. Thuc. 2. 67. 4: the Athenians captured some Corinthian envoys and ἀκρίτους καὶ βουλομένους ἔστιν ἅ εἰπεῖν αὐθημερὸν (cf. Orestes' εὐθύς at *El.* 1505) ἀπέκτειναν πάντας καὶ ἐς φάραγγα ἐσέβαλον (as Aegisthus' body is to be thrown away ἄποπτον ἡμῶν, *El.* 1489), δικαιοῦντες τοῖς αὐτοῖς ἀμύνεσθαι οἷσπερ καὶ οἱ Λακεδαιμόνιοι ὑπῆρξαν (the Athenians were applying the revenge-principle, but the historian's dry narrative implies an ironic, unfavourable comment).

comment upon their ensnared enemies: 'This is the penalty that all should pay *forthwith*, everyone who undertakes to act beyond the laws – Kill them! Then you wouldn't have many rascals!' (1505–7). Indeed no! And you wouldn't have many laws either! Was Sophocles thinking of the men who were shortly to take over the government of Athens, the Thirty Tyrants of 404/3, who 'simplified' the laws, suspended the courts, and executed men 'without trial' (ἀκρίτους), beginning with 'the bad', but ending up by killing the good indiscriminately?[1] Is this why Orestes talks throughout like a soldier of limited imagination and even like a Spartan? For the Athenian oligarchs' thinking was based on the Spartan 'orderliness' (εὐνομία) with its emphasis upon social uniformity, an all-pervasive militarism, and its dislike of intellectual theorising (cf. the notes to 15f., Index s.v. *military terminology*).

But there can scarcely be a definitive 'interpretation' of this strange but moving masterpiece, of which Virginia Woolf wrote: '(Sophocles) chose a design which, if it failed, would show its failure in gashes and ruin, not in the gentle blurring of some insignificant detail; which, if it succeeded, would cut each stroke to the bone, would stamp each fingerprint in marble.'

## 2. THE STYLE OF SOPHOCLES

Apart from the peculiar feature that it almost always has a mythological setting, Greek tragedy, like all poetic drama, differs from prose-drama in that it tends more to universalise its themes, to be less realistic, and at the same time more quintessential. The characters speak more obviously in language that the poet has devised for them; and this language is the language of poetry, which may carry overtones transcending what the particular character concerned, speaking at a particular moment of the play, might have been expected to mean or say.[2] And all the characters speak in language which bears overall

---

[1] Cf. Aristotle, *Const. Ath.* chap. 35, and, for execution without trial, Hdt. 3.80; Lys. 12.82, 25.26. In the latter part of the Peloponnesian War the oligarchs were especially associated in the minds of the democrats with execution without trial, cf. Thuc. 8. 48. 6.

[2] A good example of this occurs, it seems to me, at *El.* 456: Pray for Orestes ἐχθροῖσιν αὐτοῦ ζῶντ' ἐπεμβῆναι ποδί. Electra, *qua* character, cannot know at this point that there is any question of Orestes not being alive. But

the individual poet's stamp. Just as Beethoven's early music has generally an unmistakable character which belongs also to late Beethoven, so all Sophocles has a certain tone or style, which distinguishes it from Aeschylus on the one hand or Euripides on the other.

Much has been written about Sophocles' style, but most of it is not readily available, and none of it exists in a succinct form which might be of use to general readers, cf. the remarks of A. A. Long, *Language and thought* 4. It seems desirable therefore to try to specify here briefly a few of the aspects of Sophocles' style, especially those which have most impressed this editor as being features with which a modern reader would not be familiar from experience of his own literature. Modes of expression, on the other hand, which are common with modern literatures (including many figures of speech) will not be treated here, except incidentally. I have also attempted to draw attention to some general differences between Greek prose and poetic style, where these seemed relevant.

### (i) *Hyperbaton*

Ancient Greek literary style (and Latin too, for that matter) differs from modern in its capacity to *vary its word-order*. There is a 'natural' word-order, but this can be departed from, within certain limits, but to a degree that would be impossible in a modern language. This mannerism was known to the Greeks as *hyperbaton*. Its presence constitutes a unique feature of the classical languages, and one which is continually neglected. I have written elsewhere about hyperbaton,[1] attributing it (as well as certain other stylistic elements of classical literature) to the way in which the ancients read and generally understood their literature, namely vocally and aurally, as opposed to the modern technique of understanding words in strict sequence by their (largely visual) proximity. But, whatever the explanation, the phenomenon exists and is constantly to be observed. Sometimes it is not possible to say whether it serves any particular purpose. In some instances it may be guessed that it arises merely for its own sake, as a kind of play on words or for variety. Usually, however, the disturbance of the normal word-order has a more important function.

her words would seem here to have been affected by the general atmosphere of the play, in which the supposed death of Orestes is paramount.

[1] In *C.R.* n.s. 11 (1961) 188–95; 12 (1962) 111–12; 19 (1969) 65–7.

In prose, hyperbaton would seem to be used most frequently in order to achieve euphony or a particular rhythm. Consequently, the departure from normal word-order is usually slight. In poetry, hyperbaton is used more frequently and more variously. Sometimes the disturbance is slight, but often it is much more extensive. One type of this poetic hyperbaton may be described as 'interlacing': e.g. *El.* 296 ἥτις ἐκ χερῶν | κλέψασ' Ὀρέστην τῶν ἐμῶν ὑπεξέθου (for ἥτις κλέψασα Ὀρέστην ἐκ τῶν ἐμῶν χερῶν ὑπεξέθου (Ὀρέστην) – the figure of *economy* (see below) being here combined with the hyperbaton). Sometimes again two expressions, which belong together grammatically, are separated from one another by a long stretch of intervening words (as in the opening sentence of *Electra* five words separate ὦ from its complementary Ἀγαμέμνονος παῖ). Not infrequently the two complementary elements are at maximum separation, one being placed at the very beginning of the sentence, the other at the end. I call this 'circular' hyperbaton, since in it the end of the sentence returns, as it were, upon its beginning. Examples are *O.T.* 295 τὰς σὰς ἀκούων οὐ μενεῖ τοιάσδ' ἀράς, 1056f. τὰ δὲ | ῥηθέντα βούλου μηδὲ μεμνῆσθαι μάτην (where Jebb, construing by visual proximity, takes μάτην with μεμνῆσθαι), *El.* 328f. τίν' αὖ σὺ τήνδε πρὸς θυρῶνος ἐξόδοις | ἐλθοῦσα φωνεῖς, ὦ κασιγνήτη, φάτιν;

It seems to me tolerably clear that long hyperbaton and circular hyperbaton almost always serve to emphasise the idea represented by the distantly separated words (e.g. at *El.* 328 Chrysothemis' question is indignant: she thinks her sister *talks too much*; this idea, and her associated feeling, is conveyed by the separation of τίνα...τήνδε... φάτιν). The source of the emphasis is the suspense produced in the reader or hearer by being made to wait for the completion of a vital idea. The suspense makes him pay more acute attention.

(ii) ἀπο κοινοῦ, '*economy*', *anacoluthon or sense-construction*

Though often regarded as the original storehouses of 'grammar', the classical languages tend, on occasion, to break or dispense with their own grammatical rules in certain more or less stereotyped ways. Sometimes, for instance, a word which is required to complete the sense in two clauses is stated only once and left 'in common' to both: cf. Aesch. *Sept.* 467 στείχει πρὸς ἐχθρῶν πύργον ἐκπέρσαι θέλων (πύργον goes equally with ἐχθρῶν and with ἐκπέρσαι: no such use of language is to be found in modern English). Sometimes the 'in common' word is not placed (as in the preceding example) in an indeterminate position between its two relevant constructions, but is actually *included* in one, and has to be 'understood' in the other: cf. Aesch. *Ag.* 532 Πάρις γὰρ οὔτε συντελὴς πόλις (for οὔτε Πάρις κτλ.), Soph. *El.* 1498 τά τ' ὄντα καὶ μέλλοντα Πελοπιδῶν κακά (for τά τ' ὄντα καὶ τὰ μέλλοντα). Both usages were known to ancient Greek grammarians and scholiasts as ἀπὸ κοινοῦ constructions. A modern German investigator of this kind of phenomenon (Kiefner, *Die Versparung*) collects a great number of instances (mainly from Greek tragedy) and retains the term ἀπὸ κοινοῦ for the first type, naming the second 'economy' (*Versparung*). Similar to the above constructions, but differing from them in that the element involved has to be understood from one clause to another *in a different case*, or (more remarkably) in the form of a different word, from that expressed, is the construction known to the ancients as *zeugma* or *epezeugmenon*.[1] Cf. Hdt. 3. 81 ὠθέει τε ἐμπεσὼν τὰ πρήγματα (understand, from τὰ πρήγματα, τοῖς πρήγμασι with ἐμπεσών); Soph. *El.* 435f. ἀλλ' ἢ πνοαῖσιν ἢ βαθυσκαφεῖ κόνει | κρύψον νιν (see n.).

Constructions also occur in which the grammatical form of the sentence breaks down, or is more seriously incomplete, the reader being left to supply the meaning himself. This phenomenon is technically known as *anacoluthon*. I prefer to describe it as 'sense-construction'. I believe that it too is closely related to the aural nature of the ancients' reading and appreciation of literature.

### (iii) *Variatio*

In this figure (a favourite of Sophocles), instead of a word being repeated, an exact synonym of it is substituted. Examples are *O.T.* 54 ὡς εἴπερ ἄρξεις τῆσδε γῆς, ὥσπερ κρατεῖς, κτλ. (κρατεῖς for ἄρχεις), *El.* 350 οὔτε ξυνέρδεις τήν τε δρῶσαν ἐκτρέπεις (δρῶσαν for ἔρδουσαν). (Modern English, while seeking variety, does not characteristically substitute an *exactly synonymous* word for another.) On the other hand, Sophocles not infrequently repeats words at short intervals, such repetition being, this editor thinks, in some cases at least, 'vain': cf. the note to line 487, and the Index under 'repetition'.

[1] Cf. L. Spengel, *Rhetores graeci* III 35, 17; 172, 18; Quintilian 9. 3. 62–4.

## (iv) *Figures in general*[1]

These are more frequent in poetry than in prose, as one would expect. Much of Sophocles' individuality is due to the extreme economy as well as the effectiveness with which he uses figures, together with the other resources of the Greek language: as Kitto says, 'the reason why he can move so fast and yet so easily is, I imagine, that he knows exactly, at every moment, what he wants to do, and what is the most economical and therefore the most telling way of doing it'.[2] In other words Sophocles is a supremely artistic writer, deeply versed in his craft, as well as dedicated to it. Kitto, in the passage referred to, discusses the opening fourteen lines of the *Electra*, pointing out how much is achieved in them, and the reader cannot do better than refer to these comments.

## (v) *Diction*

It should be remarked in the first place that Greek has a poetic language, in many ways different from that of prose. For instance, οἶκος often means a physical house in poetry; but in prose, the word used is generally οἰκία. Similarly, στρατός in poetry means 'army'; in prose, στράτευμα or στρατιά is more usual.

Within poetry itself, one poet's language may be more 'poetic' than another's. Thus Sophocles' diction, though not so magniloquent as that of Aeschylus, is more ἐξηλλαγμένη[3] (i.e. more distinguished from the language of everyday life) than that of Euripides – though Euripides also of course is poetic. The result is that it lends itself to a more poetic treatment of his themes. It is not that Sophocles cannot be 'realistic' (indeed, he is far more so than he is allowed by critics to be). But his realism is constantly modified and controlled by his poetic use of language.

---

[1] Any artistic mode of literary expression which differed from the plain, direct expression of the same general sense was known to the ancient literary critics as a 'figure' (in Greek σχῆμα, i.e. an 'attitude' of language), cf. Ps.-Longinus, *On the sublime* 16ff., Quintilian 9. 1. 1ff.

[2] *Sophocles: dramatist and philosopher* 4.

[3] Cf. Arist. *Rhet.* 3. 1404b8, 1406a15.

## (vi) *Character-drawing*

In a famous passage,[1] Sophocles is quoted as saying that his style had evolved through several stages to a form which he himself regarded as ἠθικωτάτη καὶ βελτίστη. Opinions differ as to how far the stages can be plausibly detected in the surviving work. But it is interesting (and conforms to observation, cf. the ancient *Life* 21) that he regarded his mature style as 'pertaining to, or conveying character'. Perhaps this feature of his style shows up most in the succinctness and epigrammatic quality of some of the general remarks made by his characters, remarks which not merely identify them, but also seem to summarise memorably a situation, a characteristic viewpoint, or a vital experience of life: examples are Antigone's οὔτοι συνέχθειν, ἀλλὰ συμφιλεῖν ἔφυν (*Ant.* 523), and Odysseus' inimitable 'We shall be "just" – *another day*!' (*Phil.* 82 δίκαιοι δ' αὖθις ἐκφανούμεθα).

## (vii) *Irony*

Sophocles is markedly an *ironic* writer, and this feature has helped to incline this editor towards adopting an 'ironic' interpretation of the *Electra*. But irony is a complex phenomenon which is not easy to define, and is perhaps best left undefined. Kirkwood (*A study of Sophoclean drama* 247) puts it well when he says '"Sophoclean irony" is a well-worn term, often used to mean that kind of verbal irony wherein the speaker's words have one meaning for him and another, significantly different and in some way contrasting, for the audience'. An outstanding example is the words of Teiresias to Oedipus (*O.T.* 337f.) ὀργὴν ἐμέμψω τὴν ἐμήν, τὴν σὴν δ' ὁμοῦ | ναίουσαν οὐ κατεῖδες. Teiresias means, and Oedipus understands him to mean, 'you have found fault with my temper, but you haven't discerned your own (temper) which dwells with you'. But in the context of the whole play the words ominously convey 'you haven't discerned that your own (*wife–mother*) is living with you!'.

For further discussion the reader is referred to the whole of Kirkwood's excellent essay, 'The irony of Sophocles' (*op. cit.* 247ff.).

---

[1] Plutarch, *De profectibus in virtute* 7: discussion in C. M. Bowra, *Problems in Greek poetry* (1953) 108ff.

## 3. STAGE PRODUCTION

Sophocles' *Electra* was first produced in the 'Periclean' Theatre of Dionysus at Athens in which the audience sat around a circular dancing floor (*orchestra*), behind which was a stage, slightly raised above the *orchestra* and backed by a long wall. In the wall was a central door, which served as the 'palace-door' through which the characters so often make their entrances and exits. Between the long wall and the seats of the (roughly semi-circular) auditorium were passages (*parodoi*), by which the chorus entered the *orchestra*, and the characters from 'outside' the palace made their entrances and exits to or from the stage. In the foreground of the stage stood an altar of Apollo. For the details see T. B. L. Webster, *Greek theatre production* (1970).

The date of the first production of the *Electra* is not known for certain, nor are the names of the other plays, or the tragedians against whom Sophocles competed. He had available by the rules of the competition three speaking actors, who no doubt played the following parts:

*Protagonist*:     Electra

*Deuteragonist*:  { Orestes
                         Clytaemnestra

*Tritagonist*:    { the Paedagogus
                       Chrysothemis
                       Aegisthus

The Protagonist on this occasion was an accomplished singer, to judge by the demands made upon his voice by the long passages sung, or spoken in recitative by him.

## 4. SELECT BIBLIOGRAPHY

### General

H. Friis Johansen, 'Sophocles 1939–1959', *Lustrum* 7 (1962) 94ff.

F. Solmsen, *Electra and Orestes: three recognitions in Greek tragedy* (Amsterdam 1967).

L. Campbell, *Paralipomena Sophoclea* (London 1907: reprinted Hildesheim 1969).

## Texts

Ed. R. C. Jebb (Cambridge 1897).

Ed. A. C. Pearson (Oxford Classical Texts 1924; reprinted with corrections several times up to 1967).

Ed. A. Dain trans. P. Mazon (*Sophocle, tome II*, Paris 1958).

## Editions

*The plays and fragments of Sophocles*, II, ed. L. Campbell (Oxford 1881).

Sophocles *Electra* ed. R. C. Jebb (large ed.: Cambridge 1894).

Sophokles *Elektra* ed. A. W. Schneidewin rev. A. Nauck (Berlin 1912).

Sophokles *Elektra* ed. G. Kaibel (Leipzig 1896).

## Fragments

*Tragicorum graecorum fragmenta* ed. A. Nauck, 2nd ed. (Leipzig 1889).

*The fragments of Sophocles* ed. A. C. Pearson (Cambridge 1917), 3 vols. (In this edition of the *Electra* all Sophoclean fragments are cited as from Pearson.)

## Lexicographical

F. Ellendt, *Lexicon Sophocleum* (2nd ed., rev. H. Genthe, Frankfurt 1872; reprinted Hildesheim 1965).

## Legal

R. J. Bonner and G. Smith, *The administration of justice from Homer to Aristotle* (2 vols., Chicago 1930–8).

J. H. Lipsius, *Das attische Recht* (3 vols., Leipzig 1905–15).

D. M. MacDowell, *Athenian homicide law in the age of the orators* (Manchester 1963)

## Grammar and Style

P. T. Stevens, 'Colloquial expressions in Aeschylus and Sophocles', *Classical Quarterly* 39 (1945) 95–105.

J. D. Denniston, *The Greek particles*, 2nd ed. (Oxford 1954 and 1959).

G. Kiefner, *Die Versparung* (Wiesbaden 1964).

A. A. Long, *Language and thought in Sophocles* (London 1968).

## Philosophical and Ethical

*Die Fragmente der Vorsokratiker* ed. H. Diels rev. W. Kranz, 6th ed. (Berlin 1951–2), 3 vols.

A. W. H. Adkins, *Merit and responsibility* (Oxford 1960).

## General Books and Essays

The literature is enormous. A short list would inevitably include the following:

T. B. L. Webster, *An introduction to Sophocles* (London 1936; 2nd ed. 1969).

Virginia Woolf, 'On Not Knowing Greek' (in *The common reader*, London 1925. Contains a masterly description of Sophocles' *Electra*, and the world of Greek tragedy generally, as seen through the imagination of a modern creative writer.)

R. P. Winnington-Ingram, 'Sophocles' *Electra*: prolegomena to an interpretation', *Proceedings of the Cambridge Philological Society*, n.s. 3 (1954–5) 20–6.

G. M. Kirkwood, *A study of Sophoclean drama* (New York 1958).

H. D. F. Kitto, *Sophocles: dramatist and philosopher* (Oxford 1958).

R. Lattimore, *The poetry of Greek tragedy* (Baltimore 1958).

G. Ronnet, *Sophocle poète tragique* (Paris 1969).

# SIGLA

L = Laur. xxxii. 9 saec. x, ut videtur
A = Paris. 2712 saec. xiii

---

Γ = Abbat. Flor. 152 (olim 2725) saec. xiii
Δ = Abbat. Flor. 41 (olim 2788) saec. xiv
Aug b = Augustanus saec. xiv
Aug c = Augustanus saec. xv
Bodl = Barocc. 66 saec. xv
C = Paris. 2794 saec. xv
Chig = olim Chigianus R viii 59 hodie ut ferunt Vaticanus saec. xv
D = Paris. 2820 saec. xv
Dresd a = Dresd. D 183 saec. xiv
Dresd b = Dresd. D 181 saec. xv
E = Paris. 2884 saec. xiv
Farn = Neapolitanus olim Farnesianus II F 34 saec. xv
Harl = Harleiensis 5744 saec. xv
Jen = Jenensis B 7 saec. xiv
K = Abbat. Flor. 66 saec. xiv
Laud = Bodl. C 89 (54) saec. xv
Lb = Laur. xxxi. 10 saec. xiv
Lc = Laur. xxxii. 2 saec. xiv
Lips a = Lipsiensis Senat. I. 4. 44 saec. xiv
Lips b = Lipsiensis Senat. I. 4. 44 saec. xv
Liv p ⎫ = lectiones duorum codicum in margine exemplaris Aldini
Liv v ⎬ a Ioh. Livineio (1546–1599) scriptae et in Diar. Class.
         ⎭ xiv. 428 editae
M = Ambros. G 56 sup. saec. xiv
Mb = Ambros. L 39 sup. saec. xiv ineuntis
Mc = Ambros. E 77 sup. saec. xv exeuntis
Md = Ambros. C 24 sup. saec. xv
Monac = Monacensis teste Doederlinio in Specim. ed. Soph.
Mosq b = Mosquensis 392 saec. xv
Pal = Heidelbergensis cod. Pal. gr. 40 saec. xiv

[ 21 ]

Ricc a = Riccardianus Flor. 34 saec. xiv
Ricc b = Riccardianus Flor. 77 saec. xv
      T = Paris. 2711 saec. xiv
   Trin = Cantabrigiensis cod. Trin. Coll. R. 3. 31 saec. xiv et xv
  Vat a = Vaticanus 40 saec. xiv vel xv
  Vat c = Urbin. 140 saec. xiv
  Vat d = Vat. 47 saec. xv
    Ven = Marcianus 468 saec. xiii
  Ven b = Marcianus 616 saec. xv
  Ven c = Marcianus 467 saec. xv ineuntis
  Ven d = Marcianus 472 saec. xiv
 Vindob = Vindob. 281 saec. xiv vel xv

---

    Ald = Aldina Venet. 1502
 Turneb = Turnebus Paris. 1553
 Lond I = ed. Londinensis 1722
Lond II = ed. Londinensis 1747

---

    $L^{ac}$ = ante correctionem
     $L^c$ = post correctionem ⎫ sive a pr. man. sive ab alia antiqua
     $L^s$ = supra lineam        ⎭   profecta
     $L^2$ = a recentiore manu
   $L^{\gamma\rho}$ = varia lectio add. γρ(ἄφεται) vel καὶ γρ
    $L^{mg}$ = in margine scripta
        Σ = scholia antiqua Laurentiani a διορθωτοῦ manu profecta
Tricl vel σ = scholia recentiora Triclinii aliorum a Dindorfio edita
       $\Sigma^1$ = in lemmate scholiorum
   $\Sigma^{\gamma\rho}$ = varia lectio add. γρ vel καὶ γρ a διορθωτοῦ manu
      rec = duo vel plures codicum quorum praeter L et A notitiam
            habemus
    codd. = omnes codices quorum notitiam habemus

---

    Πd = Pap. Oxy. 639 saec. iii [El. 993–1007]

# ΗΛΕΚΤΡΑ

## ΥΠΟΘΕΣΙΣ ΗΛΕΚΤΡΑΣ

Ὑπόκειται ὧδε· τροφεὺς δεικνὺς τῷ Ὀρέστῃ τὰ ἐν Ἄργει. μικρὸν γὰρ αὐτὸν ὄντα κλέψασα ἡ Ἠλέκτρα, ἡνίκα ὁ πατὴρ ἐσφάζετο, δέδωκε τῷ τροφεῖ, φοβουμένη μὴ καὶ αὐτὸν φονεύσωσι σὺν τῷ πατρί. ἔπεμψε δὲ αὐτὸν εἰς Φωκίδα εἰς τὸν τοῦ πατρὸς αὐτοῦ [... ἐπὶ Ἀναξιβίαν ἀδελφὴν αὐτοῦ] ἐξάδελφον Στροφίον.                                                           5

## ΚΑΙ ΑΛΛΩΣ

Τροφεύς ἐστιν ὁ προλογίζων πρεσβύτης παιδαγωγὸς ὁ ὑποκείμενος καὶ ὑπεκθέμενος τὸν Ὀρέστην εἰς τὴν Φωκίδα πρὸς Στροφίον καὶ ὑποδεικνὺς αὐτῷ τὰ ἐν Ἄργει. μικρὸν γὰρ αὐτὸν κλέψας ἐκ τοῦ Ἄργους ὁ παιδα- γωγὸς ἔφυγεν καὶ διὰ εἴκοσι ἐτῶν ἐπανελθὼν εἰς τὸ Ἄργος μετ᾽ αὐτοῦ   10 δείκυσιν αὐτῷ τὰ ἐν Ἄργει.

Ἡ σκηνὴ τοῦ δράματος ὑπόκειται ἐν Ἄργει. ὁ δὲ χορὸς συνέστηκεν ἐξ ἐπιχωρίων παρθένων. προλογίζει δὲ ὁ παιδαγωγὸς Ὀρέστου.

Argumentum habent L A rec      2 ὄντα αὐτὸν A rec      3 φοβουμένη] δείσασα A rec      φονεύσωσι] κτείνωσιν A rec      σὺν τῷ πατρί om. A rec 3–5 ἔπεμψε ... στρόφιον (sic) solus habet Vindob      6 καὶ ἄλλως om. L A rec      7–10 τροφεύς ... ἔφυγεν om. A rec: cetera habent A rec sed paullum immutata      8 στροφίον L Lb: στρόφιον rec      12–13 ἡ σκηνὴ ... Ὀρέστου habent A rec: om. L rec

## ΤΑ ΤΟΥ ΔΡΑΜΑΤΟΣ ΠΡΟΣΩΠΑ

Παιδαγωγός
Ὀρέστης
Ἠλέκτρα
Χορὸς ἐξ ἐπιχωρίων παρθένων
Χρυσόθεμις
Κλυταιμήστρα
Αἴγισθος

Personarum laterculum om. L    παρόντος δράματος rec

# ΗΛΕΚΤΡΑ

ΠΑΙΔΑΓΩΓΟΣ

Ὦ τοῦ στρατηγήσαντος ἐν Τροίᾳ ποτὲ
Ἀγαμέμνονος παῖ, νῦν ἐκεῖν' ἔξεστί σοι
παρόντι λεύσσειν, ὧν πρόθυμος ἦσθ' ἀεί.
τὸ γὰρ παλαιὸν Ἄργος οὑπόθεις τόδε,
τῆς οἰστροπλῆγος ἄλσος Ἰνάχου κόρης·          5
αὕτη δ', Ὀρέστα, τοῦ λυκοκτόνου θεοῦ
ἀγορὰ Λύκειος· οὑξ ἀριστερᾶς δ' ὅδε
Ἥρας ὁ κλεινὸς ναός· οἷ δ' ἱκάνομεν,
φάσκειν Μυκήνας τὰς πολυχρύσους ὁρᾶν,
πολύφθορόν τε δῶμα Πελοπιδῶν τόδε,          10
ὅθεν σε πατρὸς ἐκ φόνων ἐγώ ποτε
πρὸς σῆς ὁμαίμου καὶ κασιγνήτης λαβὼν
ἤνεγκα κἀξέσωσα κἀξεθρεψάμην
τοσόνδ' ἐς ἥβης, πατρὶ τιμωρὸν φόνου.
νῦν οὖν, Ὀρέστα καὶ σὺ φίλτατε ξένων          15
Πυλάδη, τί χρὴ δρᾶν ἐν τάχει βουλευτέον·
ὡς ἡμὶν ἤδη λαμπρὸν ἡλίου σέλας
ἑῷα κινεῖ φθέγματ' ὀρνίθων σαφῆ
μέλαινά τ' ἄστρων ἐκλέλοιπεν εὐφρόνη.
πρὶν οὖν τιν' ἀνδρῶν ἐξοδοιπορεῖν στέγης,          20
ξυνάπτετον λόγοισιν· ὡς ἐνταῦθ' †ἐμὲν†
ἵν' οὐκέτ' ὀκνεῖν καιρός, ἀλλ' ἔργων ἀκμή.

1 τυραννήσαντος Σʸᴾ      4 τόδε γὰρ E      10 τε] δὲ T   Πελοπιδᾶν
Lᵃᶜ   11 φονῶν Dindorf      13 καί σ' ἐθρεψάμην schol. B Hom. I 485
14 τιμωρῶν φθόνου Lᵃᶜ      15 in L omissum sed in mg. a m. pr. additum
16 Πυλάδης Lᵃᶜ   βουλεύετον coni. Porson      21 ξυναπτέον E   ἐνταῦθ'
ἐμὲν vix sana: ἐνταῦθ' ἐσμέν rec: ἐλήλυθμεν M. Schmidt: ἐνταῦθ' ἵμεν
Dawes

[ 25 ]

ΟΡΕΣΤΗΣ

ὦ φίλτατ' ἀνδρῶν προσπόλων, ὥς μοι σαφῆ
σημεῖα φαίνεις ἐσθλὸς εἰς ἡμᾶς γεγώς.
ὥσπερ γὰρ ἵππος εὐγενής, κἂν ᾖ γέρων,                    25
ἐν τοῖσι δεινοῖς θυμὸν οὐκ ἀπώλεσεν,
ἀλλ' ὀρθὸν οὖς ἵστησιν, ὡσαύτως δὲ σὺ
ἡμᾶς τ' ὀτρύνεις καὐτὸς ἐν πρώτοις ἔπῃ.
τοιγὰρ τὰ μὲν δόξαντα δηλώσω, σὺ δὲ
ὀξεῖαν ἀκοὴν τοῖς ἐμοῖς λόγοις διδούς,                    30
εἰ μή τι καιροῦ τυγχάνω, μεθάρμοσον.
ἐγὼ γὰρ ἡνίχ' ἱκόμην τὸ Πυθικὸν
μαντεῖον, ὡς μάθοιμ' ὅτῳ τρόπῳ πατρὸς
δίκας ἀροίμην τῶν φονευσάντων πάρα,
χρῇ μοι τοιαῦθ' ὁ Φοῖβος ὧν πεύσῃ τάχα·                  35
ἄσκευον αὐτὸν ἀσπίδων τε καὶ στρατοῦ
δόλοισι κλέψαι χειρὸς ἐνδίκους σφαγάς.
ὅτ' οὖν τοιόνδε χρησμὸν εἰσηκούσαμεν,
σὺ μὲν μολών, ὅταν σε καιρὸς εἰσάγῃ,
δόμων ἔσω τῶνδ', ἴσθι πᾶν τὸ δρώμενον,                  40
ὅπως ἂν εἰδὼς ἡμὶν ἀγγείλῃς σαφῆ.
οὐ γάρ σε μὴ γήρᾳ τε καὶ χρόνῳ μακρῷ
γνῶσ', οὐδ' ὑποπτεύσουσιν ὧδ' ἠνθισμένον.
λόγῳ δὲ χρῶ τοιῷδ', ὅτι ξένος μὲν εἶ
Φωκέως παρ' ἀνδρὸς Φανοτέως ἥκων· ὁ γὰρ                45
μέγιστος αὐτοῖς τυγχάνει δορυξένων.
ἄγγελλε δ' ὅρκον προστιθεὶς ὁθούνεκα
τέθνηκ' Ὀρέστης ἐξ ἀναγκαίας τύχης,
ἄθλοισι Πυθικοῖσιν ἐκ τροχηλάτων
δίφρων κυλισθείς· ὧδ' ὁ μῦθος ἐστάτω.                   50
ἡμεῖς δὲ πατρὸς τύμβον, ὡς ἐφίετο,

28 ἡμᾶς τ' L (τ' in litura) rec: ἡμᾶς A rec: ἡμᾶς δ' rec   ἔπῃ] ἔσῃ Pal:
quid Σ voluerit (δι (sscr. χ) ἔσῃ διὰ τὴν ἀπὸ τοῦ γήρως εὐβουλίαν)
incertum     33 πατρός Lᶜ A rec: πατρὶ Lb et fort. Lᵃᶜ     42 μακρῷ
χρόνῳ rec     43 ὑποπτεύουσιν vel ὑποπτεύσωσιν rec     45 Φωκέως
Bentley et fort. noverat Σ: φωκεὺς codd.     47 ὅρκον Reiske: ὅρκῳ codd.:
ἔργῳ Vahlen: ὄγκον Musgrave

λοιβαῖσι πρῶτον καὶ καρατόμοις χλιδαῖς
στέψαντες, εἶτ᾽ ἄψορρον ἥξομεν πάλιν,
τύπωμα χαλκόπλευρον ἠρμένοι χεροῖν,
ὃ καὶ σὺ θάμνοις οἶσθά που κεκρυμμένον,           55
ὅπως λόγῳ κλέπτοντες ἡδεῖαν φάτιν
φέρωμεν αὐτοῖς, τοὐμὸν ὡς ἔρρει δέμας
φλογιστὸν ἤδη καὶ κατηνθρακωμένον.
τί γάρ με λυπεῖ τοῦθ᾽, ὅταν λόγῳ θανὼν
ἔργοισι σωθῶ κἀξενέγκωμαι κλέος;           60
δοκῶ μέν, οὐδὲν ῥῆμα σὺν κέρδει κακόν.
ἤδη γὰρ εἶδον πολλάκις καὶ τοὺς σοφοὺς
λόγῳ μάτην θνήσκοντας· εἶθ᾽, ὅταν δόμους
ἔλθωσιν αὖθις, ἐκτετίμηνται πλέον·
ὡς κἄμ᾽ ἐπαυχῶ τῆσδε τῆς φήμης ἄπο           65
δεδορκότ᾽ ἐχθροῖς ἄστρον ὣς λάμψειν ἔτι.
ἀλλ᾽, ὦ πατρῷα γῆ θεοί τ᾽ ἐγχώριοι,
δέξασθέ μ᾽ εὐτυχοῦντα ταῖσδε ταῖς ὁδοῖς,
σύ τ᾽, ὦ πατρῷον δῶμα· σοῦ γὰρ ἔρχομαι
δίκῃ καθαρτὴς πρὸς θεῶν ὡρμημένος·           70
καὶ μή μ᾽ ἄτιμον τῆσδ᾽ ἀποστείλητε γῆς,
ἀλλ᾽ ἀρχέπλουτον καὶ καταστάτην δόμων.
εἴρηκα μέν νυν ταῦτα· σοὶ δ᾽ ἤδη, γέρον,
τὸ σὸν μελέσθω βάντι φρουρῆσαι χρέος.
νὼ δ᾽ ἔξιμεν· καιρὸς γάρ, ὅσπερ ἀνδράσιν           75
μέγιστος ἔργου παντός ἐστ᾽ ἐπιστάτης.

ΗΛΕΚΤΡΑ
    ἰώ μοί μοι δύστηνος.

ΠΑ. καὶ μὴν θυρῶν ἔδοξα προσπόλων τινὸς
    ὑποστενούσης ἔνδον αἰσθέσθαι, τέκνον.

ΟΡ. ἆρ᾽ ἐστὶν ἡ δύστηνος Ἠλέκτρα; θέλεις           80

52 λοιβαῖσι L rec Σ¹ Suidae v. χλιδή E, Eustath. 692, 59: λοιβαῖς τε
L²ˢ A rec: λοιβαῖς τὸ Suidae A B     54 ἠρμένοι rec     55 που Lᶜ A rec:
μοι Lᵃᶜ: rec     56 κλέπτοντες] θνήσκοντες rec     57 φέρωμεν Γ: φέροιμεν
L A rec     61 μὲν ὡς οὐδὲν L rec Suidae v. τί γάρ et v. λύπη codd.
nonnulli     64 αὖτις Lb     65 ὡς] ὣς L     66 δεδορκότ᾽ Palᵞᵖ
77 δύστηνος del. Dindorf     80 ἠλέκτρας L (σ eraso)

      μείνωμεν αὐτοῦ κἀπακούσωμεν γόων;

ΠΑ.  ἥκιστα. μηδὲν πρόσθεν ἢ τὰ Λοξίου
      πειρώμεθ' ἔρδειν κἀπὸ τῶνδ' ἀρχηγετεῖν,
      πατρὸς χέοντες λουτρά· ταῦτα γὰρ φέρειν
      νίκην τέ φημι καὶ κράτος τῶν δρωμένων.      85

ΗΛ.  ὦ φάος ἁγνὸν
      καὶ γῆς ἰσόμοιρ' ἀήρ, ὥς μοι
      πολλὰς μὲν θρήνων ᾠδάς,
      πολλὰς δ' ἀντήρεις ᾔσθου
      στέρνων πλαγὰς αἱμασσομένων,      90
      ὁπόταν δνοφερὰ νὺξ ὑπολειφθῇ·
      τὰ δὲ παννυχίδων ἤδη στυγεραὶ
      ξυνίσασ' εὐναὶ μογερῶν οἴκων,
      ὅσα τὸν δύστηνον ἐμὸν θρηνῶ
      πατέρ', ὃν κατὰ μὲν βάρβαρον αἶαν      95
      φοίνιος "Αρης οὐκ ἐξένισεν,
      μήτηρ δ' ἡμὴ χὠ κοινολεχὴς
      Αἴγισθος ὅπως δρῦν ὑλοτόμοι
      σχίζουσι κάρα φονίῳ πελέκει.
      κοὐδεὶς τούτων οἶκτος ἀπ' ἄλλης      100
      ἢ 'μοῦ φέρεται, σοῦ, πάτερ, οὕτως
      αἰκῶς οἰκτρῶς τε θανόντος.
      ἀλλ' οὐ μὲν δὴ
      λήξω θρήνων στυγερῶν τε γόων,
      ἔστ' ἂν παμφεγγεῖς ἄστρων      105
      ῥιπάς, λεύσσω δὲ τόδ' ἦμαρ,

81 κἀπακούσωμεν Nauck (ἐπακούσωμεν Σ<sup>gl</sup>): κἀνακούσωμεν codd. 84 sq. χεσοντες (sscr. ευ) L    φέρειν νίκην τέ φημι Tournier: φέρει νίκην τ' ἐφ' ἡμῖν codd.    87 ἰσόμοιρ' (quod coni. Porson) Vindob: ἰσόμοιρος L A rec Suid. v. φάος    90 πληγὰς rec Suid. v. ἀντήρεις 92 κήδη Froehlich    93 μογερῶν οἴκων L<sup>c</sup> A rec: μογερῶν οἰκιῶν (vel οἰκίων) L<sup>ac</sup> rec: μογέρ' οἰκείων Kaibel    96 ἐξένισε(ν) L<sup>ac</sup> rec Σ Suid. s.v. et v. ξένια: ἐξείνισε(ν) L<sup>c</sup> A rec    99 φοινίῳ L rec    102 αἰκῶς (ἀϊκῶς Brunck) Hermann: ἀεικῶς Σ (ἔν τισιν ὑπόκειται ἀντὶ τοῦ ἀδίκως): ἀδίκως codd. et testatur Dio Cass. lii. 18    105 λεύσσω παμφεγγεῖς ἄστρων codd. Suid. v. ῥιπάς: om. λεύσσω Reisig: om. ἄστρων Dobree

μὴ οὐ τεκνολέτειρ' ὥς τις ἀηδών
ἐπὶ κωκυτῷ τῶνδε πατρῴων
πρὸ θυρῶν ἠχὼ πᾶσι προφωνεῖν.
ὦ δῶμ' Ἀίδου καὶ Περσεφόνης,                   110
ὦ χθόνι' Ἑρμῆ καὶ πότνι' Ἀρά,
σεμναί τε θεῶν παῖδες Ἐρινύες,
αἳ τοὺς ἀδίκως θνήσκοντας ὁρᾶθ',
αἳ τοὺς εὐνὰς ὑποκλεπτομένους,
ἔλθετ', ἀρήξατε, τείσασθε πατρὸς               115
φόνον ἡμετέρου,
καί μοι τὸν ἐμὸν πέμψατ' ἀδελφόν.
μούνη γὰρ ἄγειν οὐκέτι σωκῶ
λύπης ἀντίρροπον ἄχθος.                         120

ΧΟΡΟΣ

    ὦ παῖ, παῖ δυστανοτάτας                 στρ.
     Ἠλέκτρα ματρός, τίν' ἀεὶ τάκεις
     ὧδ' ἀκόρεστον οἰμωγὰν
    τὸν πάλαι ἐκ δολερᾶς ἀθεώτατα
    ματρὸς ἁλόντ' ἀπάταις Ἀγαμέμνονα         125
    κακᾷ τε χειρὶ πρόδοτον; ὡς ὁ τάδε πορὼν
    ὄλοιτ', εἴ μοι θέμις τάδ' αὐδᾶν.

ΗΛ.    ὦ γενέθλα γενναίων,
    ἥκετ' ἐμῶν καμάτων παραμύθιον·          130
    οἶδά τε καὶ ξυνίημι τάδ', οὔ τί με
    φυγγάνει, οὐδ' ἐθέλω προλιπεῖν τόδε,
    μὴ οὐ τὸν ἐμὸν στενάχειν πατέρ' ἄθλιον.
     ἀλλ' ὦ παντοί-
    ας φιλότητος ἀμειβόμεναι χάριν,

108 κωκυτῶν L<sup>ac</sup>: κωκυτοῖς Suidae B E G     111 ποινία ἀρὰ Σγρ
113 sq. ὁρᾶθ' αἳ τοὺς Dobree: ὁρᾶτε τοὺς codd. (τούς τ' rec: τοὺς τὰς
Suidae v. Περσεφόνη A): τοὺς εὐνὰς ὑποκλ. del. Porson     117 κἀμοὶ
Brunck     121 ὦ T: ἰὼ L A rec     122 Ἠλέκτρας A     123 ἀκόρετον
A rec     124 ἀθεωτάτας codd. Σ: corr. Porson     126 ὡς] ὡς L rec
128 γενναίων Monk: γενναίων πατέρων L A rec: γενναίων τοκέων rec
132 οὐδ' αὖ θέλω L (sscr. δὲ) rec     133 στενάχειν (στεναχεῖν rec)
Elmsley: στοναχεῖν L A rec

ἐᾶτέ μ' ὧδ' ἀλύειν,                                    135
αἰαῖ, ἱκνοῦμαι.


ΧΟ.      ἀλλ' οὔτοι τόν γ' ἐξ Ἀΐδα                        ἀντ.
παγκοίνου λίμνας πατέρ' ἀνστάσεις
οὔτε γόοισιν οὔτ' εὐχαῖς·
ἀλλ' ἀπὸ τῶν μετρίων ἐπ' ἀμήχανον            140
ἄλγος ἀεὶ στενάχουσα διόλλυσαι,
ἐν οἷς ἀνάλυσίς ἐστιν οὐδεμία κακῶν.
τί μοι τῶν δυσφόρων ἐφίη;
ΗΛ.      νήπιος ὃς τῶν οἰκτρῶς                            145
οἰχομένων γονέων ἐπιλάθεται.
ἀλλ' ἐμέ γ' ἁ στονόεσσ' ἄραρεν φρένας,
ἃ Ἴτυν, αἰὲν Ἴτυν ὀλοφύρεται,
ὄρνις ἀτυζομένα, Διὸς ἄγγελος.
ἰὼ παντλά-
μων Νιόβα, σὲ δ' ἔγωγε νέμω θεόν,              150
ἅτ' ἐν τάφῳ πετραίῳ,
αἰαῖ, δακρύεις.


ΧΟ.      οὔτοι σοὶ μούνᾳ,                                  στρ.
τέκνον, ἄχος ἐφάνη βροτῶν,
πρὸς ὅ τι σὺ τῶν ἔνδον εἶ περισσά,            155
οἷς ὁμόθεν εἶ καὶ γονᾷ ξύναιμος,
οἷα Χρυσόθεμις ζώει καὶ Ἰφιάνασσα,
κρυπτᾷ τ' ἀχέων ἐν ἥβᾳ
ὄλβιος, ὃν ἁ κλεινὰ                                160
γᾶ ποτε Μυκηναίων
δέξεται εὐπατρίδαν, Διὸς εὔφρονι

137 τόν γ'] τόνδ' A rec     139 γόοισιν οὔτ' εὐχαῖς Erfurdt: γόοις οὔτε
λιταῖσιν L rec: γόοις οὔτε λιταῖς A rec: γόοισιν οὐ λιταῖς T Tricl: γόοισιν
οὔτ' ἄνταις Hermann     145 οἰκτρῶς αἰκῶς τ' Porson: οἰκτρῶς οὕτως
Kaibel     152 αἰαῖ] αἰεὶ Tricl^γρ: αἰὲν rec     157 οἷα L rec     160 sqq.
Electrae cum sequentibus tribuunt codd., choro reddidit Tyrwhitt
162 διὸς] ποδὸς Haupt

βήματι μολόντα τάνδε γᾶν Ὀρέσταν.

ΗΛ.  ὅν γ' ἐγὼ ἀκάματα προσμένουσ' ἄτεκνος,
    τάλαιν' ἀνύμφευτος αἰὲν οἰχνῶ,                    165
      δάκρυσι μυδαλέα, τὸν ἀνήνυτον
      οἶτον ἔχουσα κακῶν· ὃ δὲ λάθεται
      ὧν τ' ἔπαθ' ὧν τ' ἐδάη. τί γὰρ οὐκ ἐμοὶ
      ἔρχεται ἀγγελίας ἀπατώμενον;                    170
          ἀεὶ μὲν γὰρ ποθεῖ,
    ποθῶν δ' οὐκ ἀξιοῖ φανῆναι.


ΧΟ.      θάρσει μοι, θάρσει,                          ἀντ.
      τέκνον. ἔτι μέγας οὐρανῷ
    Ζεύς, ὃς ἐφορᾷ πάντα καὶ κρατύνει·                175
    ᾧ τὸν ὑπεραλγῆ χόλον νέμουσα
    μήθ' οἷς ἐχθαίρεις ὑπεράχθεο μήτ' ἐπιλάθου·
      χρόνος γὰρ εὐμαρὴς θεός.
      οὔτε γὰρ ὁ τὰν Κρίσᾳ                            180
      βούνομον ἔχων ἀκτὰν
    παῖς Ἀγαμεμνονίδας ἀπερίτροπος
    οὔθ' ὁ παρὰ τὸν Ἀχέροντα θεὸς ἀνάσσων.

ΗΛ.  ἀλλ' ἐμὲ μὲν ὁ πολὺς ἀπολέλοιπεν ἤδη            185
    βίοτος ἀνέλπιστος, οὐδ' ἔτ' ἀρκῶ·
      ἅτις ἄνευ τεκέων κατατάκομαι,
      ἇς φίλος οὔτις ἀνὴρ ὑπερίσταται,
    ἀλλ' ἀπερεί τις ἔποικος ἀναξία
    οἰκονομῶ θαλάμους πατρός, ὧδε μὲν                 190


163 βήματι] σήματι Musgrave    164 ὅν γ' ἐγὼ Hermann: ὃν ἔγωγ' codd.
168 ὃ δὲ λάθεται L°A rec: ὧδ' ἐλάθεται Lᵃᶜ: ὃ δ' ἐλάθετο LˢΔ
169 ἔπαθεν Lᵃᶜ rec Σ¹    173 τέκνον θάρσει Σ (ad v. 823)    174 ἔτι
μέγας οὐρανῷ Heath: ἔστι μέγας ἐν οὐρανῷ L (ἔτι Lᵃᶜ) A rec Σ (ad v.
823): ἔστι μέγας οὐρανῷ rec: μέγας ἔτ' ἐν οὐρανῷ Hermann    180 Κρίσᾳ
Musgrave: Κρίσαν L A rec: Κρίσσαν rec: Κρίσσα Pal: Κρίσαν Hermann
181 βούνομον Lᵃᶜ: βουνόμον L° A rec Suid. s.v.    186 ἀνέλπιστον, quod
Σ legisse suspicatur, Nauck    187 τεκέων Vindobˢ (coniecerat Meineke): τοκέων cett.

      ἀεικεῖ σὺν στολᾷ,
κεναῖς δ' ἀμφίσταμαι τραπέζαις.


XO.    οἰκτρὰ μὲν νόστοις αὐδά,            στρ.
        οἰκτρὰ δ' ἐν κοίταις πατρῴαις
        ὅτε οἱ παγχάλκων ἀνταία          195
        γενύων ὡρμάθη πλαγά.
        δόλος ἦν ὁ φράσας, ἔρος ὁ κτείνας,
        δεινὰν δεινῶς προφυτεύσαντες
        μορφάν· εἴτ' οὖν θεὸς εἴτε βροτῶν
         ἦν ὁ ταῦτα πράσσων.           200

ΗΛ.    ὦ πασᾶν κείνα πλέον ἀμέρα
        ἐλθοῦσ' ἐχθίστα δή μοι·
        ὦ νύξ, ὦ δείπνων ἀρρήτων
         ἔκπαγλ' ἄχθη·
         τοὺς ἐμὸς ἴδε πατὴρ          205
        θανάτους αἰκεῖς διδύμαιν χειροῖν,
         αἳ τὸν ἐμὸν εἷλον βίον
         πρόδοτον, αἵ μ' ἀπώλεσαν·
        οἷς θεὸς ὁ μέγας Ὀλύμπιος
        ποίνιμα πάθεα παθεῖν πόροι,      210
        μηδέ ποτ' ἀγλαΐας ἀποναίατο
        τοιάδ' ἀνύσαντες ἔργα.


XO.    φράζου μὴ πόρσω φωνεῖν.         ἀντ.
        οὐ γνώμαν ἴσχεις ἐξ οἵων
        τὰ παρόντ' οἰκείας εἰς ἄτας      215
        ἐμπίπτεις οὕτως αἰκῶς;

---

192 ἀμφίσταμαι rec Eustath. 1692, 57: ἀφίσταμαι Lᵃᶜ: ἐφίσταμαι Lᶜ A rec
195 ὅτε οἱ Hermann: ὅτε σοι codd. Σ Suid v. γένυς     197 ἔρος ... δόλος
Wakefield    204 ἔκπαγλα πάθη Σᵞᵖ    205 ἴδε Brunck: εἴδε codd.
(οἴδε Γ)    206 αἰκεῖς Seidler: ἄικεῖς L: ἀεικεῖς A rec    χειροῖν Liv p: χεροῖν
cett.     215 τὰ παρόντ' οἰκείας vulgo sine distinctione leguntur: τὰ
παρόντ'; οἰκείας L A rec: δ' post οἰκείας add. Bergk    216 ἐμπίπτουσ'
A. Seyffert   αἰκῶς Seidler: ἄικῶς rec: ἀεικῶς L A rec

πολὺ γάρ τι κακῶν ὑπερεκτήσω,
σᾷ δυσθύμῳ τίκτουσ' αἰεὶ
ψυχᾷ πολέμους· τὰ δὲ τοῖς δυνατοῖς
οὐκ ἐριστὰ πλάθειν.                                   220

ΗΛ.    δείν' ἐν δεινοῖς ἠναγκάσθην·
ἔξοιδ', οὐ λάθει μ' ὀργά.
ἀλλ' ἐν γὰρ δεινοῖς οὐ σχήσω
    ταύτας ἄτας,
    ὄφρα με βίος ἔχῃ.                                  225
τίνι γάρ ποτ' ἄν, ὦ φιλία γενέθλα,
πρόσφορον ἀκούσαιμ' ἔπος,
τίνι φρονοῦντι καίρια;
ἄνετέ μ' ἄνετε παράγοροι.
τάδε γὰρ ἄλυτα κεκλήσεται·                          230
οὐδέ ποτ' ἐκ καμάτων ἀποπαύσομαι
ἀνάριθμος ὧδε θρήνων.

ΧΟ.    ἀλλ' οὖν εὐνοίᾳ γ' αὐδῶ,                     ἐπ.
μάτηρ ὡσεί τις πιστά,
μὴ τίκτειν σ' ἄταν ἄταις.                             235

ΗΛ.    καὶ τί μέτρον κακότατος ἔφυ; φέρε,
πῶς ἐπὶ τοῖς φθιμένοις ἀμελεῖν καλόν;
ἐν τίνι τοῦτ' ἔβλαστ' ἀνθρώπων;
μήτ' εἴην ἔντιμος τούτοις
μήτ', εἴ τῳ πρόσκειμαι χρηστῷ,                      240
ξυνναίοιμ' εὔκηλος, γονέων
ἐκτίμους ἴσχουσα πτέρυγας
    ὀξυτόνων γόων.
εἰ γὰρ ὁ μὲν θανὼν γᾶ τε καὶ οὐδὲν ὢν              245
    κείσεται τάλας,

221 ἐν δεινοῖς ἠναγκάσθην ἐν δεινοῖς codd. (ἐν δεινοῖς ἠ. δή T Tricl):
δεινοῖς ἠ. δεινοῖς Brunck: post Wolffium (δειν. ἠ. ἐν δεινοῖς) et Kaibelium
(ἐν δεινοῖς δείν' ἠ. ) correxi       226 ἂν A rec Σ (ut videtur): om. L rec
Suid. v. καίρια       232 ἀνάνομος Σ (ἔν τισι κεῖται): ἀνήριθμος Σ (κεῖται
δὲ καὶ ἀνήριθμος)       236 κακότατος L rec Hesych. ii. 394: κακότητος A rec
238 ἔβλαστεν L rec.       245 γᾷ A

οἳ δὲ μὴ πάλιν
δώσουσ' ἀντιφόνους δίκας,
ἔρροι τ' ἂν αἰδὼς
ἁπάντων τ' εὐσέβεια θνατῶν.                              250

ΧΟ. ἐγὼ μέν, ὦ παῖ, καὶ τὸ σὸν σπεύδουσ' ἅμα
καὶ τοὐμὸν αὐτῆς ἦλθον· εἰ δὲ μὴ καλῶς
λέγω, σὺ νίκα· σοὶ γὰρ ἑψόμεσθ' ἅμα.

ΗΛ. αἰσχύνομαι μέν, ὦ γυναῖκες, εἰ δοκῶ
πολλοῖσι θρήνοις δυσφορεῖν ὑμῖν ἄγαν.                     255
ἀλλ' ἡ βία γὰρ ταῦτ' ἀναγκάζει με δρᾶν,
σύγγνωτε. πῶς γὰρ ἥτις εὐγενὴς γυνή,
πατρῷ' ὁρῶσα πήματ', οὐ δρῴη τάδ' ἄν,
ἁγὼ κατ' ἦμαρ καὶ κατ' εὐφρόνην ἀεὶ
θάλλοντα μᾶλλον ἢ καταφθίνονθ' ὁρῶ;                       260
ἦ πρῶτα μὲν τὰ μητρός, ἥ μ' ἐγείνατο,
ἔχθιστα συμβέβηκεν· εἶτα δώμασιν
ἐν τοῖς ἐμαυτῆς τοῖς φονεῦσι τοῦ πατρὸς
ξύνειμι, κἀκ τῶνδ' ἄρχομαι κἀκ τῶνδέ μοι
λαβεῖν θ' ὁμοίως καὶ τὸ τητᾶσθαι πέλει.                   265
ἔπειτα ποίας ἡμέρας δοκεῖς μ' ἄγειν,
ὅταν θρόνοις Αἴγισθον ἐνθακοῦντ' ἴδω
τοῖσιν πατρῴοις, εἰσίδω δ' ἐσθήματα
φοροῦντ' ἐκείνῳ ταὐτά, καὶ παρεστίους
σπένδοντα λοιβὰς ἔνθ' ἐκεῖνον ὤλεσεν,                     270
ἴδω δὲ τούτων τὴν τελευταίαν ὕβριν,
τὸν αὐτοφόντην ἡμῖν ἐν κοίτῃ πατρὸς
ξὺν τῇ ταλαίνῃ μητρί, μητέρ' εἰ χρεὼν
ταύτην προσαυδᾶν τῷδε συγκοιμωμένην·
ἣ δ' ὧδε τλήμων ὥστε τῷ μιάστορι                          275
ξύνεστ', Ἐρινὺν οὔτιν' ἐκφοβουμένη·
ἀλλ' ὥσπερ ἐγγελῶσα τοῖς ποιουμένους,

256 ἀλλ' ἡ βία με ταῦτ' ἀναγκάζει ποιεῖν Arist. metaph. iv. 1015ᵃ31
257 ἥτις L A rec (cf. Ai. 478): εἴ τις rec    272 αὐτοφόντην] αὐτοέντην Σγρ
(item Σ ad v. 271) Lbγρ    275 omissum in margine add. L

τηροῦσ' ἐκείνην ἡμέραν, ἐν ᾗ τότε
πατέρα τὸν ἁμὸν ἐκ δόλου κατέκτανεν,
ταύτῃ χοροὺς ἵστησι καὶ μηλοσφαγεῖ     280
θεοῖσιν ἔμμην' ἱερὰ τοῖς σωτηρίοις.
ἐγὼ δ' ὁρῶσα δύσμορος κατὰ στέγας
κλαίω, τέτηκα, κἀπικωκύω πατρὸς
τὴν δυστάλαιναν δαῖτ' ἐπωνομασμένην
αὐτὴ πρὸς αὐτήν· οὐδὲ γὰρ κλαῦσαι πάρα     285
τοσόνδ' ὅσον μοι θυμὸς ἡδονὴν φέρει.
αὕτη γὰρ ἡ λόγοισι γενναία γυνὴ
φωνοῦσα τοιάδ' ἐξονειδίζει κακά,
ὦ δύσθεον μίσημα, σοὶ μόνῃ πατὴρ
τέθνηκεν; ἄλλος δ' οὔτις ἐν πένθει βροτῶν;     290
κακῶς ὄλοιο, μηδέ σ' ἐκ γόων ποτὲ
τῶν νῦν ἀπαλλάξειαν οἱ κάτω θεοί.
τάδ' ἐξυβρίζει· πλὴν ὅταν κλύῃ τινὸς
ἥξοντ' Ὀρέστην· τηνικαῦτα δ' ἐμμανὴς
βοᾷ παραστᾶσ', οὐ σύ μοι τῶνδ' αἰτία;     295
οὐ σὸν τόδ' ἐστὶ τοὔργον, ἥτις ἐκ χερῶν
κλέψασ' Ὀρέστην τῶν ἐμῶν ὑπεξέθου;
ἀλλ' ἴσθι τοι τείσουσά γ' ἀξίαν δίκην.
τοιαῦθ' ὑλακτεῖ, σὺν δ' ἐποτρύνει πέλας
ὁ κλεινὸς αὐτῇ ταῦτα νυμφίος παρών,     300
ὁ πάντ' ἄναλκις οὗτος, ἡ πᾶσα βλάβη,
ὁ σὺν γυναιξὶ τὰς μάχας ποιούμενος.
ἐγὼ δ' Ὀρέστην τῶνδε προσμένουσ' ἀεὶ
παυστῆρ' ἐφήξειν ἡ τάλαιν' ἀπόλλυμαι.
μέλλων γὰρ αἰεὶ δρᾶν τι τὰς οὔσας τέ μου     305
καὶ τὰς ἀπούσας ἐλπίδας διέφθορεν.
ἐν οὖν τοιούτοις οὔτε σωφρονεῖν, φίλαι,
οὔτ' εὐσεβεῖν πάρεστιν· ἀλλ' ἐν τοῖς κακοῖς

278 τηροῦσ' Reiske: εὑροῦσ' codd.: φρουροῦσ' Nauck    279 ἁμὸν Lᶜ
A rec: ημερον (sic) Aˢ: ἐμὸν Lᵃᶜ rec    281 ἱρὰ rec    282 ὁρῶσα Aᵃᶜ rec:
ὁρῶσ' ἢ L Aᶜ rec    293 κλύει ut videtur Lᵃᶜ    295 αἰτίαι L Lb
300 ταῦτα Blomfield    303 Ὀρέστην προσμένουσ' ἀεί ποτε Σʸᴾ
305 μου] μοι Δ    308 ἕν τοι Hermann

πολλή 'στ' ἀνάγκη κἀπιτηδεύειν κακά.

ΧΟ. φέρ' εἰπέ, πότερον ὄντος Αἰγίσθου πέλας     310
λέγεις τάδ' ἡμῖν, ἢ βεβῶτος ἐκ δόμων;

ΗΛ. ἦ κάρτα. μὴ δόκει μ' ἄν, εἴπερ ἦν πέλας,
θυραῖον οἰχνεῖν· νῦν δ' ἀγροῖσι τυγχάνει.

ΧΟ. ἦ κἂν ἐγὼ θαρσοῦσα μᾶλλον ἐς λόγους
τοὺς σοὺς ἱκοίμην, εἴπερ ὧδε ταῦτ' ἔχει.     315

ΗΛ. ὡς νῦν ἀπόντος ἱστόρει· τί σοι φίλον;

ΧΟ. καὶ δή σ' ἐρωτῶ, τοῦ κασιγνήτου τί φής,
ἥξοντος, ἢ μέλλοντος; εἰδέναι θέλω.

ΗΛ. φησίν γε· φάσκων δ' οὐδὲν ὧν λέγει ποεῖ.

ΧΟ. φιλεῖ γὰρ ὀκνεῖν πρᾶγμ' ἀνὴρ πράσσων μέγα.     320

ΗΛ. καὶ μὴν ἔγωγ' ἔσωσ' ἐκεῖνον οὐκ ὄκνῳ.

ΧΟ. θάρσει· πέφυκεν ἐσθλός, ὥστ' ἀρκεῖν φίλοις.

ΗΛ. πέποιθ', ἐπεί τἂν οὐ μακρὰν ἔζων ἐγώ.

ΧΟ. μὴ νῦν ἔτ' εἴπῃς μηδέν· ὡς δόμων ὁρῶ
τὴν σὴν ὅμαιμον, ἐκ πατρὸς ταὐτοῦ φύσιν,     325
Χρυσόθεμιν, ἔκ τε μητρός, ἐντάφια χεροῖν
φέρουσαν, οἷα τοῖς κάτω νομίζεται.

ΧΡΥΣΟΘΕΜΙΣ

τίν' αὖ σὺ τήνδε πρὸς θυρῶνος ἐξόδοις
ἐλθοῦσα φωνεῖς, ὦ κασιγνήτη, φάτιν,
κοὐδ' ἐν χρόνῳ μακρῷ διδαχθῆναι θέλεις     330
θυμῷ ματαίῳ μὴ χαρίζεσθαι κενά;
καίτοι τοσοῦτόν γ' οἶδα κἀμαυτήν, ὅτι
ἀλγῶ 'πὶ τοῖς παροῦσιν· ὥστ' ἄν, εἰ σθένος
λάβοιμι, δηλώσαιμ' ἂν οἷ' αὐτοῖς φρονῶ.
νῦν δ' ἐν κακοῖς μοι πλεῖν ὑφειμένῃ δοκεῖ,     335
καὶ μὴ δοκεῖν μὲν δρᾶν τι, πημαίνειν δὲ μή.
τοιαῦτα δ' ἄλλα καὶ σὲ βούλομαι ποεῖν.
καίτοι τὸ μὲν δίκαιον, οὐχ ᾗ 'γὼ λέγω,

309 πολλήστ' L : πολλή τ' A rec : πολλή γ' rec     314 ἤ κἂν Lᶜ A rec : ἢ δὴ ἂν (δ' ἂν vel δἂν) Lᵃᶜ rec. : ἢ τἂν Monk     316 primus quod sciam interpunxit Jebb : ἱστορεῖν τί σοι φίλον; Madvig     φίλον] φίλων Lᵃᶜ 320 πρᾶγμ'] πᾶς Suid. v. ὀκνῶν     321 ἔσωσ' ἔγωγ' rec     325 φύσαν vel φύσαν rec     331 ψυχῆι ματαίαι Σγρ     337 ἄλλα Dindorf : ἀλλὰ codd.

ἀλλ᾽ ἢ σὺ κρίνεις. εἰ δ᾽ ἐλευθέραν με δεῖ

ζῆν, τῶν κρατούντων ἐστὶ πάντ᾽ ἀκουστέα.　　　340

ΗΛ. δεινόν γέ σ᾽ οὖσαν πατρὸς οὗ σὺ παῖς ἔφυς

κείνου λελῆσθαι, τῆς δὲ τικτούσης μέλειν.

ἅπαντα γάρ σοι τἀμὰ νουθετήματα

κείνης διδακτά, κοὐδὲν ἐκ σαυτῆς λέγεις.

ἔπειθ᾽ ἑλοῦ γε θάτερ᾽, ἢ φρονεῖν κακῶς,　　　345

ἢ τῶν φίλων φρονοῦσα μὴ μνήμην ἔχειν·

ἥτις λέγεις μὲν ἀρτίως ὡς, εἰ λάβοις

σθένος, τὸ τούτων μῖσος ἐκδείξειας ἄν·

ἐμοῦ δὲ πατρὶ πάντα τιμωρουμένης

οὔτε ξυνέρδεις τήν τε δρῶσαν ἐκτρέπεις.　　　350

οὐ ταῦτα πρὸς κακοῖσι δειλίαν ἔχει;

ἐπεὶ δίδαξον, ἢ μάθ᾽ ἐξ ἐμοῦ, τί μοι

κέρδος γένοιτ᾽ ἂν τῶνδε ληξάσῃ γόων.

οὐ ζῶ; κακῶς μέν, οἶδ᾽, ἐπαρκούντως δ᾽ ἐμοί.

λυπῶ δὲ τούτους, ὥστε τῷ τεθνηκότι　　　355

τιμὰς προσάπτειν, εἴ τις ἔστ᾽ ἐκεῖ χάρις.

σὺ δ᾽ ἡμὶν ἡ μισοῦσα μισεῖς μὲν λόγῳ,

ἔργῳ δὲ τοῖς φονεῦσι τοῦ πατρὸς ξύνει.

ἐγὼ μὲν οὖν οὐκ ἄν ποτ᾽, οὐδ᾽ εἴ μοι τὰ σὰ

μέλλοι τις οἴσειν δῶρ᾽, ἐφ᾽ οἷσι νῦν χλιδᾷς,　　　360

τούτοις ὑπεικάθοιμι· σοὶ δὲ πλουσία

τράπεζα κείσθω καὶ περιρρείτω βίος.

ἐμοὶ γὰρ ἔστω τοὐμὲ μὴ λυπεῖν μόνον

βόσκημα· τῆς σῆς δ᾽ οὐκ ἐρῶ τιμῆς λαχεῖν.

οὐδ᾽ ἂν σύ, σώφρων γ᾽ οὖσα. νῦν δ᾽ ἐξὸν πατρὸς　　　365

πάντων ἀρίστου παῖδα κεκλῆσθαι, καλοῦ

τῆς μητρός. οὕτω γὰρ φανῇ πλείστοις κακή,

θανόντα πατέρα καὶ φίλους προδοῦσα σούς.

ΧΟ. μηδὲν πρὸς ὀργὴν πρὸς θεῶν· ὡς τοῖς λόγοις

340 ἀκουστέον rec　　　345 θάτερ᾽ ἤ] θάτερον rec　　　354 ἀπαρκούντως
Thom. Mag. v. ἀπαρκεῖ 24, 16　　δ᾽ ἐμοί Ven: δέ μοι L A rec　　　355 post v.
356 habet sed ordinem nota marginali correxit L　　　359 μὲν οὖν L²ˢ A rec:
μὲν L Lb　　360 μέλλει rec　　363 λυπεῖν codd. Σ: λυποῦν Erfurdt et
fort. Σ　　364 λαχεῖν Lˢ rec: τυχεῖν L A rec

ἔνεστιν ἀμφοῖν κέρδος, εἰ σὺ μὲν μάθοις     370
τοῖς τῆσδε χρῆσθαι, τοῖς δὲ σοῖς αὕτη πάλιν.

ΧΡ. ἐγὼ μέν, ὦ γυναῖκες, ἠθάς εἰμί πως
τῶν τῆσδε μύθων· οὐδ' ἂν ἐμνήσθην ποτέ,
εἰ μὴ κακὸν μέγιστον εἰς αὐτὴν ἰὸν
ἤκουσ', ὃ ταύτην τῶν μακρῶν σχήσει γόων.     375

ΗΛ. φέρ' εἰπὲ δὴ τὸ δεινόν. εἰ γὰρ τῶνδέ μοι
μεῖζόν τι λέξεις, οὐκ ἂν ἀντείποιμ' ἔτι.

ΧΡ. ἀλλ' ἐξερῶ σοι πᾶν ὅσον κάτοιδ' ἐγώ.
μέλλουσι γάρ σ', εἰ τῶνδε μὴ λήξεις γόων,
ἐνταῦθα πέμψειν ἔνθα μή ποθ' ἡλίου     380
φέγγος προσόψῃ, ζῶσα δ' ἐν κατηρεφεῖ
στέγῃ χθονὸς τῆσδ' ἐκτὸς ὑμνήσεις κακά.
πρὸς ταῦτα φράζου κἀμὲ μή ποθ' ὕστερον
παθοῦσα μέμψῃ. νῦν γὰρ ἐν καλῷ φρονεῖν.

ΗΛ. ἦ ταῦτα δή με καὶ βεβούλευνται ποεῖν;     385

ΧΡ. μάλισθ'· ὅταν περ οἴκαδ' Αἴγισθος μόλῃ.

ΗΛ. ἀλλ' ἐξίκοιτο τοῦδέ γ' οὕνεκ' ἐν τάχει.

ΧΡ. τίν', ὦ τάλαινα, τόνδ' ἐπηράσω λόγον;

ΗΛ. ἐλθεῖν ἐκεῖνον, εἴ τι τῶνδε δρᾶν νοεῖ.

ΧΡ. ὅπως πάθῃς τί χρῆμα; ποῦ ποτ' εἶ φρενῶν;     390

ΗΛ. ὅπως ἀφ' ὑμῶν ὡς προσώτατ' ἐκφύγω.

ΧΡ. βίου δὲ τοῦ παρόντος οὐ μνείαν ἔχεις;

ΗΛ. καλὸς γὰρ οὑμὸς βίοτος ὥστε θαυμάσαι.

ΧΡ. ἀλλ' ἦν ἄν, εἰ σύ γ' εὖ φρονεῖν ἠπίστασο.

ΗΛ. μή μ' ἐκδίδασκε τοῖς φίλοις εἶναι κακήν.     395

ΧΡ. ἀλλ' οὐ διδάσκω· τοῖς κρατοῦσι δ' εἰκαθεῖν.

ΗΛ. σὺ ταῦτα θώπευ'· οὐκ ἐμοὺς τρόπους λέγεις.

ΧΡ. καλόν γε μέντοι μὴ 'ξ ἀβουλίας πεσεῖν.

371 αὕτη rec: αὐτὴ L A rec    373 οὐδ'] κοὑκ T    376 γὰρ] δὲ Elmsley
378 σοι L rec: τοι Lˢ A rec    379 λήξεις Lᶜ A rec: λήξηισ Lᵃᶜ rec   γόων]
λόγων Σγρ    381 κατόψει Eustath. 1839, 61: καθορῇ Ammon. p. 51
κατηρεφεῖ] κατώρυχι coni. Nauck: κατασκαφεῖ Bruhn    382 χθονὸς
στέγῃ Kaibel: στέγῃ πόλεως coni. Nauck    383 κἀμὲ] καί με codd.:
κοὔ με Blaydes    385 δή] γάρ rec   με] μοι rec   βεβούλευται rec
387 εἵνεκ' Lb    396 εἰκάθειν codd.: corr. Elmsley

ΗΛ. πεσούμεθ', εἰ χρή, πατρὶ τιμωρούμενοι.

ΧΡ. πατὴρ δὲ τούτων, οἶδα, συγγνώμην ἔχει.                    400

ΗΛ. ταῦτ' ἐστὶ τἄπη πρὸς κακῶν ἐπαινέσαι.

ΧΡ. σὺ δ' οὐχὶ πείσῃ καὶ συναινέσεις ἐμοί;

ΗΛ. οὐ δῆτα. μή πω νοῦ τοσόνδ' εἴην κενή.

ΧΡ. χωρήσομαί τἄρ' οἷπερ ἐστάλην ὁδοῦ.

ΗΛ. ποῖ δ' ἐμπορεύῃ; τῷ φέρεις τάδ' ἔμπυρα;         405

ΧΡ. μήτηρ με πέμπει πατρὶ τυμβεῦσαι χοάς.

ΗΛ. πῶς εἶπας; ἦ τῷ δυσμενεστάτῳ βροτῶν;

ΧΡ. ὃν ἔκταν' αὐτή· τοῦτο γὰρ λέξαι θέλεις.

ΗΛ. ἐκ τοῦ φίλων πεισθεῖσα; τῷ τοῦτ' ἤρεσεν;

ΧΡ. ἐκ δείματός του νυκτέρου, δοκεῖν ἐμοί.         410

ΗΛ. ὦ θεοὶ πατρῷοι, συγγένεσθέ γ' ἀλλὰ νῦν.

ΧΡ. ἔχεις τι θάρσος τοῦδε τοῦ τάρβους πέρι;

ΗΛ. εἴ μοι λέγοις τὴν ὄψιν, εἴποιμ' ἂν τότε.

ΧΡ. ἀλλ' οὐ κάτοιδα πλὴν ἐπὶ σμικρὸν φράσαι.

ΗΛ. λέγ' ἀλλὰ τοῦτο. πολλά τοι σμικροὶ λόγοι         415
       ἔσφηλαν ἤδη καὶ κατώρθωσαν βροτούς.

ΧΡ. λόγος τις αὐτήν ἐστιν εἰσιδεῖν πατρὸς
       τοῦ σοῦ τε κἀμοῦ δευτέραν ὁμιλίαν
       ἐλθόντος ἐς φῶς· εἶτα τόνδ' ἐφέστιον
       πῆξαι λαβόντα σκῆπτρον οὑφόρει ποτὲ         420
       αὐτός, τανῦν δ' Αἴγισθος· ἔκ τε τοῦδ' ἄνω
       βλαστεῖν βρύοντα θαλλόν, ᾧ κατάσκιον
       πᾶσαν γενέσθαι τὴν Μυκηναίων χθόνα.
       τοιαῦτά του παρόντος, ἡνίχ' Ἡλίῳ
       δείκνυσι τοὔναρ, ἔκλυον ἐξηγουμένου.         425
       πλείω δὲ τούτων οὐ κάτοιδα, πλὴν ὅτι
       πέμπει με κείνη τοῦδε τοῦ φόβου χάριν.
       πρός νυν θεῶν σε λίσσομαι τῶν ἐγγενῶν

399 τιμωρούμεναι Γ      405 ποῖ] ποῦ rec    τῷ φέρεις rec: ποῖ φέρεις
L A rec: ποῦ (vel πῆ) φέρεις rec      407 ἦ Lᶜ A rec: εἰ Lᵃᶜ: ἦ rec
413 λέγοις Turneb: λέγεις L A T rec      414 σμικρὸν Lᶜ (ον in litura)
rec: σμικρῷ A rec: σμικρῶν Lˢ      421 δ' om. A ἔκ τε] ἔκ δὲ Γ
422 ᾧ A Lᵃ ᵞᵖ rec  τῷ L rec      424 τοιαῦτα τοῦ Lᵃᶜ rec Σ ad O.C. 477
425 δείκνυε Σ ad O.C. 477    ἐξηγουμένου L rec: ἐξηγουμένης Lˢ A rec
427 μ' ἐκείνη rec  φόβου] τάρβους Jen      428 sqq. Electrae tribuunt
codd. plurimi, Chrys. continuant Γ T Turneb

ἐμοὶ πιθέσθαι μηδ' ἀβουλίᾳ πεσεῖν·
εἰ γάρ μ' ἀπώσῃ, σὺν κακῷ μέτει πάλιν.　　　　430

ΗΛ.　ἀλλ', ὦ φίλη, τούτων μὲν ὧν ἔχεις χεροῖν
τύμβῳ προσάψῃς μηδέν· οὐ γάρ σοι θέμις
οὐδ' ὅσιον ἐχθρᾶς ἀπὸ γυναικὸς ἱστάναι
κτερίσματ' οὐδὲ λουτρὰ προσφέρειν πατρί·
ἀλλ' ἢ πνοαῖσιν ἢ βαθυσκαφεῖ κόνει　　　　435
κρύψον νιν, ἔνθα μή ποτ' εἰς εὐνὴν πατρὸς
τούτων πρόσεισι μηδέν· ἀλλ' ὅταν θάνῃ,
κειμήλι' αὐτῇ ταῦτα σῳζέσθω κάτω.
ἀρχὴν δ' ἄν, εἰ μὴ τλημονεστάτη γυνὴ
πασῶν ἔβλαστε, τάσδε δυσμενεῖς χοὰς　　　　440
οὐκ ἄν ποθ' ὅν γ' ἔκτεινε τῷδ' ἐπέστεφε.
σκέψαι γὰρ εἴ σοι προσφιλῶς αὐτῇ δοκεῖ
γέρα τάδ' οὖν τάφοισι δέξεσθαι νέκυς
ὑφ' ἧς θανὼν ἄτιμος ὥστε δυσμενὴς
ἐμασχαλίσθη κἀπὶ λουτροῖσιν κάρα　　　　445
κηλῖδας ἐξέμαξεν. ἆρα μὴ δοκεῖς
λυτήρι' αὐτῇ ταῦτα τοῦ φόνου φέρειν;
οὐκ ἔστιν. ἀλλὰ ταῦτα μὲν μέθες· σὺ δὲ
τεμοῦσα κρατὸς βοστρύχων ἄκρας φόβας
κἀμοῦ ταλαίνης, σμικρὰ μὲν τάδ', ἀλλ' ὅμως　　　　450
ἄχω, δὸς αὐτῷ, τήνδε, λιπαρῶ, τρίχα
καὶ ζῶμα τοὐμὸν οὐ χλιδαῖς ἠσκημένον.
αἰτοῦ δὲ προσπίτνουσα γῆθεν εὐμενῆ
ἡμῖν ἀρωγὸν αὐτὸν εἰς ἐχθροὺς μολεῖν,
καὶ παῖδ' Ὀρέστην ἐξ ὑπερτέρας χερὸς　　　　455
ἐχθροῖσιν αὐτοῦ ζῶντ' ἐπεμβῆναι ποδί,
ὅπως τὸ λοιπὸν αὐτὸν ἀφνεωτέραις

433 ἀπὸ L²ˢ A rec: om. L rec　　　435 πνοαῖσιν] ῥοαῖσιν Heath
436 ἔνθα] ἔνθεν coni. Meineke　　438 σῳζέσθων rec　　439 δ' ἄν] γάρ Lˢ rec
443 δέξασθαι codd.: corr. Heath　　　445 ἐμασχαλίσθην A: ἐμασχαλίσθης
Etym. M. 118,30　　　κάρα rec Σ: κάρα L A rec Σ　　446 ἐξαίμαξεν Lᵃᶜ
rec Σ¹　　449 φόβας] κόμας Lˢ Γ　　451 τήνδε, λιπαρῶ, Kells:
τήνδε λιπαρῇ Σ (ἐν τῷ ὑπομνήματι): τήνδ' ἀλιπαρῇ codd. Σ Hesych.
i. 123, Suid. s.v. et v. ζῶμα, Eustath. 787, 50: τήνδ' ἀνηλιφῇ Blaydes
456 ἐπιβῆναι Lᵃᶜ Lb

χερσὶ στέφωμεν ἢ τανῦν δωρούμεθα.
οἶμαι μὲν οὖν, οἶμαί τι κἀκείνῳ μέλον
πέμψαι τάδ' αὐτῇ δυσπρόσοπτ' ὀνείρατα·        460
ὅμως δ', ἀδελφή, σοί θ' ὑπούργησον τάδε
ἐμοί τ' ἀρωγά, τῷ τε φιλτάτῳ βροτῶν
πάντων, ἐν Ἅιδου κειμένῳ κοινῷ πατρί.

ΧΟ. πρὸς εὐσέβειαν ἡ κόρη λέγει· σὺ δέ,
εἰ σωφρονήσεις, ὦ φίλη, δράσεις τάδε.        465

ΧΡ. δράσω· τὸ γὰρ δίκαιον οὐκ ἔχει λόγον
δυοῖν ἐρίζειν, ἀλλ' ἐπισπεύδειν τὸ δρᾶν.
πειρωμένη δὲ τῶνδε τῶν ἔργων ἐμοὶ
σιγὴ παρ' ὑμῶν πρὸς θεῶν ἔστω, φίλαι·
ὡς εἰ τάδ' ἡ τεκοῦσα πεύσεται, πικρὰν        470
δοκῶ με πεῖραν τήνδε τολμήσειν ἔτι.

ΧΟ. εἰ μὴ 'γὼ παράφρων μάντις ἔφυν        στρ.
καὶ γνώμας λειπομένα σοφᾶς,
εἶσιν ἁ πρόμαντις        475
Δίκα, δίκαια φερομένα χεροῖν κράτη·
μέτεισιν, ὦ τέκνον, οὐ μακροῦ χρόνου.
    ὕπεστί μοι θάρσος,
    ἁδυπνόων κλύουσαν        480
    ἀρτίως ὀνειράτων.
    οὐ γάρ ποτ' ἀμναστεῖ γ' ὁ φύ-
    σας ⟨σ'⟩ Ἑλλάνων ἄναξ,
    οὐδ' ἁ παλαιὰ χαλκόπλα-
    κτος ἀμφάκης γένυς,        485
    ἅ νιν κατέπεφνεν αἰσχί-
    σταις ἐν αἰκείαις.

459 οἶμαί τι] εἶναί τι coni. Nauck    μέλον codd.: μέλειν Nauck
460 δυσπρόσοπτ' Vindob        467 ἐπισπεύδει Stob. flor. 11. 9
479 θάρσος Lᶜ A rec: θράσος Lᵃᶜ rec    480 κλύουσαν L rec: κλύουσα A
Γ: κλυούσᾳ et κλυούσῃ rec    482 ἀμναστεῖ A rec: ἀμνηστεῖ L rec Suid.
s.v. γ' codd.: σ' Wakefield        483 σ' add. Froehlich        484 sq. χαλκό-
πλακτος rec.: χαλκόπληκτος L A rec: χαλκόπακτος Erfurdt    ἀμφάκης ex
Hesych. i. 155 (ἀμφακῆς· ἀξίνη) Brunck: ἀμφήκης codd.        487 αἰσχίσταις ἐν L rec: αἰσχίσταις εἶν (h. e. ἐν sscr. 1) A rec: αἰσχίσταισιν rec
αἰκίαις codd.: corr. Porson

ἥξει καὶ πολύπους καὶ πολύχειρ                                    ἀντ.
ἁ δεινοῖς κρυπτομένα λόχοις                                        490
    χαλκόπους Ἐρινύς.
ἄλεκτρ' ἄνυμφα γὰρ ἐπέβα μιαιφόνων
γάμων ἁμιλλήμαθ' οἷσιν οὐ θέμις.
    πρὸ τῶνδέ τοι θάρσος                                          495
    μήποτε μήποθ' ἡμῖν
    ἀψεγὲς πελᾶν τέρας
    τοῖς δρῶσι καὶ συνδρῶσιν. ἤ-
    τοι μαντεῖαι βροτῶν
    οὐκ εἰσὶν ἐν δεινοῖς ὀνεί-
    ροις οὐδ' ἐν θεσφάτοις,                                       500
    εἰ μὴ τόδε φάσμα νυκτὸς
    εὖ κατασχήσει.


    ὦ Πέλοπος ἁ πρόσθεν                                           ἐπ.
    πολύπονος ἱππεία,                                             505
    ὡς ἔμολες αἰανὴς
        τᾷδε γᾷ.
    εὖτε γὰρ ὁ ποντισθεὶς
    Μυρτίλος ἐκοιμάθη,
    παγχρύσων δίφρων                                              510
    δυστάνοις αἰκείαις
    πρόρριζος ἐκριφθείς,
        οὔ τί πω
    ἔλιπεν ἐκ τοῦδ' οἴκου
    πολύπονος αἰκεία.                                             515

488 πολύπαις Σ (ἐν τῷ ὑπομνήματι κεῖται)      495 θάρσος Wilamowitz:
μ' ἔχει L A rec Σ: μ' ἔχει θάρσος Σ¹ rec: μ' ἴσχει Kaibel      496 μήποτε
μήποθ' A rec: μήποθ' L rec   ἡμῖν suspectum      497 ἀψεγὲς ] ἀψεφὲς
coni. Bergk    πελᾶν] πελᾷ Froehlich      498 sq. ἤτοι] ἤτοι Lbᶜ et fort. Lᵃᶜ
506 αἰανὴς LᵃᶜLbᶜ: αἰανὴ LᶜA rec: αἰανᾷ Σ    511 αἰκίαις codd.   512 ἐκριφείς
Lᵃᶜ rec Suid. v. πρόρριζος      513 οὔ τίς πω codd.: corr. Hermann
514 ἔλιπεν rec: ἔλειπεν L A rec   οἴκου] οἴκους Lᵃᶜ rec Σ (ad v. 508)
515 πολύπονος] πολυπάμονας (πολυπήμονας Bothe) Bergk ex Σ ad v. 508
(τοὺς πολυκτήμονας δόμους)    αἰκία codd

ΚΛΥΤΑΙΜΗΣΤΡΑ

ἀνειμένη μέν, ὡς ἔοικας, αὖ στρέφῃ.

οὐ γὰρ πάρεστ' Αἴγισθος, ὅς σ' ἐπεῖχ' ἀεὶ

μή τοι θυραίαν γ' οὖσαν αἰσχύνειν φίλους·

νῦν δ' ὡς ἄπεστ' ἐκεῖνος, οὐδὲν ἐντρέπῃ

ἐμοῦ γε· καίτοι πολλὰ πρὸς πολλούς με δὴ                    520

ἐξεῖπας ὡς θρασεῖα καὶ πέρα δίκης

ἄρχω, καθυβρίζουσα καὶ σὲ καὶ τὰ σά.

ἐγὼ δ' ὕβριν μὲν οὐκ ἔχω, κακῶς δέ σε

λέγω κακῶς κλύουσα πρὸς σέθεν θαμά.

πατὴρ γάρ, οὐδὲν ἄλλο, σοὶ πρόσχημ' ἀεί,              525

ὡς ἐξ ἐμοῦ τέθνηκεν. ἐξ ἐμοῦ· καλῶς

ἔξοιδα· τῶνδ' ἄρνησις οὐκ ἔνεστί μοι.

ἡ γὰρ Δίκη νιν εἷλεν, οὐκ ἐγὼ μόνη,

ᾗ χρῆν σ' ἀρήγειν, εἰ φρονοῦσ' ἐτύγχανες.

ἐπεὶ πατὴρ σὸς οὗτος, ὃν θρηνεῖς ἀεί,                          530

τὴν σὴν ὅμαιμον μοῦνος Ἑλλήνων ἔτλη

θῦσαι θεοῖσιν, οὐκ ἴσον καμὼν ἐμοὶ

λύπης, ὅτ' ἔσπειρ', ὥσπερ ἡ τίκτουσ' ἐγώ.

εἶεν· δίδαξον δή με τοῦ χάριν, τίνων

ἔθυσεν αὐτήν. πότερον Ἀργείων ἐρεῖς;                         535

ἀλλ' οὐ μετῆν αὐτοῖσι τήν γ' ἐμὴν κτανεῖν.

ἀλλ' ἀντ' ἀδελφοῦ δῆτα Μενέλεω κτανὼν

τἄμ' οὐκ ἔμελλε τῶνδέ μοι δώσειν δίκην;

πότερον ἐκείνῳ παῖδες οὐκ ἦσαν διπλοῖ,

οὓς τῆσδε μᾶλλον εἰκὸς ἦν θνῄσκειν, πατρὸς          540

καὶ μητρὸς ὄντας, ἧς ὁ πλοῦς ὅδ' ἦν χάριν;

ἢ τῶν ἐμῶν Ἅιδης τιν' ἵμερον τέκνων

ἢ τῶν ἐκείνης ἔσχε δαίσασθαι πλέον;

ἢ τῷ πανώλει πατρὶ τῶν μὲν ἐξ ἐμοῦ

516 αὖ στρέφῃ A rec Suidae v. ἀνειμέναι plures: αὖ τρέφῃ L rec Eustath. 168, 36: ἐκτρέφῃ Suidae A      528 εἷλεν οὐκ A rec: εἶλεν κοὐκ Lᵃᶜ Aug c: εἷλε κοὐκ Lᶜ rec      534 δή] δέ Lᵃᶜ rec τοῦ χάριν τίνων Lᵃᶜ rec: τοῦ χάριν τίνος Lᶜ A rec: τοῦτο, τοῦ χάριν Schmalfeld      540 πατρός suspectum: πάρος Nauck: fort. ὕπερ      541 del. Nauck καὶ] ἐκ Hermann 543 πλέων Lᵃᶜ: πλέω rec

παίδων πόθος παρεῖτο, Μενέλεω δ' ἐνῆν;     545
οὐ ταῦτ' ἀβούλου καὶ κακοῦ γνώμην πατρός;
δοκῶ μέν, εἰ καὶ σῆς δίχα γνώμης λέγω.
φαίη δ' ἂν ἡ θανοῦσά γ', εἰ φωνὴν λάβοι.
ἐγὼ μὲν οὖν οὐκ εἰμὶ τοῖς πεπραγμένοις
δύσθυμος· εἰ δὲ σοὶ δοκῶ φρονεῖν κακῶς,     550
γνώμην δικαίαν σχοῦσα τοὺς πέλας ψέγε.

ΗΛ. ἐρεῖς μὲν οὐχὶ νῦν γέ μ' ὡς ἄρξασά τι
λυπηρὸν εἶτα σοῦ τάδ' ἐξήκουσ' ὕπο·
ἀλλ' ἢν ἐφῇς μοι, τοῦ τεθνηκότος θ' ὕπερ
λέξαιμ' ἂν ὀρθῶς τῆς κασιγνήτης θ' ὁμοῦ.     555

ΚΛ. καὶ μὴν ἐφίημ'· εἰ δέ μ' ὧδ' ἀεὶ λόγους
ἐξῆρχες, οὐκ ἂν ἦσθα λυπηρὰ κλύειν.

ΗΛ. καὶ δὴ λέγω σοι. πατέρα φῂς κτεῖναι. τίς ἂν
τούτου λόγος γένοιτ' ἂν αἰσχίων ἔτι,
εἴτ' οὖν δικαίως εἴτε μή; λέξω δέ σοι,     560
ὡς οὐ δίκῃ γ' ἔκτεινας, ἀλλά σ' ἔσπασεν
πειθὼ κακοῦ πρὸς ἀνδρός, ᾧ τανῦν ξύνει.
ἐροῦ δὲ τὴν κυναγὸν Ἄρτεμιν τίνος
ποινὰς τὰ πλοῖ' ἀπνεύματ' ἔσχ' ἐν Αὐλίδι·
ἢ 'γὼ φράσω· κείνης γὰρ οὐ θέμις μαθεῖν.     565
πατήρ ποθ' οὑμός, ὡς ἐγὼ κλύω, θεᾶς
παίζων κατ' ἄλσος ἐξεκίνησεν ποδοῖν
στικτὸν κεράστην ἔλαφον, οὗ κατὰ σφαγὰς
ἐκκομπάσας ἔπος τι τυγχάνει βαλών.
κἀκ τοῦδε μηνίσασα Λητῴα κόρη     570
κατεῖχ' Ἀχαιούς, ὡς πατὴρ ἀντίσταθμον
τοῦ θηρὸς ἐκθύσειε τὴν αὑτοῦ κόρην.
ὧδ' ἦν τὰ κείνης θύματ'· οὐ γὰρ ἦν λύσις

545 Μενελέῳ σ (Bodl)     548 φαίην A     554 θ' rec: γ' A rec: om.
L rec     556 λόγους Lᵃᶜ: λόγοις cett. Σ¹     559 ἔτι L (in rasura)
560 λέξω] δείξω Morstadt     562 πιθὼ L Σ¹     564 ποινὰς Lᵃᶜ rec:
ποινᾶς rec: ποινῆς Lᶜ A rec     τὰ πλοῖ' ἀπνεύματ' Froehlich: τὰ πλοῖα
πνεύματ' Housman: τὰ πολλὰ πνεύματ' codd.   ἔσχ' ἐν] ἔσχεν rec   Αὐλίδι
L (in rasura)     567 ἐξενίκησεν rec Suidae v. ἐξεκίνησεν B     569 τι om.
A Ven     572 αὑτοῦ Pal: αὐτοῦ L A rec

ἄλλη στρατῷ πρὸς οἶκον οὐδ' εἰς Ἴλιον.
ἀνθ' ὧν βιασθεὶς πολλὰ κἀντιβὰς μόλις                    575
ἔθυσεν αὐτήν, οὐχὶ Μενέλεω χάριν.
εἰ δ' οὖν, ἐρῶ γὰρ καὶ τὸ σόν, κεῖνον θέλων
ἐπωφελῆσαι ταῦτ' ἔδρα, τούτου θανεῖν
χρῆν αὐτὸν οὕνεκ' ἐκ σέθεν; ποίῳ νόμῳ;
ὅρα τιθεῖσα τόνδε τὸν νόμον βροτοῖς                      580
μὴ πῆμα σαυτῇ καὶ μετάγνοιαν τίθης.
εἰ γὰρ κτενοῦμεν ἄλλον ἀντ' ἄλλου, σύ τοι
πρώτη θάνοις ἄν, εἰ δίκης γε τυγχάνοις.
ἀλλ' εἰσόρα μὴ σκῆψιν οὐκ οὖσαν τίθης.
εἰ γὰρ θέλεις, δίδαξον ἀνθ' ὅτου τανῦν                   585
αἴσχιστα πάντων ἔργα δρῶσα τυγχάνεις,
ἥτις ξυνεύδεις τῷ παλαμναίῳ, μεθ' οὗ
πατέρα τὸν ἀμὸν πρόσθεν ἐξαπώλεσας,
καὶ παιδοποιεῖς, τοὺς δὲ πρόσθεν εὐσεβεῖς
κἀξ εὐσεβῶν βλαστόντας ἐκβαλοῦσ' ἔχεις.                  590
πῶς ταῦτ' ἐπαινέσαιμ' ἄν; ἢ καὶ ταῦτ' ἐρεῖς
ὡς τῆς θυγατρὸς ἀντίποινα λαμβάνεις;
αἰσχρῶς γ', ἐάν περ καὶ λέγῃς. οὐ γὰρ καλὸν
ἐχθροῖς γαμεῖσθαι τῆς θυγατρὸς οὕνεκα.
ἀλλ' οὐ γὰρ οὐδὲ νουθετεῖν ἔξεστί σε,                    595
ἢ πᾶσαν ἵῃς γλῶσσαν ὡς τὴν μητέρα
κακοστομοῦμεν. καί σ' ἔγωγε δεσπότιν
ἢ μητέρ' οὐκ ἔλασσον εἰς ἡμᾶς νέμω,
ἢ ζῶ βίον μοχθηρόν, ἔκ τε σοῦ κακοῖς
πολλοῖς ἀεὶ ξυνοῦσα τοῦ τε συννόμου.                     600
ὁ δ' ἄλλος ἔξω, χεῖρα σὴν μόλις φυγών,

575 μόλις] μόγις rec      581 τίθης A rec: τίθηις L: τιθῇς (τιθῆς) rec
Aelian. (fr. 64) ap. Suid. v. ὁμοῦ      583 τυγχάνοις Turneb: τυγχάνεις
L A rec T: τυγχάνοι (praemisso δίκη) Jen      584–6 omissos in margine
add. L      584 τίθης L rec Suid. v. σκῆψις: τίθεις A: τιθῇς (τιθῆς) rec
588 ἀμὸν Lᶜ A rec: ἀμὸν rec: ἐμὸν Lᵃᶜ rec      590 βλαστῶντας L rec
591 ἐπαινέσωμεν Σγρ καὶ ταῦτ' Dobree: καὶ τοῦτ' codd.      592 λαμ-
βάνει Lˢ: τυγχάνει L (postea erasum) Γ Lb      593 γ' Hartung: δ' codd. (om.
Γ) λέγεις Lᵃᶜ rec      595 σε Lᶜ A rec: σοι Lᵃᶜ rec      596 ἵῃς rec: ἵεις
L A rec      601 ἄλλος] ἀμὸς Wex

τλήμων Ὀρέστης δυστυχῆ τρίβει βίον·
ὃν πολλὰ δή μέ σοι τρέφειν μιάστορα
ἐπῃτιάσω· καὶ τόδ᾽, εἴπερ ἔσθενον,
ἔδρων ἄν, εὖ τοῦτ᾽ ἴσθι. τοῦδέ γ᾽ οὕνεκα     605
κήρυσσέ μ᾽ εἰς ἅπαντας, εἴτε χρῇς κακὴν
εἴτε στόμαργον εἴτ᾽ ἀναιδείας πλέαν.
εἰ γὰρ πέφυκα τῶνδε τῶν ἔργων ἴδρις,
σχεδόν τι τὴν σὴν οὐ καταισχύνω φύσιν.

ΧΟ. ὁρῶ μένος πνέουσαν· εἰ δὲ σὺν δίκῃ     610
ξύνεστι, τοῦδε φροντίδ᾽ οὐκέτ᾽ εἰσορῶ.

ΚΛ. ποίας δ᾽ ἐμοὶ δεῖ πρός γε τήνδε φροντίδος,
ἥτις τοιαῦτα τὴν τεκοῦσαν ὕβρισεν,
καὶ ταῦτα τηλικοῦτος; ἆρά σοι δοκεῖ
χωρεῖν ἂν ἐς πᾶν ἔργον αἰσχύνης ἄτερ;     615

ΗΛ. εὖ νυν ἐπίστω τῶνδέ μ᾽ αἰσχύνην ἔχειν,
κεἰ μὴ δοκῶ σοι· μανθάνω δ᾽ ὁθούνεκα
ἔξωρα πράσσω κοὐκ ἐμοὶ προσεικότα.
ἀλλ᾽ ἡ γὰρ ἐκ σοῦ δυσμένεια καὶ τὰ σὰ
ἔργ᾽ ἐξαναγκάζει με ταῦτα δρᾶν βίᾳ·     620
αἰσχροῖς γὰρ αἰσχρὰ πράγματ᾽ ἐκδιδάσκεται.

ΚΛ. ὦ θρέμμ᾽ ἀναιδές, ἦ σ᾽ ἐγὼ καὶ τἄμ᾽ ἔπη
καὶ τἄργα τἀμὰ πόλλ᾽ ἄγαν λέγειν ποεῖ;

ΗΛ. σύ τοι λέγεις νιν, οὐκ ἐγώ. σὺ γὰρ ποεῖς
τοὔργον· τὰ δ᾽ ἔργα τοὺς λόγους εὑρίσκεται.     625

ΚΛ. ἀλλ᾽ οὐ μὰ τὴν δέσποιναν Ἄρτεμιν θράσους
τοῦδ᾽ οὐκ ἀλύξεις, εὖτ᾽ ἂν Αἴγισθος μόλῃ.

ΗΛ. ὁρᾷς; πρὸς ὀργὴν ἐκφέρῃ, μεθεῖσά μοι
λέγειν ἃ χρήζοιμ᾽, οὐδ᾽ ἐπίστασαι κλύειν.

ΚΛ. οὔκουν ἐάσεις οὐδ᾽ ὑπ᾽ εὐφήμου βοῆς     630
θῦσαί μ᾽, ἐπειδὴ σοί γ᾽ ἐφῆκα πᾶν λέγειν;

606 χρῇς Wunder: χρὴ codd.    608 ἔργων] κακῶν rec Eustath. 1969, 18: λόγων Suid. v. ἴδριας    612 δέ μοι codd. Σ    614 ἆρα Lᵃᶜ rec: ἆρ᾽ οὐ Lᶜ A rec    618 προσεικότα rec: προσηκότα L rec Suidae v. ἔξωρα plerique: προσήκοντα A rec Suidae ed. Med.    623 interrogandi signum quod in fine versus habet L del. Schaefer    628 μεθεῖσα] παρεῖσα rec    630 ὑπ᾽] ἐπ᾽ A

ΗΛ. ἐῶ, κελεύω, θῦε, μηδ᾽ ἐπαιτιῶ
τοὐμὸν στόμ᾽· ὡς οὐκ ἂν πέρα λέξαιμ᾽ ἔτι.

ΚΛ. ἔπαιρε δὴ σὺ θύμαθ᾽ ἡ παροῦσά μοι
πάγκαρπ᾽, ἄνακτι τῷδ᾽ ὅπως λυτηρίους            635
εὐχὰς ἀνάσχω δειμάτων, ἃ νῦν ἔχω.
κλύοις ἂν ἤδη, Φοῖβε προστατήριε,
κεκρυμμένην μου βάξιν. οὐ γὰρ ἐν φίλοις
ὁ μῦθος, οὐδὲ πᾶν ἀναπτύξαι πρέπει
πρὸς φῶς παρούσης τῆσδε πλησίας ἐμοί,            640
μὴ σὺν φθόνῳ τε καὶ πολυγλώσσῳ βοῇ
σπείρῃ ματαίαν βάξιν ἐς πᾶσαν πόλιν.
ἀλλ᾽ ὧδ᾽ ἄκουε· τῇδε γὰρ κἀγὼ φράσω.
ἃ γὰρ προσεῖδον νυκτὶ τῇδε φάσματα
δισσῶν ὀνείρων, ταῦτά μοι, Λύκει᾽ ἄναξ,          645
εἰ μὲν πέφηνεν ἐσθλά, δὸς τελεσφόρα,
εἰ δ᾽ ἐχθρά, τοῖς ἐχθροῖσιν ἔμπαλιν μέθες·
καὶ μή με πλούτου τοῦ παρόντος εἴ τινες
δόλοισι βουλεύουσιν ἐκβαλεῖν, ἐφῇς,
ἀλλ᾽ ὧδέ μ᾽ αἰεὶ ζῶσαν ἀβλαβεῖ βίῳ                650
δόμους Ἀτρειδῶν σκῆπτρά τ᾽ ἀμφέπειν τάδε,
φίλοισί τε ξυνοῦσαν οἷς ξύνειμι νῦν
εὐημεροῦσαν καὶ τέκνων ὅσων ἐμοὶ
δύσνοια μὴ πρόσεστιν ἢ λύπη πικρά.
ταῦτ᾽, ὦ Λύκει᾽ Ἄπολλον, ἵλεως κλύων              655
δὸς πᾶσιν ἡμῖν ὥσπερ ἐξαιτούμεθα.
τὰ δ᾽ ἄλλα πάντα καὶ σιωπώσης ἐμοῦ
ἐπαξιῶ σε δαίμον᾽ ὄντ᾽ ἐξειδέναι·
τοὺς ἐκ Διὸς γὰρ εἰκός ἐστι πάνθ᾽ ὁρᾶν.

ΠΑ. ξέναι γυναῖκες, πῶς ἂν εἰδείην σαφῶς          660
εἰ τοῦ τυράννου δώματ᾽ Αἰγίσθου τάδε;

ΧΟ. τάδ᾽ ἐστίν, ὦ ξέν᾽· αὐτὸς ἤκασας καλῶς.

636 ἃ L Aˢ rec: ὧν A rec          641 παλιγλώσσῳ coni. Meineke
644 τῇδε νυκτὶ rec          645 δισσῶν] δεινῶν Schenkl          646 πέφηνεν]
πέφυκεν Vindob Σ ad v. 645          649 ἐφεῖς Lᵃᶜ (ut videtur) Lbᵃᶜ
653 εὐημεροῦσιν Lˢ          662 εἴκασας codd.: corr. Brunck

ΠΑ. ἦ καὶ δάμαρτα τήνδ' ἐπεικάζων κυρῶ
κείνου; πρέπει γὰρ ὡς τύραννος εἰσορᾶν.

ΧΟ. μάλιστα πάντων· ἥδε σοι κείνη πάρα.     665

ΠΑ. ὦ χαῖρ', ἄνασσα. σοὶ φέρων ἥκω λόγους
ἡδεῖς φίλου παρ' ἀνδρὸς Αἰγίσθῳ θ' ὁμοῦ.

ΚΛ. ἐδεξάμην τὸ ῥηθέν· εἰδέναι δέ σου
πρώτιστα χρῄζω τίς σ' ἀπέστειλεν βροτῶν.

ΠΑ. Φανοτεὺς ὁ Φωκεύς, πρᾶγμα πορσύνων μέγα.     670

ΚΛ. τὸ ποῖον, ὦ ξέν'; εἰπέ. παρὰ φίλου γὰρ ὢν
ἀνδρός, σάφ' οἶδα, προσφιλεῖς λέξεις λόγους.

ΠΑ. τέθνηκ' Ὀρέστης· ἐν βραχεῖ ξυνθεὶς λέγω.

ΗΛ. οἲ 'γὼ τάλαιν', ὄλωλα τῇδ' ἐν ἡμέρᾳ.

ΚΛ. τί φής, τί φής, ὦ ξεῖνε; μὴ ταύτης κλύε.     675

ΠΑ. θανόντ' Ὀρέστην νῦν τε καὶ τότ' ἐννέπω.

ΗΛ. ἀπωλόμην δύστηνος, οὐδέν εἰμ' ἔτι.

ΚΛ. σὺ μὲν τὰ σαυτῆς πρᾶσσ', ἐμοὶ δὲ σύ, ξένε,
τἀληθὲς εἰπέ, τῷ τρόπῳ διόλλυται;

ΠΑ. κἀπεμπόμην πρὸς ταῦτα καὶ τὸ πᾶν φράσω.     680
κεῖνος γὰρ ἐλθὼν ἐς τὸ κλεινὸν Ἑλλάδος
πρόσχημ' ἀγῶνος Δελφικῶν ἄθλων χάριν,
ὅτ' ᾔσθετ' ἀνδρὸς ὀρθίων κηρυγμάτων
δρόμον προκηρύξαντος, οὗ πρώτη κρίσις,
εἰσῆλθε λαμπρός, πᾶσι τοῖς ἐκεῖ σέβας·     685
δρόμου δ' ἰσώσας τἀφέσει τὰ τέρματα
νίκης ἔχων ἐξῆλθε πάντιμον γέρας.
χὤπως μὲν ἐν πολλοῖσι παῦρά σοι λέγω,
οὐκ οἶδα τοιοῦδ' ἀνδρὸς ἔργα καὶ κράτη·
ἓν δ' ἴσθ'· ὅσων γὰρ εἰσεκήρυξαν βραβῆς     690

675 ξένε A    676 τότ' ἐννέπω L²ˢ ᵧᵖ A rec: πάλαι λέγω L rec Eustath.
702, 4: πάλιν λέγω rec    681 κλεινὸν] κοινὸν Thom. Mag. 286, 4
684 δρόμον rec: δρόμου L A rec    686 δρόμου L A rec T Σ¹: δρόμῳ
Suid. v. δρόμοις: δρόμοις Ven: δρόμον Pearson    τἀφέσει Musgrave (qui τῇ
'φέσει scripsit): τῇ φύσει codd.    τὰ τέρματα] τὰ πράγματα Suid.: τά τ'
ἔργματα Pearson    688 ἐν παύροισι πολλά Bergk    689 τοιάδ' A rec
690 ὅσον Lbᵃᶜ Suid. v. βραβεῖς    βραβῆς L Ven: βραβεῖς Lˢ A rec
Suid.

†δρόμων διαύλων πένταθλ' ἃ νομίζεται,†
ἄθλων ἐνεγκὼν πάντα τἀπινίκια
ὠλβίζετ', Ἀργεῖος μὲν ἀνακαλούμενος,
ὄνομα δ' Ὀρέστης, τοῦ τὸ κλεινὸν Ἑλλάδος
Ἀγαμέμνονος στράτευμ' ἀγείραντός ποτε.                    695
καὶ ταῦτα μὲν τοιαῦθ'· ὅταν δέ τις θεῶν
βλάπτῃ, δύναιτ' ἂν οὐδ' ἂν ἰσχύων φυγεῖν.
κεῖνος γὰρ ἄλλης ἡμέρας, ὅθ' ἱππικῶν
ἦν ἡλίου τέλλοντος ὠκύπους ἀγών,
εἰσῆλθε πολλῶν ἁρματηλατῶν μέτα.                          700
εἷς ἦν Ἀχαιός, εἷς ἀπὸ Σπάρτης, δύο
Λίβυες ζυγωτῶν ἁρμάτων ἐπιστάται·
κἀκεῖνος ἐν τούτοισι Θεσσαλὰς ἔχων
ἵππους, ὁ πέμπτος· ἕκτος ἐξ Αἰτωλίας
ξανθαῖσι πώλοις· ἕβδομος Μάγνης ἀνήρ·                     705
ὁ δ' ὄγδοος λεύκιππος, Αἰνιὰν γένος·
ἔνατος Ἀθηνῶν τῶν θεοδμήτων ἄπο·
Βοιωτὸς ἄλλος, δέκατον ἐκπληρῶν ὄχον.
στάντες δ' ὅθ' αὐτοῖς οἱ τεταγμένοι βραβῆς
κλήρους ἔπηλαν καὶ κατέστησαν δίφρους,                    710
χαλκῆς ὑπαὶ σάλπιγγος ᾖξαν· οἱ δ' ἅμα
ἵπποις ὁμοκλήσαντες ἡνίας χεροῖν
ἔσεισαν· ἐν δὲ πᾶς ἐμεστώθη δρόμος
κτύπου κροτητῶν ἁρμάτων· κόνις δ' ἄνω
φορεῖθ'· ὁμοῦ δὲ πάντες ἀναμεμειγμένοι                    715
φείδοντο κέντρων οὐδέν, ὡς ὑπερβάλοι
χνόας τις αὐτῶν καὶ φρυάγμαθ' ἱππικά.
ὁμοῦ γὰρ ἀμφὶ νῶτα καὶ τροχῶν βάσεις

691 versum corruptum damnaverunt Burges alii    πένταθλ' ἃ L rec Suidae
plerique: πεντάεθλ' ἃ A rec Suidae E: ἄθλ' ἅπερ Porson    692 ἄθλων
Tournier: τούτων codd.    697 δύναι...τ' L (cum rasura)
706 Αἰνιὰν rec Eustath. 335, 20; 524 31: Αἰνειὰν A rec Eustath. 335, 21:
Αἰνειᾶν L rec Σ¹    707 ἔνατος] ἔνατος rec: ἔνατος (vel ἔννατος) δ' rec
709 στάντες] πάντες Koechly    ὅθ' αὐτοῖς Kells (ἵν' αὐτοῖς Blaydes):
ὅθ' αὐτοὺς L A rec: ὅτ' αὐτοὺς rec: ὅθεν αὐτοὺς Vindob: ὅθ' ἀγνοὺς
Housman    βραβῆς L Venˢ: βραβεῖς Lˢ A rec    710 κλήρους Wunder:
κλήροις codd.    713 ἐν] ἐκ rec

ἤφριζον, εἰσέβαλλον ἱππικαὶ πνοαί.
κεῖνος δ᾽ ὑπ᾽ αὐτὴν ἐσχάτην στήλην ἔχων      720
ἔχριμπτ᾽ ἀεὶ σύριγγα, δεξιὸν δ᾽ ἀνεὶς
σειραῖον ἵππον εἶργε τὸν προσκείμενον.
καὶ πρὶν μὲν ὀρθοὶ πάντες ἔστασαν δίφροι·
ἔπειτα δ᾽ Αἰνιᾶνος ἀνδρὸς ἄστομοι
πῶλοι βίᾳ φέρουσιν, ἐκ δ᾽ ὑποστροφῆς      725
τελοῦντες ἕκτον ἕβδομόν τ᾽ ἤδη δρόμον
μέτωπα συμπαίουσι Βαρκαίοις ὄχοις·
κἀντεῦθεν ἄλλος ἄλλον ἐξ ἑνὸς κακοῦ
ἔθραυε κἀνέπιπτε, πᾶν δ᾽ ἐπίμπλατο
ναυαγίων Κρισαῖον ἱππικῶν πέδον.      730
γνοὺς δ᾽ οὑξ Ἀθηνῶν δεινὸς ἡνιοστρόφος
ἔξω παρασπᾷ κἀνοκωχεύει παρεὶς
κλύδων᾽ ἔφιππον ἐν μέσῳ κυκώμενον.
ἤλαυνε δ᾽ ἔσχατος μὲν ὑστέρας δ᾽ ἔχων
πώλους Ὀρέστης, τῷ τέλει πίστιν φέρων·      735
ὅπως δ᾽ ὁρᾷ μόνον νιν ἐλλελειμμένον,
ὀξὺν δι᾽ ὤτων κέλαδον ἐνσείσας θοαῖς
πώλοις διώκει, κἀξισώσαντε ζυγὰ
ἠλαυνέτην, τότ᾽ ἄλλος, ἄλλοθ᾽ ἅτερος
κάρα προβάλλων ἱππικῶν ὀχημάτων.      740
καὶ τοὺς μὲν ἄλλους πάντας ἀσφαλεῖς δρόμους
ὠρθοῦθ᾽ ὁ τλήμων ὀρθὸς ἐξ ὀρθῶν δίφρων·
ἔπειτα λύων ἡνίαν ἀριστερὰν

720–2 post v. 740 traiecit E. Piccolomini     720 ἔσχατος coni. Kaibel
721 ἔχριπτ᾽ rec: ἔγχριμπτ᾽ (vel ἔγχριπτ᾽) rec Suidae v. σῦριγξ
codd. nonnulli     δεξιὸν δ᾽ L² A rec: δεξιὸν L Pal Suidae v. σειραῖος
A V: δεξιόν τ᾽ rec     722 προκείμενον A Suidae A     723 δίφροις rec:
δίφρῳ Kaibel     724 Αἰνιᾶνος rec Plut. mor. 521 c, Eustath. (v. 706):
Αἰνειᾶνος L A rec Eustath.     725 φοροῦσιν Plut.     726 τελοῦντος
coni. Musgrave     730 Κρισαῖον Pal: κρισσαῖον L A rec     ἱππικὸν L Γ
732 περισπᾷ Aug c Suid. v. περισπᾶν     κἀνακωχεύει codd. Σ: corr. Cobet
734 ὑστέρας δ᾽ L² A rec: ὑστέρας L rec     736 ὅπως δ᾽ Lac Γ: ὃ δ᾽ ὡς
A rec: ὃ δ᾽ ὡς δ᾽ Lc Lb     738 κἀξισώσαντες ᾽A rec     741 ἀσφα-
λὴς coni. Reiske     743 ἔπειτα λύων multis suspectum (ἔπειτα τανύων
Toepfer)

κάμπτοντος ἵππου λανθάνει στήλην ἄκραν
παίσας· ἔθραυσε δ' ἄξονος μέσας χνόας, 745
κἀξ ἀντύγων ὤλισθε· σὺν δ' ἑλίσσεται
τμητοῖς ἱμᾶσι· τοῦ δὲ πίπτοντος πέδῳ
πῶλοι διεσπάρησαν ἐς μέσον δρόμον.
στρατὸς δ' ὅπως ὁρᾷ νιν ἐκπεπτωκότα
δίφρων, ἀνωλόλυξε τὸν νεανίαν, 750
οἷ' ἔργα δράσας οἷα λαγχάνει κακά,
φορούμενος πρὸς οὖδας, ἄλλοτ' οὐρανῷ
σκέλη προφαίνων, ἔστε νιν διφρηλάται,
μόλις κατασχεθόντες ἱππικὸν δρόμον,
ἔλυσαν αἱματηρόν, ὥστε μηδένα 755
γνῶναι φίλων ἰδόντ' ἂν ἄθλιον δέμας.
καί νιν πυρᾷ κέαντες εὐθὺς ἐν βραχεῖ
χαλκῷ μέγιστον σῶμα δειλαίας σποδοῦ
φέρουσιν ἄνδρες Φωκέων τεταγμένοι,
ὅπως πατρῴας τύμβον ἐκλάχῃ χθονός. 760
τοιαῦτά σοι ταῦτ' ἐστίν, ὡς μὲν ἐν λόγοις
ἀλγεινά, τοῖς δ' ἰδοῦσιν, οἵπερ εἴδομεν,
μέγιστα πάντων ὧν ὄπωπ' ἐγὼ κακῶν.
ΧΟ. φεῦ φεῦ· τὸ πᾶν δὴ δεσπόταισι τοῖς πάλαι
πρόρριζον, ὡς ἔοικεν, ἔφθαρται γένος. 765
ΚΛ. ὦ Ζεῦ, τί ταῦτα, πότερον εὐτυχῆ λέγω,
ἢ δεινὰ μέν, κέρδη δέ; λυπηρῶς δ' ἔχει,
εἰ τοῖς ἐμαυτῆς τὸν βίον σῴζω κακοῖς.
ΠΑ. τί δ' ὧδ' ἀθυμεῖς, ὦ γύναι, τῷ νῦν λόγῳ;
ΚΛ. δεινὸν τὸ τίκτειν ἐστίν· οὐδὲ γὰρ κακῶς 770
πάσχοντι μῖσος ὧν τέκῃ προσγίγνεται.
ΠΑ. μάτην ἄρ' ἡμεῖς, ὡς ἔοικεν, ἥκομεν.

746 ὤλισθε σὺν δ' A rec: ὤλισθεν σὺν δ' L Lb: ὤλισθεν ἐν δ' Nauck
751 τυγχάνει Lb Σγρ 754 κατασχέθοντες codd.: corr. Elmsley
757 κέαντες Brunck: κήαντες L rec: κήαντες A: κείαντες rec 758 μεγί-
στου σώματος Lˢ δειλαίαν σποδὸν coni. Neue 760 ἐκλάχῃ rec:
ἐκλάχοι L A rec 761 λόγοις Lˢ A rec: λόγωι L rec 768 τῶν ἐμαυτῆς
coni. Seidler 769 τῷ νῦν A rec: τῶι ναῦ L: ποίῳ rec 771 τέκῃ
(η) Lᶜ A rec: τέκει Lᵃᶜ Lb: τέκοι Liv v

52    ΣΟΦΟΚΛΕΟΥΣ

ΚΛ.  οὔτοι μάτην γε. πῶς γὰρ ἂν μάτην λέγοις;
     εἴ μοι θανόντος πίστ᾽ ἔχων τεκμήρια
     προσῆλθες, ὅστις τῆς ἐμῆς ψυχῆς γεγώς,                    775
     μαστῶν ἀποστὰς καὶ τροφῆς ἐμῆς, φυγὰς
     ἀπεξενοῦτο· καί μ᾽, ἐπεὶ τῆσδε χθονὸς
     ἐξῆλθεν, οὐκέτ᾽ εἶδεν· ἐγκαλῶν δέ μοι
     φόνους πατρῴους δείν᾽ ἐπηπείλει τελεῖν·
     ὥστ᾽ οὔτε νυκτὸς ὕπνον οὔτ᾽ ἐξ ἡμέρας                    780
     ἐμὲ στεγάζειν ἡδύν, ἀλλ᾽ ὁ προστατῶν
     χρόνος διῆγέ μ᾽ αἰὲν ὡς θανουμένην.
     νῦν δ᾽ – ἡμέρᾳ γὰρ τῇδ᾽ ἀπηλλάγην φόβου
     πρὸς τῆσδ᾽ ἐκείνου θ᾽· ἥδε γὰρ μείζων βλάβη
     ξύνοικος ἦν μοι, τοὐμὸν ἐκπίνουσ᾽ ἀεὶ                     785
     ψυχῆς ἄκρατον αἷμα – νῦν δ᾽ ἕκηλά που
     τῶν τῆσδ᾽ ἀπειλῶν οὕνεχ᾽ ἡμερεύσομεν.
ΗΛ.  οἴμοι τάλαινα· νῦν γὰρ οἰμῶξαι πάρα,
     Ὀρέστα, τὴν σὴν ξυμφοράν, ὅθ᾽ ὧδ᾽ ἔχων
     πρὸς τῆσδ᾽ ὑβρίζῃ μητρός. ἆρ᾽ ἔχει καλῶς;                790
ΚΛ.  οὔτοι σύ· κεῖνος δ᾽ ὡς ἔχει καλῶς ἔχει.
ΗΛ.  ἄκουε, Νέμεσι τοῦ θανόντος ἀρτίως.
ΚΛ.  ἤκουσεν ὧν δεῖ κἀπεκύρωσεν καλῶς.
ΗΛ.  ὕβριζε· νῦν γὰρ εὐτυχοῦσα τυγχάνεις.
ΚΛ.  οὔκουν Ὀρέστης καὶ σὺ παύσετον τάδε;                    795
ΗΛ.  πεπαύμεθ᾽ ἡμεῖς, οὐχ ὅπως σε παύσομεν.
ΚΛ.  πολλῶν ἂν ἥκοις, ὦ ξέν᾽, ἄξιος τυχεῖν,
     εἰ τήνδ᾽ ἔπαυσας τῆς πολυγλώσσου βοῆς.
ΠΑ.  οὐκοῦν ἀποστείχοιμ᾽ ἄν, εἰ τάδ᾽ εὖ κυρεῖ.
ΚΛ.  ἥκιστ᾽· ἐπείπερ οὔτ᾽ ἐμοῦ κατάξι᾽ ἂν                    800
     πράξειας οὔτε τοῦ πορεύσαντος ξένου.
     ἀλλ᾽ εἴσιθ᾽ εἴσω· τήνδε δ᾽ ἔκτοθεν βοᾶν

780 ἐξ] ἐφ᾽ Eˢ    781 προσστατῶν coni. Meineke    783 ἀπηλλάγην
rec Suid. v. προστατῶν et fort. Lᵃᶜ: ἀπήλλαγμαι Lᶜ A rec    792 νέμεσις
rec    795 interrogandi nota primus distinxit Monk    797 ἥκεις rec
τυχεῖν Lᶜ A rec: φιλεῖν Lᵃᶜ Lb: φίλος Γ    798 τήνδε παύσαις Wunder
800 κατάξι᾽ ἂν Monk: κατ᾽ ἀξίαν rec: καταξίως L A rec    802 ἔκτοθεν
L rec: ἔκτοσθεν A rec

ἔα τά θ' αὑτῆς καὶ τὰ τῶν φίλων κακά.

ΗΛ. ἆρ' ὑμὶν ὡς ἀλγοῦσα κὠδυνωμένη
δεινῶς δακρῦσαι κἀπικωκῦσαι δοκεῖ                             805
τὸν υἱὸν ἡ δύστηνος ὧδ' ὀλωλότα;
ἀλλ' ἐγγελῶσα φροῦδος. ὢ τάλαιν' ἐγώ·
'Ορέστα φίλταθ', ὥς μ' ἀπώλεσας θανών.
ἀποσπάσας γὰρ τῆς ἐμῆς οἴχῃ φρενὸς
αἵ μοι μόναι παρῆσαν ἐλπίδων ἔτι,                            810
σὲ πατρὸς ἥξειν ζῶντα τιμωρόν ποτε
κἀμοῦ ταλαίνης. νῦν δὲ ποῖ με χρὴ μολεῖν;
μόνη γάρ εἰμι, σοῦ τ' ἀπεστερημένη
καὶ πατρός. ἤδη δεῖ με δουλεύειν πάλιν
ἐν τοῖσιν ἐχθίστοισιν ἀνθρώπων ἐμοί,                         815
φονεῦσι πατρός. ἆρά μοι καλῶς ἔχει;
ἀλλ' οὔ τι μὴν ἔγωγε τοῦ λοιποῦ χρόνου
ξύνοικος εἴσειμ', ἀλλὰ τῇδε πρὸς πύλῃ
παρεῖσ' ἐμαυτὴν ἄφιλος αὐανῶ βίον.
πρὸς ταῦτα καινέτω τις, εἰ βαρύνεται,                        820
τῶν ἔνδον ὄντων· ὡς χάρις μέν, ἢν κτάνῃ,
λύπη δ', ἐὰν ζῶ· τοῦ βίου δ' οὐδεὶς πόθος.

ΧΟ.      ποῦ ποτε κεραυνοὶ Διός, ἢ ποῦ                     στρ.
φαέθων Ἅλιος, εἰ ταῦτ' ἐφορῶντες
κρύπτουσιν ἔκηλοι;                                          825
ΗΛ.      ἒ ἔ, αἰαῖ.
ΧΟ.      ὢ παῖ, τί δακρύεις;
ΗΛ.      φεῦ. ΧΟ. μηδὲν μέγ' ἀΰσῃς.                         830
ΗΛ.      ἀπολεῖς. ΧΟ. πῶς;
ΗΛ.      εἰ τῶν φανερῶς οἰχομένων εἰς
'Αίδαν ἐλπίδ' ὑποίσεις,

---

809 οἴχῃ φρενὸς L² (in rasura) A rec: φρενὸς οἴχῃ L rec      810 μόνον
A Ven      818 ξύνοικος εἴσειμ' Hermann: ξύνοικος ἔσσομ' Lᶜ A rec (ἔσομ'
Lᵃᶜ): ξύνοικος ἔσσομαι rec: ἔσσομαι ξύνοικος Dawes      819 ἄφιλον Vindobᶜ
821 κτάνῃ] θάνω Σ ad v. 975      824 ἅλιος A rec: ἥλιος Suid. v. κεραυνοί:
ἀέλιος L rec

κατ' ἐμοῦ τακομένας μᾶλλον ἐπεμβάσῃ.                    835


ΧΟ.    οἶδα γὰρ ἄνακτ' ᾽Αμφιάρεων χρυ-                         ἀντ.
       σοδέτοις ἕρκεσι κρυφθέντα γυναικῶν
          καὶ νῦν ὑπὸ γαίας
ΗΛ.       ἒ ἔ, ἰώ.                                            840
ΧΟ.    πάμψυχος ἀνάσσει.
ΗΛ.    φεῦ. ΧΟ. φεῦ δῆτ'· ὀλοὰ γὰρ
ΗΛ.       ἐδάμη. ΧΟ. ναί.                                     845
ΗΛ.    οἶδ' οἶδ'· ἐφάνη γὰρ μελέτωρ ἀμ-
       φὶ τὸν ἐν πένθει· ἐμοὶ δ' οὔ-
       τις ἔτ' ἔσθ'· ὃς γὰρ ἔτ' ἦν, φροῦδος ἀναρπασθείς.


ΧΟ.    δειλαία δειλαίων κυρεῖς.                               στρ.
ΗΛ.    κἀγὼ τοῦδ' ἴστωρ, ὑπερίστωρ,                          850
       πανσύρτῳ παμμήνῳ πολλῶν
       δεινῶν στυγνῶν τ' αἰῶνι.
ΧΟ.       εἴδομεν ἃ θροεῖς.
ΗΛ.    μή μέ νυν μηκέτι
       παραγάγῃς, ἵν' οὐ  ΧΟ. τί φής;                        855
ΗΛ.    πάρεισιν ἐλπίδων ἔτι κοινοτόκων
          εὐπατρίδων τ' ἀρωγαί.


ΧΟ.    πᾶσι θνατοῖς ἔφυ μόρος.                               ἀντ.
ΗΛ.    ἦ καὶ χαλαργοῖς ἐν ἁμίλλαις                           861
       οὕτως, ὡς κείνῳ δυστάνῳ,


838 γυναικῶν] γυναικῶν ἀπάταις codd.: corr. Brunck   843 γὰρ] γοῦν T
Vat d      845 ἐδάμη γάρ...ναί T      851 πανσύρτων in libris vetustissimis se invenisse testatur Tricl      852 αἰῶνι Hermann: ἀχέων Lᶜ rec Σ
Suid. v. ἴστωρ: ἀχαίων A (habuisse Lᵃᶜ non constat) Tricl: ἀχαιῶν T:
ἀρχαίων Tˢ quod in vetustissimis quibusdam libris invenisset commendat
Tricl      853 ἀθρήνεις (ἃ θρηνεῖς Gernhard) Dindorf      856 αὐδᾷς δὲ
ποῖον post τί φής in codicibus additum del. T      859 εὐπατρίδων τ'
Neue: εὐπατριδᾶν τ' codd. Σ: εὐπατριδῶν Suidae v. παραγάγῃς A C:
εὐπατριδᾶν ap. Suidam vulgo      ἀρωγαί Γ Σ : ἀρωγοί cett. Suid.
861 χαλάργοις Dindorf      862 δυστήνῳ A rec

τμητοῖς ὁλκοῖς ἐγκῦρσαι;

ΧΟ.     ἄσκοπος ἁ λώβα.

ΗΛ.     πῶς γὰρ οὔκ; εἰ ξένος                                      865
        ἄτερ ἐμᾶν χερῶν   ΧΟ. παπαῖ.

ΗΛ.     κέκευθεν, οὔτε του τάφου ἀντιάσας
        οὔτε γόων παρ' ἡμῶν.                                        870

ΧΡ.     ὑφ' ἡδονῆς τοι, φιλτάτη, διώκομαι
        τὸ κόσμιον μεθεῖσα σὺν τάχει μολεῖν.
        φέρω γὰρ ἡδονάς τε κἀνάπαυλαν ὧν
        πάροιθεν εἶχες καὶ κατέστενες κακῶν.

ΗΛ.     πόθεν δ' ἂν εὕροις τῶν ἐμῶν σὺ πημάτων               875
        ἄρηξιν, οἷς ἴασις οὐκ ἔνεστ' ἔτι;

ΧΡ.     πάρεστ' Ὀρέστης ἡμίν, ἴσθι τοῦτ' ἐμοῦ
        κλύουσ', ἐναργῶς, ὥσπερ εἰσορᾷς ἐμέ.

ΗΛ.     ἀλλ' ἦ μέμηνας, ὦ τάλαινα, κἀπὶ τοῖς
        σαυτῆς κακοῖσι κἀπὶ τοῖς ἐμοῖς γελᾷς;                   880

ΧΡ.     μὰ τὴν πατρῴαν ἑστίαν, ἀλλ' οὐχ ὕβρει
        λέγω τάδ', ἀλλ' ἐκεῖνον ὡς παρόντα νῷν.

ΗΛ.     οἴμοι τάλαινα· καὶ τίνος βροτῶν λόγον
        τόνδ' εἰσακούσασ' ὧδε πιστεύεις ἄγαν;

ΧΡ.     ἐγὼ μὲν ἐξ ἐμοῦ τε κοὐκ ἄλλης σαφῆ                     885
        σημεῖ' ἰδοῦσα τῷδε πιστεύω λόγῳ.

ΗΛ.     τίν', ὦ τάλαιν', ἰδοῦσα πίστιν; ἐς τί μοι
        βλέψασα θάλπῃ τῷδ' ἀνηκέστῳ πυρί;

ΧΡ.     πρός νυν θεῶν ἄκουσον, ὡς μαθοῦσά μου
        τὸ λοιπὸν ἢ φρονοῦσαν ἢ μώραν λέγῃς.                    890

ΗΛ.     σὺ δ' οὖν λέγ', εἴ σοι τῷ λόγῳ τις ἡδονή.

ΧΡ.     καὶ δὴ λέγω σοι πᾶν ὅσον κατειδόμην.

863 ἐγκῦρσαι rec: ἐγκύρσαι A rec: ἐνκύρσαι Lᶜ Lb: ἐνκύσαι Lᵃᶜ
866 χεροῖν rec     871 τοι] σοι Brunck     876 ἴασις Lˢ rec Suidae s.v.
AV: ἴασιν L A rec     οὐκ ἔνεστ' ἔτι Lˢ rec: οὐκ ἔνεστ' ἰδεῖν L A rec:
οὐκέτ' ἔστ' ἰδεῖν Thiersch     881 ὕβριν Lᵃᶜ     882 νῷν] νόει rec: νῦν rec
885 ἄλλης L Γ: ἄλλου L² A rec     890 λοιπὸν ἢ rec: λοιπόν μ' ἢ L
(ὁ ex ὁ facto) rec: λοιπὸν ἵν' ἢ A rec     μώραν L A rec: μῶραν rec   λέγῃς
(-ης) L²ˢ A rec: λέγοις L Lbˢ: λέγεις rec

ἐπεὶ γὰρ ἦλθον πατρὸς ἀρχαῖον τάφον,
ὁρῶ κολώνης ἐξ ἄκρας νεορρύτους
πηγὰς γάλακτος καὶ περιστεφῆ κύκλῳ      895
πάντων ὅσ' ἔστιν ἀνθέων θήκην πατρός.
ἰδοῦσα δ' ἔσχον θαῦμα, καὶ περισκοπῶ
μή πού τις ἡμῖν ἐγγὺς ἐγχρίμπτει βροτῶν.
ὡς δ' ἐν γαλήνῃ πάντ' ἐδερκόμην τόπον,
τύμβου προσεῖρπον ἄσσον· ἐσχάτης δ' ὁρῶ      900
πυρᾶς νεώρη βόστρυχον τετμημένον·
κεὐθὺς τάλαιν' ὡς εἶδον, ἐμπαίει τί μοι
ψυχῇ σύνηθες ὄμμα, φιλτάτου βροτῶν
πάντων Ὀρέστου τοῦθ' ὁρᾶν τεκμήριον·
καὶ χερσὶ βαστάσασα δυσφημῶ μὲν οὔ,      905
χαρᾷ δὲ πίμπλημ' εὐθὺς ὄμμα δακρύων.
καὶ νῦν θ' ὁμοίως καὶ τότ' ἐξεπίσταμαι
μή του τόδ' ἀγλάισμα πλὴν κείνου μολεῖν.
τῷ γὰρ προσήκει πλήν γ' ἐμοῦ καὶ σοῦ τόδε;
κἀγὼ μὲν οὐκ ἔδρασα, τοῦτ' ἐπίσταμαι,      910
οὐδ' αὖ σύ· πῶς γάρ; ᾗ γε μηδὲ πρὸς θεοὺς
ἔξεστ' ἀκλαύτῳ τῆσδ' ἀποστῆναι στέγης.
ἀλλ' οὐδὲ μὲν δὴ μητρὸς οὔθ' ὁ νοῦς φιλεῖ
τοιαῦτα πράσσειν οὔτε δρῶσ' ἐλάνθαν' ἄν·
ἀλλ' ἔστ' Ὀρέστου ταῦτα τἀπιτύμβια.      915
ἀλλ', ὦ φίλη, θάρσυνε. τοῖς αὐτοῖσί τοι
οὐχ αὑτὸς αἰεὶ δαιμόνων παραστατεῖ.
νῷν δ' ἦν τὰ πρόσθεν στυγνός· ἡ δὲ νῦν ἴσως
πολλῶν ὑπάρξει κῦρος ἡμέρα καλῶν.

ΗΛ. φεῦ, τῆς ἀνοίας ὥς σ' ἐποικτίρω πάλαι.      920
ΧΡ. τί δ' ἔστιν; οὐ πρὸς ἡδονὴν λέγω τάδε;

896 ἔστιν] εἰσὶν Lˢ     898 ἐγχρίμπτει] ἐγχρίπτει rec: ἐγχρίπτη L A
rec: ἐγχρίμπτη rec: ἐγχρίμπτοι vel ἐγχρίπτοι rec     901 νεωρῆ codd.:
corr. Dindorf     902 μου L     903 ψυχῆς Lᵃᶜ rec     912 ἀκλαύστῳ
codd.: corr. Dindorf     914 ἐλάνθαν' ἄν Heath: ἐλάνθανεν codd.
915 τἀπιτύμβια Dindorf: τἀπιτίμια codd.: τἀγλαΐσματα Σγρ     917 οὐκ
αὑτὸς codd.: corr. Brunck     918 νῷν δ' A rec: νῶν L     πρόσθεν A rec:
πρόσθε L rec

ΗΛ. οὐκ οἶσθ' ὅποι γῆς οὐδ' ὅποι γνώμης φέρῃ.

ΧΡ. πῶς δ' οὐκ ἐγὼ κάτοιδ' ἅ γ' εἶδον ἐμφανῶς;

ΗΛ. τέθνηκεν, ὦ τάλαινα· τἀκείνου δέ σοι
σωτήρι' ἔρρει· μηδὲν ἐς κεῖνόν γ' ὅρα.     925

ΧΡ. οἴμοι τάλαινα· τοῦ τάδ' ἤκουσας βροτῶν;

ΗΛ. τοῦ πλησίον παρόντος, ἡνίκ' ὤλλυτο.

ΧΡ. καὶ ποῦ 'στιν οὗτος; θαῦμά τοί μ' ὑπέρχεται.

ΗΛ. κατ' οἶκον, ἡδὺς οὐδὲ μητρὶ δυσχερής.

ΧΡ. οἴμοι τάλαινα· τοῦ γὰρ ἀνθρώπων ποτ' ἦν     930
τὰ πολλὰ πατρὸς πρὸς τάφοις κτερίσματα;

ΗΛ. οἶμαι μάλιστ' ἔγωγε τοῦ τεθνηκότος
μνημεῖ' Ὀρέστου ταῦτα προσθεῖναί τινα.

ΧΡ. ὦ δυστυχής· ἐγὼ δὲ σὺν χαρᾷ λόγους
τοιούσδ' ἔχουσ' ἔσπευδον, οὐκ εἰδυῖ' ἄρα     935
ἵν' ἦμεν ἄτης· ἀλλὰ νῦν, ὅθ' ἱκόμην,
τά τ' ὄντα πρόσθεν ἄλλα θ' εὑρίσκω κακά.

ΗΛ. οὕτως ἔχει σοι ταῦτ'· ἐὰν δ' ἐμοὶ πίθῃ,
τῆς νῦν παρούσης πημονῆς λύσεις βάρος.

ΧΡ. ἦ τοὺς θανόντας ἐξαναστήσω ποτέ;     940

ΗΛ. οὐκ ἐς τόδ' εἶπον· οὐ γὰρ ὧδ' ἄφρων ἔφυν.

ΧΡ. τί γὰρ κελεύεις ὧν ἐγὼ φερέγγυος;

ΗΛ. τλῆναί σε δρῶσαν ἂν ἐγὼ παραινέσω.

ΧΡ. ἀλλ' εἴ τις ὠφέλειά γ', οὐκ ἀπώσομαι.

ΗΛ. ὅρα, πόνου τοι χωρὶς οὐδὲν εὐτυχεῖ.     945

ΧΡ. ὁρῶ. ξυνοίσω πᾶν ὅσονπερ ἂν σθένω.

ΗΛ. ἄκουε δή νυν ᾗ βεβούλευμαι τελεῖν.
παρουσίαν μὲν οἶσθα καὶ σύ που φίλων
ὡς οὔτις ἡμῖν ἐστιν, ἀλλ' Ἅιδης λαβὼν
ἀπεστέρηκε καὶ μόνα λελείμμεθον.     950
ἐγὼ δ' ἕως μὲν τὸν κασίγνητον βίῳ

922 φέρηι] φόρηι Lᵃᶜ: ἔφυς Σᵞᵖ     924 τἀκ κείνου Canter     929 δυσμενής Σᵞᵖ     931 τάφον codd.: corr. Housman (τάφῳ iam Blaydes)
934 δὲ] γὰρ A     938 δέ μοι codd.: corr. Brunck     941 ἐς τόδ' M:
ἔσθ' ὅδ' L Lb: ἔσθ' ὅ γ' Lˢ A rec     947 τελεῖν A L²ᵞᵖ rec: ποεῖν L Γ
Vindobˢ     948 παρουσία rec καὶ σύ που L²ᵞᵖ A rec: καὶ ποῦ σοι
L Aᵞᵖ     950 λελείμμεθον L A rec: λελείμμεθα Monac

θάλλοντ' ἔτ' εἰσήκουον, εἶχον ἐλπίδας
φόνου ποτ' αὐτὸν πράκτορ' ἵξεσθαι πατρός·
νῦν δ' ἡνίκ' οὐκέτ' ἔστιν, ἐς σὲ δὴ βλέπω,
ὅπως τὸν αὐτόχειρα πατρῴου φόνου                    955
ξὺν τῇδ' ἀδελφῇ μὴ κατοκνήσεις κτανεῖν
Αἴγισθον· οὐδὲν γάρ σε δεῖ κρύπτειν μ' ἔτι.
ποῖ γὰρ μενεῖς ῥάθυμος, ἐς τίν' ἐλπίδων
βλέψασ' ἔτ' ὀρθήν; ᾗ πάρεστι μὲν στένειν
πλούτου πατρῴου κτῆσιν ἐστερημένη,                  960
πάρεστι δ' ἀλγεῖν ἐς τοσόνδε τοῦ χρόνου
ἄλεκτρα γηράκουσαν ἀνυμέναιά τε.
καὶ τῶνδε μέντοι μηκέτ' ἐλπίσῃς ὅπως
τεύξῃ ποτ'· οὐ γὰρ ὧδ' ἄβουλός ἐστ' ἀνὴρ
Αἴγισθος ὥστε σόν ποτ' ἢ κἀμὸν γένος                965
βλαστεῖν ἐᾶσαι, πημονὴν αὑτῷ σαφῆ.
ἀλλ' ἢν ἐπίσπῃ τοῖς ἐμοῖς βουλεύμασιν,
πρῶτον μὲν εὐσέβειαν ἐκ πατρὸς κάτω
θανόντος οἴσῃ τοῦ κασιγνήτου θ' ἅμα·
ἔπειτα δ', ὥσπερ ἐξέφυς, ἐλευθέρα                    970
καλῇ τὸ λοιπὸν καὶ γάμων ἐπαξίων
τεύξῃ· φιλεῖ γὰρ πρὸς τὰ χρηστὰ πᾶς ὁρᾶν.
λόγων γε μὴν εὔκλειαν οὐχ ὁρᾷς ὅσην
σαυτῇ τε κἀμοὶ προσβαλεῖς πεισθεῖσ' ἐμοί;
τίς γάρ ποτ' ἀστῶν ἢ ξένων ἡμᾶς ἰδὼν               975
τοιοῖσδ' ἐπαίνοις οὐχὶ δεξιώσεται,
ἴδεσθε τώδε τὼ κασιγνήτω, φίλοι,
ὣ τὸν πατρῷον οἶκον ἐξεσωσάτην,
ὣ τοῖσιν ἐχθροῖς εὖ βεβηκόσιν ποτὲ
ψυχῆς ἀφειδήσαντε προυστήτην φόνου.                 980
τούτω φιλεῖν χρή, τώδε χρὴ πάντας σέβειν·
τώδ' ἔν θ' ἑορταῖς ἔν τε πανδήμῳ πόλει

952 θάλλοντ' ἔτ' Reiske: θάλλοντά τ' L A rec: θάλλοντά γ' D
956 κατοκνήσεις A rec: κατοκνήσῃς L rec        961 πάρεστιν L<sup>ac</sup> Lb
973 λόγων Dobree: λόγῳ (vel λόγω) codd.        974 πεισθεῖσά μοι rec
981 χρή] χρῆν L (sscr. η et sequente rasura)

τιμᾶν ἅπαντας οὕνεκ' ἀνδρείας χρεών.
τοιαῦτά τοι νὼ πᾶς τις ἐξερεῖ βροτῶν,
ζώσαιν θανούσαιν θ' ὥστε μὴ 'κλιπεῖν κλέος.      985
ἀλλ', ὦ φίλη, πείσθητι, συμπόνει πατρί,
σύγκαμν' ἀδελφῷ, παῦσον ἐκ κακῶν ἐμέ,
παῦσον δὲ σαυτήν, τοῦτο γιγνώσκουσ', ὅτι
ζῆν αἰσχρὸν αἰσχρῶς τοῖς καλῶς πεφυκόσιν.

ΧΟ. ἐν τοῖς τοιούτοις ἐστὶν ἡ προμηθία      990
καὶ τῷ λέγοντι καὶ κλύοντι σύμμαχος.

ΧΡ. καὶ πρίν γε φωνεῖν, ὦ γυναῖκες, εἰ φρενῶν
ἐτύγχαν' αὕτη μὴ κακῶν, ἐσῴζετ' ἂν
τὴν εὐλάβειαν, ὥσπερ οὐχὶ σῴζεται.
ποῖ γάρ ποτε βλέψασα τοιοῦτον θράσος      995
αὐτή θ' ὁπλίζῃ κἄμ' ὑπηρετεῖν καλεῖς;
οὐκ εἰσορᾷς; γυνὴ μὲν οὐδ' ἀνὴρ ἔφυς,
σθένεις δ' ἔλασσον τῶν ἐναντίων χερί.
δαίμων δὲ τοῖς μὲν εὐτυχεῖ καθ' ἡμέραν,
ἡμῖν δ' ἀπορρεῖ κἀπὶ μηδὲν ἔρχεται.      1000
τίς οὖν τοιοῦτον ἄνδρα βουλεύων ἑλεῖν
ἄλυπος ἄτης ἐξαπαλλαχθήσεται;
ὅρα κακῶς πράσσοντε μὴ μείζω κακὰ
κτησώμεθ', εἴ τις τοῦσδ' ἀκούσεται λόγους.
λύει γὰρ ἡμᾶς οὐδὲν οὐδ' ἐπωφελεῖ      1005
βάξιν καλὴν λαβόντε δυσκλεῶς θανεῖν.
οὐ γὰρ θανεῖν ἔχθιστον, ἀλλ' ὅταν θανεῖν
χρήζων τις εἶτα μηδὲ τοῦτ' ἔχῃ λαβεῖν.
ἀλλ' ἀντιάζω, πρὶν πανωλέθρους τὸ πᾶν
ἡμᾶς τ' ὀλέσθαι κἀξερημῶσαι γένος,      1010

985 μὴ 'κλιπεῖν L rec: μὴ λιπεῖν A rec: μοι λιπεῖν Lᵃᵞρ      986 πίσθητι
L      987 ἀδελφῇ rec      991 κλύοντι] τῶι κλύοντι L (τῶι postea
deleto) A rec      993 ἐσῴζετ' L (ι servato velut in vv. 994, 1257) Σ Lb
995 ποτε βλέψασα Pd Monac: ποτ' ἐμβλέψασα L A rec: ποτ' ἐκβλέψασα
Lbᵃᶜ      998 ἔλασσον Pd: ἔλαττον codd.      999 εὐτυχεῖ L rec: εὐτυχὴς
Lˢ A rec      1003 πράσσοντε] πάσχοντε Σ ad O.C. 1676      1005 ἡμᾶς]
ἡμῖν Elmsley      1007 omissum in margine supplevit Σ      1008 χρήζων
Lᶜ A rec: χρήζῃ Lᵃᶜ rec  ἔχῃ Lᶜ A rec: ἔχει Lᵃᶜ Γ

κατάσχες ὀργήν. καὶ τὰ μὲν λελεγμένα
ἄρρητ' ἐγώ σοι κἀτελῆ φυλάξομαι,
αὐτὴ δὲ νοῦν σχὲς ἀλλὰ τῷ χρόνῳ ποτέ,
σθένουσα μηδὲν τοῖς κρατοῦσιν εἰκαθεῖν.

ΧΟ. πείθου. προνοίας οὐδὲν ἀνθρώποις ἔφυ          1015
κέρδος λαβεῖν ἄμεινον οὐδὲ νοῦ σοφοῦ.

ΗΛ. ἀπροσδόκητον οὐδὲν εἴρηκας· καλῶς δ'
ἤδη σ' ἀπορρίψουσαν ἀπηγγελλόμην.
ἀλλ' αὐτόχειρί μοι μόνη τε δραστέον
τοὔργον τόδ'· οὐ γὰρ δὴ κενόν γ' ἀφήσομεν.          1020

ΧΡ. φεῦ·
εἴθ' ὤφελες τοιάδε τὴν γνώμην πατρὸς
θνήσκοντος εἶναι· πᾶν γὰρ ἂν κατειργάσω.

ΗΛ. ἀλλ' ἦ φύσιν γε, τὸν δὲ νοῦν ἥσσων τότε.

ΧΡ. ἄσκει τοιαύτη νοῦν δι' αἰῶνος μένειν.

ΗΛ. ὡς οὐχὶ συνδράσουσα νουθετεῖς τάδε.          1025

ΧΡ. εἰκὸς γὰρ ἐγχειροῦντα καὶ πράσσειν κακῶς.

ΗΛ. ζηλῶ σε τοῦ νοῦ, τῆς δὲ δειλίας στυγῶ.

ΧΡ. ἀνέξομαι κλύουσα χὤταν εὖ λέγῃς.

ΗΛ. ἀλλ' οὔ ποτ' ἐξ ἐμοῦ γε μὴ πάθῃς τόδε.

ΧΡ. μακρὸς τὸ κρῖναι ταῦτα χὠ λοιπὸς χρόνος.          1030

ΗΛ. ἄπελθε· σοὶ γὰρ ὠφέλησις οὐκ ἔνι.

ΧΡ. ἔνεστιν· ἀλλὰ σοὶ μάθησις οὐ πάρα.

ΗΛ. ἐλθοῦσα μητρὶ ταῦτα πάντ' ἔξειπε σῇ.

ΧΡ. οὐδ' αὖ τοσοῦτον ἔχθος ἐχθαίρω σ' ἐγώ.

ΗΛ. ἀλλ' οὖν ἐπίστω γ' οἷ μ' ἀτιμίας ἄγεις.          1035

ΧΡ. ἀτιμίας μὲν οὔ, προμηθίας δὲ σοῦ.

ΗΛ. τῷ σῷ δικαίῳ δῆτ' ἐπισπέσθαι με δεῖ;

1014 εἰκάθειν codd.: corr. Elmsley    1015 πιθοῦ rec    ἀνθρώποις ἔφυ]
ἔφυ βροτοῖς Suid. v. πρόνοια    1018 ἤδη] ἤδη Thom. Mag. 143. 7:
ἤδειν L A rec: ἤιδην Lb    ἀπηγγειλάμην Thom. Mag.    1019 ἀλλ'
οὐδὲν ἧσσόν μοι Σγρ    1022 πᾶν γὰρ ἂν Dawes: πάντα γὰρ ἂν L
(ἂν eraso) rec: πάντα γὰρ A rec: πάντα γ' ἂν Musgrave: πάντα τᾶν
R. Arnold    1023 ἦν codd.: corr. Elmsley    1024 νοῦν] γοῦν L (ut
videtur)    1029 πάθῃς L⁸ A rec: μάθῃς (-ης) L rec    τόδε] τότε Lᵃᶜ
1036 προμηθείας rec

ΧΡ. ὅταν γὰρ εὖ φρονῇς, τόθ' ἡγήσῃ σὺ νῷν.
ΗΛ. ἦ δεινὸν εὖ λέγουσαν ἐξαμαρτάνειν.
ΧΡ. εἴρηκας ὀρθῶς ᾧ σὺ πρόσκεισαι κακῷ.                     1040
ΗΛ. τί δ'; οὐ δοκῶ σοι ταῦτα σὺν δίκῃ λέγειν;
ΧΡ. ἀλλ' ἔστιν ἔνθα χἠ δίκη βλάβην φέρει.
ΗΛ. τούτοις ἐγὼ ζῆν τοῖς νόμοις οὐ βούλομαι.
ΧΡ. ἀλλ' εἰ ποήσεις ταῦτ', ἐπαινέσεις ἐμέ.
ΗΛ. καὶ μὴν ποήσω γ' οὐδὲν ἐκπλαγεῖσά σε.                   1045
ΧΡ. καὶ τοῦτ' ἀληθές, οὐδὲ βουλεύσῃ πάλιν;
ΗΛ. βουλῆς γὰρ οὐδέν ἐστιν ἔχθιον κακῆς.
ΧΡ. φρονεῖν ἔοικας οὐδὲν ὧν ἐγὼ λέγω.
ΗΛ. πάλαι δέδοκται ταῦτα κοὐ νεωστί μοι.
ΧΡ. ἄπειμι τοίνυν· οὔτε γὰρ σὺ τἄμ' ἔπη                      1050
    τολμᾷς ἐπαινεῖν οὔτ' ἐγὼ τοὺς σοὺς τρόπους.
ΗΛ. ἀλλ' εἴσιθ'. οὔ σοι μὴ μεθέψομαί ποτε,
    οὐδ' ἢν σφόδρ' ἱμείρουσα τυγχάνῃς· ἐπεὶ
    πολλῆς ἀνοίας καὶ τὸ θηρᾶσθαι κενά.
ΧΡ. ἀλλ' εἰ σεαυτῇ τυγχάνεις δοκοῦσά τι                      1055
    φρονεῖν, φρόνει τοιαῦθ'· ὅταν γὰρ ἐν κακοῖς
    ἤδη βεβήκῃς, τἄμ' ἐπαινέσεις ἔπη.

ΧΟ. τί τοὺς ἄνωθεν φρονιμωτάτους οἰω-                        στρ.
    νοὺς ἐσορώμενοι τροφᾶς
    κηδομένους ἀφ' ὧν τε βλά-                                1060
    στωσιν ἀφ' ὧν τ' ὄνασιν εὕ-
    ρωσι, τάδ' οὐκ ἐπ' ἴσας τελοῦμεν;
    ἀλλ' οὐ τὰν Διὸς ἀστραπὰν
    καὶ τὰν οὐρανίαν Θέμιν
    δαρὸν οὐκ ἀπόνητοι.                                      1065
    ὦ χθονία βροτοῖσι φά-
    μα, κατά μοι βόασον οἰ-

1047 γὰρ ἐστιν οὐδὲν rec        1050 sq. e Sophoclis Phaedra citare videtur
Stob. flor. 2. 29 (28)     1052 οὔ σοι] οὔ σοι L Lbᵃᶜ     1053 ἦν] εἰ rec
τυγχάνεις Lˢ rec       1061 ὄνησιν codd. Suid. v. ἄνωθεν: corr. Brunck
1063 ἀλλ' οὐ τὰν T Liv p: ἀλλ' οὐ μὰ τὰν cett.

κτράν ὄπα τοῖς ἔνερθ᾽ Ἀτρεί-
δαις, ἀχόρευτα φέρουσ᾽ ὀνείδη·

ὅτι σφὶν ἤδη τὰ μὲν ἐκ δόμων νοσεῖ                    ἀντ.
δή, τὰ δὲ πρὸς τέκνων διπλῇ                          1071
φύλοπις οὐκέτ᾽ ἐξισοῦ-
ται φιλοτασίῳ διαί-
τα. πρόδοτος δὲ μόνα σαλεύει
ἀ παῖς, οἶτον ἀεὶ πατρὸς                             1075
δειλαία στενάχουσ᾽ ὅπως
ἀ πάνδυρτος ἀηδών,
οὔτε τι τοῦ θανεῖν προμη-
θὴς τό τε μὴ βλέπειν ἑτοί-
μα, διδύμαν ἑλοῦσ᾽ Ἐρι-                              1080
νύν. τίς ἂν εὔπατρις ὧδε βλάστοι;

οὐδεὶς τῶν ἀγαθῶν ζῶν                                στρ.
κακῶς εὔκλειαν αἰσχῦναι θέλει
νώνυμος, ὦ παῖ παῖ,
ὡς καὶ σὺ πάγκλαυτον αἰ-                             1085
ῶνα κοινὸν εἵλου,
τὰ μὴ κάλ᾽ οὐ καθοπλίσα-
σα δύο φέρειν ⟨ἐν⟩ ἑνὶ λόγῳ,
σοφά τ᾽ ἀρίστα τε παῖς κεκλῆσθαι.

1070 sq. σφιν ἤδη Schaefer: σφίσιν ἤδη L A rec Σ¹: σφίσι γ᾽ ἤδη rec: σφίσ᾽
ἤδη T: σφίσιν δὴ Erfurdt    νοσεῖ δὴ T: νοσεῖ L A rec: νοσεῖται C: νο-
σοῦσι rec: νοσοῦντ᾽ ἦν Pearson    1075 ἀ παῖς οἶτον ἀεὶ πατρὸς Heath:
Ἠλέκτρα τὸν ἀεὶ πατρὸς (πρς L) codd. Σ: Ἠλέκτρα τό γ᾽ ἀεὶ πάρος
Pearson    1077 πανόδυρτος L A rec: corr. Porson    1078 τοῦ μὴ θανεῖν
C Eustath. 645, 16 fort. Σ Tricl ᵞᵖ    1079 μὴ] μὴν Lᵃᶜ    1081 τίς ἂν
T Tricl: τίς ἂν οὖν L A rec    1082 τῶν ἀγαθῶν codd. Stob. flor. 37.
4, Orion 7. 11: τῶν γὰρ ἀγαθῶν Grotius: τῶν ἀγαθῶν γὰρ Hermann
1084 νώνυμος Lᵃᶜ Σ    1085 sq. ὡς] ὡς Σ: ὥστε T Tricl    πάγκλαυτον
L T Tricl Σ: πάγκλαυστον A rec    αἰῶνα κοινὸν] fort. αἰῶν᾽ ἄοικον
(quod coni. Lindner) vel ἄνοικον: cf. 817 sqq.    1087 τὰ μὴ κάλ᾽ οὐ Kells:
τὸ μὴ καλὸν codd.: ἄκος καλὸν Lloyd-Jones    καθοπλίσασα] ἀπολακτί-
σασα J. H. H. Schmidt: καθιππάσασα Hermann    1088 sq. ἐν add.
Brunck (gl. Lips a b)

ӡῴης μοι καθύπερθεν        ἀντ.
χερὶ πλούτῳ τε τῶν ἐχθρῶν ὅσον    1091
  νῦν ὑπόχειρ ναίεις ·
  ἐπεί σ' ἐφηύρηκα μοί-
  ρᾳ μὲν οὐκ ἐν ἐσθλᾷ
  βεβῶσαν, ἃ δὲ μέγιστ' ἔβλα-    1095
  στε νόμιμα, τῶνδε φερομέναν
ἄριστα τᾷ Ζηνὸς εὐσεβείᾳ.

ΟΡ. ἆρ', ὦ γυναῖκες, ὀρθά τ' εἰσηκούσαμεν
  ὀρθῶς θ' ὁδοιποροῦμεν ἔνθα χρῄζομεν;
ΧΟ. τί δ' ἐξερευνᾷς καὶ τί βουληθεὶς πάρει;    1100
ΟΡ. Αἴγισθον ἔνθ' ᾤκηκεν ἱστορῶ πάλαι.
ΧΟ. ἀλλ' εὖ θ' ἱκάνεις χὠ φράσας ἀӡήμιος.
ΟΡ. τίς οὖν ἂν ὑμῶν τοῖς ἔσω φράσειεν ἂν
  ἡμῶν ποθεινὴν κοινόπουν παρουσίαν;
ΧΟ. ἥδ', εἰ τὸν ἀγχιστόν γε κηρύσσειν χρεών.    1105
ΟΡ. ἴθ', ὦ γύναι, δήλωσον εἰσελθοῦσ' ὅτι
  Φωκῆς ματεύουσ' ἄνδρες Αἴγισθόν τινες.
ΗΛ. οἴμοι τάλαιν', οὐ δή ποθ' ἧς ἠκούσαμεν
  φήμης φέροντες ἐμφανῆ τεκμήρια;
ΟΡ. οὐκ οἶδα τὴν σὴν κληδόν' · ἀλλά μοι γέρων    1110
  ἐφεῖτ' Ὀρέστου Στροφίος ἀγγεῖλαι πέρι.
ΗΛ. τί δ' ἔστιν, ὦ ξέν'; ὥς μ' ὑπέρχεται φόβος.
ΟΡ. φέροντες αὐτοῦ σμικρὰ λείψαν' ἐν βραχεῖ
  τεύχει θανόντος, ὡς ὁρᾷς, κομίӡομεν.
ΗΛ. οἲ 'γὼ τάλαινα, τοῦτ' ἐκεῖν' ἤδη σαφές ·    1115
  πρόχειρον ἄχθος, ὡς ἔοικε, δέρκομαι.

1090 καθύπερθεν T Liv v Eustath. 1083, 17: καθύπερθε L A rec
1091 χερὶ] χειρὶ Eustath.   πλούτῳ τε τῶν T Liv v: καὶ πλούτῳ τῶν L A
rec: καὶ πλούτῳ τεῶν Hermann   1092 ὑπὸ χεῖρα codd.: ὑπὸ χέρα
Erfurdt: corr. Musgrave   1094 ἐν A rec: ἐπ' rec: om. L rec
1096 τῶνδε] τῶν Erfurdt   1097 ἄριστα] ἐριστὰ Σ  Ζηνὸς T Vat d Liv
v Σγρ: Διὸς L A rec   1099 θ' rec: δ' L A rec   1101 ἱστορῶ] μασ-
τεύω Σγρ   1102 ἀλλ' εὖ θ'] ὀρθῶς rec   1107 ματεύουσ' A rec:
μαστεύουσ' L rec   1111 Στροφίος L Lb: Στρόφιος vulgo
1113 σμικρὰ L T: μικρὰ A rec

ΟΡ. εἴπερ τι κλαίεις τῶν Ὀρεστείων κακῶν,
    τόδ' ἄγγος ἴσθι σῶμα τοὐκείνου στέγον.

ΗΛ. ὦ ξεῖνε, δός νυν πρὸς θεῶν, εἴπερ τόδε
    κέκευθεν αὐτὸν τεῦχος, ἐς χεῖρας λαβεῖν,     1120
    ὅπως ἐμαυτὴν καὶ γένος τὸ πᾶν ὁμοῦ
    ξὺν τῇδε κλαύσω κἀποδύρωμαι σποδῷ.

ΟΡ. δόθ', ἥτις ἐστί, προσφέροντες· οὐ γὰρ ὡς
    ἐν δυσμενείᾳ γ' οὖσ' ἐπαιτεῖται τόδε,
    ἀλλ' ἢ φίλων τις, ἢ πρὸς αἵματος φύσιν.     1145

ΗΛ. ὦ φιλτάτου μνημεῖον ἀνθρώπων ἐμοὶ
    ψυχῆς Ὀρέστου λοιπόν, ὥς ⟨σ'⟩ ἀπ' ἐλπίδων
    οὐχ ὧνπερ ἐξέπεμπον εἰσεδεξάμην.
    νῦν μὲν γὰρ οὐδὲν ὄντα βαστάζω χεροῖν,
    δόμων δέ σ', ὦ παῖ, λαμπρὸν ἐξέπεμψ' ἐγώ.     1130
    ὡς ὤφελον πάροιθεν ἐκλιπεῖν βίον,
    πρὶν ἐς ξένην σε γαῖαν ἐκπέμψαι χεροῖν
    κλέψασα τοῖνδε κἀνασώσασθαι φόνου,
    ὅπως θανὼν ἔκεισο τῇ τόθ' ἡμέρᾳ,
    τύμβου πατρῴου κοινὸν εἰληχὼς μέρος.     1135
    νῦν δ' ἐκτὸς οἴκων κἀπὶ γῆς ἄλλης φυγὰς
    κακῶς ἀπώλου, σῆς κασιγνήτης δίχα·
    κοὔτ' ἐν φίλαισι χερσὶν ἡ τάλαιν' ἐγὼ
    λουτροῖς σ' ἐκόσμησ' οὔτε παμφλέκτου πυρὸς
    ἀνειλόμην, ὡς εἰκός, ἄθλιον βάρος,     1140
    ἀλλ' ἐν ξένῃσι χερσὶ κηδευθεὶς τάλας
    σμικρὸς προσήκεις ὄγκος ἐν σμικρῷ κύτει.
    οἴμοι τάλαινα τῆς ἐμῆς πάλαι τροφῆς
    ἀνωφελήτου, τὴν ἐγὼ θάμ' ἀμφὶ σοὶ
    πόνῳ γλυκεῖ παρέσχον. οὔτε γάρ ποτε     1145

1124 ἐπαιτεῖται A rec: ἐπαιτεῖ L Γ: ἀπαιτεῖται Aug b: ἀπαιτεῖ Monac
τόδε L rec: τάδε Lˢ A rec   1127 σ' add. Brunck   ὑπ' ἐλπίδων Schaefer
1128 οὐχ ὧνπερ L A rec: οὐχ ὥσπερ rec: οὐχ ὄνπερ Harl.   εἰσέπεμπον
Lᵃᶜ rec   1129 οὐδέν σ' ὄντα Δ   1131 ὤφελες L² rec   1132 ἐκπέμψω L²ˢ
1133 κλέψασαν L²ˢ   τοῖνδε codd.   κἀνασώσασα L²ˢ rec     1139 σ' add.
rec     1141 ξένῃσι L rec: ξένῃσι rec: ξέναισι A rec     1142 μικρὸς
Suid. v. ὄγκος   σμικρῷ L rec: μικρῷ A rec Suid.

μητρὸς σύ γ' ἦσθα μᾶλλον ἢ κἀμοῦ φίλος,
οὔθ' οἱ κατ' οἶκον ἦσαν ἀλλ' ἐγὼ τροφός,
ἐγὼ δ' ἀδελφὴ σοὶ προσηυδώμην ἀεί.
νῦν δ' ἐκλέλοιπε ταῦτ' ἐν ἡμέρᾳ μιᾷ
θανόντι σὺν σοί. πάντα γὰρ συναρπάσας,                1150
θύελλ' ὅπως, βέβηκας. οἴχεται πατήρ,
τέθνηκ' ἐγὼ σοί· φροῦδος αὐτὸς εἶ θανών·
γελῶσι δ' ἐχθροί· μαίνεται δ' ὑφ' ἡδονῆς
μήτηρ ἀμήτωρ, ἧς ἐμοὶ σὺ πολλάκις
φήμας λάθρᾳ προύπεμπες ὡς φανούμενος              1155
τιμωρὸς αὐτός. ἀλλὰ ταῦθ' ὁ δυστυχὴς
δαίμων ὁ σός τε κἀμὸς ἐξαφείλετο,
ὅς σ' ὧδέ μοι προύπεμψεν ἀντὶ φιλτάτης
μορφῆς σποδόν τε καὶ σκιὰν ἀνωφελῆ.
οἴμοι μοι.                                                             1160
ὦ δέμας οἰκτρόν. φεῦ φεῦ.
ὦ δεινοτάτας, οἴμοι μοι,
πεμφθεὶς κελεύθους, φίλταθ', ὥς μ' ἀπώλεσας·
ἀπώλεσας δῆτ', ὦ κασίγνητον κάρα.
τοιγὰρ σὺ δέξαι μ' ἐς τὸ σὸν τόδε στέγος,          1165
τὴν μηδὲν ἐς τὸ μηδέν, ὡς σὺν σοὶ κάτω
ναίω τὸ λοιπόν. καὶ γὰρ ἡνίκ' ἦσθ' ἄνω,
ξὺν σοὶ μετεῖχον τῶν ἴσων· καὶ νῦν ποθῶ
τοῦ σοῦ θανοῦσα μὴ ἀπολείπεσθαι τάφου.
τοὺς γὰρ θανόντας οὐχ ὁρῶ λυπουμένους.            1170
ΧΟ. θνητοῦ πέφυκας πατρός, Ἠλέκτρα, φρόνει·
θνητὸς δ' Ὀρέστης· ὥστε μὴ λίαν στένε·
πᾶσιν γὰρ ἡμῖν τοῦτ' ὀφείλεται παθεῖν.
ΟΡ. φεῦ φεῦ, τί λέξω; ποῖ λόγων ἀμηχανῶν

1148 σοὶ L A rec: σὴ Lˢ rec    1150 θανόντα rec    1151–2 ita interpunxit Kells, ut σοί cum οἴχεται intellegatur: πατήρ· τέθνηκ'
codd.    1152 ἐγὼ· σὺ φροῦδος Erfurdt    1158 φιλτάτης Lˢ A rec:
φιλτάτου L    1163 κελεύθους Lᶜ rec: κελεύθου Lᵃᶜ A rec    1168 κατ-
εῖχον Lᵃᶜ    1173 eadem verba ex Aristophanis Polyido citat Stob. flor.
118. 16: del. Bergk    1174 ποῖ] ποίων A    ἀμηχανῶν C: ἀμηχάνων
cett.

3                                                                              KSE

ἔλθω; κρατεῖν γὰρ οὐκέτι γλώσσης σθένω.     1175

ΗΛ. τί δ' ἔσχες ἄλγος; πρὸς τί τοῦτ' εἰπὼν κυρεῖς;

ΟΡ. ἦ σὸν τὸ κλεινὸν εἶδος Ἠλέκτρας τόδε;

ΗΛ. τόδ' ἔστ' ἐκεῖνο, καὶ μάλ' ἀθλίως ἔχον.

ΟΡ. οἴμοι ταλαίνης ἆρα τῆσδε συμφορᾶς.

ΗΛ. οὐ δή ποτ', ὦ ξέν', ἀμφ' ἐμοὶ στένεις τάδε;     1180

ΟΡ. ὦ σῶμ' ἀτίμως κἀθέως ἐφθαρμένον.

ΗΛ. οὔτοι ποτ' ἄλλην ἢ 'μὲ δυσφημεῖς, ξένε.

ΟΡ. φεῦ τῆς ἀνύμφου δυσμόρου τε σῆς τροφῆς.

ΗΛ. τί δή ποτ', ὦ ξέν', ὧδ' ἐπισκοπῶν στένεις;

ΟΡ. ὡς οὐκ ἄρ' ᾔδη τῶν ἐμῶν οὐδὲν κακῶν.     1185

ΗΛ. ἐν τῷ διέγνως τοῦτο τῶν εἰρημένων;

ΟΡ. ὁρῶν σὲ πολλοῖς ἐμπρέπουσαν ἄλγεσιν.

ΗΛ. καὶ μὴν ὁρᾷς γε παῦρα τῶν ἐμῶν κακῶν.

ΟΡ. καὶ πῶς γένοιτ' ἂν τῶνδ' ἔτ' ἐχθίω βλέπειν;

ΗΛ. ὁθούνεκ' εἰμὶ τοῖς φονεῦσι σύντροφος.     1190

ΟΡ. τοῖς τοῦ; πόθεν τοῦτ' ἐξεσήμηνας κακόν;

ΗΛ. τοῖς πατρός. εἶτα τοῖσδε δουλεύω βίᾳ.

ΟΡ. τίς γάρ σ' ἀνάγκη τῇδε προστρέπει βροτῶν;

ΗΛ. μήτηρ καλεῖται· μητρὶ δ' οὐδὲν ἐξισοῖ.

ΟΡ. τί δρῶσα; πότερα χερσίν, ἢ λύμῃ βίου;     1195

ΗΛ. καὶ χερσὶ καὶ λύμαισι καὶ πᾶσιν κακοῖς.

ΟΡ. οὐδ' οὑπαρήξων οὐδ' ὁ κωλύσων πάρα;

ΗΛ. οὐ δῆθ'· ὃς ἦν γάρ μοι σὺ προὔθηκας σποδόν.

ΟΡ. ὦ δύσποτμ', ὡς ὁρῶν σ' ἐποικτίρω πάλαι.

ΗΛ. μόνος βροτῶν νυν ἴσθ' ἐποικτίρας ποτέ,     1200

ΟΡ. μόνος γὰρ ἥκω τοῖσι σοῖς ἀλγῶν κακοῖς.

ΗΛ. οὐ δή ποθ' ἡμῖν ξυγγενὴς ἥκεις ποθέν;

1175 γλώσσης Lᶜ A rec: γνώσσης Lᵃᶜ: γνώμης Lˢ rec     1177 Ἠλέκτρα Lᵃᶜ rec     1180 οὐ δή Lˢ Σ rec: τί δή L A rec     1184 δή Lˢ A rec: μοί Lᵃᶜ rec Suid. v. ἐπισκοπῶν     1185 ᾔδειν codd.     οὐδὲν] ἐγὼ Lᵃᶜ     1187 σὲ Jebb: σε codd.     1189 τῶνδ' ἔτ' rec: τῶνδέ τ' L A rec     1193 ἀνάγκῃ rec: ἀνάγκη L A rec et fort Σ     προστρέπει Reiske: προτρέπει codd.     1197 οὐδ' ὁ rec: οὔθ' ὁ L A rec     1198 ἦν γάρ L rec: γάρ ἦν A rec     1200 ποτέ L A rec: ἐμέ Δ: με σύ Harl     1201 τοῖσι σοῖς Lᶜ A rec: τοῖς ἴσοις Lᵃᶜ Pal

ΟΡ. ἐγὼ φράσαιμ' ἄν, εἰ τὸ τῶνδ' εὔνουν πάρα.

ΗΛ. ἀλλ' ἐστὶν εὔνουν, ὥστε πρὸς πιστὰς ἐρεῖς.

ΟΡ. μέθες τόδ' ἄγγος νυν, ὅπως τὸ πᾶν μάθῃς.　　　　1205

ΗΛ. μὴ δῆτα πρὸς θεῶν τοῦτό μ' ἐργάσῃ, ξένε.

ΟΡ. πιθοῦ λέγοντι κοὐχ ἁμαρτήσῃ ποτέ.

ΗΛ. μὴ πρὸς γενείου μὴ 'ξέλῃ τὰ φίλτατα.

ΟΡ. οὔ φημ' ἐάσειν.　ΗΛ. ὦ τάλαιν' ἐγὼ σέθεν,
　　　'Ορέστα, τῆς σῆς εἰ στερήσομαι ταφῆς.　　　　1210

ΟΡ. εὔφημα φώνει· πρὸς δίκης γὰρ οὐ στένεις.

ΗΛ. πῶς τὸν θανόντ' ἀδελφὸν οὐ δίκῃ στένω;

ΟΡ. οὔ σοι προσήκει τήνδε προσφωνεῖν φάτιν.

ΗΛ. οὕτως ἄτιμός εἰμι τοῦ τεθνηκότος;

ΟΡ. ἄτιμος οὐδενὸς σύ· τοῦτο δ' οὐχὶ σόν.　　　　1215

ΗΛ. εἴπερ γ' 'Ορέστου σῶμα βαστάζω τόδε.

ΟΡ. ἀλλ' οὐκ 'Ορέστου, πλὴν λόγῳ γ' ἠσκημένον.

ΗΛ. ποῦ δ' ἔστ' ἐκείνου τοῦ ταλαιπώρου τάφος;

ΟΡ. οὐκ ἔστι· τοῦ γὰρ ζῶντος οὐκ ἔστιν τάφος.

ΗΛ. πῶς εἶπας, ὦ παῖ;　ΟΡ. ψεῦδος οὐδὲν ὧν λέγω.　　　1220

ΗΛ. ἦ ζῇ γὰρ ἁνήρ;　ΟΡ. εἴπερ ἔμψυχός γ' ἐγώ.

ΗΛ. ἦ γὰρ σὺ κεῖνος;　ΟΡ. τήνδε προσβλέψασά μου
　　　σφραγῖδα πατρὸς ἔκμαθ' εἰ σαφῆ λέγω.

ΗΛ. ὦ φίλτατον φῶς.　ΟΡ. φίλτατον, ξυμμαρτυρῶ.

ΗΛ. ὦ φθέγμ', ἀφίκου;　ΟΡ. μηκέτ' ἄλλοθεν πύθῃ.　　　1225

ΗΛ. ἔχω σε χερσίν;　ΟΡ. ὡς τὰ λοίπ' ἔχοις ἀεί.

ΗΛ. ὦ φίλταται γυναῖκες, ὦ πολίτιδες,
　　　ὁρᾶτ' 'Ορέστην τόνδε, μηχαναῖσι μὲν
　　　θανόντα, νῦν δὲ μηχαναῖς σεσωσμένον.

ΧΟ. ὁρῶμεν, ὦ παῖ, κἀπὶ συμφοραῖσί μοι　　　　1230
　　　γεγηθὸς ἕρπει δάκρυον ὀμμάτων ἄπο.

1207 πιθοῦ rec: πείθου L A rec　　　1208 μὴ 'ξέλῃ L A rec Eustath. 129,
15: μὴ 'ξέλῃς Monac· μ' ἐξέλῃ Elmsley　　　1210 ὑστερήσομαι Ven b
1220 ψεῦδος δ' A　　　1221 ἁνήρ codd.　　　1222 προσβλέψουσά μου Lb
1226 χερσίν A rec L²ᵞρ: χεροῖν L rec　　ἔχοις Lᵃᶜ: ἔχεις Lᶜ Aᶜ rec: ἄχοις
Aᵃᶜ　　　1229 σεσωσμένον codd.: corr. Wecklein

ΗΛ.                 ἰὼ γοναί,                                                    στρ.
               γοναὶ σωμάτων ἐμοὶ φιλτάτων
                  ἐμόλετ᾿ ἀρτίως,
          ἐφηύρετ᾿, ἤλθετ᾿, εἴδεθ᾿ οὓς ἐχρῄζετε.                               1235
ΟΡ.  πάρεσμεν· ἀλλὰ σῖγ᾿ ἔχουσα πρόσμενε.
ΗΛ.                 τί δ᾿ ἔστιν;
ΟΡ.  σιγᾶν ἄμεινον, μή τις ἔνδοθεν κλύῃ.
ΗΛ.                 ἀλλ᾿ οὐ τὰν Ἄρτεμιν
                  τὰν ἀεὶ ἀδμήταν
               τόδε μὲν οὔ ποτ᾿ ἀξιώσω τρέσαι,                                  1240
               περισσὸν ἄχθος ἔνδον
               γυναικῶν ὂν αἰεί.
ΟΡ.  ὅρα γε μὲν δὴ κἀν γυναιξὶν ὡς Ἄρης
          ἔνεστιν· εὖ δ᾿ ἔξοισθα πειραθεῖσά που.
ΗΛ.                 ὀττοτοῖ ὀττοτοῖ,                                            1245
          ἀνέφελον ἐνέβαλες οὔ ποτε καταλύσιμον,
               οὐδέ ποτε λησόμενον ἁμέτερον
               οἷον ἔφυ κακόν.                                                  1250
ΟΡ.  ἔξοιδα καὶ ταῦτ᾿· ἀλλ᾿ ὅταν παρουσία
          φράζῃ, τότ᾿ ἔργων τῶνδε μεμνῆσθαι χρεών.


ΗΛ.                 ὁ πᾶς ἐμοὶ                                                  ἀντ.
               ὁ πᾶς ἂν πρέποι παρὼν ἐννέπειν
                  τάδε δίκᾳ χρόνος.                                            1255
          μόλις γὰρ ἔσχον νῦν ἐλεύθερον στόμα.
ΟΡ.  ξύμφημι κἀγώ. τοιγαροῦν σῴζου τόδε.
ΗΛ.                 τί δρῶσα;


1233 γοναὶ LˢA rec: om. L rec        1235 ἐφεύρετ᾿ codd.: corr. Dindorf
1239 τὰν] μὰ τὰν rec: cf. 1063   ἀεὶ Hartung: αἰὲν codd.        1244 om. T
1245 ὀττοτοῖ ὀττοτοῖ Bergk: ὀτοττοῖ L Σ¹: ὀττοτοῖ (vel ὀττοτοί) A rec:
ὀτοτοττοῖ Pal: ὀτοτοτοτοῖ τοτοῖ Hermann        1246 ἐνέβαλες Σ (ut
videtur): ἐπέβαλες L A rec: ὑπέβαλες Vat a        1248 οὐδέ] οὐ δή A
1251 παρουσία L A rec: παρρησία rec: παρρησίᾳ Pearson        1255 δίκᾳ
(δίκα Σᵞ) rec Tricl (ἔν τινι τῶν παλαιῶν βιβλίων): δίκαια (h. e.
δίκαι (sscr. α) L A rec

ΟΡ.　οὗ μή 'στι καιρὸς μὴ μακρὰν βούλου λέγειν.

ΗΛ.　　　τίς οὖν ἀντάξι' ἂν　　　　　　　　1260
　　　　σοῦ γε πεφηνότος
　　　μεταβάλοιτ' ἂν ὧδε σιγὰν λόγων;
　　　ἐπεί σε νῦν ἀφράστως
　　　ἀέλπτως τ' ἐσεῖδον.

ΟΡ.　τότ' εἶδες, ὅτε θεοί μ' ἐπώτρυναν μολεῖν

　　　·　·　·　·　·　·　·　·　·　·

ΗΛ.　　　ἔφρασας ὑπερτέραν　　　　　　　1265
　　　τᾶς πάρος ἔτι χάριτος, εἴ σε θεὸς ἐπόρισεν
　　　ἀμέτερα πρὸς μέλαθρα· δαιμόνιον
　　　αὐτὸ τίθημ' ἐγώ.　　　　　　　　　1270

ΟΡ.　τὰ μέν σ' ὀκνῶ χαίρουσαν εἰργαθεῖν, τὰ δὲ
　　　δέδοικα λίαν ἡδονῇ νικωμένην.

ΗΛ.　　　ἰὼ χρόνῳ　　　　　　　　　　ἐπ.
　　　μακρῷ φιλτάταν ὁδὸν ἐπαξιώ-
　　　σας ὧδέ μοι φανῆναι,
　　　μή τί με, πολύπονον ὧδ' ἰδὼν　　　　1275

ΟΡ.　τί μὴ ποήσω; ΗΛ. μή μ' ἀποστερήσῃς
　　　τῶν σῶν προσώπων ἀδονὰν μεθέσθαι.

ΟΡ.　ἦ κάρτα κἂν ἄλλοισι θυμοίμην ἰδών.

ΗΛ.　ξυναινεῖς; ΟΡ. τί μὴν οὔ;　　　　　1280

ΗΛ.　ὦ φίλ', ἔκλυον ἂν ἐγὼ οὐδ' ἂν ἤλπισ' αὐδάν.
　　　ἔσχον ὀργὰν ἄναυδον
　　　οὐδὲ σὺν βοᾷ κλύουσ' ἀ τάλαινα.

1260 τίς] τί A　οὖν ἀντάξι' ἂν scripsi (ἀνταξίαν iam Arndt): οὖν ἀξίαν
L rec: οὖν ἂν ἀξίαν L²ˢ A rec: ἂν οὖν ἀξίαν rec　　1261 σοῦ γε Seidler:
γε σοῦ codd.　　1263 τ' om. A rec　　1264 ἐπώτρυναν Reiske: ὤτρυναν
codd.　post hunc v. lacunam indicavit Heath　　1267 ἐπόρισεν Dindorf:
ἐπῶρεν Lᵃᶜ A rec: ἐπόρσεν Lᶜ　　1271 εἰργάθειν codd.: corr. Elmsley
1275 με om. rec　πολύπονον Jen: πολύστονον L A rec　ὧδ'] τῶιδ' Lᵃᶜ
1277 ἀδονὰν Dindorf: ἡδονὰν vel ἡδονὴν codd.: ἡδονῇ legisse Σ sunt
qui existimant　　1280 μὴν Seidler: μὴ codd.　　1281 ὦ φίλ' Wunder:
ὦ φίλαι (unde ὦ φίλε olim exstitisse censeas) L A rec Σ: ἀλλ' ὦ
φίλαι M　　1284 κλύουσ' ἀ Hartung (κλύουσα | ἀ Hermann): κλύουσα
codd.

νῦν δ' ἔχω σε· προυφάνης δὲ                    1285
φιλτάταν ἔχων πρόσοψιν,
ἃς ἐγὼ οὐδ' ἂν ἐν κακοῖς λαθοίμαν.

ΟΡ. τὰ μὲν περισσεύοντα τῶν λόγων ἄφες,
καὶ μήτε μήτηρ ὡς κακὴ δίδασκέ με
μήθ' ὡς πατρῴαν κτῆσιν Αἴγισθος δόμων          1290
ἀντλεῖ, τὰ δ' ἐκχεῖ, τὰ δὲ διασπείρει μάτην·
χρόνου γὰρ ἄν σοι καιρὸν ἐξείργοι λόγος.
ἃ δ' ἁρμόσει μοι τῷ παρόντι νῦν χρόνῳ
σήμαιν', ὅπου φανέντες ἢ κεκρυμμένοι
γελῶντας ἐχθροὺς παύσομεν τῇ νῦν ὁδῷ.          1295
οὕτως δ' ὅπως μήτηρ σε μὴ 'πιγνώσεται
φαιδρῷ προσώπῳ νῷν ἐπελθόντοιν δόμους·
ἀλλ' ὡς ἐπ' ἄτῃ τῇ μάτην λελεγμένη
στέναζ'· ὅταν γὰρ εὐτυχήσωμεν, τότε
χαίρειν παρέσται καὶ γελᾶν ἐλευθέρως.          1300

ΗΛ. ἀλλ', ὦ κασίγνηθ', ὧδ' ὅπως καὶ σοὶ φίλον
καὶ τοὐμὸν ἔσται τῇδ'· ἐπεὶ τὰς ἡδονὰς
πρὸς σοῦ λαβοῦσα κοὐκ ἐμὰς ἐκτησάμην.
κοὐδ' ἄν σε λυπήσασα δεξαίμην βραχὺ
αὐτὴ μέγ' εὑρεῖν κέρδος· οὐ γὰρ ἂν καλῶς      1305
ὑπηρετοίην τῷ παρόντι δαίμονι.
ἀλλ' οἶσθα μὲν τἀνθένδε, πῶς γὰρ οὔ; κλύων
ὁθούνεκ' Αἴγισθος μὲν οὐ κατὰ στέγας,
μήτηρ δ' ἐν οἴκοις· ἣν σὺ μὴ δείσῃς ποθ' ὡς
γέλωτι τοὐμὸν φαιδρὸν ὄψεται κάρα.            1310
μῖσός τε γὰρ παλαιὸν ἐντέτηκέ μοι,
κἀπεί σ' ἐσεῖδον, οὔ ποτ' ἐκλήξω χαρᾷ

1287 λαθοίμαν L rec: λαθοίμην A: λάθοιμ' ἂν rec      1292 ἐξείργοι]
ἐξαίροι Suidae v. χρόνου πόδα codd. plerique      1296 οὕτως] οὕτω rec
1297 ἐπελθόντοιν Lᶜ A rec: ἐπελθόντων Lᵃᶜ rec: ἐσελθόντοιν Nauck
1298 λελεγμένη Lˢ A rec: δεδεγμένη L      1304 δεξαίμην rec: λεξαίμην
L: βουλοίμην A rec L²ᵞᵖ      1306 ὑπηρετοίμην codd.: corr. Musgrave
1310 τοὐμὸν φαιδρὸν L rec: φαιδρὸν τοὐμὸν A rec: φαιδρῷ τοὐμὸν rec
1311 τε om. Lᵃᶜ      1312 χαρᾷ Schaefer: χαρᾶς L A rec

δακρυρροοῦσα. πῶς γὰρ ἂν λήξαιμ' ἐγώ,
ἥτις μιᾷ σε τῇδ' ὁδῷ θανόντα τε
καὶ ζῶντ' ἐσεῖδον; εἴργασαι δέ μ' ἄσκοπα·      1315
ὥστ', εἰ πατήρ μοι ζῶν ἵκοιτο, μηκέτ' ἂν
τέρας νομίζειν αὐτό, πιστεύειν δ' ὁρᾶν.
ὅτ' οὖν τοιαύτην ἡμὶν ἐξήκεις ὁδόν,
ἄρχ' αὐτὸς ὥς σοι θυμός. ὡς ἐγὼ μόνη
οὐκ ἂν δυοῖν ἥμαρτον· ἢ γὰρ ἂν καλῶς      1320
ἔσωσ' ἐμαυτήν, ἢ καλῶς ἀπωλόμην.

ΟΡ. σιγᾶν ἐπήνεσ'· ὡς ἐπ' ἐξόδῳ κλύω
τῶν ἔνδοθεν χωροῦντος.   ΗΛ. εἴσιτ', ὦ ξένοι,
ἄλλως τε καὶ φέροντες οἷ' ἂν οὔτε τις
δόμων ἀπώσαιτ' οὔτ' ἂν ἡσθείη λαβών.      1325

ΠΑ. ὦ πλεῖστα μῶροι καὶ φρενῶν τητώμενοι,
πότερα παρ' οὐδὲν τοῦ βίου κήδεσθ' ἔτι,
ἢ νοῦς ἔνεστιν οὔτις ὑμὶν ἐγγενής,
ὅτ' οὐ παρ' αὐτοῖς ἀλλ' ἐν αὐτοῖσιν κακοῖς
τοῖσιν μεγίστοις ὄντες οὐ γιγνώσκετε;      1330
ἀλλ' εἰ σταθμοῖσι τοῖσδε μὴ 'κύρουν ἐγὼ
πάλαι φυλάσσων, ἦν ἂν ὑμὶν ἐν δόμοις
τὰ δρώμεν' ὑμῶν πρόσθεν ἢ τὰ σώματα·
νῦν δ' εὐλάβειαν τῶνδε προυθέμην ἐγώ.
καὶ νῦν ἀπαλλαχθέντε τῶν μακρῶν λόγων      1335
καὶ τῆς ἀπλήστου τῆσδε σὺν χαρᾷ βοῆς
εἴσω παρέλθεθ', ὡς τὸ μὲν μέλλειν κακὸν
ἐν τοῖς τοιούτοις ἔστ', ἀπηλλάχθαι δ' ἀκμή.

ΟΡ. πῶς οὖν ἔχει τἀντεῦθεν εἰσιόντι μοι;

ΠΑ. καλῶς· ὑπάρχει γάρ σε μὴ γνῶναί τινα.      1340

ΟΡ. ἤγγειλας, ὡς ἔοικεν, ὡς τεθνηκότα.

ΠΑ. εἷς τῶν ἐν Ἅιδου μάνθαν' ἐνθάδ' ὢν ἀνήρ.

ΟΡ. χαίρουσιν οὖν τούτοισιν; ἢ τίνες λόγοι;

1315 εἰργάσω L^{ac}   1320 καλῶς] κακῶς Nauck   1322 sq. choro
nonnullos tribuisse testatur Σ   1325 ἀπώσαιτ' L^{s}A rec: ἀπώσετ' L rec
1328 ἐγγενής A rec Σ: ἐκγενής L rec   1332 ὑμὶν] ἡμὶν Lb
1336 ἀπλήστου rec: ἀπλείστου L A: ἀλήκτου M   1337 μέλειν L Γ
1343 οὖν A rec: ἐν L rec

ΠΑ. τελουμένων εἴποιμ' ἄν· ὡς δὲ νῦν ἔχει,
    καλῶς τὰ κείνων πάντα, καὶ τὰ μὴ καλῶς.     1345

ΗΛ. τίς οὗτός ἐστ', ἀδελφέ; πρὸς θεῶν φράσον.

ΟΡ. οὐχὶ ξυνίης;   ΗΛ. οὐδέ γ' ἐς θυμὸν φέρω.

ΟΡ. οὐκ οἶσθ' ὅτῳ μ' ἔδωκας ἐς χεῖράς ποτε;

ΗΛ. ποίῳ; τί φωνεῖς;   ΟΡ. οὗ τὸ Φωκέων πέδον
    ὑπεξεπέμφθην σῇ προμηθίᾳ χεροῖν.     1350

ΗΛ. ἦ κεῖνος οὗτος ὅν ποτ' ἐκ πολλῶν ἐγὼ
    μόνον προσηῦρον πιστὸν ἐν πατρὸς φόνῳ;

ΟΡ. ὅδ' ἐστί. μή μ' ἔλεγχε πλείοσιν λόγοις.

ΗΛ. ὦ φίλτατον φῶς, ὦ μόνος σωτὴρ δόμων
    Ἀγαμέμνονος, πῶς ἦλθες; ἦ σὺ κεῖνος εἶ,     1355
    ὃς τόνδε κἄμ' ἔσωσας ἐκ πολλῶν πόνων;
    ὦ φίλταται μὲν χεῖρες, ἥδιστον δ' ἔχων
    ποδῶν ὑπηρέτημα, πῶς οὕτω πάλαι
    ξυνών μ' ἔληθες οὐδ' ἔφαινες, ἀλλά με
    λόγοις ἀπώλλυς, ἔργ' ἔχων ἥδιστ' ἐμοί;     1360
    χαῖρ', ὦ πάτερ· πατέρα γὰρ εἰσορᾶν δοκῶ·
    χαῖρ'· ἴσθι δ' ὡς μάλιστά σ' ἀνθρώπων ἐγὼ
    ἤχθηρα κἀφίλησ' ἐν ἡμέρᾳ μιᾷ.

ΠΑ. ἀρκεῖν δοκεῖ μοι· τοὺς γὰρ ἐν μέσῳ λόγους
    πολλαὶ κυκλοῦνται νύκτες ἡμέραι τ' ἴσαι,     1365
    αἳ ταῦτά σοι δείξουσιν, Ἠλέκτρα, σαφῆ.
    σφῷν δ' ἐννέπω γε τοῖν παρεστώτοιν ὅτι
    νῦν καιρὸς ἔρδειν· νῦν Κλυταιμήστρα μόνη·
    νῦν οὔτις ἀνδρῶν ἔνδον· εἰ δ' ἐφέξετον,
    φροντίζεθ' ὡς τούτοις τε καὶ σοφωτέροις     1370
    ἄλλοισι τούτων πλείοσιν μαχούμενοι.

ΟΡ. οὐκ ἂν μακρῶν ἔθ' ἡμῖν οὐδὲν ἂν λόγων,
    Πυλάδη, τόδ' εἴη τοὔργον, ἀλλ' ὅσον τάχος
    χωρεῖν ἔσω, πατρῷα προσκύσανθ' ἕδη

1347 ξυνίης rec: ξυνιείς L A rec    1348 χέρας L    1350 προμηθίᾳ
L Γ Σ : προμηθείᾳ Lˢ A rec: προθυμίᾳ Pal    1352 προσεῦρον codd.:
corr. Dindorf    1359 ἔφανες A    1362 ἴσθι δ'] ἴσθ' Lᵃᶜ: ἴσθι Γ
1365 κυκλοῦνται Lᵃᶜ rec: κυκλοῦσι Lᶜ A rec    1367 ἐννέπω 'γὼ Hermann    1368 Κλυταιμήστρα L: Κλυταιμνήστρα A rec

θεῶν, ὅσοιπερ πρόπυλα ναίουσιν τάδε.          1375

ΗΛ. ἄναξ Ἄπολλον, ἵλεως αὐτοῖν κλύε,
ἐμοῦ τε πρὸς τούτοισιν, ἥ σε πολλὰ δὴ
ἀφ᾽ ὧν ἔχοιμι λιπαρεῖ προύστην χερί.
νῦν δ᾽, ὦ Λύκει᾽ Ἄπολλον, ἐξ οἵων ἔχω
αἰτῶ, προπίτνω, λίσσομαι, γενοῦ πρόφρων          1380
ἡμῖν ἀρωγὸς τῶνδε τῶν βουλευμάτων
καὶ δεῖξον ἀνθρώποισι τἀπιτίμια
τῆς δυσσεβείας οἷα δωροῦνται θεοί.

ΧΟ.          ἴδεθ᾽ ὅπου προνέμεται          στρ.
τὸ δυσέριστον αἷμα φυσῶν Ἄρης.          1385
βεβᾶσιν ἄρτι δωμάτων ὑπόστεγοι
μετάδρομοι κακῶν πανουργημάτων
          ἄφυκτοι κύνες·
          ὥστ᾽ οὐ μακρὰν ἔτ᾽ ἀμμενεῖ
τοὐμὸν φρενῶν ὄνειρον αἰωρούμενον.          1390

          παράγεται γὰρ ἐνέρων          ἀντ.
δολιόπους ἀρωγὸς εἴσω στέγας,
ἀρχαιόπλουτα πατρὸς εἰς ἑδώλια,
νεακόνητον αἷμα χειροῖν ἔχων·
          ὁ Μαίας δὲ παῖς          1395
Ἑρμῆς σφ᾽ ἄγει δόλον σκότῳ
κρύψας πρὸς αὐτὸ τέρμα, κοὐκέτ᾽ ἀμμένει.

ΗΛ. ὦ φίλταται γυναῖκες, ἄνδρες αὐτίκα          στρ.

1375 ὅσοιπερ rec: ὅσοι L A Γ          1378 πρόστην Lᵃᶜ          1380 προπιτνῶ
Lᶜ A rec: προσπιτνῶ Lᵃᶜ rec Suid. v. ἐξ οἵων et eiusdem v. λιπαρεῖ
codd. A E          1384 ὅπου] ὅπῃ Δ          1389 ἀμμενεῖ legisse videtur Σ:
ἀμμένει L A rec          1390 αἰωρούμενον L (-ον ex -ων facto)
1393 ἑδώλια L rec Suid. s. v.: ἑδράσματα A rec Σʸᴾ          1394 νεακόνητον
αἷμα vitio laborant nondum sanato: αἷμα testantur etiam Hesych. i. 79,
Etym. M. 35, 4, Suid. s. v., Bekk. anecd. 356, 20: νεοκόμιστον coni.
Kaibel: malim νεόκμητον quod eidem quoque in mentem venerat          χειροῖν
Lᵃᶜ: χεροῖν Lᶜ A rec          1396 σφ᾽ ἄγει rec T: ἐ.ἄγει L: ἐπάγει A rec:
ἐπεισάγει E: σφ᾽ ἐπάγει Pal          1398 ἄνδρες codd.

τελοῦσι τοὔργον· ἀλλὰ σῖγα πρόσμενε.

ΧΟ. πῶς δή; τί νῦν πράσσουσιν;   ΗΛ. ἡ μὲν ἐς τάφον   1400
λέβητα κοσμεῖ, τὼ δ' ἐφέστατον πέλας.

ΧΟ. σὺ δ' ἐκτὸς ᾖξας πρὸς τί;   ΗΛ. φρουρήσουσ' ὅπως
Αἴγισθος ἡμᾶς μὴ λάθῃ μολὼν ἔσω.

ΚΛ.   αἰαῖ. ἰὼ στέγαι
φίλων ἐρῆμοι, τῶν δ' ἀπολλύντων πλέαι.   1405

ΗΛ. βοᾷ τις ἔνδον. οὐκ ἀκούετ', ὦ φίλαι;

ΧΟ.   ἤκουσ' ἀνήκουστα δύ-
στανος, ὥστε φρῖξαι.

ΚΛ. οἴμοι τάλαιν'· Αἴγισθε, ποῦ ποτ' ὢν κυρεῖς;

ΗΛ. ἰδοὺ μάλ'· αὖ θροεῖ τις.   ΚΛ. ὦ τέκνον τέκνον,   1410
οἴκτιρε τὴν τεκοῦσαν.   ΗΛ. ἀλλ' οὐκ ἐκ σέθεν
ᾠκτίρεθ' οὗτος οὐδ' ὁ γεννήσας πατήρ.

ΧΟ. ὦ πόλις, ὦ γενεὰ τάλαινα, νῦν σοι
μοῖρα καθαμερία φθίνει φθίνει.

ΚΛ. ὤμοι πέπληγμαι.   ΗΛ. παῖσον, εἰ σθένεις, διπλῆν.   1415

ΚΛ. ὤμοι μάλ' αὖθις.   ΗΛ. εἰ γὰρ Αἰγίσθῳ θ' ὁμοῦ.

ΧΟ.   τελοῦσ' ἀραί· ζῶσιν οἱ
γᾶς ὑπαὶ κείμενοι.

παλίρρυτον γὰρ αἷμ' ὑπεξαιροῦσι τῶν   1420
κτανόντων οἱ πάλαι θανόντες.

καὶ μὴν πάρεισιν οἵδε· φοινία δὲ χεὶρ   ἀντ.
στάζει θυηλῆς Ἄρεος, οὐδ' ἔχω ψέγειν.

ΗΛ. Ὀρέστα, πῶς κυρεῖτε;   ΟΡ. τἀν δόμοισι μὲν

1399 τελοῦσι L (sscr. ἔσω )   1403 ἡμᾶς Jenˢ: om. cett: αὐτὸς coni.
Tricl: αὐτοὺς Kaibel   1404 αἲ αἲ αἲ αἲ A rec: αἲ αἲ L rec Σ¹
1409 ποῦ A rec: ποῖ L Pal   1410 ὦ τέκνον τέκνον T: ὦ τέκνον ὦ
τέκνον L A rec   1412 οὐδ' Vindob: οὔθ' L A rec   1413 σοι
Hermann: σε codd.   1414 καθαμερία rec: καθημερία A rec: καθ' ἡμερία
L φθίνει φθίνει L rec: φθίνει A rec   1416 θ' L A rec: δ' rec: γ' Hermann
1417 τελοῦσ' T: τελοῦσιν L A rec   ἀραί L rec: ἀράς rec: ἀραίας A
1419 ὑποκείμενοι codd.: corr. Brunck   1420 παλίρρυτον Bothe:
πολύρρυτον (πολλύρυτον L Lb) codd.   1422 sq. Electrae tribuunt
codd.: corr. Hermann   ψέγειν Erfurdt: λέγειν codd.   1424 κυρεῖτε
Elmsley: κυρεῖ L A rec σ: κυρεῖ γε T Liv ν: κυρεῖς rec

καλῶς, Ἀπόλλων εἰ καλῶς ἐθέσπισεν.                    1425

ΗΛ. τέθνηκεν ἡ τάλαινα;     ΟΡ. μηκέτ' ἐκφοβοῦ
μητρῷον ὥς σε λῆμ' ἀτιμάσει ποτέ.

ΗΛ. .    .    .    .

.    .    .    .    .    .    .

ΟΡ. .    .    .    .    .    .

ΧΟ.     παύσασθε, λεύσσω γὰρ Αἴγισθον ἐκ προδήλου.

ΟΡ. .    .    .    .    .    .

ΗΛ. ὦ παῖδες, οὐκ ἄψορρον;     ΟΡ. εἰσορᾶτέ που      1430
τὸν ἄνδρ' ἐφ' ἡμῖν ... ΗΛ. .  .  .  .  .  .  .
χωρεῖ γεγηθὼς οὗτος ἐκ προαστίου.

ΧΟ. βᾶτε κατ' ἀντιθύρων ὅσον τάχιστα,
νῦν, τὰ πρὶν εὖ θέμενοι, τάδ' ὡς πάλιν.

ΟΡ. θάρσει· τελοῦμεν.     ΗΛ. ᾗ νοεῖς ἔπειγέ νυν.      1435

ΟΡ. καὶ δὴ βέβηκα.     ΗΛ. τἀνθάδ' ἂν μέλοιτ' ἐμοί.

ΧΟ.     δι' ὠτὸς ἂν παῦρά γ' ὡς
ἡπίως ἐννέπειν
πρὸς ἄνδρα τόνδε συμφέροι, λαθραῖον ὡς      1440
ὁρούσῃ πρὸς δίκας ἀγῶνα.

ΑΙΓΙΣΘΟΣ

τίς οἶδεν ὑμῶν ποῦ ποθ' οἱ Φωκῆς ξένοι,
οὕς φασ' Ὀρέστην ἡμὶν ἀγγεῖλαι βίον
λελοιπόθ' ἱππικοῖσιν ἐν ναυαγίοις;
σέ τοι, σὲ κρίνω, ναὶ σέ, τὴν ἐν τῷ πάρος      1445
χρόνῳ θρασεῖαν· ὡς μάλιστα σοὶ μέλειν

---

1426 Orestae continuant codd.: corr. Erfurdt     1427 post hunc v. trium
versuum lacunam indicavit Erfurdt     1429 post hunc v. lacunam indicavit
Seidler     1430 εἰσορᾶτε ποῦ rec     1431 sq. secundum Pal. disposui:
τὸν ἄνδρ' ἐφ' ἡμῖν; ΗΛ. οὗτος ἐκ π. | χ. γ. L A rec: post quae lacunam
primus indicavit Hermann: textum explere possis scribendo στάντα; ΗΛ.
καὶ γὰρ οὐ μακρὰν προαστίου L Aᶜ Suid. s.v.: προαστείου Aᵃᶜ rec
1433 βᾶτε κατ' ἀντιθύρων (κατάντι θυρῶν Γ) vix sana: fort. βᾶτε
θυρῶν κατένανθ'     1435 ᾗ νοεῖς Orestae continuant codd.: corr. Erfurdt
1437 sqq. choro tribuit T: Electrae continuant L A rec     ἡπίως]
νηπιωι (sscr. ·ον·) Σγρ (νήπιον et νηπίῳ pariter explicans): ἤπιον rec
1442 Φωκῆς Lˢ: Φωκεῖς L A rec     1445 ναὶ Reiske: καὶ codd.

οἶμαι, μάλιστα δ' ἂν κατειδυῖαν φράσαι.

ΗΛ. ἔξοιδα· πῶς γὰρ οὐχί; συμφορᾶς γὰρ ἂν
ἔξωθεν εἴην τῶν ἐμῶν γε φιλτάτων.

ΑΙ. ποῦ δῆτ' ἂν εἶεν οἱ ξένοι; δίδασκέ με.      1450

ΗΛ. ἔνδον· φίλης γὰρ προξένου κατήνυσαν.

ΑΙ. ἦ καὶ θανόντ' ἤγγειλαν ὡς ἐτητύμως;

ΗΛ. οὔκ, ἀλλὰ κἀπέδειξαν, οὐ λόγῳ μόνον.

ΑΙ. πάρεστ' ἄρ' ἡμῖν ὥστε κἀμφανῆ μαθεῖν;

ΗΛ. πάρεστι δῆτα καὶ μάλ' ἄζηλος θέα.      1455

ΑΙ. ἦ πολλὰ χαίρειν μ' εἶπας οὐκ εἰωθότως.

ΗΛ. χαίροις ἄν, εἴ σοι χαρτὰ τυγχάνει τάδε.

ΑΙ. σιγᾶν ἄνωγα κἀναδεικνύναι πύλας
πᾶσιν Μυκηναίοισιν 'Αργείοις θ' ὁρᾶν,
ὡς εἴ τις αὐτῶν ἐλπίσιν κεναῖς πάρος      1460
ἐξῆρετ' ἀνδρὸς τοῦδε, νῦν ὁρῶν νεκρὸν
στόμια δέχηται τἀμά, μηδὲ πρὸς βίαν
ἐμοῦ κολαστοῦ προστυχὼν φύσῃ φρένας.

ΗΛ. καὶ δὴ τελεῖται τἀπ' ἐμοῦ· τῷ γὰρ χρόνῳ
νοῦν ἔσχον, ὥστε συμφέρειν τοῖς κρείσσοσιν.      1465

ΑΙ. ὦ Ζεῦ, δέδορκα φάσμ' ἄνευ φθόνου μὲν οὐ
πεπτωκός· εἰ δ' ἔπεστι νέμεσις οὐ λέγω.
χαλᾶτε πᾶν κάλυμμ' ἀπ' ὀφθαλμῶν, ὅπως
τὸ συγγενές τοι κἀπ' ἐμοῦ θρήνων τύχῃ.

ΟΡ. αὐτὸς σὺ βάσταζ'· οὐκ ἐμὸν τόδ', ἀλλὰ σόν,      1470
τὸ ταῦθ' ὁρᾶν τε καὶ προσηγορεῖν φίλως.

ΑΙ. ἀλλ' εὖ παραινεῖς, κἀπιπείσομαι· σὺ δέ,
εἴ που κατ' οἶκόν μοι Κλυταιμήστρα, κάλει.

1449 γε φιλτάτων rec: τε φιλτάτων L A rec: τῆς φιλτάτης Lˢ rec
1450 δίδασκέ με] μήνυέ μοι Σγρ   1451 καθήνυσαν Dobree   1456 μ'
om. A rec   1457 τυγχάνει A rec: τυγχάνοι L   1458 σιγᾶν] οἴγειν
Wecklein (οἴγειν πύλας ἄν. κἀν. Wilamowitz)  κἀναδεικνύναι] ἀναγνύναι
(antecedente ἄνωγ') Δ: καὶ διοιγνύναι Froehlich: κἀξανοιγνύναι Blaydes:
κἀναφραγνύναι Postgate: fort. καὶ πύλας ἀνοιγνύναι  πύλας] πύλαις
Monac: πέλας Reiske   1465 κρείττοσιν A rec   1466 φθόνου] θεοῦ
Gomperz  οὐ] εὖ Tyrwhitt   1469 τοι rec: τε L A rec T: γε Turneb
1471 φίλως Lᵃᶜ rec: φίλος Lᶜ A rec

ΟΡ. αὕτη πέλας σοῦ· μηκέτ' ἄλλοσε σκόπει.

ΑΙ. οἴμοι, τί λεύσσω;   ΟΡ. τίνα φοβῇ; τίν' ἀγνοεῖς;   1475

ΑΙ. τίνων ποτ' ἀνδρῶν ἐν μέσοις ἀρκυστάτοις
πέπτωχ' ὁ τλήμων;   ΟΡ. οὐ γὰρ αἰσθάνῃ πάλαι
ζῶντας θανοῦσιν οὕνεκ' ἀνταυδᾷς ἴσα;

ΑΙ. οἴμοι, ξυνῆκα τοὔπος· οὐ γὰρ ἔσθ' ὅπως
ὅδ' οὐκ Ὀρέστης ἔσθ' ὁ προσφωνῶν ἐμέ.   1480

ΟΡ. καὶ μάντις ὢν ἄριστος ἐσφάλλου πάλαι;

ΑΙ. ὄλωλα δὴ δείλαιος. ἀλλά μοι πάρες
κἂν σμικρὸν εἰπεῖν.   ΗΛ. μὴ πέρα λέγειν ἔα,
πρὸς θεῶν, ἀδελφέ, μηδὲ μηκύνειν λόγους.
τί γὰρ βροτῶν ἂν σὺν κακοῖς μεμειγμένων   1485
θνήσκειν ὁ μέλλων τοῦ χρόνου κέρδος φέροι;
ἀλλ' ὡς τάχιστα κτεῖνε καὶ κτανὼν πρόθες
ταφεῦσιν ὧν τόνδ' εἰκός ἐστι τυγχάνειν,
ἄποπτον ἡμῶν. ὡς ἐμοὶ τόδ' ἂν κακῶν
μόνον γένοιτο τῶν πάλαι λυτήριον.   1490

ΟΡ. χωροῖς ἂν εἴσω σὺν τάχει· λόγων γὰρ οὐ
νῦν ἐστιν ἀγών, ἀλλὰ σῆς ψυχῆς πέρι.

ΑΙ. τί δ' ἐς δόμους ἄγεις με; πῶς, τόδ' εἰ καλὸν
τοὔργον, σκότου δεῖ, κοὐ πρόχειρος εἶ κτανεῖν;

ΟΡ. μὴ τάσσε· χώρει δ' ἔνθαπερ κατέκτανες   1495
πατέρα τὸν ἀμόν, ὡς ἂν ἐν ταὐτῷ θάνῃς.

ΑΙ. ἦ πᾶσ' ἀνάγκη τήνδε τὴν στέγην ἰδεῖν
τά τ' ὄντα καὶ μέλλοντα Πελοπιδῶν κακά;

ΟΡ. τὰ γοῦν σ'· ἐγὼ σοι μάντις εἰμὶ τῶνδ' ἄκρος.

ΑΙ. ἀλλ' οὐ πατρῴαν τὴν τέχνην ἐκόμπασας.   1500

ΟΡ. πόλλ' ἀντιφωνεῖς, ἡ δ' ὁδὸς βραδύνεται.
ἀλλ' ἔρφ'.   ΑΙ. ὑφηγοῦ.   ΟΡ. σοὶ βαδιστέον πάρος.

ΑΙ. ἦ μὴ φύγω σε;   ΟΡ. μὴ μὲν οὖν καθ' ἡδονὴν

1478 ζῶντας Tyrwhitt: ζῶν τοῖς codd.     1481 καὶ] ὡς Tzetzes Epist.
p. 19 ἐσφάλου L rec     1483 κἂν σμικρὸν A rec Σ: κἂν ἐπὶ μικρὸν L rec
1485 sq. in L omissos in margine add. Σ (vel m. pr.): fere idem in Lb
accidit: secl. Dindorf   μεμιγμένον rec   οὐ χρόνου Vahlen   φέροι]
φέερι L^c rec     1487 πρόσθες L^ac rec     1492 ἀγών codd.: corr.
Heath 1496 ἂν ἐν rec: ἂν Lb: ἐν L A rec

θάνῃς· φυλάξαι δεῖ με τοῦτό σοι πικρόν.
χρῆν δ' εὐθὺς εἶναι τήνδε τοῖς πᾶσιν δίκην,                    1505
ὅστις πέρα πράσσειν γε τῶν νόμων θέλοι,
κτείνειν· τὸ γὰρ πανοῦργον οὐκ ἂν ἦν πολύ.

ΧΟ.  ὦ σπέρμ' Ἀτρέως, ὡς πολλὰ παθὸν
       δι' ἐλευθερίας μόλις ἐξῆλθες
       τῇ νῦν ὁρμῇ τελεωθέν.                                    1510

1505 ἐχρῆν A rec Nicephorus ap. Walz i. 461      1506 πέρα τι τῶν νόμων
πράσσειν Niceph. (πράσσειν τι coni. Wunder)      θέλοι L^{ac} rec: θέλει L^{c} A
rec Niceph.      1507 κακοῦργον Niceph.      1508 παθὼν A

# COMMENTARY

The Scene: Mycenae. Enter the Paedagogus (an ancient, faithful servant from the household of Agamemnon, who has been responsible for Orestes' upbringing), leading Orestes and Orestes' guest-friend and inseparable companion, Pylades.

**1f** ὦ τοῦ στρατηγήσαντος ἐν Τροίᾳ ποτὲ κτλ. For the hyperbaton cf. Introduction, p. 14. The natural, or prose word-order would be ὦ παῖ ᾿Αγαμέμνονος τοῦ στρατηγήσαντος κτλ. The present word-order puts an emphasis on τοῦ στρατηγήσαντος ἐν Τροίᾳ, hence upon the fact that Orestes was a young man of brilliant parentage of whom much was to be expected. For the supreme στρατηγία against Troy was the highest of offices, and the taking of Troy the most famous of military achievements. For a similar effect, cf. *Phil.* 3f. ὦ κρατίστου πατρὸς Ἑλλήνων τραφεὶς | ᾿Αχιλλέως παῖ Νεοπτόλεμε.

**2ff** Orestes has now an opportunity to view 'in the flesh' places (associated with his home) which he (as an exile) had only been able to dream of (οὑπόθεις) before. ἔξεστί μοι properly means 'I am allowed' (opp. to πάρεστί μοι='I have the opportunity'), but is frequently used as the equivalent of πάρεστι.

**4ff** The list of places and people appeals to the imagination as well as to the senses, and we should not be too realistic in interpreting it. The Paedagogus refers first with a sweeping gesture to an 'ancient' (because old in story) plain of Argos, the 'grove' (as he describes it) of Inachus' daughter Io (i.e. the territory over which Io roamed when metamorphosed into a cow and driven on by the gadfly). The plain is in the background, to the south and west. In the middle distance lies the city of Argos with its two most famous features, the agora dedicated to 'Lycean' Apollo, the 'wolf-killing' god (but see 645n.), and the celebrated temple of Hera. In the immediate foreground of the travellers (coming from the north) lies Mycenae.

[ 79 ]

**9** φάσκειν: the infinitive used (as frequently) as a mild imperative. 'Whither we are coming, here you may say you behold Mycenae the golden.'

**10** πολύφθορον 'murderous' (literally 'which has suffered much destruction, many deaths': for the passive meaning of the word so accented, see the Lexicon). At last we are brought up sharply upon a piece of stage-reality. For there in the actual background of the set stands the grim palace of the Atridae, the house which had seen the murders of Agamemnon, Cassandra, and also Thyestes' children by Agamemnon's father Atreus.

**11** ἐκ φόνων 'out of', i.e. just after and out of the murderous situation (plural for singular), in which the child Orestes might also have been killed, had not Electra given him to the Paedagogus.

**12** 'Having received you from her hands.' πρός, as often in verse, for ὑπό or ἀπό.

**13** ἤνεγκα...κἀξεθρεψάμην: the accumulation of verbs emphasises the Paedagogus' services to Orestes in rearing him etc., and his consequent dominance over Orestes' ideas and purposes.

**14** Orestes has now grown into a strapping young man of about 19 or 20, since Aegisthus was killed in the eighth year of his usurpation (*Od.* 3. 303ff.), and Orestes was born before Agamemnon went to Troy, and he has been reared and educated by the P. to one purpose, that of avenging his father's death.

**15f** 'So now...you must quickly take counsel as to what is to be *done*.' From this line to its end (85) the Prologue acquires a *leit-motif* expressing the preference of the Paedagogus (and his pupil, Orestes) for *action* (δρᾶν) rather than 'words' (which for the Greeks include thought, theorising, subtle moral distinctions).

**17ff** ἡμῖν: 'ethic' dative: 'the sun's ray arouses the clear birds' songs of morning *for* us', i.e. we find (experience) it doing so. The freshness of the morning, of the dawn-chorus of birds, and of Sophocles' verse contrasts ironically with the grim mission of the three adventurers.

**19** ἐκλέλοιπεν 'has died away', intransitive.

**20** ἀνδρῶν: men (excluding women); for them it is a man's world.

**21** ξυνάπτετον (used absolutely) = 'fix together', i.e. arrange (matters).

λόγοισιν: even the man of action cannot do without λόγοι. But these λόγοι are only preparatory to action, and their effect is immediately overshadowed by the insistence on καιρός (time for *action*, also at 39), and ἔργων ἀκμή (ἀκμή = καιρός) in the following line.

**21f** The meaning is straightforward, but the MS reading ὡς ἐνταῦθ᾽ ἐμέν cannot be right, since ἐμέν is not Attic for ἐσμέν (which would not scan). Sophocles could have written ὡς ἵν᾽ ἕσταμεν, | ἔσθ᾽ οὐκέτ᾽ ὀκνεῖν καιρός (cf. *O.T.* 1442f., *Trach.* 1145). But it is not clear how this could have produced the MS corruption.

ὀκνεῖν 'to shrink', 'draw back' (from an enterprise), not merely physically, but also morally (cf. *Phil.* 111 ὅταν τι δρᾷς ἐς κέρδος, οὐκ ὀκνεῖν πρέπει where the 'shrinking' is from telling a lie).

## 23–38

From the Paedagogus' speech we have garnered certain information about himself and his companions. We see that they are men of action, dedicated to vengeance upon Agamemnon's murderers, impatient of hindrance to that action: λόγοι for them are useful as preliminaries to, counsels for, action (ξυνάπτετον λόγοισιν). They are interested in men, not women, since men spell action. In Orestes' following speech we now see these characteristics further developed, and also a new trait which goes along with them to make up a consistent picture: namely, a tendency to military terminology and military thinking. Orestes is primarily a soldier, trained in the Spartan fashion of strict discipline and obedience to orders.

**23f** 'O dearest of *men*-servants, what clear directives you issue (lit. 'show') to me, splendid fellow that you are to me.'

ἡμᾶς: plural for singular, as often.

σημεῖα φαίνειν in this context is a military term: cf. 1294; Aesch. *Eum.* 569; Hdt. 7. 128; Xen. *Hell.* 3. 2. 23 φρουρὰν ἔφηναν οἱ ἔφοροι (cf. *El.* 74 φρουρῆσαι), *Anab.* 2. 1. 2 οἱ στρατηγοὶ ἐθαύμαζον ὅτι Κῦρος οὔτε ἄλλον πέμπει σημανοῦντα ὅτι χρὴ ποιεῖν, κτλ.

**25ff** 'Just as a thoroughbred horse, even if he is aged, does not lose (οὐκ ἀπώλεσεν – gnomic aorist) his courage in the moment of battle [τὰ δεινά = the 'terrible moment', when the enemy has to be met face to face], but pricks up (ὀρθὸν ἵστησιν) his ear, just so you both spur me on and are yourself in the forefront of those following up (my commands).'

**30f** 'giving sharp ear to my words, if I in any respect (τι) fail to hit the target (καιρός = right point, not merely of time, but of anything), bring me back (μεθ-) into line'. μεθάρμοσον again recalls Orestes' liking for discipline, especially of the Spartan variety. After the Peloponnesian war the Spartans appointed governors of the Greek cities over which they ruled: these governors were called ἁρμοσταί. Orestes uses the verb again at 1293f.

**32ff** Orestes describes how he arrived at the Delphic oracle, 'in order to learn how I should exact vengeance for my father from those who murdered him'. For the implications of the leading question, see Introduction 4f.

**33f** μάθοιμ᾽: the elided iota makes a quasi-caesura with the following syllable, cf. *Ant.* 44, *Phil.* 276.

πάρα: the preposition placed after its substantive by the kind of inversion known as *anastrophe*: hence the throwing forward of the accent.

**35ff** 'Apollo issued an oracle to me (χρῇ, the historic present used, as often, when reporting a critical or striking act or occurrence) the gist of which (τοιαῦθ᾽, ὧν) you will quickly learn from me: that myself alone, without panoply of arms or army, I should stealthily accomplish (κλέψαι), using stratagem (δόλοισι) this personally executed deed of justifiable slaughter.' χειρός (lit. 'of my hand', 'accomplished by my hand') emphasises that Orestes was to do the killing himself. The account of the oracle is so managed that we do not know exactly what it said (notice the vagueness of τοιαῦθ᾽ (35) and τοιόνδε (38)). We do not know (from the structure of the sentence) whether it was the oracle which called the proposed killing ἔνδικοι, or whether χειρὸς ἐνδίκους σφαγάς represents Orestes' own words and Orestes' own estimation of the killing (which he assumed the oracle would agree with).

**38ff** 'Since, then, we have had such an oracle addressed to us.'

ὅτε here is not simply temporal, but = Latin *quandoquidem*, and gives a *subjective* reason (cf. 1318). The oracle is the reason for Orestes' feeling secure in his plans to commit matricide.

## 39–76

*The plan.* The Paedagogus is to gain admittance to the palace, saying that he is a friendly messenger sent from Phocis to deliver the news that Orestes is dead, killed in an accident at the Pythian games. Sooner or later Orestes will turn up, disguised as a fellow-Phocian, to back up the Paedagogus' story with visible evidence of his own death in the shape of the funeral urn containing his supposed ashes. The stratagem is a good one, better thought out and leaving less to chance than either of the parallel stories constructed by Aeschylus and Euripides respectively. The Paedagogus is unlikely to be recognised, not merely because age has changed him so much since he left Argos, but also because he is a relatively unimportant person, less likely to attract attention than Orestes. By establishing himself as a spy in the enemy camp, he will be in a position to keep Orestes and Pylades informed of the enemy's actions (cf. 40–1), and so to indicate to them when a favourable moment arrives to carry out the killings. Finally, Aegisthus and Clytaemnestra are to be put off their guard by having a story told them which is in itself plausible and just what they wish to hear.

**41** ὅπως ἄν... σαφῆ 'in order that you may, from sure knowledge, let me have true information'. σαφής frequently means not 'clear' but 'true'. ὅπως final may have, or not have, ἄν without affecting the meaning.

**42f** 'For, by reason of your years and the length of time (since you left Argos), they will certainly not recognise you, or suspect you, matured (ἠνθισμένον) as you are.' The well-known idiom, οὐ μή with aorist subjunctive, to express a strong future denial, is here linked with an ordinary future denial, using οὐ and the future indicative (οὐδ' ὑποπτεύσουσιν).

**44f** 'A friend come from the household of the Phocian gentleman, Phanoteus.' Phanoteus or Panopeus, the eponymous hero of a town in Phocis, is said to have fought in the womb with his brother Crisus (Tzetzes *ad Lyc.* 300. 24f., 303. 18f.). Crisus was the father of Strophius, the father of Orestes' friend Pylades, who lodged and entertained Orestes in exile. Since Phanoteus was thus at hereditary feud with

Strophius it was plausible to represent Phanoteus as the friend of Aegisthus and Clytaemnestra who sends them advance news of Orestes' death, and Strophius as the one who actually tends Orestes' supposed remains, and sends them to his home for burial (1110ff.).

**45** ὅ: not the article (as the accent shows), but a demonstrative pronoun (='he', i.e. Phanoteus).

**46** τυγχάνει: ὤν is easily supplied.

**47** The MSS have ὅρκῳ, which is usually emended to ὅρκον, since the construction requires an accusative. Probably the source of the corruption was the proximity of προσ- ('in addition'). 'Tell them, adding an oath (in support of your story)' must be the meaning, if ὅρκον is right. That the Paedagogus, when he does come to report Orestes' death (673ff.) in fact uses no oath, need not hinder this interpretation. For in *Trachiniae* 378 the false tale of Lichas is referred to as ὥσπερ οὐπάγων διώμνυτο, though in fact Lichas had taken no oath. In such cases 'taking one's oath' to an assertion may be only an exaggerated way of saying 'to assert confidently'. Nevertheless, ὅρκον προστιθείς sounds odd here, and Musgrave's excellent emendation, ὄγκον – 'adding *bulk* (to my sketch)' – may well be right. 'Bulk' (or 'padding') is just what the Paedagogus does add, when he comes to tell his story (681ff.).

**48** ἐξ ἀναγκαίας τύχης 'as a result of an accident that there was no resisting', i.e. a fatal accident.

**49** Notice the ornamental epithet, τροχηλάτων. The idea of ornamenting, expanding the story of Orestes' death in a chariot-race, is already hinted at.

**50** 'Let the story be firmly established (ἑστάτω) to this effect.'

**51** ὡς ἐφίετο (sc. Apollo). Evidently the oracle had told Orestes to pay his respects to his father's tomb.

**52** καρατόμοις χλιδαῖς 'decking with indulgence of shorn locks'. As in the *Choephori* (168f.) and Euripides' *Electra* (91), Orestes dedicates a lock of his hair (symbolising his youthful strength) at his father's grave. The gift of the lock is a *luxury* in which the dead Agamemnon will delight (cf. *Cho.* 320f. χάριτες...κέκληνται γόος εὐκλεὴς | προσθοδόμοις Ἀτρείδαις).

**53**  ἄψορρον: adverbial, cf. 1430.

**54f**  'taking up a brazen-walled urn (lit. casting) which you as well as I (καί) know, I imagine (που), is hidden away in bushes'. που cannot here be the indefinite *somewhere*, since Orestes would not say that if he had hidden the urn in a definite place.

χεροῖν: redundant, as so often.

**56f**  'in order that, cheating (κλέπτοντες) them in words, we may bring them a story that will be sweet to their ears'. Orestes is evidently attracted by the idea of κλέπτειν (cf. 37). Compare the young Neoptolemus' dislike of it, and of telling lies (*Phil.* 108).

**59f**  'For what harm does it do me, when, through dying merely in word, I achieve salvation in *deeds* and win fame?' To the ancient Greeks, with their belief in omens, spreading a report of one's own death must have seemed an even more sinister proceeding than it does to us. Cf. Eur. *Hel.* 1050ff.: ΕΛ. βούλει λέγεσθαι μὴ θανὼν τεθνηκέναι; | ΜΕ. κακὸς μὲν ὄρνις· εἰ δὲ κερδανῶ, λέγειν | ἕτοιμός εἰμι μὴ θανὼν λόγῳ θανεῖν, which A. M. Dale (cf. her note *ad loc.*) thinks was suggested by our passage, and written immediately after it.

**61**  'I suppose nothing one *says* which brings profit is a bad thing.' δοκῶ μέν (with following δέ suppressed) conveys 'this is what *I* think (whatever others may say)'. For the sentiment and its implications cf. Introduction 6.

**62ff**  'For I have before now (ἤδη) often seen even clever people reported dead when there was no truth in it (μάτην). Then, when they turn up at their homes again, why! they are lauded to the skies more (than they were before).' (The vivid gnomic perfect has a dramatic exclamatory effect.) Jebb and others see here an allusion to various historical persons who were rumoured to have mysteriously vanished and re-appeared (cf. Hdt. 4. 95). But how could Orestes have 'seen' such happenings? I think there is some contemporary allusion in these lines which is now lost. One thinks perhaps of soldiers (for the play was written in the depth of a long war) who are reported missing (even deliberately allow themselves to be reported missing), then enjoy the fuss when they come home safe and well. σοφός frequently can mean educated, 'clever' people.

**65f** 'as I trust (lit. 'boast') that I too from this mighty word (φήμης = an important, ominous saying, ἄπο = both 'after' and 'because of') will yet flash forth, as a living person (δεδορκότ') like a star upon my enemies'.

**67** πατρῴα: the general distinction is that πατρῷος means 'of my *father*', πάτριος 'of my *fathers*'. But there is occasionally some interchange.

**68** εὐτυχοῦντα ταῖσδε ταῖς ὁδοῖς 'fortunate in (or 'by') this journey' (plural for singular).

**69f** For the returned exile praying to his native land, home, or gods cf. Aesch. *Ag.* 503 and 810. 'For I come as your purifier, in all justice, sped by the gods.' πρός used of the agent (as often in verse) instead of ὑπό.

**71f** 'Do not send me away dishonoured from this land, but (receive me) as commander of the wealth of this home and its stablisher': *zeugma* (see Introduction (Style)). Orestes looks forward, when he has accomplished the vengeance, to a peaceful, untroubled rule over the Palace of the Atridae, which would thus be settled or 'established', after its troubles.

**73f** 'Those are my *words* on the matter. But now, old friend, make sure that *you* go and attend closely to (φρουρῆσαι, lit. 'keep watch upon') your *job*.' Again, there is the contrast between deeds (χρέος – 'duty', 'task' – being a mere variant on ἔργον) and words, it being implied that the latter are inferior to the former. Again, there is a military overtone in φρουρῆσαι.

**75f** '*We* two shall withdraw. For it is exact season to do so, exact season, which is to men the greatest presiding officer over every deed they do.' Everything is to be 'timed', as in a carefully-planned military operation.

### 77-120

From the doorway of the palace suddenly there sounds a muffled but passionate cry, the voice of Electra lamenting, in a heavily grief-stricken lyric strain, the never-forgotten death of her father. The sound contrasts vividly and dramatically with the prosaic iambic trimeters that have preceded and are to follow. The contrast (con-

ventional in tragedy) between lyrics and iambics is rendered more
than usually dramatically significant in this play by the two facts that
the preceding iambics have insisted so much on *time* and *precision of
time* (Electra conspicuously lacks a sense of time), and that the 'world'
which we have seen introduced by Electra's lyric outburst is a world
of women.

**78f** 'Why! [καὶ μήν introduces a new, striking, thought or occur-
rence] I thought I heard, from the direction of the doors [the simple
genitive of source is sometimes used without a preposition in verse]
some maidservant or other moaning softly (ὑπο-) within the palace.'

**80f** 'Can it be that poor creature, Electra? Should we perhaps stay
here and lend our ears (ἐπακούσωμεν) to her lamentations?' Notice
the studied *prosaic* quality of the remark (θέλεις μείνωμεν – a mixture
of 'will you (stay)?' and 'are we to stay?' – is *colloquial* Greek for a
polite suggestion, cf. Stevens, 'Colloquial expressions' 103) which
contrasts ironically with Electra's passionate lament of which 77 is the
prelude. In this context the young man's dissociation from his sister's
troubles (of which he evidently knows full well) seems to reflect a
remarkable callousness.

**82ff** 'Not at all! Let us attempt to do nothing before (we do) the
behests of Apollo, let us attempt to *lead off* from these, pouring lustra-
tions to (lit. 'of' – πατρός, possessive genitive) your father. For it is
such actions, I say, that bring us victory and mastery in our *doings*.'

ἀρχηγετεῖν means to start off in a disciplined way from some
central authority. The word had special Spartan associations (their
kings were called ἀρχαγέται).

λουτρά: cf. Hesychius, χθόνια λουτρά· τὰ τοῖς νεκροῖς ἐπιφερόμενα·
ἐκόμιζον γὰρ ἐπὶ τοὺς τάφους λουτρά. So the word is used for the more
usual χοαί here and at 434. This sense seems to be confined to this
play. Elsewhere (as at Eur. *Phoen.* 1667), when used of the dead, it
means '*washing*'.

**86ff** 'O sacred light of the sun, and air whose bounds are as wide as
earth's, how many keening songs you have known (ᾔσθου), how many
straight-dealt (ἀντήρεις) blows upon my breast that runs blood with
them, whenever the dark night ceases. But as to the vigils I spend *all
through the nights*, with these it is the chill couch in my wretched home

that is by now (ἤδη) familiar, (knowing) how much I lament my
unhappy father, to whom the bloody god of war gave no resting-place
in a foreign land, but my mother and her concubine Aegisthus, as
woodmen fell an oak, cleft his skull with bloody axe.' Electra, at dawn,
brings her grief out into the open daylight. But she has not been
asleep. Her lamentation has continued all through the night. παννυχίς
normally means an all-night *festival* and must be used here ironically.
Electra means 'No enjoyment for me. *My* παννυχίδες are sessions of
lonely lamentation.'

**95f** Electra means she regrets that Agamemnon was not killed in
battle at Troy, thus receiving a ceremonial burial there and settlement
as a kind of permanent resident-alien (μέτοικος or ξένος). This would
have been better for him and his children than for him to come home
and be murdered there, disgracefully, by Clytaemnestra and
Aegisthus: cf. 776f., Aesch. *Cho.* 345ff.: εἰ γὰρ ὑπ᾽ ᾽Ιλίῳ | πρός τινος
Λυκίων, πάτερ, | δορίτμητος κατηναρίσθης κτλ. and 683ff. But
Sophocles, trusting to the context, has here boldly used the word
ξενίζω in an unusual sense (not 'entertain', but 'afford (lasting)
hospitality to'). That he can use words in this way illustrates the
extreme 'creativity' of his use of language. To take ἐξένισεν in its
normal sense of 'entertain', makes nonsense of the passage.

**99** So the murder-weapon was an *axe*. This is one of the features
which distinguish Sophocles' version from the Homeric, according to
which Agamemnon was killed with a *sword* (cf. *Od.* 11. 424). In
Aeschylus the weapon would seem to have been a sword, in Euripides
an axe; but in both cases there is some ambiguity: see J. D. Denniston
on Eur. *El.* 164, E. Fraenkel, App. B to ed. of Aesch. *Ag.*

**101** φέρεται 'is borne' (upon the air).

**103** μὲν δή 'I swear!' (μέν asseverative, like μήν).

**105f** 'As long as I look upon the brilliant-shining sweep of the
constellations in the heavens, as long as I look upon this daylight.'
παμφεγγεῖς ἄστρων ῥιπάς is a phrase marvellously suggestive of the
mysterious and awe-inspiring beauty of the heavenly dome: ordinarily
the constellations may appear to move slowly across the sky; but at
other times they may appear to move quickly and even to sweep (like
winds) upon their way: cf. Pind. *Pyth.* 4. 194f. and Eur. *Hel.* 1498.

λεύσσω is understood from the second limb of the sentence in the first by the figure of 'economy' (cf. Introduction (Style)).

**107ff** '(I shall not leave off keening) so as to fail to publish the sound of my voice to all, like some nightingale that has lost her child, in lamentation before these doors of my father's house.' A 'sense' construction. The previous lines have suggested 'I shall not be prevented from', and on this suggested meaning is made to depend a result infinitive (προφωνεῖν) introduced by the double negative μὴ οὐ usual with infinitives dependent upon verbs of preventing which are themselves negatived. (For τεκνολέτειρ' Jebb gives 'slayer of her child'. But 'loss' fits the context better. The child was Itys, whom the mother, Procne, in the Greek legend, killed for revenge on the father, Tereus, for the latter's treatment of Philomela. Procne was changed into the nightingale.) Note μὴ οὐ treated as one syllable (synizesis).

**110ff** Electra invokes the powers of darkness to help her against her enemies.

**111** ʼAρά = the (hypothetical) curse which Agamemnon is supposed to have pronounced upon his killers. πότνια ('mistress') shows that it is being invoked as if it were a divinity.

**112** The Erinyes are spirits of ancient tradition whose function is to punish crimes *to do with the family*, thus including not merely homicide but also adultery.

**113f** 'You who look upon those who are unjustly done to death, who look upon those who have their marriage-beds beguiled.' Verbs of stealing take two accusatives, the person stolen from, and the object stolen (or involved in a process of stealth: for this 'extended' use of κλέπτειν cf. 37, 56). The second accusative is often, as here, retained, when such verbs are used passively. Aegisthus had seduced Agamemnon's wife, as his father Thyestes had seduced the wife of Agamemnon's father, Atreus.

**119f** 'For I have no longer the strength to hold in balance (ἀντίρ-ροπον – predicative) the weight of my grief.' When an object in one scale of a balance counterbalances that in the other, it is said ἄγειν ('to draw') the other: cf. Dem. 22. 76 (χρυσίδες) ἄγουσα ἑκάστη μνᾶν. Electra sees her own fortitude (in one scale) as counterbalancing her grief in the other. But she is afraid that the grief will soon outweigh her, overpower her.

### 121–250

*The Parodos.* Electra's song from the stage is now answered by that of the Chorus as they enter the Orchestra. They are women of the neighbourhood, friends of Electra, who have come to offer her consolation and support in her troubles. They sing in a more intricate rhythm (aeolic and dactylic in character, but with some iambic lines, e.g. 126f., for variety) than the simpler 'melic' anapaests which Electra has been using, and as they sing to this rhythm they also dance (mainly through gestures?). Electra responds in the same dancing or dance-like rhythm, so that the whole lyrical interlude becomes a *kommos* or operatic dialogue between actor and chorus. See further Appendix 1. The Chorus address Electra as older women with a maternal concern for her. They refer twice in their opening address to the deficiencies of her own mother (122 and 125).

**122ff** 'What is (i.e. What is the *meaning of it*? Why do you *do* it?) this insatiable lamentation...?'

τάκειν (Doricistic lyric form for τήκειν) οἰμωγάν is no more normal Greek than 'pine a lamentation' is normal English. But Sophocles often departs slightly from normal usage (provided that the context makes the meaning clear): cf. Introduction (ἐξηλλαγμένη λέξις). Similarly the accusative ᾿Αγαμέμνονα τὸν πάλαι κτλ. is loosely the object of the whole phrase τάκεις οἰμωγάν (as if the chorus had said τί οἰμώҘεις;).

ἀλόντʼ: lit. 'caught'. ἁλίσκεσθαι is often used of enemies being *worsted*, overthrown, as αἱρεῖν of worsting, overthrowing, ruining them, cf. 207.

**126f** ὁ τάδε πορών: no doubt Aegisthus, whose alliance with Clytaemnestra had nerved her to kill Agamemnon. The reason they hesitate openly to wish him ill is that, usurper or not, Aegisthus is the *de facto* ruler, the 'law' of Argos.

**129** 'You who are the (true) offspring of noble parents.' Notice that the scansion is ὦ γένέθλᾱ γεννᾱῖῶν, as the corresponding line of the antistrophe (145) shows.

**130** 'You have come as a consolation' (i.e. to console me) seems better (because less artificial) than 'You have come *in* consolation' (limitative accusative).

**131**  τάδ' 'what you imply', i.e. that my grief is excessive.

**132f**  οὐδ': adversative (Denniston, *Particles*² 191): 'but I will not give up this activity, (will not be prevented from) lamenting'.

**133**  The doubled negative μὴ οὐ as if a negatived verb of preventing had gone before: a sense-construction.

**134**  'Ah! No! (ἀλλά) You who give and take (ἀμειβόμεναι) every kind of sweetness of friendship (with me).' χάρις, like Latin *gratia*, is not only a grateful act, but also the gracious act which deserves a grateful act in return.

**135**  ἀλύειν: a strong word, almost = 'be demented'.

**137ff**  'Ah! But you will never with lamentations or prayers raise *him* – your father – again from the marsh which receives all alike.' Whereas to the Hebrews of the Old Testament the realm of death was pictured as a valley, to the Greeks it was a marshy lake or stagnant mire (Styx, Acheron, etc.). Notice the long hyperbaton τὸν . . . πατέρ', which makes the article stand by itself virtually as a demonstrative.

**140f**  'Yet (ἀλλ') you, starting from (ἀπό) reasonable beginnings waste yourself, with your constant lamentation, upon (ἐπ' lit. = 'as far as') intractable grief.'

**144**  'Why (I say) do you reach out for what is unbearable?'
μοι: ethic dative.

**145f**  Electra states her doctrine that one should never 'forget' parents who have died (οἰχομένων) pitiably.

**147**  'No! The grief-stricken bird it is that fits (lit. 'has fitted', once for all) my mind.' ἄραρεν (from the defective Epic 2nd aorist form ἤραρον normally, when intransitive, governs a dative. But Sophocles often deviates, cf. 122n.

φρένας is an accusative of further definition, lit. 'me, that is, my mind'.

**149**  'The bird of utter desolation, Zeus's messenger.' The nightingale's song introduces the spring, and so the new year, which is sacred to Zeus (as are all the seasons: cf. *Od.* 24. 344 Διὸς ὧραι).

**150** 'And you (too), all-suffering Niobe, I reckon as a god.' Electra means that Niobe *has her reverence* for her steadfastness in bereavement. Frozen to stone on Mount Sipylus in Lydia, Niobe's image (across which the coursing streams were thought to represent tears) was shown to tourists (see Jebb on *Antigone* 823ff.).

**153ff** You are not the only one who has lost a father. Think of your sisters and Orestes. The tone should be noted. The chorus are on Electra's side, but they do not approve of her behaviour, which they think is excessive and quixotic, therefore hybristic, not embodying the virtue of σωφροσύνη – 'nothing too much'.

**154f** 'a grief... in respect of which you are exceptional above those who dwell within your house'.

περισσά implies comparison and therefore takes a genitive here. The likeness to *Hamlet* (1. ii. 75): 'Why seems it so particular with thee?' is remarkable.

**158** Iphianassa appears nowhere else in this play as a living (157) daughter of Agamemnon. She was a mere name which Sophocles found in his epic sources (cf. *Il.* 9. 145: Agamemnon's daughters Chrysothemis, Laodice and Iphianassa), used here to pad out a verse, and could afterwards discard. Such was the non-realistic character of this kind of drama.

**159** I think (with Hermann) that this line means 'in his youth hidden away from (i.e. protected from) griefs'; for the construction cf. Eur. *Hipp.* 154 κρυπτὰ κοίτα λεχέων σῶν 'a bed hidden from your (marriage-)bed'. Jebb takes ἀχέων as a participle 'sorrowing in a secluded youth'.

**160ff** Orestes will one day return to assert himself against his father's murderers, because he is a 'true blue' aristocrat (εὐπατρίδαν). He will have gone forth with the 'favourable step that comes from Zeus' (Διὸς εὔφρονι βήματι), because Zeus is the protector of sceptred kings such as Agamemnon (cf. *Il.* 1. 279 σκηπτοῦχος βασιλεύς, ᾧ τε Ζεὺς κῦδος ἔδωκεν). The name of Orestes is very dramatically emphasised; it has been withheld to the very end of the sentence, and so becomes attracted into the relative clause to agree with ὅν (for the 'long' hyperbaton cf. Introduction (Style)).

**164f** 'Yes! and in waiting for whom tirelessly (ἀκάματα – neut. plur. used as adverb) I, childless, alas! unwed, ever wilt' (οἰχνέω suggests οἴχομαι, 'am gone', 'am lost').

**168ff** 'Whereas *he* forgets both what he has suffered and what he has been informed of (i.e. of the deprivations of his sister). For what do I not receive (from him) in the way of messages (lit. 'what of message'), messages that are belied? For he is always "yearning" (to come); but, yearning, he does not think fit to appear.'

**173ff** The argument between the Chorus and Electra continues. She should take heart, they say. Zeus is great in his Heaven. 'To whom assigning your excessive anger neither be over-vexed with those you hate nor yet forget them.' Time is a great healer. 'For neither is he who dwells in (ἔχει = ἐνοικεῖ) the land's edge of roaming herds at Crisa [the plain untilled as sacred to Apollo, which fell away southwards from Delphi to the Corinthian Gulf], the lad, Agamemnon's son, nor he who holds lordly state as a god by Acheron (i.e. Agamemnon) heedless.' The Chorus in Aeschylus' *Choephori* (354ff.) also reassure Orestes and Electra that Agamemnon still lives and rules underneath the earth – κατὰ χθονὸς ἐμπρέπων | σεμνότιμος ἀνάκτωρ.

**185ff** But Electra will not be soothed.

μέν (without following δέ) emphasises ἐμέ: cf. 61n. 'But from *me* (never mind Orestes and my dead father) most of my life has already departed, gone without hope, and I can no longer bear up (against my troubles), I who waste away without children, who have no man to be my friend and to stand up for me, but, like some unvalued stranger-resident, am housekeeper of the rooms of my father, thus as I am in this unsightly dress, and have to wait upon tables that (for me) are empty.' I take κεναῖς... τραπέζαις to mean not that Electra has to act as *waitress* at table, but that she has *no place* at table; she has to stand waiting for the diners to finish before she can eat: but by then the tables are empty. With the daughter of the house who cannot partake of the food of its tables compare the daughters of Oedipus, who could, *O.T.* 1463–5.

**193ff** The Chorus and Electra are now at one. Her reference to the 'empty tables' from which she now suffers has made them think of the table spread before Agamemnon, at his homecoming. 'Pitiable was the cry heard at his return, pitiable to hear in the rooms of his fathers, when the stroke of the brazen jaws (i.e. the two-bladed axe) was launched straight and true (ἀνταία) against him.' μέν and δέ are not here adversative but complementary, and reinforce the pathetic repetition οἰκτρά... οἰκτρά (= the figure known as *epanaphora*). The Aeschylean account (followed by Euripides) was that Agamemnon was killed in his bath (Aesch. *Ag.* 1540, *Cho.* 999, *Eum.* 633; Eur. *El.* 157). Sophocles, like Homer (*Od.* 11. 411 and 418ff.), has him killed at supper (cf. 284), but otherwise implies quite different circumstances (the murder-weapon is different, and in Homer Agamemnon is killed in *Aegisthus*' house, invited there by Aegisthus). One therefore need not (as Jebb does) fill in the picture here from Homer's account (as that the 'cry' referred to is that of Cassandra, or that κοῖται here refers to the dining chamber in which Agamemnon was murdered). Usually κοίτη means 'bed' or 'resting-place', cf. *Phil.* 160. Here κοίταις is best taken, by an extension of the ordinary meaning, as the bedrooms or chambers of Agamemnon's house.

**197ff** 'It was cunning that devised the killing, and lust that did it: between the two of them they bred terribly a terrible (monstrous) shape – whether it was a divinity or (some) of mortals who transacted the deed.'

εἴτ' οὖν... εἴτε: a fairly frequent variant for εἴτε... εἴτε cf. *O.T.* 1049; Denniston, *Particles*[2] 418. The 'divinity' may be a succinct remembrance of the ghostly presences, the curses, which Aeschylus had supposed haunted the house of Agamemnon: cf. *Ag.* 1090ff. and 1498ff.

**201f** πλέον as if ἐχθρά was to follow: 'more hateful than all (other) days'. But the superlative ἐχθίστα (lyric form for ἐχθίστη) is substituted, and this is emphasised, as often, by δή – 'the far most hateful day'.

**203ff** ὦ δείπνων ἀρρήτων κτλ. 'O fearful anguish (lit. burdens) of that unspeakable banquet, (that is) the hideous death which my father experienced at their twin hands – hands which ravaged my life and betrayed it.'

δείπνων... θανάτους: plural for singular. In strict grammar, τούς should have been ἅ (as relative to ἄχθη), with θανάτους in apposition. But the masculine noun θανάτους 'attracted' the relative to its own gender.

ἴδε of *metaphorical* seeing, i.e. experiencing, cf. 417. For εἶλον cf. 122 n.

**209**  οἷς = the (implied) owners of the hands, i.e. Aegisthus and Clytaemnestra, cf. 719n., Hdt. 7. 10 γ 3.

**211**  ἀποναίατο: a form found in Ionic and other Greek dialects, = ἀπόναιντο in Attic.

**212**  Scan τοϊάδ' ἄν|ύσᾶντ|ἔς ἔργ|ᾰ: cf. 232, the corresponding line of the antistrophe.

**213ff**  Once again the Chorus have parted company from Electra. Her grief and her behaviour seem to them excessive. 'Consider how not to voice (your feelings) further. Do you not perceive from what kind of behaviour as it is you plunge so dreadfully into woes of your own making? Indeed (γάρ) it is a real surfeit of suffering that you have acquired for yourself, always breeding strife in your disaffected soul. These matters in fact (δέ) are not ones that you can dispute with our rulers, so as to come into conflict with them.'

φράζου: sometimes the middle gives an inner *mental* meaning; φράζε would mean 'explain' (to someone else), cf. βουλεύω and βουλεύεσθαι.

πόρσω by metathesis for πρόσω, which would not fit the metre.

γνώμαν ἴσχεις = γιγνώσκεις.

τὰ παρόντ': adverbial accusative.

πολύ τι: the τι strengthens the adjective with which it is put – 'a really large amount of'.

πλάθειν (πλήθειν) elsewhere means to 'draw near to', not to 'compete with' (as the scholiast took it here). J. Jackson's emendation (*Marginalia Scaenica* (1955) 138) τάδε – τοῖς δυνατοῖς οὐκ ἐριστά – τλᾶθι (making the broad statement of principle – 'one should not argue with, dispute with, those in power' – a parenthesis) may be right. For the thought cf. 1465n. and Appendix 2.

**221**  'I have been compelled (to do) outrageous things in outrageous circumstances.' The dramatic importance of these and the following words has been undervalued by commentators. Electra *knows* that her conduct is abnormal. She has been *compelled* to it by her character and circumstances. Similarly, Aeschylus' Agamemnon brought himself to sacrifice his daughter, Iphigenia, because ἀνάγκας ἔδυ λέπαδνον (*Ag.* 218). The 'compulsion' there was his exaggerated sense of duty as commander-in-chief to his army.

**222** ὀργά 'my disposition, state of mind' (not 'anger').

**223** ἀλλὰ γάρ assumes an ellipse, 'But (there's an objection) for...'. Translate, 'But no! I shall not repress these ruinous ways (lit. these ruins), as long as I have life' (lit. 'as long as life has me ').

σχήσω: ἔχω is frequently used in verse in the sense of κατέχω cf. 375.

**226** τίνι (dative of interest) is here equivalent to '*from* whom?'.

**227** πρόσφορον 'remedial' (lit. 'applicable').

**228** τίνι φρονοῦντι καίρια (sc. καίρια ἄν ἀκούσαιμι), καίρια being used once only by the figure of ἀπὸ κοινοῦ. 'From whom, as having timely wisdom, could I listen to timely consolation?' (Jebb rejects this version of τίνι, which, as he says, is hard to parallel. He takes the dative to be of the person judging: 'for *in the judgment* of what person that thinks aright'. But the rhetorical repetition of τίνι (*epanaphora*) seems to me to compel us to this meaning. Electra is effectively saying, '*Who* shall dare to advise me? *Who* shall suggest timely wisdom to me?')

**229f** 'Let me be! Let me be! you who would assuage me. For these troubles of mine will be found to be (lit. 'will have been called') unresolvable.'

**232** '(being as I am) so infinite of lamentation'. Scan ἀνἄρῐθμος (cf. 212, the corresponding line of the strophe), as at *O.T.* 168 and 179.

**233ff** 'Well at any rate I speak in good-will (loyalty) to you, like some faithful mother, (telling you) not to breed direness from direness.' They conclude (by a well-known principle of Greek literary construction: ring-composition) with the same theme – the mother-image – with which they began (122).

**236ff** 'And what *degree* can there be (in nature) of evil? Come tell me, how can it be "good" to be forgetful over the dead? In what human being did this ever flourish as a natural law?' καί often introduces an indignant or expostulatory question.

ἔφυ...ἔβλαστε: she is claiming that her principles are an expression of *natural* law (φύσις), which was, in the ideological conflict of the late fifth century, often contrasted with conventional law (νόμος). Compare Antigone's ἄγραπτα κἀσφαλῆ θεῶν | νόμιμα (*Ant.* 454f.).

**239ff** 'May I neither be in honour among such men nor, if I am associated with (lit. attached to) any good, may I dwell with it in careless freedom, restraining the piercing-voiced wings of my lamentation, that they leave my parents *out* of honour.'

ἔντιμος...ἐκτίμους: a punning antithesis. ἐκτίμους is predicative, and active (though ἔντιμος was passive). γονέων goes with it as a genitive of relationship. She speaks of her 'parents', though only one is concerned.

**245ff** 'For if *he*, in death, is to lie there, poor wretch, mere earth and nothingness, and *they* are not to pay back the just penalty in requital for murder, then reverence and respect for right must be gone from all mortals.'

οὐδέν: μηδέν, in the protasis of a conditional sentence, would be more normal, and therefore οὐδέν is the more striking and emphatic.

We have here the 'logical' use of ἄν with the optative, meaning something must be, 'it follows that something is'.

εὐσέβεια: It is a mistake always to give this word a purely religious connotation. The gods are of course implied here; but only because they support the law, the principle of order in society. εὐσέβεια here means practically 'law-abidingness', 'respect for law'. Cf. 308 below, where it would be nonsense to translate εὐσεβεῖν = 'be pious' (it means 'be well-behaved', 'decent', 'law-abiding').

### 251–323

The choral lyric over, the Chorus leader begins (without quitting the Orchestra) a dialogue with Electra in ordinary iambic trimeters. The passion of the choral singing subsides into a more measured declamation. However, many of the points made in the lyric are repeated or developed in the following speeches. Their first statement in the chorus has been a rehearsal.

4

**251f** 'It was from concern at your business as well as my own that I came.' They mean that a friend has a selfish as well as an altruistic interest in another's welfare. Notice again, as at 133ff., the delicate courtesy of their conversation with Electra.

**253 σὺ νίκα:** this gently echoes a proverbial idea, namely that 'victory' should be conceded easily by friends to friends, and that then it is also a 'victory' for the former. Cf. Aesch. *Ag.* 943 κρατεῖς μέντοι παρείς γ' ἑκὼν ἐμοί, Soph. *Aj.* 1353 κρατεῖς τοι τῶν φίλων νικώμενος.

**256f** Lit. 'but, for unlawful force (βία) constrains me, forgive me'. Here the γάρ clause is fully expressed, cf. 223n.

**259** The relative ἅ in ἁγώ looks back beyond τάδε in 258 to find its antecedent in πήματα.

**261f ᾗ πρῶτα μὲν κτλ.** 'to whom first of all relations with my mother – the mother that bore me – have turned out most hostile'.

**262ff** Secondly she has to live with her father's murderers, is ruled by them, and they have the say as to whether she receives (λαβεῖν) or is deprived of necessities.

**264 κἀκ τῶνδε:** ἐκ as frequently in verse, for ὑπό.

**265 τό** is to be understood with λαβεῖν, by the figure of 'economy': cf. 991, 1498; Eur. *El.* 1351f. οἷσιν δ' ὅσιον καὶ τὸ δίκαιον | φίλον ἐν βιότῳ.

**266ff** Aegisthus sits on Agamemnon's throne (or chair?), wears his clothes, and pours the customary evening libations after dinner by the hearth at which he slew Agamemnon.

**272** '(When I see) our murderer in my father's bedroom with my abandoned mother.' (But κοίτη can also of course mean literally 'bed': cf. 193n.) Hamlet also objects to his mother sleeping with Claudius (*Ham.* III. iv. 159).

**276 ἐκφοβουμένη:** the compound verb used (as frequently in Sophocles) not intensively, but in the same sense as the simple verb, φοβουμένη.

**277 ὥσπερ ἐγγελῶσα τοῖς ποιουμένοις** 'as if exulting in her deeds'. γελᾶν and its cognates are often used in Greek of an enemy triumphing,

exulting over another (the 'laughter' is not necessarily physical: it may
be metaphorical). ἐγγελᾶν has usually a personal object in the dative.
Here Clytaemnestra triumphs at her own deeds.

**278**  τηροῦσ' (='watching out for', 'observing' the day on which
Agamemnon died) is Reiske's palmary correction of the MS reading
εὑροῦσ', a ridiculous copyist's error.

**281**  The θεοὶ σωτήριοι were certain gods (mainly Zeus and Apollo)
particularly associated with the safety of the house, its inhabitants, and
its possessions: cf. 637. Clytaemnestra celebrates the day of Agamemnon's death, each month, by choral hymns of thanksgiving and
sacrifices to these gods.

**283ff**  'I weep for, I am lost in tears over, and I bewail my father's
ill-fated banquet, as it has come to be called after him.'

τέτηκα: since the Greek perfect denotes a state achieved, even the
active perfect of some verbs tends to have an intransitive meaning.
But by a slight sense-construction the form is here used to mean
'weep at', and so governs the same accusative as the two other
(transitive) verbs. The accumulation of the three verbs meaning
practically the same thing sounds banal in any literal English
rendering, but in Greek is simply part of the 'stylistic ornament'
referred to in the Introduction (1). Eustathius (1507. 61, on
*Od.* 4. 531) says that Ἀγαμεμνόνειος δαίς was a proverbial expression
ἐπὶ τῶν ἐπ' ὀλέθρῳ εὐωχουμένων. Electra means that Clytaemnestra's
celebrations carry her back mentally even more poignantly to the
banquet at which her father was murdered. The δαίς referred to is
the (original) proverbial banquet, not the celebration feast inaugurated
by Clytaemnestra (as Jebb supposes).

**285**  οὐδέ intensive, 'not even'.
πάρα = πάρεστι, as the throwing back of the accent indicates.

**286**  'as much as my spirit pleases me (to weep)', the Greek words
being equivalent to ὅσον μοι ἀνδάνει κλαῦσαι.

**289**  δύσθεον μίσημα: 'hateful thing, unwelcome to the gods'.
δύσθεον, because Clytaemnestra thinks Agamemnon's death was a
good thing, of which the σωτήριοι θεοί (having helped to bring it
about) approve.

**289f** 'Are you the only one whose father is dead?' Again the resemblance to *Hamlet* (cf. 154n.) is remarkable. Cf. i. ii. 74f: *Ham.* Ay, madam, it is common. *Queen.* If it be, why seems it so particular with thee?

**291f** 'May the nether gods never release you from your present laments.' Since mourning was a form of dedication to the dead man (hence the lock of Orestes' hair dedicated at Agamemnon's tomb, cf. 52: the hair is a symbol of the life of the individual dedicated), the person who continued in mourning continued to be intimately associated with the nether gods, with and under whose sway the dead man lived. This would further estrange Electra from the *Olympian* gods.

**293f** τάδ' ἐξυβρίζει 'she says these things in overweening insolence'. But the succeeding lines show that fear is at least as strong a motivation.

ὅταν κλύῃ τινὸς | ἥξοντ' Ὀρέστην 'when she hears from some person that Orestes is about to come'. The slight, almost offhand touch conveys a world of meaning. We sense an infinitude of gossip, reports, speculation within the palace.

κλύῃ is given the participial construction usual with verbs of sensory perception, thus making the message more immediate and threatening.

**294f** 'Then, maddened with rage, she comes up to me, screaming "Have I not *you* to blame for all this?"'

σύ, being emphatic, would have an accent even if it were not followed by the enclitic μοι.

τῶνδε are her fears not merely of Orestes but of all the associated circumstances (evil dreams, and so on, cf. 780ff.).

**296f** ἥτις: the causal or circumstantial use, 'in that you'.

ἐκ χερῶν...τῶν ἐμῶν: it has been suggested to me that this phrase implies that Clytaemnestra would have killed *Orestes* (as well as Agamemnon), if she could have caught him, and that therefore Orestes' present attack upon *her* life is fully justified as a kind of self-defence in retrospect. Certainly, ἐκ χερῶν τῶν ἐμῶν could imply that. Equally, it could imply something quite different ('hands' can be used for endearments, tendance: cf. 1141, 1276f.), just as κλέψασ' can imply that Electra had stolen Orestes' love from Clytaemnestra (cf.

1145f.). The phrase in itself is ambivalent. For its full dramatic implication we must wait to see how Sophocles unfolds the character of his Clytaemnestra. Even if from 296f. we had taken a preliminary impression of Clytaemnestra's violent intention towards Orestes, we should be taken aback by the maternal feeling which she exhibits towards her other children at 653f., and towards Orestes himself (despite her feeling that he was μαστῶν ἀποστὰς καὶ τροφῆς ἐμῆς, 776) at 770–1. This ambivalence of ἐκ χερῶν τῶν ἐμῶν, the *unlikelier* (as we may regard it) implication of which is later taken up and emphasised by the dramatist, illustrates the Sophoclean use of dramatic irony.

ὑπεξέθου 'smuggled away'. For the hyperbatic word-order, cf. Introduction 14.

**298**  τοι: often used in threats, 'Ah! but know that.'

ἀλλ'...γ': ἀλλά and γε in the same clause are normally separated, the γε being used to emphasise a particular element (here τείσουσα): cf. Denniston, *Particles*² 11f. (Denniston cites only the usage in *apodoses*; but here is a clear instance of it in an independent sentence.)

**299f**  ὑλακτεῖ: Clytaemnestra's anger is not a pleasant thing. σὺν δ' ἐποτρύνει κτλ. 'and she has her famous marriage-partner present by her side (πέλας...παρών) spurring on, along with her, this (same) abuse of me'.

σύν is used adverbially.

αὐτῇ: ethic dative, cf. 17n.

ταῦτα 'these things'. But Blomfield was perhaps right to read ταὐτά 'the same things'.

**301**  πάντ': accusative of respect.

ἄναλκις: cf. *Od.* 3. 310 ἀνάλκιδος Αἰγίσθοιο, Aesch. *Ag.* 1224.

**302**  'he who fights his battles in company with (i.e. allies himself with) women': cf. *Ant.* 740 ὅδ', ὡς ἔοικε, τῇ γυναικὶ συμμαχεῖ.

**303f**  Hyperbatic word-order for ἐγὼ δὲ ἀεὶ προσμένουσα 'Ορέστην τῶνδε παυστῆρα ἐφήξειν.

**304**  ἐφήξειν 'to arrive on the scene'.

**305f**  'Being always about to do something' (but not doing it).

τὰς οὔσας (ἐλπίδας) 'my present hopes' (that he will come).

τὰς ἀπούσας ἐλπίδας 'the hopes that I dare not yet conceive', sc. that he will also kill Clytaemnestra and Aegisthus.

**307ff** Notice that she ends her speech with exactly the same point which she made at (almost) the end of her lyric dialogue with the Chorus. The repetition (also verbal: cf. 256 ἀναγκάζει, 221 ἠναγ-κάσθην) is of course by no means vain. It reinforces the point, which is of great dramatic significance, that she does not claim that her conduct is *right*, but merely that it is forced upon her. She disclaims σωφροσύνη and εὐσέβεια (being well-behaved, orderly, cf. 245n.).

ἀλλ' ἐν τοῖς κακοῖς κτλ. 'there is a vast necessity when one is in the midst of evils, also to practise (κἀπιτηδεύειν = καὶ ἐπιτηδεύειν) evil'. It is the same burden as that of Thucydides in the famous description of the *stasis* at Corcyra (3. 82ff.) – that men's conduct and values deteriorated under the violent circumstances of war.

**310f** 'When you say this, is Aegisthus *near at hand*, or gone from the house?'

**312** 'Indeed most assuredly' (he is away).

**312f** ἄν...θυραῖον οἰχνεῖν 'that I would be moving abroad beyond the doors'. Many references show that the women of tragedy were normally expected to stay within doors, unless accompanied by groups of other women (as, for instance, the women of the Chorus in this play). In Electra's case the normal taboo was reinforced by Aegisthus' strictness in keeping her indoors: cf. 517f. She is 'breaking bounds' by coming out of doors and talking scandal to the Chorus.

νῦν δ' ἀγροῖσι τυγχάνει: (sc. ὤν) cf. 46n. 'as it is, he happens to be in the country'. In verse (but not in prose) the dative is often used without a preposition as a locative.

**314f** 'Might I too (κἄν) pluck up courage to have further talk with you, if that is so?' (The reading ἤ κἄν is preferable to the variant ἤ δή ἄν: cf. Denniston, *Particles*² 285.)

σούς = σου '*with* you' (objective genitive).

The Chorus preserve their cautious attitude of not wanting to get into trouble with the effective ruler of Mycenae (cf. 127).

**317f** 'Very well, then! I do ask you. What do you say of your brother? Is he going to come? Or is he hesitating?'

τοῦ κασιγνήτου: Sophocles frequently has this simple genitive of reference. περί would be needed in prose, and is usual in verse.

**319** 'Well (γε) he *says* (he's coming). But though he says it, he does nothing of what he says.'

φησίν... φάσκων... λέγει: different words for the same thing, by the principle of *variatio* (cf. Introduction (Style)).

**320** 'Yes (that is to be expected), for...'

ὀκνεῖν: cf. 22n. Notice a slight 'interlacing' hyperbaton in this line.

**321** 'Well, I can tell you *I* didn't save *him* by hesitating.'

καὶ μήν: adversative.

**322** 'He is of honest stock, so as to give satisfaction to his friends' (i.e. so that he will give satisfaction).

**323** 'I am convinced of it, for I can assure you (τοι) I would not otherwise have stayed long alive.'

### 324–384

A new character is now seen coming upon the stage from the doors of the palace. She is Electra's sister, Chrysothemis. She carries in her hands objects which the Chorus immediately recognise to be offerings suitable to the dead, i.e. a pitcher or pitchers with which to make libations and 'some other articles, such as flowers, and perhaps cakes' (Jebb).

In the succeeding dialogue Chrysothemis is revealed as fundamentally different both temperamentally and in her general attitudes from Electra, and this difference leads to a dramatic clash between the sisters. (We realise, of course, that the clash has taken place many times before in their lives. But, since this is theatre, all the basic issues have to be stated as if for the first time, so that the audience may know what the significant differences are between them.) Sophocles had already dramatised the two contrasting types of sisters in the *Antigone* (Antigone versus Ismene, the doer versus the non-doer, the determined versus the placid). But while much of the characterisation here repeats that of the *Antigone*, there are certain important differences. Chrysothemis is a solider character than Ismene, more sanguine and less inclined to settle for being a shadow of her stronger-willed sister. Loyal in her innermost heart to her father's memory, she nevertheless

believes that common sense is a supreme virtue, and that she has no
strength as an isolated woman to overthrow Aegisthus as the *de facto* ruler
of Mycenae. In return for this accommodating attitude she has been
well treated by the murderers, is allowed to wear fine clothes (i.e. need
not go about like a slave), and has enough to eat.

**324ff**  ὡς δόμων κτλ. The natural order would be: ὡς ὁρῶ τὴν σὴν
ὅμαιμον, ἐκ πατρὸς ταὐτοῦ ἔκ τε μητρὸς (sc. ταὐτῆς) φύσιν, Χρυσόθεμιν
ἐντάφια, οἷα τοῖς κάτω νομίζεται, χεροῖν δόμων φέρουσαν. The
exaggerated hyperbaton probably conveys here the Chorus' heightened
sense of a new dramatic occurrence (cf. Introduction). On the other
hand, Sophocles' individual and inimitable modelling of the sentence
enables him to express ταὐτοῦ with πατρός and to suppress the
corresponding ταὐτῆς with μητρός, thus making a very subtle sense:
for it is the fact that Chrysothemis is of the same father as Electra
(therefore how could she be so different?) that is important to the
Chorus, not the fact (equally true) that she is of the same mother.

δόμων: genitive of source, cf. 78n.

φύσιν 'someone sprung from' (abstract for concrete) = 'child of'.
Cf. *O.T.* 334f. πέτρου φύσιν (though the meaning is slightly different).
(Otherwise Jebb, who takes φύσιν as accusative of respect.)

**328f** 'What is this talk that you once more, having come to the
doorway, utter there?'

πρὸς θυρῶνος ἐξόδους is to be understood with ἐλθοῦσα from the
preceding phrase, πρὸς θυρῶνος ἐξόδοις, by the figure of zeugma. The
long separation in hyperbaton of τίνα from its complement φάτιν
emphasises the latter. For both effects cf. the Introduction (Style).

**330** That rare phenomenon, a line without caesura.

**331** χαρίζεσθαι κενά 'idly indulge' (lit. 'do empty favours to').

**332** 'And yet so much I know myself, that'= 'I know this much of
myself, that' (anticipatory accusative).

**333** ἀλγῶ 'πὶ τοῖς παροῦσιν (dative of τὰ παρόντα) = 'am pained
at present circumstances' (sc. that Clytaemnestra and Aegisthus
should remain unpunished).

**335** πλεῖν ὑφειμένη 'to sail with slackened sail', 'to trim my sails
to the wind': cf. *Ant.* 715 ναὸς ὅστις ἐγκρατῆ πόδα | τείνας ὑπείκει

μηδέν. The Athenians being a nautical people, nautical imagery is very common in their literature: cf. 730, 1074, 1444.

**336** 'and not give an (idle) impression of doing something, and in fact hurt them not at all'. The repeated *simple* negatives μή...μή do not cancel out, but each retains its full force.

**337** 'I wish your pattern of behaviour too to be another of the same kind as mine' – not the remark of an underdog.

**338ff** 'Yet *right* certainly is not as I declare it, but as *you* judge it. But if I am to live as a free woman, I must heed my superiors in power in everything.' For this opinion cf. 213–20n., 396, 1013–14, 1087–9n., 1465n. In 338 Chrysothemis may be chaffing Electra over her un-yielding devotion to δίκαιον, but I think that she also has in mind the fact that Electra is the elder sister, and that it would normally be the duty of the younger to follow her judgment on matters in dispute (cf. 1035n.).

ᾗ 'in the way in which', i.e. 'as'.

**340** Notice that τῶν κρατούντων κτλ. is simply another way of expressing Thrasymachus' doctrine (Plato, *Rep.* 1. 338c f.) that justice (δικαιοσύνη) is 'the interest of the stronger', cf. 1465n. It will be seen that Chrysothemis is leading up to an ethical debate of the type which the Sophists engaged in and which was to be heard in law-courts and political assemblies of the period. That is why her speeches and Electra's abound in many of the cant terms of ethical debate of the period, and also why they sound like *debating* speeches.

**341f** 'How can you forget such a father, you his daughter, and kow-tow (μέλειν) to your mother?' Chrysothemis has represented the younger (the sophistic) ethic of Greece that one should adapt oneself to circumstances, 'live as Rome does'; Electra now asserts the older ethic, that of the true-born aristocrat (εὐγενής), that one should remain loyal to one's highest family traditions, and never budge on a matter of principle.

λελῆσθαι 'to be *in a state of* forgetfulness', i.e. to have forgotten completely.

**343f** This (like many of the things said by Electra) is neither true nor fair.

τἀμὰ νουθετήματα = τὰ νουθετήματά μου (objective genitive), 'your scolding of me'.

**345f** 'You must then choose one of two courses: either accept that you are *not right*; or that being right (φρονοῦσα, sc. εὖ), you are *unmindful of your nearest and dearest*' (and therefore doing what is not καλόν, not εὐκλεές). τῶν φίλων, i.e. Agamemnon.

The argument (with its dilemma) assails the position of the sophist Protagoras who by 'making the worse appear the better cause' could make what was σοφόν (i.e. συμφέρον, κερδαλέον, etc.) appear also δίκαιον (i.e. καλόν, ἀγαθόν, εὐκλεές). Electra means that there is an absolute καλόν, which is *either* identifiable with σοφόν, *or*, being separated from it, is to be preferred to it. She is not inviting Chrysothemis to embark upon a course of action; she is inviting her to make an admission that her present course of action is wrong in one of two ways; and by so doing she is trying to score a debating point over her sister. Jebb's note shows that he has not understood this.

**347** ἥτις: circumstantial, 'you who...!'

**349** 'While I defend my father in all things.' The middle τιμωρουμένης has the same sense as the active would have.

**350** 'You not merely do not act in concert with me but you also divert the person who *is* acting.' οὔτε...τε are often used in this adversative and complementary sense.

δρῶσαν is *variatio* on ἔρδεις: cf. Introduction (Style).

**351** 'Does this conduct not imply (ἔχει = παρέχει, cf. 466) cowardice in addition to misfortune?' (i.e. your conduct is both wrong *and* inexpedient).

**352ff** The argument amounts to '*my* conduct is κερδαλέον (hence σοφόν), since I *annoy* the murderers while retaining my own life'.

δίδαξον: cf. 534n.

**356** 'if there is any pleasure in that place' (i.e. if it is any pleasure to the dead Agamemnon in having paid to him the kind of tribute (annoying his enemies) that Electra is paying to him).

ἐκεῖ is often used euphemistically for 'in Hades' house', 'among the dead'.

For the thought cf. Aesch. *Cho.* 320f. χάριτες δ᾿ ὁμοίως | κέκληνται γόος εὐκλεὴς | προσθοδόμοις ᾿Ατρείδαις.

**357f** For the familiar antithesis λόγῳ ... ἔργῳ cf. 15–16n.

**361f** 'Let there be laid a sumptuous table for you and let your life (or livelihood) be in abundance.'

**363f** 'Let it be *my* sole sustenance that I do not vex *myself*.' A wonderfully turned verse, expressing the personality of the speaker in a nutshell. It is amazing that anyone should ever have thought of altering the MSS' λυπεῖν, which gives perfect sense.

**364** τῆς σῆς...τιμῆς 'the honour *paid to* you': σῆς = σου (objective genitive), cf. 315, 343.

**365ff** The attack has been to the effect that Chrysothemis is not σοφή. Now it is that she is not σώφρων. Immediately below, it is that she is not ἀρίστη (lit. not 'called after' a 'best' father). The conclusion is that she is κακή. It is of the essence of Greek rhetoric that all these terms are not specific, but interchangeable.

**365** ἐξόν 'when you could have been called', accus. absol.

**369ff** '(Say) nothing in passion, for Heaven's sake!' These words of the Chorus show that in the Chorus' view some at least of the reproaches Electra has levelled at Chrysothemis are exaggerated.

**372f** ἐγὼ μέν: μέν without a balancing δέ expressed: '*I* am pretty well (πως) used to (lit. 'of', genitive of relation) this one's words' (sc. however they may surprise *you*, the δέ being included in the unexpressed thought).

**374f** 'had I not heard of a very great evil advancing against her'.
σχήσει for κατασχήσει (cf. 223n.), 'will restrain this one from her long-drawn-out lamentations.'

The new evil advancing against Electra imparts a new and important movement to the drama. As often in Sophocles such movements are introduced quietly, appearing as they do to grow naturally out of the matter and events (the dramatic interest of which has for the moment been exhausted) preceding them.

**376f** 'Come tell me, please, this terrible thing' (δή ironical). 'For if you shall tell me of something worse than these things I suffer now,

then I cannot any longer contradict you.' The potential ἄν + optative
is often better represented in English by 'can' than 'could' (since its
meaning is often not by any means 'remote').

**378** ἀλλ' 'well!'

**380** ἐνταῦθα ('thither') by poetic license for ἐνταυθοῖ, ἐνθάδε or
ἐκεῖσε.

**381f** 'But you will be bewailing your misfortunes (shut up) alive in
an enclosed dwelling, somewhere outside the boundaries of this land.'

κατηρεφεῖ 'roofed' suggests in the context that the dwelling will be
*completely* enclosed, i.e. that Electra will be entombed alive, as was
Antigone in her rocky enclosure, so that there is no good reason to
emend the word. Cf. *Ant.* 773ff. ἄγων ἐρῆμος ἔνθ' ἂν ᾖ βροτῶν στίβος |
κρύψω πετρώδει ζῶσαν ἐν κατώρυχι, and 885f κατηρεφεῖ | τύμβῳ
περιπτύξαντες. *Then* (Chrysothemis means) you will have *something to
cry about*.

**383f** 'In view of this think well (about your conduct), and do not
blame me (for not having talked sense into you) some day in the
future, when you have suffered the fate' (and it is too late: for the
illogicality cf. *Aj.* 100 θανόντες ἤδη τἄμ' ἀφαιρείσθων ὅπλα). 'For now
it is high time (ἐν καλῷ sc. ἐστι) to exercise prudence.' φρονεῖν = εὖ
φρονεῖν.

## 385–404

There follows a fairly long passage of *stichomythia*, which has a slightly
artificial effect upon English ears; but this is not felt in Greek:
because Greek literature is more rhetorical than English, and
*stichomythia* is a form of rhetoric. It is used to convey heated argument
or the rapid exchange of exciting information between speakers, and
the tempo of the declamation probably increases with the excitement
of the speakers. The object of these in a piece such as that which
follows is to score debating points over each other as speedily and
effectively as possible. No words are wasted, and the grammatical
constructions are 'understood' (as far as possible) from one line to
another for the sake of speed and brevity. Here we are most aware of
what Virginia Woolf ('On not knowing Greek') calls 'the lightning-
quick, sneering, out-of-doors manner' of Greek literature.

**385** 'Have they actually (καί) planned to do *this* to me?' δή emphasises ταῦτα, and ἤ expresses Electra's astonishment at the unexpected turn of events. (No doubt she had not thought that Clytaemnestra and Aegisthus would venture to go so far against a princess of Mycenae.)

**386** ὅταν περ 'just as soon as'.

**387** 'Well, as far as *that* is concerned, may he cover the distance (ἐξίκοιτο) speedily.' At 385 she was unprepared for death. At 387 she is ready and eager for it. Her resolution is achieved in a split second, and it astonishes her sister, who is so different from Electra that she did not foresee the effect on the latter of her news.

**388** 'What proposal is this, unhappy girl, that you invoke upon yourself?' (lit. 'as what have you invoked this proposition?', τίν' being predicative after τόνδε λόγον).

ἐπηράσω: aorist, idiomatically in Greek of an event which takes place *instantaneously*, or just a moment before the time of speaking. English uses a present tense.

**389** ἐλθεῖν ἐκεῖνον 'that he should come', ἐπηρασάμην being understood from ἐπηράσω in 388, on the principle of brevity described in the general note to 385ff.

**390f** In debates in *stichomythia* one speaker tries to cap the other, and one of the ways of achieving this is rhyme or repetition, whether terminal, initial or internal: so here ὅπως...ὅπως...

ποῦ φρενῶν 'where in your mind' (lit. 'of your mind', φρενῶν being partitive genitive), i.e. 'what on earth are you thinking of?'

**391** ὑμῶν includes not merely Chrysothemis, but also everyone else 'in the house'. 391 is an aggressive remark, and we may note here that Electra's conduct becomes more and more aggressive (except for the interlude in which she expresses her love for Orestes) as the play proceeds.

**392** Jebb translates 'But hast thou no care for thy present life?' That would be a meaningful remark if Electra's life were a happy one. But we know it isn't. Sense is restored if we translate βίου τοῦ παρόντος as 'the *life which you still have left*' (upon which Electra set some store, cf. 354) – for the meaning of παρεῖναι (=ὑπάρχειν) cf. 810; *O.T.*

1476–7 λέγεις. ἐγὼ γάρ εἰμ' ὁ πορσύνας τάδε, | γνοὺς τὴν παροῦσαν τέρψιν, ἥ σ' εἶχεν πάλαι (which I explained in *Philologus* 108 (1964) 72f. as meaning 'perceiving that *it was the only delight left you*'); Democritus 191 ἐπὶ τοῖς δυνατοῖς οὖν δεῖ ἔχειν τὴν γνώμην καὶ τοῖς παρεοῦσιν ἀρκέεσθαι τῶν μὲν ζηλουμένων καὶ θαυμαζομένων ὀλίγην μνήμην ἔχοντα... ὅκως ἂν τὰ παρεόντα σοι καὶ ὑπάρχοντα μεγάλα καὶ ζηλωτὰ φαίνηται.

**μνείαν:** usually 'memory', here='care', 'thought' (just like μνήμην in the Democritus passage).

**393**   Ironic: '(Yes! I should care for it,) for –!'
**βίοτος,** by *variatio,* for βίος.

**395ff**   In the following lines the sisters are really debating what is καλόν and what is κακόν. And they are irreconcilable in their attitudes: to Electra καλόν is being unswervingly loyal to φίλοι; to Chrysothemis it is being sensible, which (in her circumstances) means yielding to superior force (τοῖς κρατοῦσιν εἰκαθεῖν).

**395**   'Don't teach me to': ἐκ- redundant, cf. 276n.
**κακήν** 'untrue to', 'base towards'.

**396**   'But I'm not teaching you' (sc. to do that). διδάσκω caps ἐκδίδασκε of 395.
**τοῖς κρατοῦσι δ' εἰκαθεῖν:** cf. 340n., 1465n.

**397**   '*You* toady to them in this way. The ways you describe are not *my* ways.'
**ταῦτα** is the adverbial (or internal) accusative.

**398**   'All the same it is Right not to end disastrously as a result of imprudence.'

**399**   'I shall end disastrously, if I have to, *supporting my father*' (sc. than which latter nothing can be more right). Plural used for the singular.

**400**   'But our father makes allowances (συγγνώμην ἔχει), I know, for this situation' (sc. where his children have to make some accommodation with his enemies). For the thought and expression cf. *Ant.* 65ff. ἐγὼ μὲν οὖν αἰτοῦσα τοὺς ὑπὸ χθονὸς | ξύγγνοιαν ἴσχειν, ὡς βιάζομαι τάδε, | τοῖς ἐν τέλει βεβῶσι πείσομαι.

**401f** 'Such words are for base persons to commend' (lit. are on the side of (πρὸς) base persons, for them to commend them (ἐπαινέσαι = epexegetic infinitive). I.e. what you say is not καλόν, but κακόν.

ἐπαινέσαι . . . συναινέσεις: internal rhyme, cf. 390n.

**402** 'But will *you* (sc. never mind what 'base' people do) not listen to them and commend them with me?' The pronoun σύ is made emphatic by being placed first in the sentence.

**403** 'Indeed no! I hope I don't ever (lit. may I never yet) find myself so vastly devoid of intelligence.' I.e. what you say is foolish, therefore κακόν.

**404** 'Well! then (τἄρα = τοι ἄρα) I shall proceed in the direction in which I was sent' (lit. 'thither of journey, whither', οἵπερ separated from ὁδοῦ in hyperbaton, ὁδοῦ unnecessary to the sense and purely decorative). Chrysothemis gives up the struggle to convince her sister.

### 405-471

As so often in Sophocles, when one theme is exhausted, another takes its place (beginning quietly) and so the action moves forward easily and almost insensibly. Attention is now switched to the sacrificial offerings which Chrysothemis carries in her hands, and thence to Clytaemnestra's evil dream.

**405** 'But whither are you going? For whom are you carrying these offerings?' But ἔμπυρα should mean 'objects for *burning*'; and these χοαί were obviously liquid. Therefore H. D. Broadhead's emendation, *Tragica* (1968) 81, τοῦ φέρεις τάδ' ἐς πυράν, may well be right (a tomb could be called a πυρά).

**406** 'to pay (these) libations, as an offering at our father's tomb'. The simple infinitive can be used in poetry in a final sense.

**407** 'What! To the one man who is her greatest enemy!' For the tense of εἶπας cf. 388n. ἦ expresses a *strong* note of question (here of surprise).

**408** 'The man she killed with her own hand. That is what you would say.' Chrysothemis is even blunter than Electra.

**409** ἐκ = ὑπό, cf. 264n. But the use of ἐκ here leads elegantly to ἐκ in the next line.

**410** 'As a result of some nightmare she had, I believe.'

δοκεῖν is a limitative use of the infinitive, closely allied to the epexegetic and consecutive uses, and would, like them, in strict grammar be preceded by ὡς or ὥστε, though this is often omitted in familiar speech: 'for it to *seem* to me', i.e. if you want my impression.

**411** For πατρῷοι cf. 67n. Zeus and Apollo were particularly πατρῷοι as guarding the legitimate succession from father to son.

συγγένεσθέ γ' ἀλλὰ νῦν involves the form of hyperbaton called *anastrophe* (inverting a preposition, adverb, connective or the like, such as ἀλλὰ νῦν), and the whole stands for ἀλλὰ νῦν γε συγγένεσθε, 'Well, now at least take my part!'

**412** πέρι: anastrophe of a disyllabic preposition, and notice that then its accent is thrown back.

**414** κάτοιδα: κατα-, as often, is intensive: 'I do not know it in exact detail, except to (be able to) indicate it to a small degree.'

**415f** ἀλλά in anastrophe, and serving to emphasise the pronoun, 'at least this'. 'You must know that often insignificant words (or tales) have been known to mean the ruin of mortals or their triumph.' πολλά, adverbial. ἤδη 'in the past', 'in history'. ἔσφηλαν and κατώρθωσαν represent what might be called the historic aorist. καί is sometimes, as here, disjunctive ('or').

The words are pregnant with meaning. The 'tale' of Clytaemnestra's evil dream does portend her end at the hands of Orestes. But we cannot help thinking of that other little λόγος (cf. 44), whereby Orestes cheats, not merely Clytaemnestra and Aegisthus, but also Electra herself, into thinking that he is dead. That λόγος is not merely to lead to the death of Clytaemnestra, but also to destroy the sanity of Electra herself.

**417ff** 'There is some word that she experienced a second (period of) intercourse with my father and yours, he having visited the light (again), and that then he (τόνδ') took the sceptre and planted it...' Jebb takes ὁμιλίαν of ordinary, social intercourse. This is rather tame. Surely sexual intercourse is meant. What more terrible for the guilty woman than to dream that she had intercourse with the man she had murdered? This also explains εἶτα (*after* the intercourse). It also fits in with the symbolism of what follows. Agamemnon struck his sceptre into the earth, and from it sprang a branch, which overshadowed all the land of Argos. The sceptre is the symbol not merely of sovereignty, but also of the potency of Agamemnon. The branch which springs from it is Orestes the offspring of the intercourse of Clytaemnestra and Agamemnon, who is to overthrow Clytaemnestra and Aegisthus and establish his own dominion in Mycenae. For εἰσιδεῖν cf. 205n., *Trach.* 151, 303. Clytaemnestra's dream has a close resemblance to Astyages' dream about Mandane, Hdt. 1. 108.

**424f** The Scholiast explains τοῖς γὰρ παλαιοῖς ἔθος ἦν ἀποτροπιαζο-μένους τῷ ἡλίῳ διηγεῖσθαι τὰ ὀνείρατα.

τοῦ παρόντος '(heard) from someone present'. Notice that του, having no accent, is indefinite.

δείκνυσι: vivid historic present, used here even in a temporal clause, since no one could mistake the sense.

**425** ἐξηγουμένου 'telling the details of'. Chrysothemis had heard a servant gossiping about her mistress's dream.

**428** 'By the gods then of the family' (the ones therefore which sanctify our relationship), cf. the θεοὶ πατρῷοι of 411. Notice that νυν (when enclitic) has an inferential, not a temporal meaning.

**429** ἀβουλίᾳ πεσεῖν, almost identical with the expression in 398.

**430** 'If you repulse me, you shall seek after me again later when the evil is with you.' Later, in suffering, Electra will recognise that her sister was right, and seek for her sympathy when it is too late to mend matters. A pathetic line. Chrysothemis is greatly concerned about her sister's welfare, as is Ismene about Antigone's (cf. *Ant.* 82 οἴμοι, ταλαίνης ὡς ὑπερδέδοικά σου).

**431f** 'Ah! But, dear sister, apply none of these things which you carry in your hands to the tomb.' Electra is not interested in Chryso-themis' warning, nor in her own safety, but only in the report of the dream, which leads her to think that the spirit of the dead Agamemnon may be ready to intervene to punish Clytaemnestra and Aegisthus. This interest is conveyed in the excitement of 431f.

ὧν, by attraction, for ἅ.

**432ff** 'For it is not lawful (θέμις) or hallowed (ὅσιον).' Enemies' gifts were unacceptable, cf. *Aj.* 665 ἐχθρῶν ἄδωρα δῶρα κοὐκ ὀνήσιμα.

**ἱστάναι,** lit. 'cause to stand there'; since they would be at the tomb permanently, and would be conspicuous objects. Cf. the note to 324f.

**λουτρά** = χοάς, cf. 84.

**πατρί** goes, ἀπὸ κοινοῦ, with both infinitives.

**435ff**   'No! Either (scatter them) to the winds, or hide them away in a deep hole in the ground (lit. in the deep-dug dust), where none of these things shall ever find their way to where our father sleeps.' A suitable verb has to be supplied from κρύψον to go with πνοαῖσιν, by the figure of zeugma (see the Introduction (Style)).

**κόνει** is often used to describe Greek soil, which was generally light and dry.

**νιν** is in verse sometimes used (curiously) for any *vague* accusative of the 3rd person pronoun. So here and at 624 it = αὐτά: for other similar uses cf. *O.T.* 868 and *O.C.* 43.

**εὐνήν:** cf. Aesch. *Cho.* 318 ἔνθα σ' ἔχουσιν εὐναί.

**ἔνθα μὴ...πρόσεισι:** a final relative clause, regularly taking the future indicative.

**437f**   'Let these things be preserved as keepsakes for herself, beneath the ground for when she dies!' Bitter sarcasm.

**439**   **ἀρχήν** 'in the very beginning' (i.e. 'at all'), adv. acc.

**440**   **ἔβλαστε** merely = 'had been'.

**δυσμενεῖς,** because the χοαί are from a hostile person (δυσμενής being a variation on ἐχθρός).

**441**   'Would never have decked (them) *on the man she killed* (lit. 'the man she *killed*, would never have decked them upon *this man*'). The early positioning of the relative pronoun (as well as the use of γε) emphasises it, but also makes necessary the statement of the antecedent (τῷδ') after it. The expressive but inverted word-order (inappropriate to a modern language) is possible in a highly inflected language such as Greek.

**ἐπέστεφε:** an economical way of saying 'got someone else to deck them'.

**442**   **προσφιλῶς αὐτῇ** (with δέξεσθαι) 'with friendly feeling towards her'. αὐτῇ is simply the 3rd person pronoun, not specially emphatic, as in prose. The accumulation of this usage in the following lines is remarkable, cf. 447, 454, 456, 457, 460. For a parallel in English Mrs Easterling refers me to Milton's *Comus* 763–6.

**444ff** ὑφ' ἧς relative of αὐτῇ in 442, despite the long separation. Again, the word-order is only possible in a highly inflected language with highly complicated sentence-structures. '...at whose hand having died disregarded, like an enemy, he had his extremities cut off and, for ablution, she wiped the blood-stains off upon his head!'

ἄτιμος is used, not merely='dishonoured' (in general), but also (in connection with homicide)='without a price (τιμή) upon one's head' (cf. G. Busolt, *Griechische Staatskunde* (Müllers Handbuch der Altertumswissenschaft, 1920) 230f.), i.e. like an outlaw, an 'enemy' in the completest sense: cf. Aesch. *Cho.* 434.

ἐμασχαλίσθη: to prevent Agamemnon's ghost 'walking', as the Scholiast explains. This detail of Agamemnon's murder is also taken from Aeschylus' account, cf. *Cho.* 439 ἐμασχαλίσθη δ' ἔθ', ὡς τόδ' εἰδῇς.

κἀπὶ λουτροῖσιν κτλ.: again a barbaric and primitive idea and ritual with regard to killing people is involved: Clytaemnestra wiped her blood-stained hands, after the killing, upon the head of the dead Agamemnon, in order to absolve (lit. 'wash') herself of the blood (and with it the blood-guiltiness – in Greek, μίασμα) and transfer it to Agamemnon himself, as we say, 'On thine own head be it!' Cf. *Od.* 19. 92 ἔρδουσα μέγα ἔργον, ὃ σῇ κεφαλῇ ἀναμάξεις; Hdt. 1. 155. The guilt would be transferable to Agamemnon because of his original killing of Iphigenia.

For the use of ἐπ', cf. *O.T.* 1457 μὴ 'πί τῳ δεινῷ κακῷ. λουτροῖσιν is used here as punning on the other sense of λουτρά = χοαί to the dead, cf. 82n. and 434. Others (much less convincingly) have taken ἐπὶ λουτροῖς='for washing' (of the corpse). Both versions involve an awkward change of subject (ἐμασχαλίσθη sc. Agamemnon, ἐξέμαξεν sc. Clytaemnestra), to which I should be glad to see a parallel (those offered by the various editors not being very convincing).

**446f** 'You do not think, do you, that you bear these offerings as absolutions for her (i.e. what will effectively absolve her) of the murder?'

**448** οὐκ ἔστιν 'it is impossible' (that that is so). μέθες 'throw away'.

σὺ δέ 'do *you yourself*' (i.e. take the initiative away from her, grasp it yourself).

**449f** 'cutting the end-strands (lit. 'foliage') of your hair from your head, and mine too, poor thing that I am'.

ἄχω = ἃ ἔχω 'all that I have to offer'. For the hair offered at the grave, cf. 52n.

**451** 'Give him this hair, I beseech you.' The MSS have τήνδ' ἀλιπαρῆ τρίχα, which would make sense if ἀλιπαρής could mean 'not sleek' (root λῑπ- = 'oily'). But ἀλιπαρής is found nowhere else, and the quantity of the iota is against Sophocles' having coined the word for this occasion and in this sense. On the other hand a scribe could have corrupted the text I have printed to the MS reading, through association of ideas.

**452** οὐ χλιδαῖς ἠσκημένον 'not worked with luxurious ornaments'. Compare 52 καρατόμοις χλιδαῖς. There is a certain irony in the fact that Orestes' offerings at the tomb of his father were to be luxurious; his sister's were not.

**453f** 'Request – supplicating him – that *he* should appear from the earth, as a beneficent helper to *us* against his *enemies*.' Notice the precision of the prayer. This is needed since the prayer is a semi-magical formula, conjuring up the dead spirit: if it were not precise, the magic might go wrong.

αὐτόν is here slightly emphatic because of the context.

**455f** 'and that his son Orestes, alive, should trample, from superior strength, with his foot on his ( = Agamemnon's) enemies'.

ζῶντ': for the dramatic irony of this word here see Introduction 12 n. 2.

For the idea of jumping upon enemies cf. Aesch. *Pers.* 515f. ὦ δυσπόνητε δαῖμον ὡς ἄγαν βαρὺς | ποδοῖν ἐνήλλου παντὶ Περσικῷ γένει.

**457f** 'may deck him with more generous hands than we now give (gifts to him)'.

δωρούμεθα, by *variatio*, for στέφομεν.

**459f** 'Nay (μὲν οὖν corrective) I believe it is because he too is not unconcerned (lit. 'it being somewhat a care to him too', acc. absol.) that he sent her...'. There is no reason why the same person should not be understood in two different grammatical relationships in the same sentence (ἐκεῖνον being understood, by 'economy', from κἀκείνῳ as the subject of πέμψαι), or why the MSS' reading μέλον should be changed. In fact Nauck's injudicious conjecture μέλειν actually weakens the sense, since (on Nauck's reading) πέμψαι is governed no longer by οἶμαι, but by μέλειν, and we are denied the important statement 'I think that *he sent* the dream.'

**δυσπρόσοπτ'**: predicative (sc. ὄντα).

**461ff** ἀρωγά in 462 goes with all the datives.

**464** πρὸς εὐσέβειαν 'with proper sentiment'.

**465** εἰ σωφρονήσεις 'if you (too) shall have proper sentiment' (σωφρονεῖν used not in the restricted sense = 'practise restraint', but in the larger sense, practically = εὖ φρονεῖν).

**466f** 'I shall do it! For that which is right (to do) does not permit of argument for two people (for them) to dispute about it, but (obliges one) to *do* it.' Chrysothemis' decision is taken as rapidly and as dramatically as Electra's at 387 and 431.

**τὸ δίκαιον**: not here 'justice' in the abstract.

**ἔχει** = παρέχει, cf. 351.

**ἐρίζειν** is epexegetic. A complementary positive verb ('obliges' or 'compels') is easily to be understood (by zeugma) in the second main clause from the negatived verb in the first (οὐκ ἔχει): cf. 1373-4, *Aj.* 11-12 καί σ' οὐδὲν εἴσω τῆσδε παπταίνειν πύλης | ἔτ' ἔργον ἐστίν, ἐννέπειν δ' (sc. χρή) ὅτου χάριν | σπουδὴν ἔθου τήνδ', Hdt. 7. 104. 2. The sentiment and the expression inevitably recall the principles of the contemporary sophist, the moral relativist, Protagoras (as W. Nestle, *C.Ph.* 5 (1910) 154 points out: editors strangely ignore this application). Protagoras was a master of ἔρις and ἐριστικοὶ λόγοι (cf. Timon 47 (Diels, *Poetarum Philosophorum Fragmenta*) Πρωταγόρης τ' ἐπίμεικτος ἐριζέμεναι εὖ εἰδώς), and said δύο λόγους εἶναι περὶ παντὸς πράγματος ἀντικειμένους ἀλλήλοις (Diels–Kranz, *Vorsokr.* 80 [74]).

A number of commentators (including Jebb) have tried to construe these lines in other ways, because of the fact that ἔχειν λόγον usually means 'be reasonable', and has not been paralleled in the sense 'permit of argument'. But their versions are forced and make much poorer sense, apart from the fact that they destroy the reference to

Protagoras. We are not bound to provide a parallel for every single phrase in Greek, and ἔχειν λόγον does not always mean 'be reasonable'.

**470f** 'Since, if my mother shall hear of this, I imagine that it will be a bitter attempt which I shall hazard, in this, from then on (ἔτι).' For πεῖρα cf. *Aj.* 1f., and for πικράν Aesch. *Pers.* 473, Soph. *Aj.* 1239.

### 472-515

Chrysothemis has left the stage, in order to make the offerings on behalf of herself and Electra at Agamemnon's tomb. Electra remains, silent, on stage. The Chorus, standing in the orchestra, address their first 'standing song' (*stasimon*) to her. The song ( = strophe, antistrophe and epode) is shorter than the previous *Parodos* (121ff.), but is, like it, aeolic in character beginning with choriambs but changing to iambics (476ff.) and ending in dochmiacs (504ff.) – see further Appendix 1. The Chorus are excited by the new developments triggered off by Clytaemnestra's dream. They foretell that Justice will soon overtake Clytaemnestra and Aegisthus.

**472f** 'If I was not born a demented prophetess lacking in wise perception.' The Greek interest in μαντική is frequently expressed in tragedy, cf. 1499.

**475** πρόμαντις: Dike, the personification of justice, is also a prophetess because she has sent advance notice (through Clytaemnestra's dream) of the reversal of affairs which she means to bring about (in vindication of Agamemnon) in Mycenae.

**476** δίκαια κτλ. 'winning [the proper meaning of the middle of φέρειν] just triumphs'.

**477** μέτεισιν 'she will go after' (sc. the κράτη). Cf. 85.

**479ff** 'Confidence supports my spirit, since I heard a moment ago of Clytaemnestra's sweet-breathing dream.' κλύουσαν follows μοι by a curious sense-construction, as if ὑπεστί μοι had been θρασύνει με: cf. Aesch. *Cho.* 410 πέπαλται δ' αὖτέ μοι φίλον κέαρ | τόνδε κλύουσαν οἴκτον.

**485** 'the two-bladed cheek' = the axe that slew Agamemnon.

**487** αἰκεία means 'outrage', 'assault', cf. Aesch. *P.V.* 93f.; the word
is repeated at 511 and 515 with no particular extra significance. Such
vain repetition of certain expressions seems to be characteristic of
Sophocles' choruses. Cf. 1389 ἀμμενεῖ... 1397 ἀμμένει, *Aj.* 624 ἦ που
παλαιᾷ μὲν σύντροφος ἀμέρα... 639f. οὐκέτι συντρόφοις | ὀργαῖς
ἔμπεδος, etc. Not quite the same is the repetition of θάρσος (479 and
495), and that of μάντις (473), πρόμαντις (475), μαντεῖαι (498). These
repetitions serve to reinforce key-ideas.

**489ff** 'She will come, both many-footed and many-handed, she
who conceals herself in dreadful ambushes, the Fury with foot shod
in bronze!' The avenging Fury is often conceived as a monster who
*stalks* her prey, like a wild animal. Cf. the picture of Ate (divinely-
inspired doom or perdition) at *Il.* 9. 505ff. ἡ δ' Ἄτη σθεναρή τε καὶ
ἀρτίπος, οὕνεκα πάσας (sc. Λιτάς) | πολλὸν ὑπεκπροθέει, φθάνει δέ τε
πᾶσαν ἐπ' αἶαν | βλάπτουσ' ἀνθρώπους. For the ambush cf. *Ant.* 1074f.
τούτων σε λωβητῆρες ὑστεροφθόροι | λοχῶσιν Ἅιδου καὶ θεῶν
Ἐρινύες.

**491** χαλκόπους: the foot of the bogey is often mentioned, as being
the prominent feature of a tracking-animal, cf. *Il.* 9. 505 quoted above,
489n., and *O.T.* 418 δεινόπους ἀρά. But χαλκόπους, I think, is here a
telescoped compound, meaning (*a*) the Fury stalks with her foot,
(*b*) she *has* χαλκός (i.e. is armed).

**492ff** Difficult Greek (as frequently in Sophoclean choruses) because of its extreme concision. 'For she is gone out against improperly-
bedding, improperly-wedding strivings after marriage (which is
soiled by bloodshed), strivings undertaken by persons who had no
rights there.' ἀμιλλήματα, though a noun, is also treated as a verb.
Therefore understand the antecedent of οἶσιν (ὑπὸ τούτων) with it.
For ἐπιβαίνω cf. *Aj.* 137f. σὲ δ' ὅταν πληγὴ Διός... ἐπιβῇ. Jebb
understands ἐπέβα differently and takes ἀμιλλήματα as its subject:
'for wicked ones have been fired with passion that hurried them to a
forbidden bed' ('ἐπέβα suggesting the violence of the passion which
seized them'.) I much prefer that ἐπέβα should describe the determined march of the Fury. The Fury avenged not merely murder, but
also adultery. Cf. 112n. For ἄλεκτρ' ἄνυμφα cf. *O.T.* 1214 ἄγαμον
γάμον.

**495ff** 'In virtue of these things (πρὸ τῶνδε) I have certainly (τοι) confidence that we shall never, never have (ἡμῖν = ethic dative) (such a) nightmare approaching the killers and their accomplices as an *innocent* vision.'

μήποτε (not οὔποτε), because the Chorus do not merely believe that the dream will be fulfilled in a sense adverse to Clytaemnestra: they also wish that it shall.

ἀψεγές: if the dream proved ineffective, and Orestes (symbolised in the dream as the branch springing from Agamemnon's sceptre) did *not* come to 'overshadow' all the land of Mycenae, then of course the vision would be 'blameless', 'innocent', from Clytaemnestra's point of view.

πελᾶν: the 'Attic' future of πελάζω.

**500** θεσφάτοις 'oracles'.

**503** εὖ κατασχήσει 'shall end up (κατέχειν used absolutely) well' (from the Chorus' point of view).

**504ff** Although the Chorus have been talking primarily of the guilt of Clytaemnestra and Aegisthus, and praying for their punishment, they now reveal that they regard the troubles of Agamemnon and his descendants as not simply the result of the individual wickedness of Clytaemnestra and Aegisthus but also as an inevitable episode in the whole history of the house of Pelops (cf. 514 ἐκ τοῦδ'), a history in which one act of bloody or treacherous reprisal has succeeded another; all creating misery because the house was accursed from its inception.

'Ah! ancient (πρόσθεν) horsemanship of Pelops, full of trouble, how you came (as a force) everlasting for this land. For ever since Myrtilus – Myrtilus sunk in the deep sea – was laid to rest, tossed headlong (πρόρριζος) out of the all-gilded chariot in grievous outrage, never yet has outrage, full of trouble, ceased from this House' (ἔλιπεν used absolutely). The scheming Pelops won the hand of Hippodamia, the daughter of Oenomaus, king of Pisa, by bribing the latter's charioteer Myrtilus to remove the linch-pin from his chariot-wheel in a race to determine whether or not Pelops' suit was to be successful. Oenomaus was thrown and killed, and Myrtilus, who claimed as his reward the favours of Hippodamia, was hurled out of his chariot into the sea and drowned by Pelops.

## 516–533

As the Chorus cease singing, the character about whom our curiosity has been building up for so long finally appears. Clytaemnestra is attended by a maid-servant who carries sacrificial gifts which her mistress intends to sacrifice before the statue of Apollo which stands in front of the house (cf. 634ff.) in order to persuade him to render the dream she has had beneficial and not injurious.

**516** 'Out and about once more you are, it seems!'

ἔοικας : personal, where the English idiom is impersonal.

στρέφῃ lit. 'you are turning', 'moving round and about', i.e. not staying quietly within the palace: cf. 312n.

**517f** 'who ever held you in check from being (as they say) an out-of-doors woman and so bringing disgrace on your own people'. τοι referring to the *proverbial* embargo on women going out.

φίλους here = relatives.

**519f** 'You don't bother at all (οὐδέν = adv. acc.) about *me*.'

**520f** πολλά : adv. acc. με = anticipatory acc., 'have reported me to many that I . . .'.

**521** θρασεῖα sc. εἰμί. πέρα δίκης 'on the other side of justice', i.e. unjustly.

**522** ἄρχω : as wife of Aegisthus, Clytaemnestra shared in the *de facto* rule of Mycenae.

καθυβρίζουσα 'treating with insolent disregard'.

**523** ὕβριν... οὐκ ἔχω 'am not insolent'.

**524** κακῶς κλύουσα κτλ. 'because I am often *spoken to* vilely by you': κλύειν serves as a passive to λέγειν. πρός: cf. 69n.

**525f** πατήρ is an anticipatory nominative, 'the fact that your father is dead at my hand'.

**527** οὐκ ἔνεστί μοι : not 'is not in me', but 'is not possible *for* me'.

**528f** 'It was *Justice* (i.e. retribution) that undid him, not just I, Justice which you ought to be assisting, had you in fact been in your senses.' For εἷλεν cf. 122n. The present or imperfect (i.e. the durative

tenses) of τυγχάνω are often used together with the present participle
with the nuance of meaning suggested in the translation.

**531f** μοῦνος: Clytaemnestra means to say that Agamemnon was
the only Greek chieftain who had the hardihood to *sacrifice his own
daughter* on behalf of the expedition against Troy. But she puts it (by
a sense-construction) in a way that could be misinterpreted to mean
that he was the only Greek to sacrifice Iphigenia. Jebb and others
(wrongly, I think) understand her literally.

**532f** 'not having laboured an equal (amount) of pain, when he
sowed her, as did I, the bearer of her (sc. when I bore her)'. Again
there is a sense-construction – Clytaemnestra means that Agamemnon
had only pleasure in the begetting of Iphigenia, whereas she had the
pain of bearing her. Sense-constructions tend to occur (as we might
expect) when the speakers are moved or excited, as is Clytaemnestra
here. The pain of giving birth is often mentioned by ancient writers
as being closely associated with the affection felt by the mother for the
child. So Aeschylus' Clytaemnestra describes Iphigenia as φιλτάτην
ἐμοὶ ὠδῖνα (*Ag.* 1417f.).

### 534–545

Clytaemnestra strikes a certain note which differentiates these lines
from the other parts of the play. It is as if she were mounting a
rostrum to initiate a public debate. And in fact her words are sprinkled
with terms and figures of speech or thought identical with those used
by actual orators in courts or assemblies of the day.

We are to remember that the oratory of debate was the one other
popular form of literary art besides drama which was flowering at
Athens at the time when drama was reaching its maturity. Since the
Athenians had learned to like listening to debates in the courts and
the assembly, they liked to listen to them also in the theatre. So the
two later tragedians (Aeschylus shows less oratorical and rhetorical
influence, he flourished a little too early) provided them with such
debate. We are now about to hear a formal contest of words (*agon*) on
the merits or demerits of Agamemnon's killing of Iphigenia, and of his
own death at the hands of Clytaemnestra.

The argument proceeds in the form of a series of suggested reasons
or motives, which Agamemnon might have given for his sacrifice of
Iphigenia. These are then answered rapidly by the speaker, who

proceeds to give other 'suggestions' which are as rapidly demolished. This technique of arguing by way of stating imaginary reasons or motivations (whether one's own or someone else's, whether singly or in a series) is a familiar oratorical one (frequent in the first professional orator Antiphon and his successors), and is called *hypophora* (Latinised as *suggestio*): cf. Quintilian 9. 2. 15; Jebb, *Attic Orators* (1876) II 284ff.; Soph. *Aj.* 46off., *Ant.* 284ff., *O.T.* 1374ff., etc.

It frequently uses the rhetorical question (sometimes answered by another rhetorical question, sometimes unanswered except by the indignant tone of voice of the speaker) and abounds in certain abrupt particles, conjunctions or interjections such as πότερον, ἀλλά (introducing the rhetorical question as well as the answer to it), δῆτα (conveying indignation at an absurdity in an opponent's argument), ἤ (introducing an alternative question). A feature of this figure (when used in a series) is its rapidity: it passes swiftly from one point to another, the idea being to sweep the audience away in a tide of rhetorical persuasiveness. Also as the series proceeds it tends to gain speed and momentum: hence in the present passage, answers are given to the earlier rhetorical questions, whereas the later ones (542-5, representing a climax) are left unanswered.

**534**  'Come now! Just (δή) enlighten me, what for, for whose sake, did he sacrifice her?'

εἶεν: an interjection, used by orators introducing a discussion.

δίδαξον: not 'teach', but 'explain to me', 'enlighten me' (also oratorical): cf. 352 and Antiphon, *Tetr.* A. β. 9 ὡς δὲ τόνδε τὸν κίνδυνον οὐκ ἀσφαλέστερον τοῦ ἀπὸ τῆς γραφῆς ἡγούμην εἶναι... διδάξω.

τοῦ χάριν, τίνων: the reading of the oldest MS L (before correction) gives excellent sense (the personal τίνων picked up by 'Αργείων at 535). Only it involves a slight zeugma of χάριν ('for the sake of what?', i.e. 'to achieve what?' with τοῦ; 'for the sake of whom?', i.e. 'to please whom?' with τίνων).

**535ff**  'Will you say that it was for the sake of the Argives? But they had no part (in her) so as to (have the right to) kill *my* daughter (γε emphasises τὴν ἐμήν). Well (ἀλλά) was it instead of his *brother*, Menelaus [i.e. instead of Agamemnon's brother Menelaus having to sacrifice *his* son or daughter], just tell me (δῆτα)! that he killed *what* *was mine*? But wasn't he going to have to pay a penalty to me for that (τῶνδε)? Didn't *he* have two (lit. 'twin') children?'

**537f** 'Well, having killed…wasn't he going to…?': Clytaemnestra in her excitement here telescopes two separate suggestions – 'maybe he killed'…'then wasn't he *going* to…?'

**538** τῶνδε refers to τἀμά: ὅδε can refer back, as well as forward.

**539** παῖδες…διπλοῖ: Homer credited Menelaus with only a daughter, Hermione (*Od.* 4. 14), but Hesiod (fr. 175 Merkelbach–West) mentioned a son as well.

**540f** 'whom it was more reasonable to put to death (lit. 'for them to die') than my daughter, being of the father and the mother, for the sake of whom this voyage was taking place'. For ἧς we should expect ὧν. But Hermione's mother, Helen, was the reason and the cause, *par excellence*, of the Trojan War. Therefore she has understandably ousted her partner (Menelaus) from the mind of Clytaemnestra in 541.

**542** 'Or did Hades have some particular desire for *my* children, to taste them…?' δαίσασθαι, epexegetic. As Jebb points out, 542 is given a specially harsh effect by the absence of early caesura.

**543** Notice that this ἤ goes with πλέον, = 'than'.

**544f** 'Or had your dastardly father's tenderness for my children slackened, while his love for Menelaus' (children) remained with him?'

**546f** The *hypophora* is now ended. She proceeds by simple rhetorical question and statement.

**547** δοκῶ μέν 'I certainly think so'; for μέν cf. 372n.

**548** 'Yes! (γε) and the girl who died would say so!'

**549f** τοῖς πεπραγμένοις δύσθυμος 'uneasy, conscience-stricken at what has been done' (i.e. at the murder of Agamemnon).

**551** 'Criticise your neighbours when (i.e. only when) you have yourself acquired a just perception.'

**552f** μ' ὡς ἄρξασά τι κτλ. 'that having *begun* some hurtful (reproach), then I had these things (i.e. the same kind of things, hurtful things) addressed to me by you'. Cf. 524–5.

μ': anticipatory accusative.

ἄρξασα: legalistic, since Greek law laid guilt on anyone who *began* a dispute: cf. Hdt. 1. 2 and Soph. fr. 368. 2 ἄρξασι Φρυξὶ τὴν κατ' Ἀργείων ὕβριν.

ἐξήκουσ' = ἤκουσα (cf. 276n.); it is used here, like κλύουσα at 524, as the passive of λέγειν.

**554** 'If you (will) allow me.'

**555** λέξαιμ' ἄν ὀρθῶς 'I should like to speak correctly' (i.e. in correction of what you have said). One of the uses of the optative with ἄν is to give a mild, deferential, future sense. Electra's tone in these lines is quiet and deferential.

**556f** 'Certainly I allow you.' Clytaemnestra is herself beguiled, by her daughter's quiet tone, into a tone of polite deference.

μ' = με (since μοι does not elide in tragedy), and, if the text is right, must be governed by λόγους ἐξῆρχες, as if the latter had been προσηγόρευες.

**557** ἐξῆρχες 'struck up', 'led off', the word made famous by Aristotle in the *Poetics* of those who 'led off' the dithyramb (*Poetics* 1449a11).

**558** 'Well! I do speak (what I have to say) to you.'

πατέρα: the father of Clytaemnestra's children, and also her husband.

**559** λόγος 'proposition'. Notice the doubling of ἄν, without particular significance. ἔτι is redundant but emphatic: when you say that, what proposition *still* remains that is more shameful?

**560** 'Whether you did it justly or not.' εἴτε δικαίως εἴτε μή is perhaps little more than a phrase meaning 'in any circumstances whatsoever' (though Electra is undoubtedly here replying to Clytaemnestra's plea (528) that 'it was Dike that undid Agamemnon'): cf. *Ant.* 666–7 ἀλλ' ὃν πόλις στήσειε, τοῦδε χρὴ κλύειν | καὶ σμικρὰ καὶ δίκαια κἄδικα, and Aesch. *Eum.* 468.

λέξω δέ σοι 'I will put it to you' (as the lawyers say).

**561f** 'It wasn't in *justice* that you killed' – γε emphasises δίκη.

ἔσπασεν 'led (lured) on'.

κακοῦ πρὸς ἀνδρός '(exercised) by', πρός for ὑπό, cf. 69n.

**563f** 'As a penalty (or, in penalty) for what she held the ships becalmed at Aulis.'

ποινάς may be regarded either as an adverbial accusative or 'accusative in apposition to the sentence'.

**564** A *locus varie vexatus*. I have accepted what seems to me the most straightforward interpretation. There were two versions of the legend: (*a*) that the ships were detained by calm; (*b*) that they were detained by winds (see Jebb's notes *ad loc.*). For ἔσχε = κατέσχε cf. 223n., and 571 κατεῖχ'.

**565** 'Or (sc. don't answer!) I shall tell you.' The ἤ, as at 542 and 543, has an argumentative, contentious effect. 'For it is not lawful to gain enlightenment from *her*.' The gods cannot be summoned to account for their actions or their motives: they cannot (in modern legal terms) be *subpoenaed* to give evidence in a case (cf. *O.T.* 280f. ἀλλ' ἀναγκάσαι θεοὺς | ἂν μὴ θέλωσιν οὐδ' ἂν εἷς δύναιτ' ἀνήρ). But then, should their evidence be *used*?

### 566–633

Agamemnon hunts for amusement, as a modern prime minister might play golf. In so doing he kills a stag (all wild animals were sacred to Artemis), and instead of seeking to appease the goddess or associate her with the triumph, he offends her by claiming the success as his own (which boast he conveys in a vainglorious, hybristic word). It is the same story as at *Aj.* 176ff. (cf. particularly 178 ἀδώροις ἐλαφαβολίαις) and 762ff., in which passages the Chorus and the messenger (instructed by Calchas) respectively suggest that Ajax was punished (by his madness) for simply offering offence to a jealous (and, we can only add, petty-minded) divinity. This was the popular belief as to how such unpleasantnesses as Ajax's madness and the Greeks' detention at Aulis came about. But did Sophocles expect an intelligent person to believe it? I do not think so, since in *Ajax*, in which such causes of Ajax's madness are ventilated, we are also given a behind-the-scenes picture of the goddess concerned in action (*Aj.* 1–133), and there we

see that the madness of Ajax was in fact inspired by no such divine
jealousy: it was simply Athena's expedient to prevent Ajax from *killing
the Greek leaders* (51) – an aim which he conceived through no divine
infatuation, but because he was angry over the bestowal of the arms
of Achilles (41).

**566ff**  ὡς ἐγὼ κλύω 'as I am *told*'. Doesn't she *know* why her father
sacrificed her sister? (Notice that hearsay evidence was not admitted
in an Athenian court: cf. Bonner and Smith, *Administration of justice* II
130.) There is something curiously legalistic and unreal about
Electra's 'pleading' on behalf of Agamemnon in these lines.

θεᾶς...κατ' ἄλσος κτλ. 'taking his recreation in a grove belonging
to the goddess he stirred up, by his foot-beats, a brindled branching-
horned stag, in killing which, boasting aloud of it, he happened to let
fall a particular expression'. So Schneidewin–Nauck. Jebb however
makes βαλών = 'after *hitting*' (sc. the stag with an arrow or javelin),
saying that, though ἐκβάλλειν ἔπος occurs often, nowhere does βάλλειν
ἔπος. But βάλλειν *can* = ἐκβάλλειν (cf. Aesch. *Ag.* 1009 ὄκνος βαλών)
and we are not obliged to parallel every single verbal formula (cf.
466n.). Jebb's version makes far worse sense (his βαλών is unbearably
tautologous after κατὰ σφαγάς; and βαλών is far more meaningful
as 'letting fall').

**571f**  ἀντίσταθμον τοῦ θηρός 'as a compensation for the slain
beast'.

ἐκθύσειε probably = θύσειε, cf. 276n.

**573**  τὰ...θύματ' = the more usual θυσία.
οὐ γὰρ ἦν λύσις κτλ.: did any intelligent Greek really believe this?

**575f**  'For which reason (ἀνθ' ὧν = ὧν ἕνεκα) having been much
constrained, and having much resisted (the idea of the sacrifice) he
brought himself, with the greatest difficulty (μόλις), to sacrifice her.'
πολλά with ἀντιβάς as well as with βιασθείς.

**577**  δ' οὖν (as usual, dismissing a topic) 'however'. She proceeds to
a second line of argument: even if Agamemnon's motives in sacrificing
Iphigenia were insufficient, that was not a sufficient reason for
Clytaemnestra's killing him.

καὶ τὸ σόν '*your* argument too' – an argument you might be expected to use. Litigants in Greek court-cases are forever trying to anticipate their opponents' arguments.

**578f**  Notice the long separation of τούτου οὔνεκ', in hyperbaton.
ἐκ σέθεν: cf. 264n.

**580f**  'Mind when you establish this law for mortals that you are not establishing suffering and repentance for yourself.' τίθεσθαι (mid.) νόμους was used of those who made laws (democratically) to use themselves; τιθέναι νόμους of those who made them for others, *de haut en bas*: τιθεῖσα is therefore more autocratic than the middle would be.

τιθεῖσα...τίθης: rhetorical repetition, to enforce the point (and cf. τίθης at 584). ὅρα μή more usually has a subjunctive or optative in the subordinate clause. But the indicative is also possible, and makes the danger to be avoided more actual.

**582f**  'For if we shall...then you would be, you know (τοι), the first to die.' A naturally occurring mixed-conditional sentence. For the meaning of τοι cf. Headlam's note to *Ag.* 374ff.

δίκης: Electra's reply to Clytaemnestra's Δίκη at 528.
*In these lines we have the crux of the whole ethical situation of the play: if retributive killing is wrong (δίκη in that sense), then Electra's and Orestes' killing of their mother is going to be just as wrong as was Clytaemnestra's killing of Agamemnon. Electra condemns herself out of her own mouth.*

**584**  Legalistic again. σκῆψις is a 'plea' at law; οὐκ οὖσαν is used at law of a case which does not 'lie', cf. Bonner and Smith, *Administration of justice* II 92.

**585**  εἰ γὰρ θέλεις 'If you will' (cold and polite).

**587**  ἥτις: circumstantial, cf. 347n.: 'you who...'
παλαμναίῳ 'the guilty man', i.e. the man who had the blood of Agamemnon on the palms (παλάμαι) of his hands.

**588**  πρόσθεν 'previously': i.e. Clytemnestra *first* used Aegisthus' help to kill Agamemnon, *then* took him to her bed in Agamemnon's place.
ἐξαπώλεσας: cf. 276n.

**589f**  'Aye! and you create a family with him, and those who were formerly respectable, and sprung from respectable parentage, you have cast out' (sc. from their inheritance). Notice the repetition of πρόσθεν, which (like the repeated ἤ of 542–4) helps to convey the speaker's indignation. Evidently Clytaemnestra had had children by Aegisthus, children who were bound (given the continuance in power of Aegisthus and Clytaemnestra) to succeed to the dominion and power of Agamemnon usurped by Aegisthus and Clytaemnestra, thus ousting the legitimate offspring of Agamemnon. These children, though doubtless included in Clytaemnestra's general reference to her children at 653, are not otherwise mentioned in this play. A daughter Erigone, who is referred to by Tzetzes on Lycophron 1374, and was mentioned by the Cyclic poet Cinaethon (cf. Paus. 2. 18. 6), was the subject of Sophocles' lost play *Erigone*: a son of Aegisthus is mentioned by Hyginus (*Fab.* 122).

εὐσεβεῖς 'those who have *done no wrong*' (cf. 250n.) (and therefore do not deserve to be disinherited); κἀξ εὐσεβῶν may have the additional implication that Electra and her brother and sisters were sprung from a legitimate marriage (ἐξ ἐννόμου γάμου, as the Scholiast explains).

ἐκβαλοῦσ' ἔχεις: this periphrastic perfect is a verse usage and a favourite one of Sophocles, cf. *Ant.* 22, *O.T.* 699.

**591** πῶς ταῦτ' ἐπαινέσαιμ' ἄν: potential ('how *can* I?' rather than 'how could I?' since the notion is by no means remote).

**593** 'Well, it will be to your shame that you will say so, if you *do* (καί) in fact (περ) say it.' Hartung's γ' is preferable to the MSS' δ', not because one cannot have δέ in answer to a rhetorical question, but because the δέ-clause should contain, not a comment, but a *new point*: cf. Eur. *El.* 377 ἀλλ' εἰς ὅπλ' ἔλθω; τίς δὲ πρὸς λόγχην βλέπων κτλ.

**594** ἐχθροῖς: as Agamemnon's hereditary ἐχθρός, Aegisthus should have been ἐχθρός to Clytaemnestra also, she being Agamemnon's φίλος (by marriage).

**595** 'But no! We are not even allowed to admonish you!' For the ellipse cf. 223n.

οὐ...οὐδέ ordinary reinforcing negatives, not cancelling out. ἔξεστι: cf. 2n.

**596ff** 'who (i.e. because you – ἤ used in an explanatory sense like ἥτις at 587) give voice to every kind of utterance (to the effect that) we (sc. Electra and Orestes) slander our mother!'

πᾶσαν: cf. 615 πᾶν ἔργον.

5                                                                                          KSE

κακοστομεῖν is found only here.

οὐκ ἔλασσον 'more', by litotes.

νέμω = νομίζω: cf. 150.

**599f** ἔκ τε σοῦ... τοῦ τε συννόμου = ἐκ σοῦ τε τοῦ τε συννόμου. The first τε hás been misplaced by a slight hyperbaton. ἐκ = ὑπό. συννόμου = 'partner, associate' (a verse usage), i.e. Aegisthus.

**601** 'And that other one (of your children).'

ἔξω 'abroad'.

**602** We have not actually seen much evidence that Orestes was suffering great hardship.

**603f** 'of fostering whom as a visitant to take vengeance upon your head (σοι – dative of disadvantage) you have often indeed accused me.'

μιάστορα: a μιάστωρ is someone connected with μίασμα (blood-guiltiness), whether as the person polluted with it, or the person who exacts vengeance for it (as here).

**605ff** 'As far as *that* is concerned, advertise me to all the world, whether you like (to advertise me) as base, or loose-mouthed, or full of shamelessness.' γε emphasises τοῦδε.

οὕνεκα = ἕνεκα, as often in verse.

κήρυσσε: the herald (like the less ancient town-crier) was a familiar feature of ancient Greek life, and the official channel by which public or semi-public information could be disseminated.

**608f** 'For, if I find it in my nature to be acquainted with such deeds, I am hardly bringing disgrace upon *your* nature' (i.e. I am no worse than the daughter you deserve).

πέφυκα... φύσιν: an obvious pun.

σχεδόν τι: understatement (litotes).

**610f** μένος πνέουσαν 'breathing fury'.

εἰ δὲ σὺν δίκη κτλ. 'but whether she is associated with Justice, I no longer see any consideration on her part'. The reference is clearly to Clytaemnestra, who, during the latter part of Electra's speech (delivered with passionate bitterness, but also with complete self-assurance), has completely lost her temper. This could be easily enough conveyed, no doubt, by the actor impersonating Clytaemnestra, through his gestures, wearing a mask though he was.

For a lucid demonstration that Clytaemnestra is referred to (and not, as Jebb and others have supposed, Electra) cf. D. B. Gregor, *C.R.* 64 (1950) 87–8.

σύν δίκη κτλ. refers, sarcastically, to Clytaemnestra's claim to be on the side of Δίκη (528).

**612** 'And what sort of consideration do *I* need (to have) towards this one!' φροντίδος picks up the Chorus's φροντίδ', at 611, thus showing that Clytaemnestra had understood the Chorus's remark to apply to herself.

**613** ἥτις circumstantial: 'why should I consider her when she etc.', cf. 347.

τοιαῦτα: adv. accus.

**614** 'and that too a grown woman as she is!' If Orestes was twenty (cf. 14n.), Electra who nursed him as a young child (1143f.), and gave him to the Paedagogus πατρὸς ἐκ φόνων (11), would now scarcely be less than thirty.

ἆρα introduces an earnest question, and here the context shows it to be equivalent to ἆρ' οὐ – '*don't* you think?'

**615** χωρεῖν 'would proceed' (Jebb: 'would go forward'): cf. Xen. *Anab.* 3. 1. 18 ἆρ' οὐκ ἂν ἐπὶ πᾶν ἔλθοι... Clytaemnestra may have lost her temper, but she has weighed Electra up shrewdly. As regards her daughter, she can have no doubt where she herself stands.

**616** τῶνδε 'this conduct of mine'.

**617** ὁθούνεκα = ὅτι.

**618** 'I practise conduct which is unseasonable to me, not becoming to me' (i.e. to my nature).

**619** 'But (I cannot help myself) for': cf. 223n.

ἡ... ἐκ σοῦ δυσμένεια 'hostility on your side'.

**620** ἐξαναγκάζει... βίᾳ 'forces me of grim necessity': cf. 221, 256, 307.

**621** 'Evil deeds are the lessons taught by evil deeds.' For ἐκ- cf. 276n. Could any words be a better warning than these coming from Electra's own lips that the path of vengefulness upon which she is engaged is no triumphal progress, but one leading to moral disaster?

**622** θρέμμ' ἀναιδές 'shameless brat'.

ἦ like ἆρα at 614, but this time presupposing a negative (= *num*, not *nonne*).

**623** ποεῖ = ἀναγκάζει.

**624** '*You*, you must know, speak them (sc. the things I say).'

νιν: cf. 435n.

**625** εὑρίσκεται 'find for themselves'.

**626f** Clytaemnestra, faced with the demonstration that she herself. and no other is the source of her daughter's ingrained animosity and her intransigent behaviour, can argue no further but merely threaten Electra. Electra has won the *agon*.

μά: the particle used in negative oaths.

δέσποιναν Ἄρτεμιν: a woman's oath, since Artemis was primarily a woman's goddess.

θράσους τοῦδ' οὐκ ἀλύξεις 'you will not escape (punishment) in respect of this brazenness'. ἀλύσκω (strictly = 'avoid') is sometimes used absolutely. I take θράσους τοῦδ' as genitive of relation, thus allowing it to be classified with the genitive at *Ant.* 488f. οὐκ ἀλύξετον | μόρου κακίστου (though that effectively means 'they (two) will not escape *from* the vilest of deaths'). Jebb, taking θράσους as 'causative' genitive, finds himself in difficulties with the *Antigone* parallel. For the genitive of relation cf. 372n.

εὖτ' ἄν = ὅταν.

**628** Seeing her advantage (that she is cool while her adversary is flustered), Electra presses it home relentlessly. 'You see? You are carried away in anger although you gave me permission to say whatever I liked [χρήζοιμι = optative in a historic sequence, reporting ἄν + the subjunctive of the direct speech: Clytaemnestra is imagined to have said at 556 'I give you permission to say ἃ ἂν χρήζῃς'], and you don't know how to *listen*.'

**630f** 'Will you not then let me even accomplish my sacrifice in an atmosphere of fair-omened (absence of) outcry?'

οὐδ' goes with θῦσαι in a long hyperbaton: cf. 1304n.

εὐφήμου βοῆς put boldly for εὐφημίας βοῆς (= fair-omenedness in regard to clamour, i.e. silence).

**632** κελεύω 'please do so!', '*je vous en prie!*', sarcastic politeness.

**633** οὐκ ἄν...λέξαιμ' κτλ. 'you won't find me saying any more'. Another nuance of the optative + ἄν, cf. 245n.

### 634–659

Once more the action moves on, gently but dynamically. Clytaemnestra moves slightly away from Electra and the Chorus to the statue and altar of Apollo which stand (in the forefront of the stage?) in front of the palace. There she bids the slave deliver the offerings, and makes her prayer. The ancient prayer was not essentially (as in the Christian religion) a form of communion with a deity; it was a request for a practical return for services rendered (i.e. the present sacrifice and previous ones). Since the prayer was thus a kind of bargain with the deity and nothing more, it could contain (according to popular belief) wicked and immoral, as well as innocent, proposals. The deity was supposed to tolerate such propositions: cf. Persius (*Sat.* 2. 3ff.). When a person prayed for something improper, he prayed silently or murmured *sotto voce*, so that the public might not hear him and become aware of his evil intent. For this reason, other people's 'silent prayers' were regarded with suspicion by the ancients: cf. Lucan 5. 105f.

**634** ἔπαιρε '*raise*, as with a gesture of solemn oblation' (Jebb).
ἡ παροῦσά μοι: i.e. her maid-servant.

**635f** πάγκαρπ': the sacrifice is not a burnt offering, but consists of a variety of seasonable fruits.
ἄνακτι 'lord', i.e. Apollo.
λυτηρίους goes with δειμάτων in hyperbaton; 'giving release from the fears'.

**636** εὐχὰς ἀνάσχω 'may offer up a prayer': cf. Eur. *El.* 592 ἄνεχε χέρας, ἄνεχε λόγον.

**637** 'Please, will you now hear me': the polite respectful use of ἄν + optative. Apollo is Προστατήριος as standing in front of the house and guarding it: cf. Photius *Lex.* 141.

**638** κεκρυμμένην βάξιν 'not for all the world to hear', 'secretive' (first, because the prayer is directed away from Electra, so that she cannot hear it distinctly; secondly, because some parts of it are not expressed in words, but merely alluded to).

ἐν φίλοις 'among friends', the preposition being used metaphorically.

**639** μῦθος: by *variatio* for βάξις (638).

ἀναπτύξαι 'unfold' (like a writing-tablet or papyrus-roll).

**640** πρὸς φῶς: with ἀναπτύξαι, the sense over-running the verse by the process known as *enjambement*.

**641** μή = ἵνα μή: cf. 1238.

**642** ματαίαν not 'idle' but (by litotes) '*bad*', 'malicious' (cf. Aesch. *Pers.* 217 εἴ τι φλαῦρον εἶδες, αἰτοῦ τῶνδ' ἀποτροπὴν τελεῖν). Notice the repetition (vain) of βάξιν after βάξιν 638: cf. 487n.

**643** 'Listen to me in this sense. For it is in this sense that I for my part (lit. 'I *also*') shall communicate (my prayer).'

ὧδε...τῇδε: i.e. *sotto voce*. But in the passage which Jebb cites as parallel (*Trach.* 553f. ἣ δ' ἔχω, φίλαι, | λυτήριον λώφημα, τῇδ' ὑμῖν φράσω) the adverbs refer to the content rather than the manner of the following explanation.

κἀγώ: the redundant καί indicates that the two actions involved are complementary to each other – 'as I *explain*, so shall you *listen*' – by an idiom common in Greek, but not used in English.

**644** γάρ: redundant. Cf. 681.

**645** δισσῶν ὀνείρων: probably neuter, cf. Eur. *H.F.* 518 ὄνειρα. δισσός, besides its more obvious meanings, can mean 'ambiguous', 'ambivalent'. So here: Clytaemnestra's dream might mean that a son of Aegisthus would rule over Mycenae (since Aegisthus *now held* the sceptre from which the branch over-shadowed Mycenae, 420f.); or it might mean that Orestes, the descendant of the rightful owner of the sceptre, would do so.

Λύκει' ἄναξ: probably 'god of light'; but the derivation of the ancient title of Λύκειος is not really known: cf. Jebb's note to line 6 of this play.

**646f** 'If their appearance bodes good (lit. 'if they have appeared as good'), bring them to pass; if evil, cast them (from me) backwards upon (the heads of) my enemies.' If of evil portent, the dream is a product of the hostile wishes of Clytaemnestra's enemies, which, by a kind of evil-eye magic, may affect her. But let the god (she prays) interfere (with overriding magic) to throw its effect 'back upon' them.

**648f**  μή με: μή with ἐφῇς, με with ἐκβαλεῖν, both phrases in 'long' hyperbaton.

δόλοισι (with ἐκβαλεῖν): her intuition squares with the truth of events. Cf. 37.

**650ff**  'but grant that I, living always as I am now in an unharmed way of life, shall (rule) the house of the Atridae and wield this sceptre, in close association (enjoying fair prosperity!) both with the friends I associate with now and with all those children from whose side there is no hostility attaching to me, or sore vexation'. (Understand a word such as δός (from ἐφῇς in 649), by zeugma, to govern ἀμφέπειν.)

**650**  ἀβλαβεῖ: such compounds can be either active or passive. Here obviously passive: cf. *Trach.* 168 ζῆν ἀλυπήτῳ βίῳ.

**653**  εὐημεροῦσαν goes adverbially with ξυνοῦσαν.

τέκνων ὅσων stands for τοσούτοις (τῶν) τέκνων ὅσων. τοσούτοις is omitted, since it can be understood from ὅσων.

**654**  μή not οὐ, because the usage is classificatory.

**656**  πᾶσιν: she speaks as if she were the representative of a solid phalanx of persons who owe loyalty to herself and hostility to her enemies. So she reassures herself, feeling as she does guilty, frightened, and craving for friends.

ὥσπερ ἐξαιτούμεθα 'as we ask for them', 'in the sense in which we ask for them'. The prayer being a kind of magical formula or contract, it is necessary that its terms should be understood *as specified*.

**657f**  'All the rest (of my prayers) I expect you, being a god, to know full well, even though I keep silent about them.' In this truly *silent* part of her prayer she plainly prays for the death of her son Orestes. That, she thinks, would end her troubles and her fears (cf. 774ff.).

Clytaemnestra's prayer is a unique document from classical antiquity, illustrating some of the basic ideas and attitudes of common religious belief. It is also of the greatest dramatic significance. Sinister, ignoble, furtive, even pathetic (because of the woman's manifest obsession with fear of the vengeance coming from Orestes), it draws attention to one strong, natural, human characteristic in her otherwise weak or perverted character – her need for children and the love of children. If we think that her concern for wealth, position, comfort is odious, let us remember that Orestes too prayed for wealth (72), and that the Greeks on the whole had a high regard for material prosperity.

### 660–679

As the women stand separated – Clytaemnestra before the statue of Apollo, Electra to one side of the stage beside the Chorus, a new person (apparently!) enters from the wings: the Paedagogus pretending to be a messenger from Phocis. He has evidently judged this moment to be the καιρός alluded to at 39.

**660** ξέναι γυναῖκες 'dear ladies'. Since one had obligations towards the ξένος, ξέναι implies respect and politeness. Compare the similarly courteous exchanges at *O.T.* 924f.

ἄν εἰδείην 'can I learn?', cf. 591n.

σαφῶς 'surely', 'correctly' (as often).

**661** τυράννου 'sovereign': in the Heroic world depicted by the tragic poets the word most frequently has its old, non-depreciatory sense: cf. Aesch. *Cho.* 479 τρόποισιν οὐ τυρρανικοῖς ( = 'not royally').

**663f** 'Can it be that, if I also guess this lady to be his wife, I am not wide of the mark? For she looks like a royal personage to behold.'

ἐπεικάζων neatly picks up the ἤκασας of 663 and shows the 'messenger' to be a person of courtly address.

κυρῶ = τυγχάνω (sc. σκοποῦ). Notice that the words of 663–4 are interlaced in hyperbaton.

**665** 'Most assuredly. Here you find her standing before you.'

πάρα = πάρεστι.

Notice that the Chorus is perfectly deferential to Clytaemnestra in public. She is after all the 'queen', and behaves like it, as 664 shows.

**666** 'Greetings, my lady.'

σοὶ φέρων ἤκω κτλ. = ἤκω παρὰ φίλου ἀνδρὸς φέρων λόγους ἡδεῖς σοὶ Αἰγίσθῳ θ' ὁμοῦ. Again, interlaced hyperbaton. With the Paedagogus' words compare those of Aeschylus' Orestes (*Cho.* 658–9) ἄγγελλε τοῖσι κυρίοισι δωμάτων, | πρὸς οὕσπερ ἤκω καὶ φέρω καινοὺς λόγους.

**668** 'I accept the word.' Clytaemnestra means that she will not refuse to accept the good fortune presaged by the Messenger's words, she will not (as we say) look a gift-horse in the mouth.

ἐδεξάμην: 'instantaneous' aorist: cf. 388n.

**669** τίς for ὅστις – the direct interrogative is sometimes used instead of the indirect in dependent questions: cf. 679, 1442, *Trach.* 430 (φράσον) τίς ποτ' ἐστὶν ὁ ξένος.

**670** For Phanoteus cf. 44n. In Aeschylus (*Cho.* 679) the news of Orestes' supposed death is brought as from *Strophius*.

πορσύνων 'conveying (lit. 'forwarding') a matter of mighty significance'.

**671f** φίλου...προσφιλεῖς: the pun must be preserved – 'For being from the house of a well-liked man, you will, I know well, speak likeable news.'

**673** 'Orestes is dead! I tell you (the matter), condensing it in short.'

**674** The short summary announcement of Orestes' death is utterly shattering to Electra, sweeping away as it does in a moment all that she loved, and all that her hopes and aspirations depended upon.

**675** By contrast with Electra, Clytaemnestra is *excited* (as the repeated τί φής; shows) at the news. She can scarcely believe it; it is too good to be true.

**678** σὺ μὲν κτλ. 'You attend to your own affairs!' i.e. I am not interested in how the news affects you, Electra.

**679** τῷ = τίνι, for ᾧτινι, cf. 669n.

διόλλυται: she wants to see the event *as it occurred*. So she uses the vivid historic present.

### 680–763

The Messenger's speech is one of the most splendid and effective in Sophocles. We see, as it were before our eyes, the glitter and pageantry of a meeting for the Games at Delphi. We sense the varying emotions of the multitude of spectators and share the excitement of the drivers in the chariot race; we visualise and are involved with their triumphs as well as their moments of danger and their hair-breadth escapes. Above all, we identify with the young and brilliant hero of the occasion, Orestes, and we shudder with horror at his sudden fall from glory, and at the detailed description of the accident which fatally mangles his body. Sophocles' description has a fore-runner in Homer's description of the chariot-race in the Funeral Games for Patroclus (*Il.* 23. 271ff.), from which Sophocles has borrowed freely for this composition. Something of the same kind of excitement and tragic *feeling* has also gone into the description of the horse-race in Tolstoy's novel *Anna Karenina* (vol. 1 189ff. in the Everyman edition).

What is the purpose of this long narrative coming at this particular point in the *Electra*? Is it simply that Sophocles has seized an opportunity to reveal his power of sustaining a highly ornate narrative, a sort of Greek literary baroque?

The excitement and success of the great narrative would be enough to justify its central position here in the play. But in fact it is far from being told for itself alone and fits in most beautifully with the plot of the play and with its dramatic development. The Paedagogus may have been told by Orestes to add ὄγκος (bulk, embroidery, ornamentation) to the simple announcement that 'Orestes is dead', cf. 47n. This narrative shows him doing it brilliantly. The detailed persuasive account was intended to involve Clytaemnestra so deeply in an impression of the death of Orestes, that she will be convinced of its reality, and so thrown off her guard when the living Orestes comes to attack her. So far the strategy of Orestes and the Paedagogus succeeds splendidly. But there is another effect of the narrative, which they could not have foreseen and is of the utmost dramatic importance: that is, its emotional effect upon the two women who stand upon the stage listening to it. Curiously, critics and interpreters, while they have seen the importance of the narrative to Electra's emotional state, have altogether failed to appreciate its relevance to Clytaemnestra's. They have even supposed that it was devised by Sophocles specifically for the effect it would produce on Electra. And it is true that its effect upon her is profound, and that that effect is of the highest significance. But the effect upon Clytaemnestra is even more important.

Here is a depraved woman who has had the villainy to murder her husband, and to pray for the death of her own son. She has welcomed joyfully the simple report that he is dead (675), and now listens while the details of that fatal occurrence (as she takes it to be) are borne in upon her. We are to remember that she has not seen Orestes for many

years, that even as a child he was 'closer' (cf. 1145f.) to Electra than
to his mother and that she has been accustomed to regard him as
inexorably threatening her life (775ff.). All these factors have made it
possible for her to regard him as an ἐχθρός. Now suddenly she is
presented with a picture of Orestes whom she only remembers as a
little boy, now grown to manhood, now distinguishing himself before
a multitude of Greeks, now behaving as a son *of whom she might be
proud*. Then, when her interest and her admiration are at last engaged,
in spite of herself, this new-found emotion is again dashed to the
ground, as she hears of the horrible accident, and the mangling of her
son's limbs in the wreck of his chariot and beneath the hooves of his
horses. Only such an account as Sophocles has put into the Paedagogus' mouth could have moved and wrung the mother's heart to
that terrible *cri de cœur*, that amazing *peripeteia* of emotion, which
766ff. and 770 represent. It was with Clytaemnestra in mind that the
great narrative was above all devised.

**680  κἀπεμπόμην...καί:** καί...καί has a co-ordinating (which here
is equivalent to a subordinating) effect: 'as I was sent on my way for
this, so I shall describe it to you'. Notice the durative effect of the
imperfect ἐπεμπόμην.

**681f**  'Having come to Greece's famous show-piece of a contest, to
join in the Delphic games...' The typical 'messenger's speech' is
ornamental and grandiloquent (in its search for descriptive effect),
often using constructions which are involved and intricate. So here.

**683  ἀνδρός:** the herald or umpire.
    ὀρθίων 'shrill'.

**684  δρόμον προκηρύξαντος:** notice the repetition (ornamental)
of κηρυγμάτων...κηρύξαντος.
    οὗ πρώτη κρίσις 'the deciding of which comes first', i.e. which is
held first. That the foot-race was the first contest is known only from
this passage.

**685  εἰσῆλθε:** a technical term for taking one's place as a contestant,
cf. Dem. 18. 319.
    λαμπρός 'glowing' or 'eager' (with health).
    πᾶσι κτλ. 'an object of wondering admiration to all those present'.
So the process of glamourising her son to Clytaemnestra begins.

**686** 'Equalling his finishing with his starting-off.' I have adopted Musgrave's excellent solution of the obviously corrupt MS reading, and I take it to mean that, as Orestes started off first of the field, so he ended up first: he was right from the start a clear winner; there was never any doubt at any part of the race but that he would come in first.

τἀφέσει by crasis for τῇ ἀφέσει ('start'). τῆς ἀφέσεως is found corrupted elsewhere to τῆς φύσεως (see Jebb's note).

**687** ἐξῆλθε 'finished'. There is a slight, decorative, hyperbaton in this line.

**689** οὐκ οἶδα 'I have never heard of'.
κράτη 'victories', 'triumphs', cf. 476.

**690f** Line 691 stands as the wreck of a meaning that once was, whether of a line of Sophocles or of a scholiast's explanation or explanations, written in the margin and then jumbled together to form the gibberish that now remains. If an original Sophoclean line underlies it, that line is probably (barring some remarkable papyrus discovery) no longer recoverable. In 692 I have adopted Tournier's ἄθλων, which allows 691 to be ignored and 692 to make continuous sense with 690. It is impossible to say whether ἄθλων is genitive of ἄθλος or ἄθλον, since the latter (properly = *prize*) is also used, in verse, for 'contest'.

εἰσεκήρυξαν: the umpires heralded 'in' the contests as the contestants entered 'into' them.

**692ff** 'he received the felicitations (of the assembled people) for winning all the prizes, being proclaimed as a man of Argos, one Orestes by name, son of Agamemnon, him who assembled the glorious Greek army in days gone by'.

ἐνεγκών: causative participle. φέρω can mean 'win' in the active as well as the middle voice (cf. 476n.).

At Greek games a proclamation was made after each contest, giving the names of the winner, his father's name, and his nationality (in this case 'Argive', because Mycenae was in the territory of Argos). Cf. Eur. *H.F.* 960, etc.

**694f** Notice again the hyperbaton in a grandiloquent, arresting title: cf. 1n.

**696f** 'And so much for those happenings. But when some god or other undertakes to undo a man, then not even a strong man can possibly escape.'

βλάπτῃ: the oldest meaning is 'to hinder', 'impede', cf. *Il.* 6. 39. I have tried to bring out the *durative* force of the present.

ἄν...ἄν: the repetition perhaps emphasises the impossibility.

ἰσχύων: τις omitted (as rarely).

**698** ἄλλης ἡμέρας: not 'on *the next* day' (which would require the article, but 'on another day'.

ἱππικῶν: as Jebb says, probably neuter, cf. Xen. *Hell.* 7. 4. 29 τὰ δρομικά. Translate 'of the chariot-event' (plural for singular).

**701ff** There are ten competitors, of different nationalities, in the chariot-race. They are (according to the number of each one's *entry*) as follows:

1. A man from Achaea, 2. a Spartan, 3. a Libyan, 4. a second Libyan, 5. Orestes, the Argive, 6. an Aetolian, 7. a man from Magnesia, 8. an Aenianian, 9. an Athenian, 10. a Boeotian. All are of course Greeks, since only Greeks could compete at any of the Greek games. It is interesting to see which were the districts which Sophocles regarded as likely to send teams of fine horses to the Pythian games. Two are Peloponnesians, two from the Greek colonies in North Africa, and five from northern Greece: Orestes is anomalous since, although he comes from Argos, his horses are of northern breed.

**701** Ἀχαιός: since the whole list looks (from Sophocles' standpoint) rather 'modern' (witness the importance of the African colonies), probably Sophocles had in mind the contemporary region of Achaea on the southern shore of the Corinthian Gulf, rather than the historic 'Achaea' (= Phthiotis, in South Thessaly).

**702** Λίβυες: these could be from any of the Greek cities of Cyrenaica, of which the principal city was Cyrene: cf. 727n.

ζυγωτῶν ἀρμάτων ἐπιστάται 'masters of yoked chariots': ζυγωτῶν ornamental: cf. 49n.

**703f** ἐν τούτοισι: i.e. among the ten: a redundant phrase.

Θεσσαλὰς...ἵππους: Thessaly was famous for its horses. It has wide plains, favourable for horse-rearing. Jebb may be right in saying that mares were most often used for chariot-racing; but (as he also notices) horses are also prominent both in the Games in *Il.* 23 and in this passage. The picture of Orestes possessing Thessalian (doubtless expensive!) mares is hardly that of a penurious exile. Cf. 159.

**705** '(Was a competitor) with chestnut mares'.

ξανθαῖσι πώλοις: a 'sociative' dative, by which that object *along with* or *together with* which an action is done is expressed as if it had been the instrument *by* which (the true instrumental dative) it is done, cf. *Od.* 24. 463 ἀνήϊξαν μεγάλῳ ἀλαλητῷ and Gow's note on Theocr. 15. 135. This dative is less frequent than the instrumental dative and is generally confined to cases of *vigorous* action (e.g. springing up in assembly, marching with an army, and the like).

ξανθαῖσι: more descriptive detail; cf. λεύκιππος at 706. πῶλος is used throughout this narrative as a synonym for ἵππος.

Μάγνης = of Magnesia in Thessaly.

**706** γένος as a limiting accusative with a word of local significance indicates that a person *originates* from such-and-such a place, cf. *Phil.* 239f. ἐγὼ γένος μέν εἰμι τῆς περιρρύτου | Σκύρου, and Gow's note in *C.R.* n.s. 9 (1959) 5. The Αἰνιᾶνες were a tribe of southern Thessaly, to the south-west of Homeric Achaea.

**707** θεοδμήτων: cf. Eur. *I.T.* 1449, *Hipp.* 974. No details of the 'building' are recorded (apart from the well-known legends that Poseidon created a well upon the Acropolis, and Athena an olive tree). Notice the scansion ὁδμ. Although a mute followed by a liquid usually has the value of one consonant only, a *middle* mute (β, γ, δ) followed by μ or ν counts as two consonants and therefore lengthens a preceding short syllable; the same is normally true of β, γ, δ followed by λ.

**708** ἐκπληρῶν 'manning'.

**709** I have preferred the text printed as giving the most straight-forward sense available. I would translate as follows: 'Having taken up position (in the places) where the appointed umpires, drawing lots for them, stationed their chariots...' Just as sometimes an aorist participle replaces a finite verb plus a connective (e.g. 'having spoken, he left' for 'he spoke and left'), so here I think Sophocles has reversed the process, putting κλήρους ἔπηλαν καί for κλήρους πήλαντες, by a sense-construction.

ὅθ': ὅθι ('where') occurs elsewhere in tragedy only in lyrical passages. Nor is the *iota* even there ever elided. Jebb therefore thinks that δθ' here 'can hardly be right'. But Homer has δθ' (cf. *Il.* 2. 572, and – highly significant – *Od.* 4. 426 δθ' ἕστασαν ἐν ψαμάθοισιν), and, in a passage such as our present one (epic and Homeric in atmosphere) the homericism would hardly appear out of place.

The lots were placed in some hollow container, shaken up (πάλλω), and drawn out at random (cf. *Il.* 23. 352f.). This proceeding was of vital importance (particularly in a race with chariots, which had to wheel round a marking-post (στήλη) at each end of the course), because the competitor who drew out the first lot had the advantage of driving in the inmost lane, the second in the next farthest out, and so on. In *Iliad* 23 the most prominent person in the narrative, Antilochus, wins the first lot and so the inmost lane. He is advised by his father, Nestor, to stay in it, not to go wandering all over the course, to dog the leader and to hug the marking-post (319ff.). In our narrative we are not told at the beginning that Orestes drew the first lot; but 720–2 implies that he did, and his whole strategy is intelligible only on that assumption.

**711f** ὑπαί (for ὑπό) with the genitive, of the conditions or circumstances under which a thing is done: 'at the brazen trumpet's blast'.

οἳ δ' ἅμα κτλ.: cf. *Il.* 23. 363f. πέπληγόν θ' ἱμᾶσιν (reins), ὁμόκλησάν τ' ἐπέεσσιν | ἐσσυμένως. Notice that ὁμοκλεῖν is used *only here* in tragedy – another instance of epic colouring.

**713** ἐν... ἐμεστώθη for ἐνεμεστώθη, by tmesis, cf. *Ant.* 420 ἐν δ' ἐμεστώθη.

δρόμος here = the race-*track*.

**714** κροτητῶν 'rattling' (lit. 'rattled'): cf. *Il.* 15. 453, Soph. fr. 241 κροτητὰ πηκτίδων μέλη.

**715f** Cf. *Il.* 23. 365f. ὑπὸ δὲ στέρνοισι κονίη | ἵστατ' ἀειρομένη κτλ.

φορεῖθ' and φείδοντο for ἐφορεῖθ' and ἐφείδοντο – the syllabic augment is often omitted in the narratives of tragedy, cf. Jebb's note on *O.T.* 1249.

**716ff** 'in order that a man (τις) among them might outstrip (ὑπερβάλοι) the naves and steeds' snortings (of the others). For, in a

common mass, the horses frothed about the drivers' backs and their
moving wheels, the horses' breaths fell upon their backs.'

**χνόας...φρυάγμαθ':** outstanding features of the chariots and the
horses that draw them put for those horses and the chariots themselves; at the same time these terms draw attention to vivid details in
the race.

**718f** Cf. *Il.* 23. 380f. πνοιῇ δ' Εὐμήλοιο μετάφρενον εὐρέε τ' ὤμω |
θέρμετ' (sc. Diomede).

**τροχῶν βάσεις:** lit. 'goings of the wheels': abstract for concrete.

**ἤφριζον:** the subject ἵπποι is understood from the following
ἱππικαί, cf. 209.

**720f** 'And *he* (= Orestes) keeping just under (i.e. just *off*) the very
edge of the pillar ever grazed his wheel upon it, and letting his right-
hand trace-horse have his head reined in the horse (i.e. the left-hand
trace-horse) that pressed towards it.'

In the four-horse racing-chariot, the two middle horses were yoked,
the two outer were controlled only by traces (σειραί), so that the driver
could the more easily control the chariot when making his turn at the
turning-post (στήλη, καμπτήρ or νύσσα). Here Orestes does just what
Antilochus is advised to do by Nestor in *Il.* 23: enjoying the advantage
of the inmost lane he makes sure of keeping this advantage where it
was most felt, that is, at the sharp turn around the turning-post, by
controlling his left-hand trace-horse so that it causes the inner wheel
just to graze the post, while letting the right-hand trace-horse have
its head, so as to pull the whole chariot round smartly (cf. *Il.* 23. 334ff.
τῷ (sc. the turning-post) σὺ μάλ' ἐγχρίμψας ἐλάαν σχεδὸν ἅρμα καὶ
ἵππους... ἀτὰρ τὸν δεξιὸν ἵππον | κένσαι ὁμοκλήσας, εἶξαί τέ οἱ ἡνία
χερσίν. | ἐν νύσσῃ δέ τοι ἵππος ἀριστερὸς ἐγχριμφθήτω, | ὡς ἄν τοι
πλήμνη γε δοάσσεται ἄκρον ἱκέσθαι | κύκλου ποιητοῖο. But whereas
Antilochus had only one turn to execute, Orestes had at least twelve
(since there were twelve courses to be completed: cf. Pind. *Ol.* 2. 50;
*Pyth.* 5. 33). Hence Sophocles makes him execute the same manoeuvre
'ever' (i.e. at each of the turns). Lines 720–2 are most injudiciously
transposed in Pearson's Oxford Text so as to come after line 740.
They are not needed there, but they *are* needed here, in order that
we may visualise, at this relatively early stage of the race, how
Orestes is supposed to have been driving, and, above all, grasp the

vital fact (which we have not been told already) that he was in *the inmost lane* (as we do know of Antilochus: *Il.* 23. 353f. πάλλ' Ἀχιλεύς, ἐκ δὲ κλῆρος θόρε Νεστορίδαο | Ἀντιλόχου· μετὰ τὸν δ' ἔλαχε κρείων Εὔμηλος – so Antilochus had the place of choice).

ὑπ' αὐτήν: cf. *Il.* 13. 615 ἄκρον ὑπὸ λόφον αὐτόν.

ἐσχάτην: this is usually taken to mean 'the pillar *at the end of* the course' (so Jebb). But that is to labour the obvious, and I would prefer to interpret 'the pillar at its extremity', '*the edge of* the pillar' (like *summus mons*, and ἐσχάτην reinforcing αὐτήν). For this use of ἔσχατος cf. 900f. ἐσχάτης πυρᾶς n. and 744 στήλην ἄκραν.

ἔχων: absolute, cf. *Il.* 23. 325 ἀλλ' ἔχει ἀσχαλέως καὶ τὸν προύχοντα δοκεύει.

**721f** σύριγγα ( = lit. the opening in the nave) for the nave itself, by metonymy: cf. 716n.

δεξιὸν...σειραῖον...τὸν προσκείμενον: notice the masculines, whereas Orestes' horses were mares (cf. 705, 734 ὑστέρας, 737 θοαῖς). Greek is curiously inexact about genders in certain instances (cf. 770n.), and it so happens that trace-horses are normally treated as masculine.

**723** ὀρθοί...ἔστασαν: i.e. 'kept upright', suffered no disaster.

**724** ἄστομοι '(being) hard-mouthed': i.e. insensitive to the bit, and therefore not properly under the control of their driver.

**725ff** 'bore (him away) out of control, and wheeling round, as they were completing their sixth circuit and already (beginning upon) their seventh, collided head-on with the chariot of the Barcaean'. We notice again in this description how historic presents are especially used to denote critical events. Cf. 35n. For horses 'bolting' cf. Eur. *Hipp.* 1223f. αἱ δ' ἐνδακοῦσαι στόμια πυριγενῆ γνάθοις | βίᾳ φέρουσιν.

**726** The idea of 'beginning upon' (the seventh course) is supplied from τελοῦντες, by zeugma.

**727** Lit. 'struck their foreheads together with'.

Βαρκαίοις: we cannot be sure that the man really came from Barca, since the adjective could be used (by a kind of metonymy) for 'Cyrenaean'.

**728ff** 'And thereupon one smashed and knocked into another, as a result of one original mishap, and the whole plain of Crisa was filled with the broken remnants of chariot-teams.'

κἀνέπιπτε: supply ἄλλῳ from ἄλλον, by zeugma.

ναυαγίων: cf. 335n.

The words of 730 are scrambled in hyperbaton.

**731ff** 'But the man from Athens, deft driver that he was, taking in the situation, wrested (his team) sideways (παρ-) to the outside and reined in, thus by-passing the equestrian torrent that milled about in the centre.' As the pile-up occupied the *middle* of the race-track there were only two ways left round it. One was on the outermost lane, into which the Athenian, by braking his chariot, managed to sidetrack his horses. The other was by the innermost lane, which Orestes occupied already, so that he also missed the pile-up.

οὑξ ᾿Αθηνῶν δεινὸς ἡνιοστρόφος = ὁ ἐξ ᾿Αθηνῶν ἀνὴρ δεινὸς ἡνιοστρόφος ὤν.

κἀνοκωχεύει: he had to *hold his horses back* somewhat as he switched to the outer lane. Cf. Hdt. 6. 116 ἀνακωχεύσαντες τὰς νέας ('resting' their ships, ceasing to press them).

παρείς: lit. 'having let slip by him'.

**734f** ἔσχατος is 'last' *of the row of chariots* (seen horizontally), i.e. *inmost*. Hence the contrast ἔσχατος μὲν (an advantage)... ὑστέρας δέ (a disadvantage). At the same time the two phrases explain each other: Orestes was 'lying back' in the field (lit. 'having his mares later'), because, having the advantage of the inner lane, he knew that he had less far to go. Of course, 'later' need not (and cannot) imply that his mares were *much* behind the others; otherwise, one of the leaders would have cut in upon him. There is no reason to think that Orestes' mares were slower to *begin with* than the other horses (as were Antilochus' horses in *Il.* 23, cf. 310, 322, 572), since (*a*) it is forcing ὑστέρας to make it mean 'slower' (as some have taken it), (*b*) they are said at 703 to have been 'Thessalian mares', which (without any further qualification) would lead one to suppose that they were as good as any in the field. Also at 737 they are called θοαί. Editors have missed the point (it seems to me) of these lines by almost universally making ἔσχατος = 'last' (*of the field*) (but not so Passow and Ellendt, cf. *Lexicon Sophocleum* under ἔσχατος). So Jebb, omitting (with some MSS) δέ after ὑστέρας: 'ὑστέρας ἔχων explains *why* he was ἔσχατος:

he was purposely keeping his horses behind.' But why should he keep them behind? Jebb does not tell us. In *Anna Karenina* (p. 196) Vronsky's trainer advises: 'Get ahead at first if you can, but don't get discouraged till the last moment, if you happen to be behind.' Other versions make ὑστέρας tautologous after ἔσχατος.

τῷ τέλει πίστιν φέρων: these words are usually translated 'trusting in the finish' (i.e. he relied (for success) upon a *spurt at the end*), and this is supported by *Il.* 23. 322f. ὃς δέ κε...αἰεὶ τέρμ' ὁρόων στρέφει ἐγγύθεν κτλ. But 'trusting in the finish' (despite the *Iliad* parallel) seems a somewhat naïve expression, and the words would suit Sophocles' context better, I think, if they meant 'trusting in his *rank*' (i.e. relying upon his position in the inner lane to bring him to the front at the end). τέλος is sometimes used as (apparently) = 'rank', but always in a military or naval context, cf. *Il.* 10. 470 and Aesch. *Pers.* 47 (Paley translates 'in ranks of two or three poles abreast', but Broadhead *ad loc.* denies that τέλος can mean 'rank'). I feel no conviction either way.

**736ff** Orestes now, seeing that only the Athenian is left to contest the race with him, puts on a spurt so as to overtake him. This was the easier, of course, because the Athenian had had to 'brake' at the pile-up.

ὅπως = ἐπεί or ἐπειδή, cf. 749.

ἐλλελειμμένον 'left in' (the race).

**737f** 'having made a shrill cry to vibrate through the ears of his swift mares' (lit. *for* them – ethic dative). In *Il.* 23 (403–16), Antilochus threatens his horses that, if they do not put on a spurt, they will no longer 'get their keep', but will be killed!

**738** διώκει 'gave chase'. Again, the present used of a critical act in a narrative. Notice the scansion κἀξισώσαντε ζυγά (ζ being a double consonant). Orestes overtakes his rival, and the chariots now run 'neck and neck'.

**739f** One rider at one moment, another at another moment gets his head in front (κάρα προβάλλων) of the other's chariot.

**741** It is not otiose here, but to the point, to mention that Orestes 'stayed upright' during 'all the other courses' (which were therefore ἀσφαλεῖς for him), because (*a*) we know that Orestes had been driving

in a potentially dangerous position all along (hugging the post),
(*b*) since it was only at the beginning of the seventh course that the
pile-up occurred (726), ἄλλους πάντας δρόμους may include several
further courses during which Orestes and the Athenian ran neck-and-
neck.

**743ff** 'Then (i.e. after the unspecified number of courses run safely
by Orestes in parallel to the Athenian), allowing his left rein to slacken,
as the (inmost) horse was rounding that object, he inadvertently
struck the post.' Orestes makes a mistake, forgetting in his excitement
his previous policy of keeping a tight rein on his inner trace-horse at
the turns. λύων is antithetic to εἶργε (722).

λανθάνει: sc. ἑαυτόν.

Notice the interlacing word-order of 744-5. This bespeaks the
audience's attention, and, along with the vivid present λανθάνει,
heightens the excitement of the narrative.

**745** 'He broke the nave, in which the axle ran, through and
through' (lit. 'in the middle', but the plural emphasises the 'central',
'right-through' notion). As we say, 'break a bone', meaning 'to
suffer a breakage'.

**746ff** ἀντύγων: the rails which ran around the driver's platform of
the chariot. As the fast-moving chariot was partially arrested by the
breakdown of the wheel, Orestes' equally fast-moving body was
thrown over the chariot rim and became entangled with the horses'
reins.

ὤλισθε 'slipped out': a Homeric word, like ἄντυγες, which helps
to preserve the Homeric feel of the whole passage.

σὺν δ' ἑλίσσεται κτλ. 'and he was rolled up in a ball with the
slender reins; and as he fell upon the ground, his horses flew apart
into the centre of the race-track'. σὺν δ' ἑλίσσεται: tmesis, cf. 713n.
ἑλίσσω means to do *almost anything* connoting motion in a circle, cf.
Wilamowitz's notes on Eur. *H.F.* 398 and 690.

τμητοῖς means that the reins had been produced by cutting
leather into the slender leashes required for reins; but the word may
also convey, by suggestion, that the reins cut *into* Orestes' body, cf. 863.

διεσπάρησαν κτλ.: not having visualised Orestes as driving strictly
in the inner lane, Jebb explains that the horses 'left the track in which

the race was being run (the "course" in the narrower sense), and rushed on to the open ground between this track and the spectators'. The simple explanation is that Orestes' horses, having been confined to one narrow track, now strayed apart into the 'middle of' the course, i.e. all over it.

**749** στρατός: the early Greek citizen-assembly was often one of men serving in the army, or qualified to serve. Hence στρατός (particularly in an epic setting) can stand for λεώς, cf. *Trach.* 795.

**750** ἀνωλόλυξε: again, the narrative is devised to play upon Clytaemnestra's feelings. The host of spectators had bewailed Orestes' disaster, feeling pity for him. Why should not she?

**751** 'because, having done such deeds, he fell the victim of (lit. 'received as his lot') such misfortunes'.

οἷ' and οἷα are causative. We have no English equivalent of this qualitative relative. Cf. *O.T.* 701 (ἀντὶ) Κρέοντος (μῆνιν τοσήνδε στήσας ἔχω), οἷά μοι βεβουλευκὼς ἔχει.

**752f** 'being hurtled to the ground, and at another moment exhibiting his legs to the sky'.

φορούμενος: φορεῖν (frequentative of φέρειν) conveys more vigorous action than φέρειν.

**753** The drivers of the previously disabled chariots would be the natural persons to collar Orestes' runaway horses.

**754** κατασχεθόντες 'bringing under control'. Notice the accent which shows that the word is a 2nd aorist form (poetic, of κατέχω).

**755f** ὥστε μηδένα κτλ.: interlacing hyperbaton again.

**757ff** Orestes' corpse is in such a state that there is nothing to do with it but burn it immediately, and convey the ashes in an urn to his relatives for burial. The detail is cunning, since it makes it immediately convincing that Orestes' body should have been burnt upon the spot, not conveyed to his home in Argos as it was.

εὐθύς: with κέαντες.

ἐν βραχεῖ κτλ. 'Men of the Phocians detailed for this duty are bringing him, a mighty body (yielding poor pitiable ashes) confined in a tiny brazen urn.'

μέγιστον σῶμα δειλαίας σποδοῦ: μέγιστον σῶμα is the 'great body' of the living Orestes which now, in pathetic contrast, is compressed into the tiny urn: cf. 1113, Aesch. *Ag.* 433ff. οὓς μὲν γάρ τις ἔπεμψεν | οἶδεν, ἀντὶ δὲ φωτῶν | τεύχη καὶ σποδὸς εἰς ἑκά|στου δόμους ἀφικνεῖται, and Francis Thompson, *Essay on Shelley* 'he is shrunken into the little vessel of death'. δειλαίας σποδοῦ, a loose genitive of source: lit. '(now) consisting of'.

**761** ὡς...ἐν λόγοις: ὡς in this usage gives the standard of measurement or comparison: 'painful, merely to describe it'.

**762** 'to those who saw it, us *who saw it with our own eyes*'.

περ: intensive; it helps to identify the person who stands before Clytaemnestra and tells the tale, with 'those (abstract) who saw' the disaster.

**764f** The Chorus reveal their loyalty to the old legitimate reigning house of Mycenae, that of Agamemnon. It is now destroyed, they think, 'root and branch', because, without male stock surviving, there will be no one to represent it or assert its rights in the world (the females being at a permanent legal and social disadvantage – 'inferiors', according to Greek ideas).

δή is vivid, emphatic and untranslatable: 'there it is now, all destroyed!'

**766ff** 'O God! What am I to say of these things? Am I to call them fortunate, or...terrible, but beneficial? I am in a sad state, if I have to save my life by the sufferings of my own flesh and blood!'

λέγω is understood, by 'economy', in the first clause from the second.

Notice that Clytaemnestra uses the same word – κέρδη – as does Orestes at 61, implying (as he does) that 'gain', 'benefits' are to be accepted even at the expense of honour or natural feeling. But her next words show that she has realised (as he has not) that the 'gain' is hollow.

**768** εἰ τοῖς ἐμαυτῆς...κακοῖς: the vital phrase is emphasised by the circular hyperbaton: cf. Introduction (Style).

**769** 'And why are you so out of humour, my lady, at what I tell you now?' The Paedagogus is taken aback by Clytaemnestra's unexpected reception of his 'news'. This is not according to plan!

**770ff** 'It is a queer thing to be a mother. Even when you suffer despite at their hands, you cannot hate those you bore.' I use 'queer' in the Anglo-Irish sense, as W. B. Yeats or Synge might have understood it. It is the only single word which gives the sense of a thing being both frightening or awesome, and remarkable.

πάσχοντι: notice the masculine. Clytaemnestra is generalising, and in generalisations the masculine takes precedence over the feminine (even when, as here, the persons referred to can only be women): cf. *Trach.* 151f. τότ' ἄν τις εἰσίδοιτο, τὴν αὐτοῦ σκοπῶν | πρᾶξιν.

μῖσος...προσγίγνεται sc. τινί. Lit. 'hatred accrues to one of the children that (one) has borne'.

**772** 'So I have come in vain.' I.e. you are not pleased (as I had expected you would be) by the early message and the visible tokens (in the shape of the urn to come) of Orestes' death.

**773ff** 'No! Assuredly not in vain! How could you tell me this tale in vain! If you have come hither having sure proofs for me of his death, him who, having sprung from my life, betook himself from my bosom and my nurture, and lived as an alien and an exile in a foreign land. And, since he quit this land, never beheld me more, but, laying at my door the murder of his father, threatened that he would accomplish dreadful things upon me. So that neither by night nor by day did sweet sleep lay its protective mantle over me, but always the time that stood between him and me was only putting me off to die some other day! But now, now on this day I am freed from fear from this one's side and from his. For she was the greater bane, living at my side, a vampire ever sucking my life's blood. But now, I think, we shall pass our days in peace, as far as this one's threats are concerned.'

**773** ἄν...λέγοις: logical ἄν.

**774** θανόντος sc. Ὀρέστου.

**775** ψυχῆς: in its original (Homeric) meaning of 'life' (not 'soul').

**776f** Orestes is 'apostate' from the mother's breast and nurture. ἀποστάς is wonderfully expressive. The mother's breast is the supreme symbol to her of her relation to her child.

ἀπεξενοῦτο: cf. 95n.

**779** πατρῴους = πατρός (objective genitive): cf. 67n.

ἐπηπείλει 'threatened *against* me'.

**780** οὔτε forthe more usual μήτε, cf. 245n. ἐξ is not redundant – sleep *falls upon* one by day, and therefore (as it were) '*from* the day'.

**781** στεγάζειν: moving and expressive, like ἀποστάς (776): good sleep, sweet sleep (not nightmarish, fear-tainted sleep) '*roofs one in*', so that one is protected. In the translation, I have changed the metaphor for one which comes more easily in English – this in order to preserve the feeling of the Greek.

προστατῶν: I think the meaning is that Clytaemnestra, in her un-ceasing terror, has been living from moment to moment, and that thus the very moment which sees her safe through to the next – which thus protects her (προστατεῖ) – cannot but remind her that there is another moment to come, which will destroy her.

**782** διῆγε 'passed me on', i.e. postponed: cf. Thuc. 1. 90. 5 διῆγε καὶ προὐφασίζετο. διάγω, of course, more commonly means 'pass', and Campbell (*Paralipomena Sophoclea* 142) has a version of the passage which assumes that meaning here.

**786** So from Clytaemnestra's point of view it would seem to be Electra who has been torturing her mother, not the other way round (cf. the moral ascendancy which Electra wields over Clytaemnestra in the *agon* with her, 626n.).

ἔκηλα: neuter plural used adverbially.

**788** πάρα: cf. 285n.

**790** 'You are gloated over by this your mother.' But 'gloating' is far from a true description. Electra, obsessed by hatred for her mother, cannot now any longer see her as she really is.

ἆρ' ἔχει καλῶς: 'isn't he well off?' Bitter, passionate irony. She ceases to apostrophise Orestes and speaks of him in the third person. For ἆρα cf. 614n.

**791** 'You, I can assure you, are not well off. But *he* is well off as he is!' Goaded by Electra's spite Clytaemnestra resumes, in defiance, her previously expressed attitude.

**792** Clytaemnestra has appeared to triumph over the dead Orestes.

To triumph over the dead is unlucky and may be attended by Nemesis.

**793** 'She (= Nemesis) has heard what she ought to hear, and has ratified matters well.' She means that Orestes' death is itself a case of Nemesis for having threatened to kill his mother. Both Clytaemnestra and Aegisthus regard themselves as justified in having killed Agamemnon (Clytaemnestra for the reasons given in her speech (525ff.), Aegisthus because he supported Clytaemnestra, and also because he belonged to a faction or *stasis* hostile to Agamemnon (cf. 10n. and Introduction p. 9 n. 1). It follows that both regard Orestes' threats against both of them as unjustified aggression. Cf. 1466f. Notice the repetition of καλῶς (at 790, 791, 793) as a *leit-motif*: cf. 816, 1340, 1345, 1425 and 918n.

**795** Notice the accent of οὔκουν, which makes the negative have force – 'you will not then, will you?'

τάδε my prosperity, my power.

**796** 'We are finished ourselves, not to speak of our finishing you!'
οὐχ ὅπως elliptical for οὐ (λέγω) ὅπως.

**797** πολλῶν ἂν ἥκοις κτλ. stands for ἥκεις πολλῶν ἂν ἄξιος ὢν τυχεῖν.

**798** Again, as with καλῶς (cf. 793n.), the series παύσετον (795), πεπαύμεθ' and παύσομεν (796), and (here) ἔπαυσας is noteworthy. 'Stopping' is here a key-idea.

τῆς πολυγλώσσου βοῆς 'her outcry (against me) in every key'.

**799** 'I believe then that I will take my leave, if these matters are settled satisfactorily.' For polite ἄν with optative cf. 555n. The Paedagogus knows very well that by the laws of hospitality he will be invited into the palace.

**800f** ἐμοῦ κατάξι' ἂν πράξειας 'would fare worthily of me'. κατάξια: adverbial.

**801** πορεύσαντος 'who sent you on this journey'. The active of πορεύω is found infrequently.

**802f** 'No! Go! Go, please, inside; and leave this one to bewail her own and her "friends'" sorrows from without.'

### 804–822

The speech that follows is remarkable for the sureness of touch with which it proceeds. Every word is effective, the pith of the matter is expressed, and the whole moves with a kind of inevitability – characteristic of the greatest art and the greatest inspiration.

**804ff** Lacking the original (i.e. Sophocles') stage-directions we cannot say just how these lines were pronounced, with what particular shades of bitterness or irony, and with what emphases on particular words. I think that δεινῶς is a quotation from Clytaemnestra's δεινά at 767 and δεινόν at 770, and that Electra means 'You do not think, do you, that it was as being in (real) pain and anguish that she burst into those "terrible" tears, set up that "terrible" wail over him, the poor woman over her son thus perished?'

ἆρ': for ἆρα = ἆρα μή cf. *Trach.* 377f. ἆρ' ἀνώνυμος | πέφυκεν; . Jebb on the other hand understands οὐ as at 614 and 790, and renders '"does she *not* seem", etc., – with bitter irony'.

**808** ὡς: exclamatory. 'How you have destroyed me!'

**809f** The natural word-order would be: οἴχῃ γὰρ τῆς ἐμῆς φρενὸς ἀποσπάσας (τῶν) ἐλπίδων (ταύτας) αἵ μοι μόναι ἔτι παρῆσαν. The hyperbatic word-order helps to convey Electra's emotion: cf. Introduction (Style).

παρῆσαν: cf. 392n.

**815** ἐν: cf. 638n.
ἐχθίστοισιν: with ἐμοί.

**816** ἆρά κτλ.: almost a repetition of 790 ἆρ' ἔχει καλῶς, except that here ἔχει must be impersonal.

**817ff** 'Ah! But assuredly I shall never – not I! – in the remainder of time enter the palace to live along with them: instead I shall beside this gateway abandon myself, and, friendless, see my life wither away!' In the new circumstances Electra must think again. And, quite suddenly (as at 387), her mind is made up; and her decision marks a new step, a new movement forward of the drama: she will not any longer live under the same roof as the murderers; she will remain outside the palace, perishing, if necessary, in the process.

**817**   The abrupt first ἀλλά marks the sudden forming of her resolution.
τοῦ λοιποῦ χρόνου: genitive of 'time within which'.

**819**   αὐανῶ 'shall wither' (lit.): cf. 745 ἔθραυσε.

**820**   πρὸς ταῦτα regularly means 'therefore'.
εἰ βαρύνεται 'if he is displeased (with my action)'.

**821f**   'Since it is a favour if anyone does kill me, and a grief if I stay alive. Of life I have no further desire.'
χτάνῃ is deliberate rhetorical repetition after καινέτω (= κτεινέτω); cf. 580–1.

### 823–870

Clytaemnestra and the Paedagogus have now gone into the palace. Electra remains standing at the gate. There is a short choral interlude during which the Chorus, standing in the orchestra, begin a debate with her (in lyric metre – mainly ionic; see Appendix 1). Such choral interludes in Greek tragedy often provide intervals for reflection on the more active scenes that have gone before them, also for the expression and development of emotions connected with the preceding scenes. Here the Chorus try to *palliate*, for Electra, the news of Orestes' death and the consequent ruin of her own hopes, by comparing it with a similar *mythological situation*. They say 'You are not worse off than so-and-so' or 'So-and-so was just as badly off.' Compare the *kommos* of *Ant.* 937ff. There Antigone refuses, like Electra here, to be comforted by mythological parallels.

**823ff**   'Wherever are Zeus's thunderbolts, or where is the blazing sun, if they can look on at these things, and cheerfully cover them up?' Zeus might be expected to intervene (because of his overall responsibility for good behaviour) to punish Clytaemnestra and Aegisthus, and the Sun because, standing high in the Heaven, he *sees* everything, and cannot be unaware of Clytaemnestra's and Aegisthus' fault.
κρύπτουσιν: the word has overtones suggesting the 'burial' of Orestes: cf. 838 κρυφθέντα, 869 κέκευθεν.

**826**   Taking no notice of the Chorus' exclamation, Electra utters a loud cry of grief and despair.

**830**   μηδὲν μέγ᾿ ἀΰσῃς: 'Do not cry out *extravagantly*', i.e. 'exercise σωφροσύνη!'

**831ff**  Electra suspects that the Chorus will try to comfort her with 'Perhaps it is not as bad as all that; perhaps some influence from the dead Agamemnon or Orestes will still appear to assert your cause among your enemies.'

ἀπολεῖς 'You will be the end of me!', i.e. I cannot stand it if you do.

ὑποίσεις 'suggest to me'.

κατ' ἐμοῦ . . . ἐπεμβάσῃ 'you will plant your feet on me', i.e. you will insult me, as if you were my enemy: cf. 455n.

**837ff**  *Cho.* '(I *will* try to comfort you) for I know (= have heard) that the lord Amphiaraus was swallowed up, by reason of a woman's gold-entwined snare, and (yet) now beneath the earth' – *El.* 'Ah! Woe! Woe!' – *Cho.* 'he rules amid a throng of souls.' Amphiaraus, a famous 'seer', was cajoled into joining the expedition of the Seven against Thebes by his wife Eriphyle (who had been bribed to persuade him by the gift to her by Polynices of the famous 'necklace of Harmonia', which was an heirloom in his family). Since the expedition was foredoomed Eriphyle's treachery brought about the death of Amphiaraus. But in the rout of the Seven he was thought by the gods too good a man to be slaughtered, and was instead swallowed up in the earth.

ἄνακτ': Amphiaraus was at one time ruler of Argos (Schol. to Pind. *Nem.* 9. 30).

'Ἀμφιάρεων: the Attic second declension form of 'Ἀμφιάραον.

χρυσοδέτοις ἕρκεσι: plural for singular. Sophocles has telescoped two meanings. For ἕρκεσι describes *both* the necklace which Eriphyle put on (hence χρυσοδέτοις – 'set in gold': cf. *Trach.* 615 σφραγῖδος ἕρκει) *and* the 'snare' which the proceeding represented for Amphiaraus.

κρυφθέντα: cf. Pind. *Nem.* 9. 24f. ὁ δ' 'Ἀμφιάρει σχίσσεν κεραυνῷ παμβίᾳ | Ζεὺς τὰν βαθύστερνον χθόνα κρύψεν δ' ἅμ' ἵπποις.

γυναικῶν: plural for singular.

**840**  Electra's interjected cry of lamentation has nothing to do with Amphiaraus, but is prompted by the Chorus' ὑπὸ γαίας, which applies of course to Agamemnon as well as to Amphiaraus.

**841**  Amphiaraus lives and rules in the underworld, therefore, by implication, so does Agamemnon: cf. Aesch. *Cho.* 354ff. and *Od.* 11. 485.

πάμψυχος is *hapax legomenon* and of doubtful meaning. In the light of the parallels quoted I take it to imply that Agamemnon gathers 'all the souls' around him. Jebb thinks it means πᾶσαν τὴν ψυχὴν ἔχων 'in full possession of his soul', i.e. fully alive.

**844** Electra's φεῦ is, I think, still directed to her father, still regardless of the Chorus. The Chorus' φεῦ, on the other hand, is a quotation of Electra's φεῦ (like Electra's δεινῶς at 805, after her mother's δεινά at 767 and δεινόν at 770): 'Yes indeed! (δῆτα), it *was* "alas"'! (i.e. alas for *her*, Eriphyle). For the dire woman...' Notice the scansion ὄλὄᾱ confirmed by the corresponding syllables in the *strophe* μὄγ' ᾱῦσ(ης) (830), showing that the word is nominative, and denotes Eriphyle.

**845** The Chorus had been about to say that Eriphyle paid for her treachery with her life; but Electra, now responsive to their words, completes the sentence for them. This highly sophisticated device of splitting up a sentence between different speakers is known as *antilabe.*

ἐδάμη 'was tamed', i.e. was put to death. Cf. *Phil.* 335.

**846f** 'I know! I know. For there appeared a comforter to tend (ἀμφί) the mourning one.'

μελέτωρ: lit. 'some one to care' (about the outrage), i.e. an avenger. As Jebb says, 'the mourning one' is Amphiaraus himself, in mourning for his betrayal. The μελέτωρ was Alcmeon, see Introduction 1 n. 1.

**848** φροῦδος ἀναρπασθείς 'he (sc. Orestes) is gone, snatched up' (sc. by the Fates).

**849** 'Unhappy woman, you are the victim of unhappy circumstances': lit. 'you meet with', κυρεῖς = τυγχάνεις. Notice the scansion δεῖλαῖᾱ δεῖλαῖῶν (cretics) to match the corresponding words of the antistrophe (860 πᾶσῐ θνᾱτοῖς ἔφῡ).

**850ff** 'I too am an expert, over-and-beyond an expert in this matter (τοῦδ'), with my life-span that knows all the sweepings, all the hours of many dreadful horrors!', i.e. I know as well as you do how unfortunate I am.

ἵστωρ is a person who has expert, specialist knowledge (root ϝιδ) of a thing: hence the word occurs particularly in early legal contexts of a 'judge' or 'witness': cf. *Il.* 18. 501.

πανσύρτῳ κτλ.: as a full sea 'sweeps' many waves, so Electra's life is full of all the world's troubles, endured over all the months of the year. Notice that there are as many as three παν- compounds in this *kommos* (cf. 841 πάμψυχος).

δεινῶν is used as a substantive (loosely dependent upon πανσύρτῳ and παμμήνῳ), with πολλῶν...στυγνῶν τ᾽ agreeing with it.

αἰῶνι (Hermann's brilliant emendation of the meaningless MS readings) can be instrumental or sociative (cf. 705n.) dative with '(I am) an ἵστωρ'. αἰών is (curiously) sometimes used in the sense 'life-destiny', cf. Aesch. *Suppl.* 45f.

**853**  I.e. we are your witnesses.

θροεῖς = λέγεις. (But the word should perhaps be emended to bring it into exact responsion with λῶβᾶ in the antistrophe (864): see the critical note.)

**854ff**  *El.* 'Do not then lead me on any longer (sc. to have false hopes) in a course in which there is not' – *Cho.* 'What say you?' – *El.* 'left any longer valid support (ἀρωγαί) for hopes dependent upon a common descendant, a noble descendant.'

μή...μηκέτι: redundant reduplication of the negative.

νυν (unaccented) = οὖν.

πάρεισιν: cf. 392n.

εὐπατρίδων τ᾽: cf. 160n.

**860**  The Chorus cannot gainsay Electra's reminder that Orestes is after all *dead*. They therefore revert to the sort of comfort they had offered at 153f., that 'all must die'.

ἔφυ 'is a law of nature', cf. *Trach.* 440 χαίρειν πέφυκεν οὐχὶ τοῖς αὐτοῖς ἀεί.

**861ff**  'Is it a law of nature also that, amidst rivalry of flashing-footed horses, one should become entangled with raw-cut traces, in the way in which he did, poor fellow?'

χαλαργοῖς = the doricistic lyric form of χηλαργοῖς, lit. 'white-footed'.

τμητοῖς: certainly here suggests the active sense of *cutting* Orestes' limbs; cf. 747.

ὁλκοῖς: ὁλκός is *hapax legomenon* in the sense 'rein'.

**864**  'The outrage (offered you by Fate) is unimaginable.'
ἄσκοπος: cf. 1315 and *Trach.* 246.

**865ff**  *El.* 'Yes, indeed it is! If he, a stranger (in a foreign land), without my hands to tend him' – *Cho.* 'Ah! Spite!' – *El.* 'has sunk out of life, having met with no burial or keening from me.' There is much pathos (sensible in Greek, but not easily conveyed in English) in these words of Electra's, in which she laments that she has been deprived of the simple rights of tendance upon her dead brother. The *antilabe* doubtless fitted into the musical pattern. The subject-matter of the lines is resumed at 1135f.

κέκευθεν: second perfect forms are frequently used (where they occur) intransitively. κέκευθα *looks like* a second perfect. Therefore it can be used intransitively. 'Has hidden away' (in the world of death). Jebb translates 'lies buried', comparing *Ant.* 911 ἐν ῞Αιδου... κεκευθότοιν. But that is absurd, since Orestes' ashes were (at the moment) being, according to the Paedagogus' account, carried by 'Phocian men', so that they might receive burial in Mycenae. κέκευθεν therefore must be *metaphorical* in meaning. Orestes has died without having had Electra to tend him. He has not 'met with' (ἀντιάσας) burial or solemn lamentation (γόων – 'keening') from her, nor is he (she implies) likely to: because no doubt the urn containing his ashes will be given to *Clytaemnestra* (who has been treated hitherto by the 'Messenger' as the person responsible for him); Clytaemnestra will usurp the privilege of disposing of him (as she does of Agamemnon's body in Aeschylus' *Agamemnon* 1551ff.), and Electra will have no access to the urn. Electra is not to know that the 'Phocian men' will in fact deliver the urn to herself, and that she will have then an opportunity to 'keen' over it, cf. 1123ff.

ἀντιάσας = τυχών (Jebb says that elsewhere in Sophocles ἀντιάζω = 'entreat': but cf. *O.T.* 192).

## 871-937

There now begins a stage in the drama which was frequently a feature of great importance in Greek Tragedy, and became (because of the excitement it held for audiences) *de rigueur* in later Greek Comedy, namely, the 'Recognition' of the principal characters by each other,

or of one of them by the other. In the story of Electra and Orestes the
Recognition was one of the central elements and was told differently
by each of the three tragedians (each however making the finding of
Orestes' lock of hair, offered at Agamemnon's grave, a main feature).
Aeschylus' Electra finds the hair on the tomb herself, then goes on to
confirm her impression that it is Orestes' by the token of his footsteps
(similar in character to her own), and finally is convinced by the sight
of the garment which Orestes (now present) offers for her inspection,
and which bears the signs of her own weaving (Aesch. *Cho.* 168ff.).
In Euripides' *Electra*, on the other hand, the tell-tale hair is found by
an ancient retainer, who reports the matter to Electra, suggesting that
Orestes has returned. Electra rejects that token, and also a further
series of tokens, suggested to her by the retainer and in fact a repetition
of the Aeschylean tokens. Finally, she is convinced by the retainer's
recognition of a scar on the forehead of Orestes, who has now, as in
Aeschylus, presented himself to her (Eur. *El.* 508ff.: the passage must
be a skit on Aeschylus and some have suspected that it is not genuine
Euripides but an interpolation, cf. E. Fraenkel's Appendix D to his
edition of Aeschylus' *Agamemnon*. I see every reason for not adopting
this view: for a reply to Fraenkel see H. Lloyd-Jones in *C.Q.* n.s. 11
(1961) 171ff.).

Sophocles, like Euripides, splits up the Recognition. It has a kind
of false start in the ensuing scene with the discovery of Orestes' lock of
hair on Agamemnon's tomb off-stage by Chrysothemis (as in
Euripides' *Electra* it is discovered off-stage by the retainer). Sophocles'
Electra rejects this token (as does Euripides' *Electra*) but is finally
convinced, in the presence of Orestes, by the ring which had belonged
to their father, which he shows her.

Sophocles' Recognition is far more organic and more natural than
those of his predecessors. His treatment involves a natural interplay
between the characters involved and the outward tokens; theirs
depends upon the external tokens, which are introduced more or less
arbitrarily. Euripides' discoverer of the lock, the retainer, is a person
otherwise irrelevant to the drama. Not only is Chrysothemis, who
discovers the lock in our play, a main character, but the scene in which
she reports the finding to Electra is developed into one as significant
as any in the play, bringing to a crisis the clash of the two sisters'
personalities. In the second (the true) Recognition-scene (1125ff.) the

recognition really takes place through the dramatic exchange between Electra and the (disguised) Orestes. It comes about, as it seems, inevitably, and with a great and gradually growing sense of pathos, focusing upon the struggle of brother and sister for possession of the urn (supposed to contain the ashes of Orestes), which has become the symbolic centre of the relationship between them. The final *outward* token of recognition (the showing of the ring) comes only as a kind of finishing touch, which we accept almost unconsciously, because we have been so deeply involved in the organic growth, the mounting emotion, of the whole scene.

**871f** 'On the wings of joy it is, dearest one, that I fly, forgetting seemliness so as to arrive quickly.' Evidently running was not regarded as decorous for women.

ἡδονῆς: 'pleasure' does not convey quite the feeling here.

τοι: Jebb illustrates this by *Phil*. 245 ἐξ Ἰλίου τοι δὴ τανῦν γε ναυστολῶ and *Trach*. 234 ἔγωγέ τοι σφ' ἔλειπον ἰσχύοντα κτλ. But in these examples τοι is used in *answer to questions*, and means 'Well then, as you've asked'. τοι here is better taken as proverbial (cf. 517n.). It is not pleasant, generally, to 'be pursued'. But being pursued by ἡδονή would be another matter. I suspect that 'being pursued by ἡδονή' was a proverbial expression.

φιλτάτη: notice that Chrysothemis feels strong affection for her sister.

μεθεῖσα: lit. 'letting go'.

μολεῖν: consecutive infinitive, with ὥστε omitted.

**873f** ὧν...κακῶν = (by 'attraction' of the antecedent) τούτων τῶν κακῶν ἃ εἶχες κτλ. Notice the circular hyperbaton (cf. 768n.), which I think contributes to the decisive tone of Chrysothemis' announcement.

**875f** 'And whence could *you* find help for my sufferings, sufferings for which no cure is any longer possible?'

πόθεν ἂν εὕροις...ἀρήξιν, οἷς ἴασις κτλ.: a way of saying πῶς ἂν ἀρήγοις τοῖς ἐμοῖς πήμασιν, ἃ οὐκ ἔνεστιν ἔτι ἰᾶσθαι; Greek more readily uses simple verbs than periphrases consisting of abstract verbal nouns plus verbs (the same kind of periphrasis as is found in some styles of modern English, e.g. 'effect a junction with' for 'join'). Hence, when it does use such a periphrasis, the effect is one of

6

sophistication. Abstract verbal nouns ending in *-sis* were coming into fashion as *professional* terms in the Greek of Sophocles' day (see E. W. Handley, '*-sis* nouns in Aristophanes', *Eranos* 51 (1953) 129ff.), and Sophocles was particularly fond of them (see A. A. Long, *Language and thought in Sophocles* 31ff., 65ff.). They help to make his style concise and elegant (ἐξηλλαγμένη: see Introduction (Style)). The lines are contemptuous, and the contemptuous tone is helped by the emphasis put upon σύ by its eccentric positioning (via hyperbaton) between τῶν ἐμῶν and πημάτων, instead of before ἄν εὕροις.

ἔνεστ' this time (unlike ἔνεστι at 527) governs the expressed dative οἷς.

**877f** 'We have *Orestes present* – realise that you are hearing this from me – present visibly, just as you look upon me!'

ἡμίν: ethic dative.

ἐναργῶς with πάρεστι.

**879f** ἀλλ' ἦ expresses extreme surprise, incredulity.

τάλαινα: exclamatory. τάλας expresses anything you can pity or admire a person for, including being a fool.

κἀπὶ τοῖς ἐμοῖς γελᾷς: γελᾶν ἐπί τινι = make a mockery *over* something.

**881f** 'No! By my father's hearth-stone! No, indeed! I say this not in wantonness, but mean that the two of us have him here with us', lit. 'but (speak of) him as present for us both'. λέγω sometimes takes an accusative of the *person spoken about*, cf. 984. The first ἀλλ' is hardly antithetic to μά: rather it reinforces it, and is antithetic to Electra's γελᾷς.

**883f** 'God help you! And from whom in creation have you imbibed this tale and (now) put such reliance upon it?'

καί: cf. 236n.

λόγῳ is understood with πιστεύεις from λόγον by zeugma.

**885** 'No!' – μέν is used here, without a balancing δέ, in place of the idiomatic μὲν οὖν, correcting a previous suggestion.

ἄλλης: some MSS read ἄλλου, which is more logical than ἄλλης. But ἄλλης is perhaps more natural in the mouth of the speaker. ἄλλου would also give a rather clumsy and unpleasant internal rhyme with ἐμοῦ.

**887** πίστιν '*reason* to believe', 'proof'. Cf. *O.T.* 1420 τίς μοι φανεῖται πίστις ἔνδικος;. The word is used here as a pun on πιστεύεις (884) and πιστεύω (886).

**887f** 'Upon what, tell me, have you set your vision, that you warm to this infatuate excitement?' (lit. 'are warmed with').

βλέψασα: βλέπω may suggest abstract *consideration* as well as literal 'seeing'.

θάλπῃ suggests a *comfortable* warmth.

ἀνηκέστῳ suggests madness, cf. *Aj.* 52 τῆς ἀνηκέστου χαρᾶς (= the madman's exultation in his own frenzy).

**889** μαθοῦσά μου 'when you have *heard* what I have to say' (sc. and not before), the participle bearing the emphasis.

**891** 'Very well, then! tell it – if there is any joy for you (attaching) to the narrative.'

δ' οὖν: cf. 577.

**892** 'Very well, I *do* tell you – everything exactly as I saw it.'

κατειδόμην: Sophocles not infrequently uses the middle of ὁρᾶν in the same sense as the active. This is not a prose usage. καθορᾶν is to see things in detail, sharply.

**893** ἀρχαῖον: housing Agamemnon's ancestors as well as himself.

**894ff** 'I saw on the top of the mound fresh streamlets of milk, saw my father's grave decked round about with all the flowers that be.' The 'grave' consisted of a mound of earth, beneath which was the stone chamber in which the dead were buried.

ὁρῶ: vivid present as in the case of περισκοπῶ (897) and almost all the leading verbs in this narration.

ἐξ ἄκρας: cf. 1058n.

**897ff** 'I looked around me for fear perhaps some one or other was at hand close by me. But when I saw that the whole neighbourhood was quiet, I began walking closer up to the tomb. And there I saw, on the edge of the mound, a lock of hair but newly severed.' This description is wonderfully vivid. We see the whole scene through the girl's eyes, feel her sudden surprise at finding the tomb not as she had expected, her immediate reaction when she glances around to see if there is any interloper present, her relieved assurance that all is quiet, and her hesitant (notice the imperfect προσεῖρπον) approach to the mound itself. It is like Defoe's description of Crusoe's discovery of the foot-print: 'I stood like one thunderstruck, or as if I had seen an apparition. I listened, I looked round me, but I could hear nothing, nor see anything; I went up to a rising ground, to look farther.'

**897**  ἔσχον θαῦμα: a rather solemn way of saying ἐθαύμασα.

**898**  μὴ... ἐγχρίμπτει 'for fear that', since περισκοπῶ here implies fear. Some MSS have ἐγχρίμπτῃ. But the indicative in this construction makes the fear more vivid by suggesting that it may be *fact*.

   που: cf. 54n.

   ἡμῖν: ethic dative.

   ἐγγύς: strictly superfluous with ἐγχρίμπτει, but heightens the picture.

   ἐγχρίμπτει: lit. 'touches upon' (sc. the scene, the objects before her eyes).

**900f**  ἐσχάτης πυρᾶς: lit. '*of* the edge' (partitive genitive), for '*on* the edge': cf. 734. πυρά can mean not only a funeral pyre, but also (by association of ideas) the mound or vault within which the remains of a corpse burnt upon a pyre are buried.

   νεώρη (though in fact an adjective agreeing with βόστρυχον) goes adverbially with τετμημένον.

**902ff**  'And immediately – Heaven pity me! – as I saw it, there broke in upon my mind a familiar illumination, (thinking) that I saw in this a token of Orestes, the dearest of all mankind to me.'

   τάλαιν' in apostrophe to *herself*: cf. 879n.

   ὄμμα is not so much the '"face" or "form"' (Jebb) of her brother, as the *idea* of him, which has been accustomed to 'light up' her mind: cf. *O.T.* 987 καὶ μὴν μέγας γ' ὀφθαλμὸς οἱ πατρὸς τάφοι.

**905**  δυσφημῶ μὲν οὔ 'I uttered no word to spoil the omen of the happy situation.'

**906**  πίμπλημ' κτλ.: i.e. tears sprang to my eyes: cf. 745n.

**907**  καὶ νῦν 'even so now'.

   ἐξεπίσταμαι: ἐξ- intensive.

**908**  μή: not οὔ, because ἐξεπίσταμαι expresses confident belief; hence the construction is, virtually, one of *denying*.

ἀγλάισμα: something that adorns, cheers, cf. 52n., 211.

**909**  τῷ = τίνι.

προσήκει 'belongs properly' (by virtue of blood-relationship).

**911f**  ἥ γε: cf. 347n.

μηδέ: not οὐδέ, because the usage is also classificatory – 'a woman who is not even allowed'.

ἀκλαύτῳ: i.e. without scolding or punishment from Clytaemnestra or Aegisthus.

**913ff**  'Again, neither are our *mother*'s thoughts accustomed to busy themselves with such things, nor could she have done it without attracting attention. No! these are the grave-offerings of Orestes! Well then, take heart, my dear!'

ἀλλ' in each case indicates an abrupt change of tone: cf. 134n.

οὐδέ: if it was not you nor I, neither was it our mother.

μὲν δή serves to emphasise μητρός: cf. 372n.

μητρὸς οὔθ' ὁ νοῦς... οὔτε δρῶσ': a slight sense-construction here.

φιλεῖ: in the well-known 'philosophical' sense: 'is accustomed'.

**916f**  θάρσυνε: here, intransitive (as nowhere else). Our luck in life is produced by a δαίμων (cf. 696) which 'attends us' (παραστατεῖ). We do not always (in Greek popular belief) have the same δαίμων: there is a natural vicissitude in life, which leads the unfortunate to suffer in their turn good fortune and vice versa, cf. *Trach.* 132f.

**918f**  'The present day, on the other hand, will perhaps mark the beginning of many splendid things for us' (lit. 'will be a foundation (ὑπάρξει) as the ratification (κῦρος – nominative) of many fine things').

καλῶν: cf. 793n. The word may appear dramatically ironic since the καλά will involve the cold-blooded killing of Clytaemnestra. Line 919 is notably hyperbatic, and this gives it emphasis.

**920**  τῆς ἀνοίας: for the construction cf. Aesch. *Ag.* 1321 οἰκτίρω σε θεσφάτου μόρου.

**921**  τί δ' ἔστιν: conversational Greek for 'What's the matter?'

πρὸς ἡδονήν 'to your pleasure'.

**922**  'Whither in the world or whither in your mind you are (letting

yourself be) carried'. Broadhead (*Tragica* (1968) 82) objects to γῆς as
being inconsistent with γνώμης and emends the line. But the words
have been chosen for the repetition γ(ῆς)...γ(νώμης) which makes
the *sound* forceful: and cf. a proverb quoted by Apostolius (14. 57 in
E. L. Leutsch and F. G. Schneidewin, *Corp. Paroem. Graec.*) ποῦ γῆς
ἢ θαλάττης ὑπῆρχες; ἐπὶ τῶν ἀνοήτων.

**924** σοι 'I can assure you'.

**925** 'Look not at all to *him*' (γ' emphatic).

**928** θαῦμά τοί μ' ὑπέρχεται 'really (τοι) wonder is stealing over
me'. She wonders how on earth the offerings can have been made at
the grave, if not by Orestes' hand.

ὑπέρχεται: cf. 1112.

**929** '(The bearer of the fatal news) is at home indoors, an agreeable
guest to our mother, not at all an unpleasant one.'

μητρί: with ἡδύς as well as with δυσχερής, by 'economy'.

**930f** 'God save me! To whom on earth then belonged those lavish
offerings at our father's grave?'

γάρ: elliptical: '(I ask), for'.

**932** 'If you ask me (ἔγωγε), I am most inclined to think that someone placed them there as a remembrance of Orestes whom they knew
to be dead.'

**934** ὦ δυστυχής: (sc. ἐγώ), nominative of exclamation, cf. Jebb's
note to *Trach.* 377.

**935f** 'not knowing in what sort of plight we really were' (lit.
where of ruin we after all were'). This is the ἄρα frequently found with
the 'imperfect of sudden realisation', when a person, finding his circumstances to be different to what he had supposed them, looks back
and says 'So after all (ἄρα) things were really so-and-so.'

### 938–989

Once again the movement of the drama, having become arrested,
takes that small, but enormously significant, jolt onward. Electra,
balked of her hopes of vengeance by the hand of Orestes, conceives a
new scheme to put before her sister: that she and Chrysothemis shall
themselves alone exact the vengeance.

**939**  τῆς νῦν παρούσης κτλ. 'you will cast off the leaden weight of the suffering which now besets us.'

**940**  'What! Shall I raise the dead to life again, one day?'

ἦ in a surprised question, cf. 622.

ποτέ is really the complement of the negative implied by the rhetorical question (='I shall never recall to life' – οὔποτε ἀναστήσω).

**941**  οὐκ ἐς τόδ' εἶπον (if the correct reading) means 'I did not speak with that in mind'. I cannot see any sign in this context of the 'gentle and mournful irony' which Jebb claims to see in the alternative MS reading οὐκ ἔσθ' ὅ γ' εἶπον.

οὐ γὰρ ὧδ' ἄφρων ἔφυν: but Electra is not far from wishing that the dead *would* come to life (110f.), and in the sequel she lends herself to the illusion (1316 and 1361).

**942**  'Why (γάρ), what do you bid me do, of those things which I can reasonably undertake?' Understand εἰμί with φερέγγυος.

**943**  '(I bid you) steel yourself to do what I am going to recommend to you', lit. 'steel yourself *doing*'.

ἄν κτλ.: curiously, the indefinite construction can be used by a person of something that he is *about to say* (even though he knows very well what it is to be).

**944**  'Well! if there is any *usefulness* (emphatic γε) in it, I shall not shoulder it away.' Notice the difference between the middle (ἀπώσομαι) and the active: there might be disadvantage to Chrysothemis in what Electra is going to propose; therefore she is interested as to whether she does it or not.

**945**  'See here! Nothing, you know (τοι), succeeds without pains.'

πόνου...χωρίς: anastrophe.

**947ff**  'Very well then, let me tell you how I have determined to bring matters to a conclusion. You too know, as well as I, I imagine (που), that, as to existence of friends, we have none!'

παρουσίαν ='availability', 'forthcomingness', cf. 392n. and 810. The accusative here may be considered either as anticipatory or 'of respect'.

**950**  'We two are left alone': dual of the adjective plus first person

dual of the verb. As Jebb points out, λελείμμεθον is the only classical
instance of a first person dual, except περιδώμεθον at *Il.* 23. 485 and
ὁρμώμεθον at Soph. *Phil.* 1079.

**951f** ἐγώ emphasises what 'I' am going to do (whatever anyone
else will do); hence, expresses resolution. 'As long as I still had word
that my brother was alive and well' (lit. 'flourishing with life').

**953** φόνου...πράκτορ' an 'exactor (of vengeance) for'.

**954** 'my eyes are upon *you*'.
   δή emphasises σέ.

**955f** ὅπως with μή and the future indicative follows upon βλέπω as
if that had been a verb of exhorting – a sense-construction.

   τὸν αὐτόχειρα πατρῴου φόνου 'the very agent of our father's
murder': to kill another person deliberately and with one's own hand
(αὐτόχειρ) was regarded in Attic law as the worst possible offence and
(in the absence of certain qualifications) carried with it the death-
penalty (cf. Bonner and Smith II 229).

**957** Αἴγισθον: it is a very subtle point in the Sophoclean drama that
Electra here looks only (or only *first*) upon Aegisthus as the enemy to
be got out of the way. As the male representative of the anti-
Agamemnon faction, he was the most formidable adversary to be
coped with. The other plays on the subject therefore make him the
first victim of the avengers. So it is logical that Electra should plot her
assassination-scheme as an attempt on *his* life. But such a presentation
also brings it about that she can appear not ignoble to herself and her
sister: Aegisthus is an enemy – an outward (not a family) enemy – to
attempt to kill whom is man's work; and, by undertaking to do so she
and her sister, mere women, would be attempting what may appear a
brave adventure. But had she put Clytaemnestra first, the enterprise
might not have appeared so noble. The irony of the drama is that,
however the vengeance plot is conceived, it must (in order that the
vengeance may be complete) include Clytaemnestra (and Electra has
in fact hinted at *her* death as an object aimed at, cf. 582f. and 604).
Most of the accounts gloss over (in the early stages) the fact that
Clytaemnestra is to be slain. But Sophocles has increased the dramatic
irony by having Clytaemnestra *killed first*, and that in circumstances of
the utmost brutality after she has revealed that she has maternal

feelings for Orestes. By this construction he makes the μητροκτονία prominent, inescapable, and a leading element.

On the prominence given to Aegisthus in Electra's assassination-plan Jebb comments: 'Sophocles avoids everything that could qualify our sympathy with Electra.' Why then does he later depict her gloating over her mother's murder (1398ff.)?

**957 οὐδὲν κτλ.:** Electra has already in the past entertained thoughts of trying to assassinate Aegisthus. But, pending the arrival of Orestes, she has thought it wisest to conceal this project. Now that Orestes is dead there is no point in keeping it hidden from her sister.

οὐδέν: adverbial.

**958f** 'For to what end will you stand idly by, having fixed your gaze upon what kind of hope that still stands undefeated – you who can, etc.'

πάρεστι: cf. 2n.

**960 κτῆσιν:** cf. 875n. In Attic law, at least, women could not 'possess' property unless through the males who were their guardians (κύριοι). But it is perhaps not wise to try to equate conditions in the 'Heroic Age' too closely to later historical situations.

**961 πάρεστι:** repeated after πάρεστι (959) in a very expressive *epanaphora*, cf. 193n.

**962 ἄλεκτρα...ἀνυμέναιά τε:** neuter plurals used adverbially.

γηράσκουσαν: accusative, despite ἐστερημένη (960), because the construction has been forgotten, and the natural case for the subject of a dependent infinitive (ἀλγεῖν) is the accusative. So Chrysothemis as well as Electra is an ageing spinster!

**963f καὶ...μέντοι:** an unusual collocation, which serves as a strengthened form of καίτοι.

τῶνδε...ὅπως τεύξῃ ποτ᾽: hyperbatic word-order for ὅπως τῶνδέ ποτε τεύξῃ. ὅπως + the fut. indicative is put here irregularly for the normal future infinitive after ἐλπίσῃς because the latter here suggests a purpose or project, cf. Eur. *Hcld.* 1051f. μὴ γὰρ ἐλπίσῃς ὅπως | αὖθις πατρῴας ζῶν ἔμ᾽ ἐκβαλεῖς χθονός.

**964 ἄβουλος** 'ill-advised'.

**965** ἢ κἀμόν 'or mine either'.

γένος 'offspring'.

**966** πημονήν in apposition to γένος: '(representing) an obvious bane for himself' (because such offspring would think it their duty to avenge Agamemnon).

**968ff** 'First of all you will win the guerdon of dutiful devotion from our dead father below, and our brother at the same time. Secondly, you will, in keeping with your ancestry, be called a *freewoman* for evermore, and will gain (lit. 'light upon') marriage suitable to your rank' (lit. 'having on it the worth (ἐπαξίων) of your rank').

**968** εὐσέβειαν: not here in the broad (cf. 245n.), but in the narrow sense = respect and devotion shown to the father and brother.

**969** οἴσῃ: cf. 476n.

**971** καλῇ: future. Since καλέω is one of those few -εω verbs whose futures (being in -εω) are identical with their presents, only the context can indicate whether the present or the future is being used.

**972** 'For it is the habit of everyone to look towards that which is good and true.'

φιλεῖ: cf. 913n.

**973** 'And as for fame *on men's lips*...' – γε μήν marks a rising climax.

**975** ἀστῶν ἢ ξένων: the Heroic community of Argos is conceived by Sophocles as divided into the two classes (apart from slaves) familiar in the Greek states of his own day: citizens and resident aliens.

**976** δεξιώσεται 'hail'.

**977f** ἴδεσθε: cf. 892n.

τώδε κτλ.: for the accumulation of duals cf. 950n.

**978** οἶκον: here the 'house' in the abstract sense (as we say 'the House of Habsburg').

**979f** 'who, giving no thought to their own life, became ministers, once upon a day, of slaughter to their enemies, when those enemies were well-placed'.

εὖ βεβηκόσιν: the perfect denotes a stance taken up, a condition achieved, or a situation occupied: cf. 1057, 1095.

ψυχῆς ἀφειδήσαντε: lit. 'having not spared'. ἀφειδήσαντε is strictly the masculine form of a third declension dual participle. The proper feminine form would be ἀφειδησάσα. But the feminine forms of the nominative, vocative and accusative of such participles are rare, and the masculine was often used instead, cf. 1003 and 1006.

προυστήτην φόνου: 'represented', 'championed': cf. 781, *Aj.* 803 πρόστητ' ἀναγκαίας τύχης.

**981 φιλεῖν:** Electra compensates for the lovelessness of her actual life with the (imaginary) honours and love to be bestowed on her by her fellow-Mycenaeans.

**982 ἑορταῖς:** again in her fantasy she compensates for her present deprivations: cf. 86n., 911f.

ἐν…πανδήμῳ πόλει: at any gatherings of the city's population.

**983 ἀνδρείας:** that is the important thing to Electra: the women, in her fantasy, will be acting *like men*, showing ἀνδρεία.

χρεών (sc. ἐστι) = χρή.

**984f** 'That is the kind of thing, let me tell you (τοι), that every individual human being will be saying out aloud (ἐξερεῖ) of you and me, so that living or dead, our renown will never fail.'

νώ: a second accusative with ἐξερεῖ, cf. 881n.

πᾶς τις: the τις *individualises* the general idea 'everybody'.

ζώσαιν κτλ.: datives of the person interested.

'κλιπεῖν: used absolutely.

**986ff** 'Ah! Dear one, listen to me, labour along with our father…' The spirits of the dead Agamemnon and Orestes are conceived by Electra as actively labouring for revenge upon Aegisthus.

συμπόνει…σύγκαμν': κάμνε is put, by *variatio*, for πόνει.

παῦσον is equivalent to λῦσον.

**988 παῦσον δὲ σαυτήν:** sc. ἐκ κακῶν.

**989 ζῆν αἰσχρὸν κτλ.:** it is the watchword of the aristocratic citizens, the εὐγενεῖς, from the class of whom Sophocles' heroes and heroines are drawn. When life becomes unlivable according to his own high standards for the εὐγενής he should end it gloriously, if necessary by suicide, cf. *Aj.* 479–80 ἀλλ' ἢ καλῶς ζῆν ἢ καλῶς τεθνηκέναι | τὸν εὐγενῆ χρή. Notice the hyperbatic word-order (for αἰσχρόν (ἐστι) τοῖς καλῶς πεφυκόσιν αἰσχρῶς ζῆν) with which Electra ends her speech and compare it with the similar hyperbaton with which Chrysothemis had ended hers (918–19). In both cases the hyperbaton gives an air of conclusiveness to the speech-ending. At the same time, in 989 it serves to place αἰσχρόν and αἰσχρῶς together in a highly meaningful emphasis – an effect which could scarcely be achieved in a modern language.

### 990–1057

The predominant sense left in the mind by Electra's speech is one of unreality. She has no practical proposals for the attempt upon Aegisthus. Instead of such proposals she has preferred to dwell on the glamorous after-effects of a successful assault. Nor do we feel that even these are particularly realistic. Would the townspeople really be so keen to 'love' and to σέβειν the two sisters who had successfully assaulted (like men, like soldiers) Aegisthus? Would they like the girls if they killed their mother? (And that killing also, all the stories assume, is inextricably involved with the other killing. But Electra has said nothing about that: she has left it out of account, because it is a more difficult issue, less flattering.)

**990f** 'In matters of this kind *prudent foresight* is a useful aid both to the proposer and the person who receives the proposal.' προμηθία is the kind of prudent forethought which exposes the risks in an under-taking (cf. Hdt. 3. 36 ὦ βασιλεῦ, μὴ πάντα ἡλικίῃ καὶ θυμῷ ἐπίτρεπε, ἀλλ᾽ ἴσχε καὶ καταλάμβανε σεωυτόν. ἀγαθόν τοι πρόνοον εἶναι, σοφὸν δὲ ἡ προμηθείη). Electra has plainly not shown προμηθία. The Chorus (friends though they are and committed to Electra's cause) are warning her (politely) to do so, and to change her tune. They are also warning Chrysothemis not to listen to her.

τῷ λέγοντι καὶ κλύοντι: a second τῷ is understood, by 'economy', with κλύοντι from the first; cf. 265n.

**992ff** 'Yes, and before making her voice heard, ladies, she, had she only enjoyed good sense, would have observed due caution – as she does not observe it!'

καί. . .γε shows that Chrysothemis has read the disapproval in the Chorus' tone, and regards her own words as supporting it.

φωνεῖν: cf. Chrysothemis' emphatic φωνεῖς. . .φάτιν at 329.

φρενῶν ἐτύγχαν'...μὴ κακῶν: lit. 'had happened upon good sense' (sc. and had continued to be associated with it). The imperfect of τυγχάνω implies a continuous activity, whereas the aorist would have merely denoted a momentary association of Electra with good φρένες.

ἐσῴζετ'...σῴζεται: forceful repetition. The middle means 'preserve for herself, in her own interest'.

**994** τὴν εὐλάβειαν by *variatio*, for τὴν προμηθίαν.

**995f** 'For to whatever end having fixed your gaze do you flourish such a deed of boldness and invite me to be your helper?'

ποῖ γάρ ποτε βλέψασα: like 887f., where see the note. Notice the scansion ποτε͞ βλ-, cf. 707n.

ὁπλίζῃ: lit. 'make a weapon of it for yourself', 'bend it to your use': compare the active καθοπλίζειν at 1087.

**997** εἰσορᾷς: cf. 276n.

**999f** 'Their luck flourishes (i.e. waxes) daily, whereas ours drains away and comes to naught.' Cf. 916n.

μηδέν: the idea of 'nothingness' is conveyed; hence μηδέν, not οὐδέν. The lines here have a poetry of their own, independent of the dramatic situation or the character speaking them. For the imagery of 1000 cf. fr. 871. 8 the *moon* πάλιν διαρρεῖ κἀπὶ μηδὲν ἔρχεται.

**1001** ἐλεῖν: cf. 122n.

**1002** 'will escape scot-free', lit. 'unvexed of destruction' (a genitive of relation). Notice the force and solemnity of this line, due partly to the accumulation of alphas, partly to the long compound ἐξαπαλλαχθήσεται (passive in form, but no different in meaning from the middle -αλλάξεται).

**1003f** 'Beware lest, faring ill as we do, we get us greater ills.'
κακῶς...κακά: cf. 580n.
πράσσοντε: (masc. in form) cf. 1006 λαβόντε and 979n.

**1005** λύει 'extricates'.

**1006** 'having acquired a fine reputation then to perish ignominiously'.

**1007f** 'It is not dying that is most hateful, but when a person, longing to die, yet (εἶτα) cannot even achieve that.' For an embittered enemy, having overpowered his victim, may postpone his death in order to torture or humiliate him, as Orestes does to Aegisthus at the end of this play (1504). Cf. Xen. *Anab*. 3. 1. 29 οὐ νῦν ἐκεῖνοι παιόμενοι, κεντούμενοι, ὑβριζόμενοι οὐδὲ ἀποθανεῖν οἱ τλήμονες δύνανται καὶ μάλ' οἶμαι ἐρῶντες τούτου;

**1009** ἀντιάζω: cf. 865n.

**1010** It is perhaps best to assume a change of subject as between the two infinitives, σέ, not ἡμᾶς, being understood as the subject of ἐξερημῶσαι (for Chrysothemis has no intention of joining actively in the plot): '(relent), before we perish utterly and you altogether extirpate our household' (sc. by exasperating Aegisthus further against the sisters, and causing him to resort to extremes against them).

**1011** ὀργήν 'temper', 'spirit', not 'anger': cf. 222n.

**1012** ἄρρητ' 'a secret not to be revealed'.
σοι 'in your interest'.
ἀτελῆ 'without effect', 'going no further'.

**1013f** 'And you yourself learn sense at least at this late hour, (learn), when you are altogether powerless, to yield to those who have power over you.' For the thought and expression cf. 340, 396, 1465n., Eur. *Held*. 25, Thuc. 3. 4 and 5. 101, and Appendix 2.
ἀλλά: cf. 411n.
τῷ χρόνῳ 'in length of time' (lit.), cf. 1464.
ποτε 'For once at least' (lit.). With the whole sentence cf. 330f.

**1015f** 'Listen to her. There is no better advantage in nature for human beings to acquire than prudent foresight, or true wisdom of mind.'
προνοίας: a variant for προμηθίας (cf. 990).
ἔφυ: cf. 860.
νοῦ σοφοῦ: so Chrysothemis has displayed νοῦς σοφός. Therefore Electra, whose views contradict hers, has not: she is ἄνους, not σοφή.

**1018** ἀπορρίψουσαν: a vivid word: 'reject scornfully, out-of-hand' (as indeed Chrysothemis had).
ἀπηγγελλόμην 'the overture I made to you'.

**1019** αὐτόχειρι: not 'with my own hand' (cf. 955n.), but 'with my *sole* hand' (αὐτός, as occasionally, meaning 'alone', 'solitary'). Some αὐτο- compounds vary in meaning according to the variety of meanings αὐτός can bear.

**1020** 'For I shall certainly not let it go unfulfilled.'
κενόν = ἀτελές.

**1021f** φεῦ expresses almost any kind of strong emotion: here, Chrysothemis' astonishment and awe at her sister's determination to go to all lengths in pursuit of her one ambition. 'Would that you had been such (as you now reveal yourself) in your determination, when our father was being killed. For there is nothing that you might not have accomplished' (i.e. you might have saved his life, turned their own weapons on Aegisthus and Clytaemnestra).

εἴθ' ὤφελες... εἶναι: the well-known fusion of two constructions (εἴθε ἦσθα and ὤφελες εἶναι) to mean 'Would that such and such a thing had happened!', cf. Eur. *Med.* 1.
πᾶν: cf. 596n.

**1023** 'But I *was* such in my nature; only I was inferior in my intelligence on that day.' Electra's remark initiates a renewed bout of *stichomythia*, a new (and even more intense) *agon*, between the sisters.

**1024** 'Practise to remain of such intelligence throughout your life!'
νοῦν caps νοῦν in 1023: cf. 390n.
The following replies and answers reveal that while Electra despises Chrysothemis, the latter by no means repays the compliment. Though she has (formally) to score debating points over her sister, that is only in order to assert her point of view. She is not spiteful towards Electra, but is truly concerned for her welfare, afraid for her safety. The situation is reminiscent of the similar debate between Antigone and Ismene (*Ant.* 39–99), from which it emerges that the idealistic sister has not much feeling for the weaker sister, Ismene, but that Ismene has much genuine concern for Antigone.

**1025** 'You say that as one who does not intend to take part in the act' (sc. and that is its own condemnation of your attitude).

**1026** 'Yes! For, if I undertake it, it is likely that I shall also fare badly' (lit. 'likely for me also to fare badly').

**1028** 'I shall bear it also when you speak *well* of me!' A subtle remark. Chrysothemis knows (or thinks she knows) that there will come a time when Electra will realise (and confess) that she (Chrysothemis) was in the right. But that time will only come when Electra is at the mercy of Aegisthus – a vengeful, punishing Aegisthus. Electra's recognition of Chrysothemis' superior wisdom will be accompanied by a cry of pain or a lamentation for her own folly. Chrysothemis will put up with that too (she will have to!) just as she now puts up with being reviled by Electra. The gist then is: 'One day you will say I was right!' Jebb explains in the same sense.

**1029**  οὐ μὴ...πάθῃς: cf. 42n.

**1030** 'The rest of time *too* (χὡ) is long for forming a judgment on this', i.e. anybody but a fool could tell *now* that if you go on as you are doing, you will regret it. But there is plenty of time in the future for you to find it out!

τὸ κρῖναι: lit. 'with reference to forming a judgment' (a variant on the more usual ὥστε κρῖναι).

**1031f** 'Get you away! For there is no usefulness in you!' 'That there is! But there is no sensibleness with you!'

ὠφέλησις...μάθησις: cf. 390–1n. μάθησις: lit. 'ability to learn'. For the -*sis* nouns cf. 875n.

**1033** ἔξειπε 'reveal', 'tell on me' (as schoolchildren say). Cf. *Ant.* 86ff. οἴμοι, καταύδα· πολλὸν ἐχθίων ἔσῃ | σιγῶσ', ἐὰν μὴ πᾶσι κηρύξῃς τάδε. The taunt is, as we know, unjust.

**1034** 'Nor again, do I bear such hatred towards you!' (sc. as to do that), i.e. 'As I will not *help* you in the venture, so on the other hand, I do not *hate* you enough to give away such a terrible secret of yours, which would lead to your immediate destruction.' I think that ἔχθος ἐχθαίρω is spoken with irony – since in fact Chrysothemis, so far from hating her sister, loves her, cf. 1036. That there is a softening in her tone here is also suggested by the softer tone of Electra's reply.

**1035** 'Well then! (sc. if you do not hate me, i.e. if you care for me) just realise to what degree of dishonour you reduce me.' The point is that Electra is the elder sister, and as such has the right to 'give a lead' to Chrysothemis. Chrysothemis, by not following her leadership, is not giving her her due status (cf. 338–9n.).

ἀλλ' οὖν...γε belong together.

**1036** 'Not dishonour, cautious concern for you!'

**1037** 'Must I follow, pray, your determination of right?' For this meaning of δίκαιον cf. Eur. *Iph. Aul.* 810 τοὐμὸν μὲν οὖν δίκαιον ἐμὲ λέγειν χρεών.

δῆτ' is disdainful, implying 'who are you to tell *me* what to do?'

**1038** '(Yes) for when you are in your right mind, then you shall lead the two of us' (i.e. you will *resume* your position of seniority).

**1039** 'What a terrible thing it is to use clever talk to express wrong ideas!' Chrysothemis uses (according to Electra) skill in debate to express what is *wrong* (μὴ καλόν) – like Protagoras, who taught τὸν ἥττονα (λόγον), ὃς τἄδικα λέγων ἀνατρέπει τὸν κρείττονα (Ar. *Clouds* 883–4). For other reflections of the sophistic ἄδικος λόγος cf. Eur. *Med.* 580 ἐμοὶ γὰρ ὅστις ἄδικος ὢν σοφὸς λέγειν | πέφυκε, πλείστην ζημίαν ὀφλισκάνει; *Hipp.* 929f.; *Hec.* 1187; *Bacch.* 268–9. For ἦ exclamatory (not in a question) cf. *Ant.* 323 ἦ δεινόν, ᾧ δοκεῖ γε, καὶ ψευδῆ δοκεῖν.

**1040** 'You have described accurately the disease of which *you* are a victim' (lit. 'to which you are attached').

**1042** 'Ah! but there are times when even Justice brings harmfulness.' A memorable remark, which might serve as a motto for the whole play.

**1043** 'I do not choose to live under such laws' (i.e. Electra's laws are the eternal, unchanging 'Unwritten Laws'. Cf. *Ant.* 454–5. She does not allow that circumstance may modify conduct.)

**1044** 'But if you do what you propose, you will say I was right' (lit. commend me for having recommended the course I did).

**1045** 'And yet indeed I shall do it, not letting you stand in my way!' (lit. 'not at all dismayed at you').

καὶ μὴν...γε: cf. 1035n.

**1046** 'And is this really so, and will you not take better counsel?' (lit. 'counsel back', reverse your decision).

καί *indignantis*.

**1047**  '(Yes) for there is nothing more hateful than evil counsel!'
βουλῆς: a pun on βουλεύσῃ at 1046.

**1048**  'You have no mind, it seems, (for) anything that I say.'
φρονεῖν harks back to 1038 εὖ φρονῇς and 992 φρενῶν.

**1050f**  'I shall be off then. For neither can you bring yourself to
accept my *words*, nor can I accept your *ways*.' Chrysothemis gives up,
seeing that further argument is useless. She makes to enter the doors of
the palace. Notice that ἔπη . . . τρόπους is a substitute for the familiar
antithesis λόγος vs. ἔργον.

τολμᾷς: as frequently, τολμᾶν=have the moral courage to do
something, bring oneself to do it.

**1052ff**  'Go in! Never shall I follow after you again, even though you
may in fact happen to desire it ever so much. For it is the height of
folly even to seek after vain things.'

ἀλλ' : peremptory, and untranslatable (except in the tone in which
the line is imagined to be delivered).

οὐ . . . μὴ μεθέψομαι: the future *indicative* can substitute for the
aorist subjunctive in a strong future denial introduced by οὐ μή, cf. 42n.

πολλῆς ἀνοίας: lit. 'it is of (i.e. implies) much folly'. So Electra
replies to Chrysothemis' εὖ φρονῇς at 1038 and φρονεῖν at 1048.

**1055ff**  'Well! if you happen to think that you have some perception,
go on perceiving that kind of thing.'

τυγχάνεις picks up, and caps, τυγχάνῃς of 1053.

φρονεῖν: the continual play upon this word cannot be sustained in
English.

βεβήκῃς: cf. 979n.

### 1058-1097

As Electra remains close by the palace doors (Chrysothemis having
made her exit within) the Chorus, standing in the Orchestra, sing the
second *stasimon*. The metre is aeolic, with choriambs prominently
displayed, but including other metres (see Appendix 1). The question
what the first strophe (1058-69) means is one of the most puzzling in
Sophocles. It must be assumed that the key to some of the ideas (which
must have made sense to the Greek audience) has not survived.

'Why, when we see the most prudent birds on high caring for the
nurture (of those) from whom they are sprung and from whom they

derive benefit, do we not pay these dues on an equal footing? Ah! But, by the lightning-bolt of Zeus and Themis who rules high in the sky, they are not long untroubled. Ah! rumour that holds on earth amongst mortals, let me have you cry out the pitiable tidings to the Atridae *beneath* the earth, bearing them (news of) shames that bear no celebration' (lit. 'are not to be celebrated in dance').

**1058** ἄνωθεν = ἄνω, by a familiar 'attraction', because the sight of these birds *comes to us* 'from above'. Notice the quantity: ὀΐων-.

**1059** ἐσορώμενοι: cf. 892n.

**1062** ἐπ' ἴσας sc. μοίρας: cf. Hdt. 1. 74 διαφέρουσι δέ σφι ἐπὶ ἴσης τὸν πόλεμον.

**1063** μά has to be understood before Διὸς κτλ.

**1064** Themis is mentioned as the goddess who preserves law and order. For her as οὐρανία cf. Pind. fr. 30 (Snell) and for her (and other goddesses) as Διὸς πάρεδρος (sitting beside Zeus as he decides issues or makes judicial decisions, as an assessor might sit beside a magistrate) cf. Pind. *Ol.* 8. 21, and Soph. *O.C.* 1381f., *Ant.* 796f., Eur. *Med.* 844.

**1065** ἀπόνητοι = ἄπονοι.

**1066** βροτοῖσι: here practically = βροτῶν, cf. *Ant.* 861 ἀμετέρου πότμου | κλεινοῖς Λαβδακίδαισιν.

The questions which pose themselves in regard to the preceding strophe are as follows: (1) Who are the birds mentioned at 1058, and what are they doing? (2) Who are those 'from whom they derive benefit'? (3) Who are οὐκ ἀπόνητοι? (4) What are the Chorus complaining about? Editors, while expressing some hesitations, agree almost to a man in the answers they give to these questions.

(1) The birds are storks, or some similar bird; what they are doing is nourishing their parents: cf. Ar. *Birds* 1355ff. ἐπὴν ὁ πατὴρ ὁ πελαργὸς ἐκπετησίμους | πάντας ποήσῃ τοὺς πελαργιδῆς τρέφων | δεῖ τοὺς νεοττοὺς τὸν πατέρα πάλιν τρέφειν. Since this behaviour was so marked in storks, ἀντιπελαργεῖν was used proverbially ἐπὶ τῶν τὰς χάριτας ἀποδιδόντων (Suda s.v. ἀντιπελαργεῖν).

(2) 'Those from whom they derive benefit' are the same as those ἀφ' ὧν βλάστωσιν, i.e. their *parents*.

(3) The persons who are οὐκ ἀπόνητοι are the human beings who (unlike the storks) do not care properly for their parents. They will soon be struck by the thunderbolt of Zeus, who will be prompted so to punish them for their unfilial conduct by Themis.

(4) The Chorus are complaining about *Chrysothemis*, who, when given the chance by Electra in the preceding episode to 'defend' her father, would not do so, and therefore will be punished for it.

It is amazing that the logic inherent in these propositions should have been allowed to go so long unchallenged. To begin with, the last and most vital proposition is absurd. If only the commentators had read attentively the preceding episode they would have seen that in that scene the Chorus are deliberately aligning themselves with Chrysothemis over the proposal that she and Electra should themselves take up arms against Aegisthus: they say (or imply) that Electra's proposal is *foolish* and that Chrysothemis in rejecting it is showing νοῦς σοφός (cf. 990–1 and 1015–16). It follows that the Chorus, who have previously been *commending* Chrysothemis' attitude, cannot now be blaming her for it. The person to be punished cannot be Chrysothemis, and the thunderbolts cannot be aimed at her.

Let us retrace our steps. The birds referred to at 1058 may well be storks. But, if so, it seems very unlikely that it is only their behaviour to their *parents* that is in point. Throughout Greek literature, when ὄνησις is mentioned as between parents and children, it is the parents who are said to benefit from the children, not vice versa: cf. Ar. *Thesm.* 469 οὕτως ὀναίμην τῶν τέκνων, Eur. *Alc.* 334 τῶνδ' ὄνησιν εὔχομαι | θεοῖς γενέσθαι ('I pray to the gods that benefit will accrue to me from *these my children*'); Philemon fr. 156 (K), γένοιτό σοι τέκνων | ὄνησις. If we are to interpret 1061 according to these examples, it follows that the ὄνησις referred to is that from *children*: ἀφ' ὧν τ' ὄνασιν εὕρωσι are therefore the *offspring* as contrasted with ἀφ' ὧν τε βλάστωσιν (= the parents): the birds are said to care *both* for their parents *and* for their children.

It follows that the point at issue is not simply the debt owed by children to their parents: it is the whole *reciprocal affection* and mutual sense of obligation of parents and children. Birds, the Chorus will be singing, repay a strict debt of affection and obligation as between the generations; *we* (men) do not; we do not pay our dues ἐπ' ἴσας; we do not exhibit the same *family solidarity* as do birds. Therefore (those of us

who do not – we may assume a change of subject from τελοῦμεν to
ἀπόνητοι) are soon in trouble: Zeus's lightning strikes us.

If this logic is right, 1065 is not merely not aimed at Chrysothemis
specifically, but it is aimed at least as much at *all parents* who may
have neglected their duty to their children, as at all children who may
have neglected their duty to their parents. But the context further
suggests that it is effectively the parents who are being complained
about more than the children; and, specifically, the parent most
immediately concerned is *Agamemnon himself. He* is in fact the
'Atridae' mentioned at 1068. And what is the complaint made
against Agamemnon? Why, that he does not *intervene* to help his
struggling offspring. That he allows them to muddle on while matters
go from bad to worse. Seen from this point of view, the thought that
pervades this strophe is nothing else but a Sophoclean variant on those
numerous lyric outbursts in the early part of Aeschylus' *Choephori*,
whose avowed aim is to *stir the lethargic soul of Agamemnon* to rise up and
*take vengeance upon his enemies* (*Cho.* 315ff. and 495 ἆρ' ἐξεγείρει τοῖσδ'
ὀνείδεσιν πάτερ;).

So interpreted, the strophe will be in harmony with the preceding
*kommos* (823ff. why don't the *gods* do something about the misfortunes of the House of Atreus?) and with the Chorus' succeeding
*stasimon* (1391–2: now that Orestes *is* alive, and is moving with
Pylades into the house to exact the vengeance, it is really *the
avenging nether spirits* who are afoot and acting *through* their living
representatives)..

**1070ff** There are three ὀνείδη that affect them (σφιν, sc. the Atridae:
practically = Agamemnon): (1) that 'matters to do with their House
(τὰ μὲν ἐκ δόμων: cf. 1058 ἄνωθεν) are in a really bad state (νοσεῖ δή),
their power being usurped in an apparently decisive way by reason of
the death of Orestes; (2) 'as regards matters to do with their children
(lit. 'on the side of their children') the reciprocating strife is no longer
evened out in an amicable state of compromise'; (3) Electra is
'deserted' and ready to cast reason and life itself away.

The φύλοπις is the serious difference of opinion (depending upon
their different temperaments) that Electra and Chrysothemis have
always had as to how to behave towards Agamemnon's murderers.
That difference is διπλῆ because it takes two to make a quarrel.

Previously the sisters had managed to compromise their difference; now they can no longer do so.

**1073f**   διαίτᾳ: a *modus vivendi*.

πρόδοτος: the commentators say the 'betrayal' is by Chrysothemis. But from our examination of the strophe, it would seem to be that of Agamemnon (and any powers heavenly or otherwise that might also be expected to assist Electra): cf. 208 πρόδοτον.

σαλεύει: cf. 335n.

**1075**   ἁ παῖς οἶτον ἀεὶ πατρός: Heath's palmary emendation of the meaningless MS reading. ἁ παῖς was glossed by Ἠλέκτρα. Then this was imported into the text, and the then metrically superfluous (cf. 1063, the corresponding line of the strophe) οἶ- of οἶτον was omitted, whether through the scribe's carelessness or in an effort to make the line scan. Pearson's alternative emendation seems vastly inferior. For οἶτον cf. 167.

**1077**   ἀηδών: cf. 147.

**1078ff**   'not prudent at all to avoid death (lit. 'in regard to death'), but ready for oblivion, if only she can bring low the double Fury (that besets her House)'.

οὔτε...προμηθής and τό τε...ἑτοῖμα are complementary, and this relationship of a negative and a positive (expressed by οὔτε...τε in Greek) can best be rendered in English by a 'but' between the clauses. προμηθής recalls προμηθία at 990 and προμηθίας at 1036.

μὴ βλέπειν is 'to die', cf. 66 δεδορκότ'.

διδύμαν...Ἐρινύν: Aegisthus and Clytaemnestra. For calling persons Ἐρινύς cf. Aesch. *Ag.* 749, Eur. *Med.* 1260.

ἑλοῦσ': conditional with μὴ βλέπειν.

**1082ff**   Electra's determination in sticking uncompromisingly to her aristocratic values has been referred to at 1081. This theme is now developed. The truly aristocratic person (ὁ ἀγαθός = a variant on εὔπατρις) will prefer not to go on living rather than to compromise his aristocratic standards (lit. 'living basely, to bring shame upon his good name, being a nameless one': for αἰσχῦναι cf. 609 καταισχύνω; νώνυμος = δυσκλεής; and for the whole sentiment cf. *Aj.* 479f.).

**1085f**   'even as you too (sc. as anyone who is ἀγαθός, εὔπατρις, would) have chosen a destiny full of mourning in common (sc. with your dead ones)'. For κοινόν cf. *Aj.* 265ff. πότερα δ' ἄν, εἰ νέμοι τις αἵρεσιν, λάβοις, | φίλους ἀνιῶν αὐτὸς ἡδονὰς ἔχειν, | ἢ κοινὸς ἐν κοινοῖσι λυπεῖσθαι ξυνών;

**1087ff** The question now arises, what has Electra been doing (in the opinion of the Chorus) in choosing a life of mourning in common with Agamemnon?

The MSS all have τὸ μὴ καλὸν καθοπλίσασα κτλ., and this is translated by all editors (those that is who do not emend the words) more or less as follows: 'having warred down dishonour so as to win a twofold guerdon, namely to be called (once for all) both a wise and a very good daughter'. But this version (which goes back to the Scholiast, who explains τὸ μὴ καλὸν καθοπλίσασα as καταπολεμήσασα τὸ αἰσχρόν) gives an unexampled meaning to καθοπλίζω, which elsewhere always means 'equip'. Therefore, the text has been widely suspected, and a number of emendations have been proposed, almost all substituting another word for καθοπλίσασα, meaning 'having conquered', 'rejected', or the like.

The great objection to all these conjectures is that, apart from eliminating the 'good' (i.e. picturesque, descriptive) word καθοπλίσασα (cf. Lloyd-Jones, *C.Q.* n.s. 4 (1954) 95) they all end up by making the Chorus say that Electra has a right to be called *wise* as well as good (lit. 'best': but ἄριστα here simply replaces ἀγαθή), because of the fact that, not introducing a negative with καθοπλίσασα, they do not cancel out the result-infinitive (φέρειν) and they thus make Electra win (unqualifiedly) the *two* prizes, 'being called both wise and good'. That the Chorus should agree that Electra is to be called 'good' is natural and certain. What they cannot possibly declare is that she is also to be called wise, having themselves explicitly or implicitly said that she is *not* wise (in her present conduct – and what else can they be talking about here?) at 990–1 and 1015–16. The same charge of inconsistency naturally applies also to retaining the MS reading and rendering καθοπλίσασα = καταπολεμήσασα or the like.

What is needed is to emend 1087 in such a way as to introduce a negative along with καθοπλίσασα. This I have done, and have thus, I hope, restored the line. The meaning now is that Electra has chosen her lot of mourning '*not* having armed (or equipped) ignobility (so as) to win two prizes at once [ἐνὶ λόγῳ may mean simply 'on one account', i.e. ἅμα – but the phrase may also mean 'by one *argument*': cf. below], so as to be called once for all (= the force of the perfect κεκλῆσθαι) a daughter both wise and very good'. For the plural τά μὴ καλά='what is not good' (abstract) cf. 972 τὰ χρηστά, Eur. *Hipp.* 331 ἐκ τῶν γὰρ αἰσχρῶν ἐσθλὰ μηχανώμεθα. In saying this the Chorus of course are not *denying* that Electra is 'good'. Far from it! They are just about to say that she is supremely 'good' (1097). What they do deny is that she has tried to *combine* goodness with wisdom; they are saying that she has not tried to get the best of both of two possible worlds, by appearing *both* good *and* wise. For their judgment of course remains that she is imprudent. But they admire her for a lonely excellence, an ancient and unworldly adherence to heroic and aristocratic standards: put in modern terms, 'c'est magnifique, mais ce n'est pas la guerre'. (See Appendix 2.)

**1090ff** 'May I see you living superior to your enemies, in power (χερί) and in wealth, just as much as you now dwell subject to them, since I have discovered you to be, true, not set in an admirable walk of life, but, in regard to the laws which have the greatest origins (lit. 'originated as greatest'), here (τῶνδε) winning the first prize by reason of your pious devotion to Zeus.'

**1093f** ἐφηύρηκα: cf. *Ant.* 281 μὴ 'φευρεθῇς ἄνους τε καὶ γέρων ἅμα. μοίρᾳ μὲν οὐκ ἐν ἐσθλᾷ κτλ.: μοῖρα need not mean a fate which has attended one from birth. The word may be used of a new eventuality or manifestation of personality which develops at a critical part of a person's life (it was fated all along, of course; but it is only now that it shows itself): cf. *O.T.* 863 εἴ μοι ξυνείη φέροντι μοῖρα τὰν | εὔσεπτον ἁγνείαν λόγων (there would be no point in the *O.T.* Chorus praying for the *moira* if they had it, unshakeably, already), *Aj.* 256 τὸν αἴσ' ἄπλατος ἴσχει (αἴσα – a similar word to μοῖρα – means the *new* disaster of Ajax's madness). The whole phrase refers here, not to the general 'poorness' of Electra's situation and physical resources (that would be a very tame idea, irrelevant to this context), but to the lack of prudence, νοῦς and σωφροσύνη, which has led her to concoct her impractical scheme to overthrow Aegisthus. That defect is contrasted on the other hand with her firm adherence to the great Unwritten Laws (cf. *Ant.* 454 and *O.T.* 863), which include unswerving loyalty to one's family.

**1095** βεβῶσαν: cf. 979, 1057.

**1096** τῶνδε: genitive of relation.
φερομέναν: cf. 476n.

**1097** ἄριστα = ἀριστεῖα = 'first prize'.

τᾷ Ζηνὸς εὐσεβείᾳ: piety towards Zeus (objective genitive or genitive of relation). The Unwritten Laws were the gods' laws; therefore anyone who observed them showed exemplary piety towards the gods and particularly towards Zeus as the gods' chief representative. The reading of the oldest MS L, Διός (which doesn't scan), is an obvious gloss on the less familiar form, Ζηνός, a gloss which has found its way into the text.

For the paradox of the Chorus' compliment to Electra, which denies her prudence, but extols her idealistic loyalty, cf. *Ant.* 99 ἄνους μὲν ἔρχῃ, τοῖς φίλοις δ' ὀρθῶς φίλη.

## 1098–1175

We return to the action. Two men enter the stage from one of the wings, accompanied by one or more slave-attendants. They are Orestes and Pylades, got up to represent Phocian messengers. One of the attendants bears in his arms the urn supposed to contain the ashes of the dead Orestes. Orestes asks the way of the Chorus.

**1098** εἰσηκούσαμεν: cf. 38, 276n.

**1100** 'What is it that you are *seeking out*? And what is it that you wish, that causes you to be present?' The opening of the conversation is all the more natural for being illogical. The Chorus obviously cannot direct Orestes until they know where he wishes to go.

**1101** 'What I have been asking all along is where Aegisthus keeps his dwelling.'
Αἴγισθον: anticipatory accusative.
ᾤκηκεν: the perfect means 'where is his *permanent* residence?'

**1102** 'Why! you come well (i.e. in the right direction), and the person who directed you owes you no compensation', i.e. here you are at Aegisthus' house.

**1104** ποθεινὴν κοινόπουν παρουσίαν: i.e. that there are two of us, who have made the journey together, and that they will be glad to see us.

**1105** τὸν ἄγχιστον: the nearest relative (sc. to the inhabitants of the palace, i.e. Clytaemnestra and Aegisthus; but the word may also suggest (by dramatic irony) Electra's close relationship to *Orestes*).

κηρύσσειν: merely 'declare'.

**1107** Notice the displacement of his words in hyperbaton (giving an off-hand, aloof effect?).

**1109** ἐμφανῆ τεκμήρια: solid, concrete evidence of Orestes' death, in the shape of the actual urn containing his ashes.

**1110** 'I know nothing of your rumour': κληδόνα, by *variatio*, for φήμην, after φήμης in 1109.

**1111** ἐφεῖτ' 'enjoined upon me' (2nd aor. mid.). For Strophius cf. 44n., 670n. Again there is scrambling of the words in hyperbaton.

**1112** τί δ' ἔστιν: Here, 'What is it (that you have to announce)?' (different from the use at 921).

μ' = με.

Electra has grasped, intellectually, that Orestes is dead. But she has not *realised* the fact, in her whole being, and she dreads to see the evidence that will force her to do that.

**1113f** φέροντες with ἐν βραχεῖ τεύχει and ὡς ὁρᾷς, θανόντος with αὐτοῦ. Again, the words are scrambled in hyperbaton. I am inclined to think that the effect of all this is to make the 'messenger's' words appear frigid, formal. Sophocles has emphasised this aspect because of its contrast with the true pathos of the situation – the brother meeting the sister after so long a separation.

**1115** But *Electra's* words are not scrambled. She speaks simply and directly, from the heart. 'This is that': 'that' was the death of Orestes only intellectually apprehended and therefore remote; 'this' is the concrete evidence she sees before her and must now accept as instant reality.

**1116** πρόχειρον ἄχθος 'a burden ready to hand', 'that one can easily handle'. She means of course that it is a *small* urn (small, to hold the body of a man); but ἄχθος also means that the object is a grief to her spirit; and πρόχειρον that she longs to have it in her hands.

**1117** Again, he speaks with frigid formality, as if he at least were entirely detached from the 'Ορέστεια κακά (an Olympian, remote expression).

**1119ff** She speaks with simple sincerity, the wish of her heart: herself, and all her 'race', are bound up ξὺν τῇδε σποδῷ. There is a slight hyperbaton in ξὺν τῇδε... σποδῷ, which gives dignity and finality to her lines.

**1123ff** 'Bring it here, and give it to her, whoever she may be. For she does not make this request for herself as if she were a hostile person, but as someone of his friends, or a relative by birth.' (Therefore she has the right to handle the urn.) The omission of ταύτῃ before ἥτις, as well as the disclaimer of interest in Electra's identity expressed in ἥτις ἐστί itself, is again brusque, off-hand. The omission of οὖσα in 1125 has a similar effect.

πρὸς αἵματος: lit. 'on the side of blood' (i.e. a blood-relative).

φύσιν: in birth (accus. of respect).

At this point, we must ask ourselves an important question: *does Orestes know it is Electra he is addressing?* Is he playing a part to deceive *her* (as well as the other, less closely concerned Mycenaeans present) in order to guard against the danger (cf. 1272) of her giving him away through an emotional outburst? He is certainly playing a part. His brusqueness and indifference are an important element in that: he must not in any way indicate that he has any sympathy with or involvement in Orestes' cause. On the other hand, I do not believe that he has, at this point, recognised Electra. We must remember that she is dressed so poorly as to appear like a servant. From his point of view, obsessed as he is with the part he is playing and the stratagem he is enacting, this drudge-like woman who stands before him might be anyone. It is only as he listens to her moving speech (1126f.) over the urn which she cradles in her arms, that realisation breaks in upon him that this can be no one but his sister, Electra.

**1126ff** The words stand for: ὦ λοιπὸν μνημεῖον ψυχῆς 'Ορέστου, φιλτάτου ἐμοὶ ἀνθρώπων...'O last memorial of the spirit of Orestes, dearest to me of living souls, how I receive you into my arms differently

from the hopes with which I sent you forth!' For hyperbaton in
solemn addresses to individuals, cf. 1n. Here, the hyperbaton also
adds pathos.

**1127f** ὡς σ' ἀπ' ἐλπίδων κτλ.: the words stand for ὡς οὐ μετὰ
(τετελεσμένων) τῶν ἐλπίδων σ' εἰσεδεξάμην ἀφ' ὧνπερ ἐξέπεμπον, by
a sense construction natural to a person under deep emotion, easily
intelligible, and very expressive and moving. By contrast the reading
of the inferior late MSS (ὥσπερ, adopted by Pearson), sounds flat and
pedantic. The point of view uppermost in Electra's mind (as shown
by the lingering imperfect of duration ἐξέπεμπον) is the *hopes with
which she had sent Orestes forth* (so different from the sense of failure and
tragedy with which she receives him back). Hence ἀπ' ἐλπίδων is put
first, and absorbs the construction to itself.

εἰσεδεξάμην: instantaneous aorist, cf. 388n.

**1130** λαμπρόν: cf. 685n. With the thought compare Thetis' lament
for Achilles, *Il.* 18. 438ff. τὸν μὲν ἐγὼ θρέψασα φυτὸν ὡς γουνῷ
ἀλωῆς | νηυσὶν ἐπιπροέηκα κορωνίσιν Ἴλιον εἴσω | Τρωσὶ μαχησό-
μενον· τὸν δ' οὐχ ὑποδέξομαι αὖτις | οἴκαδε νοστήσαντα δόμον
Πηλήϊον εἴσω.

**1131ff** 'How I would that I myself had died before that moment,
before I sent you forth into a foreign land, stealing you away with
these two hands, and before I saved you from the murder that
threatened you, that you might have lain in death on that day, having
received your (due) lot, in common (with others of your family) in
your father's tomb.'

**1133** τοῖνδε: the masculine form is used for the feminine, the latter
being found (as Jebb remarks) only in Attic inscriptions.

**1134** ὅπως...ἔκεισο: a purpose-clause made to depend upon
another clause expressing a condition which was not fulfilled, has its
verb in a past tense of the *indicative*.

**1136** νῦν 'as it is'.

**1138** ἐν φίλαισι χερσίν 'with the hands of one who loved you'.

**1139f** λουτροῖς σ' ἐκόσμησ': λουτροῖς is a kind of sociative dative,
cf. 705n.: for the ceremonial washing and dressing of the corpse cf.
*Ant.* 900f., *O.C.* 1602f.

οὔτε παμφλέκτου πυρὸς κτλ. 'nor did I collect and take up (ἀνειλόμην), as was to be expected of me, the sad remnant (of your bones) from the fire raging over all'. After the funeral pyre, the bones of the dead man, now reduced to a small quantity of calcined dust, were sorted out by the mourners from the other debris, taken up by them and placed in a funerary urn for burial. Cf. *Il.* 24. 793. παμφλέκτου πυρός: for the genitive cf. 78n. The word suggests 'all-devouring', i.e. devouring *even the bones*. For a slightly different meaning cf. *Ant.* 1006 βωμοῖσι παμφλέκτοισιν.

ἄθλιον βάρος: of course the funerary ash is not weighty; it is light. But Greek poets continually refer to its weight by a kind of oxymoron which seems to condense into itself the whole tragedy of man's existence (the *light* body of ash which is a heavy *burden* to the bereaved, the *small* body of ash – enclosable in a *small* urn – which is the last state of the 'mighty' body of a hero): cf. 757n., 1116, 1142, Aesch. *Ag.* 441ff. (Ἄρης) φίλοισι πέμπει βαρὺ | ψῆγμα δυσδάκρυτον ἀν| τήνορος σποδοῦ γεμί|ζων λέβητας εὐθέτους.

**1142** Again, σμικρὸς...ὄγκος='a small *bulk*' (oxymoron).

**1143ff** τῆς ἐμῆς πάλαι τροφῆς κτλ. 'my nurture of you long ago, now proved unavailing, which I often provided, with labour of love'. τῆς ἐμῆς τροφῆς: genitive of exclamation.

ἀνωφελήτου: passive in form, but active in meaning, compare ἀνωφελῆ at 1159.

πόνῳ γλυκεῖ: oxymoron. The dative is modal or sociative.

**1145f** οὔτε γάρ ποτε κτλ.: the figure of litotes. Electra does not really mean that Orestes was 'not more' beloved; she means that he was *less* beloved of her mother than of herself. He was in fact her favourite, upon whom she doted, whom she had nursed lovingly and painstakingly as a little child. We see now with deeper insight why it is that the childless spinster, Electra, has built so much in her imagination over the years on the return of Orestes. It was not merely as Agamemnon's avenger and her own vindication that she longed for him, but as the person about whom she herself felt *maternally*. Speaking, then, of Orestes as a mother might of her own child, she makes the complaint which mothers will always make over their children who have died tragically, that they have tended them lovingly and yet the tendance has been unavailing: cf. Thetis over Achilles (in this case who is soon to die) in *Il.* 18. 436f. υἱὸν ἐπεί μοι δῶκε γενέσθαι τε τραφέμεν τε, | ...τὸν μὲν ἐγὼ θρέψασα φυτὸν ὡς γουνῷ ἀλωῆς (Sophocles' πόνῳ γλυκεῖ) κτλ. Notice the emphasis in σύ γ': sc. 'it was *you* who were my favourite – not my sisters!'

**κἀμοῦ:** the καί is redundant, as frequently in comparisons or co-ordinated statements, cf. 68on.

**1147  οἱ κατ' οἶκον** are the servants of the house, from among whom a τροφός – 'nanny' – would usually have been provided. But in Orestes' case there was no need, since Electra acted as nanny to him.

**1148**  'And it was *I* who was always called "sister" by *you*.' So the fond relationship was mutual. When the small Orestes said 'sister' he meant Electra, not one of his other sisters.

**σοί** (notice the accent) is emphatic. The dative is of the agent.

**1149  ἐκλέλοιπε:** intransitive, cf. 19, 985 'All these things have vanished, gone for nothing.'

**1151f**  We should be clear about the meaning of τέθνηκ' ἐγὼ σοί (as to which there has been much vain speculation: see Jebb's notes): σοί is the dative of the agent (as above, at 1148): the meaning is 'I am (as good as) dead *by reason of you*' (i.e. by reason of your dying). When this is understood, it will be seen that σοί (in the same sense) is also to be understood 'back' by 'economy' with οἴχεται πατήρ (meaning 'Our father is destroyed' i.e. his cause is destroyed, there is no hope of his being avenged – by reason of you). Only so understood will this series of short sentences follow logically after 1150f. 'You are gone having swept all away with you, like a whirlwind!' It follows that οἴχεται πατὴρ κτλ. *must be spoken in such a way* that the σοί can be understood both with οἴχεται and with τέθνηκ'. The series of short sentences οἴχεται πατήρ...γελῶσι δ' ἐχθροί (in which her tone is brisker) makes a very effective contrast with the longer, more pathetically lingering sentences before and after them.

**1154ff**  'the mother, who is no mother, with regard to whom you used often to send me in advance, secretly, warning words that you would appear to take vengeance upon her in person' (lit. 'as being about to appear as an avenger'). So one must render in English. And, following this pattern, Jebb (comparing 317 τοῦ κασιγνήτου τί φῄς;) says that ἧς depends primarily upon φήμας προύπεμπες. But the principles of Greek sentence-structure which we have observed suggest rather that ἧς goes directly with τιμωρός, as an objective genitive in long hyperbaton: cf. 578n.

μήτηρ ἀμήτωρ: cf. *O.T.* 1214 τὸν ἄγαμον γάμον, *Aj.* 665 ἄδωρα δῶρα.

Notice how Sophocles now begins to allow the sinister side of his action to unroll. In the *Prologue* Orestes had glossed over the fact that he intended to kill his mother with the vague τῶν φονευσάντων πάρα (34). Then Electra, making her assassination plans, had directed them against *Aegisthus* (957n.). Now it transpires that Orestes and Electra had intended all along that their mother should be killed.

**1158f** 'which sent you on to me in advance as you now are, mere dust and vain shadowy emptiness, instead of the dear (bodily) shape of you!'

**προύπεμψεν** (though προπέμπειν *can* mean simply to send forth, cf. Aesch. *Ag.* 820 σποδὸς προπέμπει πίονας πλούτου πνοάς) can scarcely have a different meaning from προύπεμπες at 1155. There Orestes sends on *messages* in advance of himself. Now the δαίμων sends on the dead Orestes' ashes in advance of (the δαίμων) himself. (When the δαίμων himself arrives, that will be to see the death of Electra herself, thus marking the completion of the doom of the House of Atreus.)

**σκιάν:** σκιά is often used (particularly in reflections on human life) of that which is vain, unsubstantial, cf. Pind. *Pyth.* 8. 95f. σκιᾶς ὄναρ ἄνθρωπος, *Aj.* 126, and *passim*.

**1160ff** Carried away by emotion, she bursts into short cries in lyric anapaests. The same happens at *Trach.* 1081ff.

**ὦ δέμας οἰκτρόν:** but it is not of course Orestes' body that she receives (or thinks she receives). It is the same ironic paradox as at 1142.

**1162f** The meaning is 'you who were sent on a fearful road' (lit. 'roads'). The 'road' is the journey upon which Electra sent Orestes when she gave him into the hands of the Paedagogus to carry him out of Argos on the night of Agamemnon's murder: it was a 'fearful road' because Orestes was only to return from it (as Electra thinks) in the form of ashes. The thought is the same as that of 1128ff. Jebb's view

that it is the road 'from Crisa to Mycenae' that is meant seems to me
to miss the point.

**1164  ἀπώλεσας δῆτ':** 'Yes! ruined me indeed!'
  **ὦ κασίγνητον κάρα:** cf. *Ant.* 1 ὦ κοινὸν αὐτάδελφον Ἰσμήνης κάρα.

**1165  τὸ σὸν τόδε στέγος** 'this your little room'. The urn has
become a metaphysical entity, representing the dead, nether world,
to which Orestes belongs. Notice the scansion τόδε στέγος, cf. 738.

**1166  τὴν μηδέν:** cf. 999n. In this sense (= a 'nothing'), μηδέν can
be used indeclinably.

**1166f**  Cf. *Ant.* 73 φίλη μετ' αὐτοῦ κείσομαι, φίλου μέτα κτλ. and
891ff.

**1167ff  καί...καί** has a co-ordinating effect: 'For even as, when you
were on earth (ἄνω), I shared all things with you on an equal footing,
even so now I desire, by my death, not to lag behind your burial.'
  **τῶν ἴσων:** the article is compendiary and all-inclusive: 'entire
equality', 'equals in all things'.
  **μὴ ἀπολείπεσθαι:** i.e. not to be left behind it, not to fail to share
in it. Note the crasis of μὴ ἀ-.

**1170**  Death is the final, and the only, release from λύπη. With this
conclusion Electra signifies her now complete acceptance of death for
herself. Notice how her mood has changed from 954ff. There she was
willing to risk her life in order to try to kill Aegisthus; now – that
unrealistic plan forgotten – death itself (by she knows not what
agency) becomes the object itself, for its own sake, of her desires.

**1171f**  'You are sprung from a *mortal* father, Electra, realise that!
And Orestes was *mortal*.' Supremely moving as has been Electra's
great speech over the urn, the Chorus stick to their role of deploring
heroics and emotionalism, and recommending restraint.

**1173  πᾶσιν...ἡμῖν:** dative of the agent with ὀφείλεται. Cf. 1148n.
  **παθεῖν:** epexegetic infinitive.

**1174f**  Orestes speaks to himself, but aloud so that Electra can hear
the words. Realising now (as he must have almost from the first words
of her speech) that she *is* Electra, and greatly moved by that speech

itself, also by her forlorn condition, he feels that he can no longer keep up his pretence with her.

**τί λέξω :** probably aorist subjunctive, though the future indicative can also be used in a deliberative question.

**ποῖ λόγων κτλ.** 'To what words (lit. 'whither of words') am I to have recourse, I who am bankrupt of words?' λόγων goes with ποῖ as well as with ἀμηχανῶν. This is the natural way to read the words, and Jebb is arbitrary in denying it here.

**σθένω** = δύναμαι, cf. 604.

For the scansion -ῐ γλ, cf. 707n., 738.

### 1176–1231

The great art and mounting excitement of this dialogue in *stichomythia* is due to its naturalness. It is perfectly natural that the characters should pick up each other's words and gestures as they do, perfectly natural that in so doing one of them (Electra) should misunderstand the other, and yet that in misunderstanding she should be drawn, gradually but ever closer, into an atmosphere of greater *understanding* with her brother, until finally the barriers to understanding are broken through, and she falls into his arms in an ecstasy of joy and recognition. So Sophocles overcomes the essential formality of Greek tragic style.

**1176** 'Why, what is this pain that you suddenly feel? What do you mean?' (lit. 'with reference to what do you happen to have said this?'). For the aorist ἔσχες cf. 388n.

**1177** The question means, 'Do I see in you the noble Electra?' (lit. 'Is this form of yours the noble form of Electra?'). Jebb is right in saying that the words do not imply that Electra was a famous beauty, but that κλεινόν is transferred epithet (τὸ κλεινὸν εἶδος 'Ηλέκτρας = τὸ εἶδος τῆς κλεινῆς 'Ηλέκτρας : Electra was κλεινή because she was the daughter of Agamemnon, cf. 1n.). But the form of the question is chosen for its dignity and solemnity.

**1178** **καί** = καίπερ.

**1179** 'Alas! then, for this wretched plight' (genitive of exclamation). ἄρα is sometimes used inferentially, like ἄρα.

7                                                                KSE

**1180** Electra is not accustomed to having strangers feeling concern over her. So she finds it hard to believe that it is herself that is the object of Orestes' pity.

**1181** 'Ah! body that is wasted so despitefully and so godlessly!' Cf. 124 ἀθεώτατα.

**1182** 'Assuredly it is never anyone but myself of whom you speak thus forbiddingly, strange gentleman!'

**1183** 'Alas! for your unwedded, wretched condition!'

**1184** ἐπισκοπῶν 'examining me', 'eyeing me'.

**1185** 'How I knew nothing, it seems, of my own ills!' Cf. 935–6n.

**1186** 'In what, of what has been spoken of, have you come to this realisation?' Electra still cannot see how her condition or her words can affect this stranger.

**1187** '(I have come to it) in that I see *you* sharply depicted against a background of many sorrows!' Cf. Aesch. *Ag.* 6 λαμπροὺς δυνάστας, ἐμπρέποντας αἰθέρι and 242 πρέπουσά θ' ὡς ἐν γραφαῖς.

**1188** καὶ μὴν...γε 'Ah! Well' cf. 556, and 1035n.

**1189** καί *indignantis.*
ἐχθίω 'more hateful'.
βλέπειν: epexegetic.

**1190** 'That I share my livelihood with the murderers!'
ὁθούνεκα can mean 'that' or 'because'.

**1191** 'Whose murderers? As of whose doing do you make known this evil thing to me?'
ἐξεσήμηνας: ἐξ- is redundant, cf. 276n. For the aorist cf. 388n.
Orestes has been deeply moved. But, well-schooled as he is in his part, he has not yet given himself away. He pretends not to know who was murdered and who murdered him.

**1192** εἶτα 'in such circumstances', i.e. *knowing* that they are his murderers.
βίᾳ 'in spite of my will to the contrary'.

**1193** 'Why! What person subjects you to this necessity?' (sc. of playing the slave).

τίς with βροτῶν in 'circular' hyperbaton.

προστρέπει: lit. 'applies you to'. Naturally the scribes of the MSS corrupted this word to the more familiar προτρέπει.

**1194** ἐξισοῖ: ἐξ- again redundant, cf. 1191.

**1195** 'Doing what (does she subject you)? Does she do it with blows, or with degradation of your daily life?'

βίου as frequently = βιότου: style, condition of living.

**1196** It is difficult to imagine the Clytaemnestra of 516ff. *beating* Electra.

**1197** 'And there is no one at hand to come to your assistance or prevent her?'

οὑπαρήξων = ὁ ἐπαρήξων: *someone* to help (the 'functional' use of the definite article).

πάρα = πάρεστι, cf. 285.

**1198** προύθηκας σποδόν 'you have placed before my eyes as ashes (in this urn)' (προτιθέναι having here a slightly different nuance from πρόθες at 1487). There is dramatic irony in this line. It is Orestes himself who, by his cruel lie, has reduced himself to ashes before his sister's eyes.

**1200** 'Know then that you are the only person alive who has ever pitied me!' (But what of the Chorus?)

ἐποικτίρας: notice the deliberate dwelling on the emotionally-charged word (which occurs at exactly the same place in the line as ἐποικτίρω, 1199).

**1201** μόνος plays on μόνος (1200); cf. 390n., 1217 etc.

ἀλγῶν κακοῖς 'feeling pain (or grief) *at* or *in*': a quasi-instrumental dative.

**1202** 'You are surely never come as a relative of ours from somewhere!'

**1203** 'I believe I will tell you, if these ladies' loyalty is to be relied on': lit. 'if *the element represented by* these ladies is present as a loyal one'. The prominent ἐγώ expresses determination and a choice made. The ἄν + optative expresses caution in the approach to doing what might prove dangerous.

τὸ τῶνδ': practically = αἵδε. Jebb cites Plato, *Laws* 657d οἱ μὲν νέοι...τὸ δὲ τῶν πρεσβυτέρων.

**1204** ἀλλ' 'Oh! indeed.'

πιστάς by *variatio*, for εὔνους.

**1205** μέθες 'let go of', 'lay aside'. To tell Electra the truth, Orestes must begin by telling her that *Orestes is not dead*. In order to do this, his first instinct is to remove the visible token of Orestes' 'death', i.e. the urn. But this leads to a further prolongation of the scene (and a heightening of its pathos and dramatic intensity), since Electra, not doubting the truth of the report of Orestes' death, cannot bear to be separated from his last remains. She thinks that the stranger, in trying to remove the urn from her, is questioning her right to exclusive possession of it.

**1208** 'ξέλῃ 'take from my embrace'.

**1209f** οὔ φημ' ἐάσειν 'I declare I will not allow you', sc. to go on believing that this urn contains Orestes' remains, to go on clinging to it: he expresses near-impatience, as he tries to wrest the urn from her.

ὦ τάλαιν' κτλ.: 'alas for me and you, Orestes, if I am to be deprived of burying your ashes!' (lit. 'alas for me in regard to you' – genitive of respect): cf. *Trach.* 971f. οἴμοι ἐγὼ σοῦ...μέλεος.

ταφῆς (='sepulture') is to be distinguished, as Jebb says, from τάφου (='sepulchre') at 1169.

**1211** 'Speak *cheerful* words (i.e. not those which accompany death and burial). For it is not with justice that you lament thus.' (πρὸς δίκης 'on the side of justice'= δίκῃ at 1212.)

**1213** 'It (sc. the urn) does not *belong to you*, that you should address this speech to it!' They are still struggling over the urn. οὔ σοι προσήκει of course really means 'you have no *business* to be clinging to the urn (since Orestes is not dead)'. But the words are so chosen that Electra can think that the stranger means 'the ashes do not belong to you' (as the nearest relative – προσήκων).

**1214** 'Am I so dishonoured of the dead?' (i.e. would he have so disowned me?)

**1216** 'Yes (γ') (surely it is), if indeed it is the body of Orestes that I bear here in my hands.'

**1216ff** Notice again the word-play Ὀρέστου (1216) – Ὀρέστου (1217), and τάφος (1218) – τάφος (1219).

**1217f** 'But it is *not* of Orestes – except in so far as it has been contrived, by a tale only (γ'), to look like it.' Cf. 59 λόγῳ θανών.

ἠσκημένον: ἀσκεῖν is 'to practise', then (by an extension of usage) to make something (or cause something to be) by practice or contrivance.

**1220** εἶπας: first aorist (= the habitual form, in Attic, of the second person indicative singular of this verb; most other parts are supplied from the second aorist form).

ὦ παῖ: since Orestes is considerably younger than Electra.

ψεῦδος κτλ. '(I speak) falsehood in nothing of what I say.'

**1221f** 'Why (γάρ), is the man living?'

ἦ introduces an eager question (cf. 622n.), as she stands on the threshold of realising the truth.

**1222f** 'Why! are *you* he?' spoken with the same eagerness, as her intuition guides her to the true realisation.

ἔκμαθ' 'make very sure'.

**1224** φῶς 'light (of *this day*)'. Cf. *Phil.* 530 ὦ φίλτατον μὲν ἦμαρ, ἥδιστος δ' ἀνήρ.

συμμαρτυρῶ 'join with you in witnessing' (that it *is* the dearest day)!

**1225f**  El.  Oh voice (that I longed to hear)! You have come!
          Or.  Never more ask news of me from elsewhere!
          El.  Do I hold you in my arms?
          Or.  As may you hold me for ever more!

**1228f** 'You see, in this man, Orestes, dead by *devising*, but now alive again – by *devising*!' Superficially, μηχαναῖς σεσωμένον means that Orestes has got back to Argos safely by stratagem. But the repetition μηχαναῖσι...μηχαναῖς strikes that sinister note which appears at intervals throughout the play (cf. 793n.). For μηχανή as a word of dubious moral significance, cf. Eur. *Hipp.* 331 ἐκ τῶν γὰρ αἰσχρῶν ἐσθλὰ μηχανώμεθα, and the formula which is technical in Greek oaths and contracts: 'I will not break this oath τέχνῃ μηδὲ μηχανῇ μηδεμιᾷ.'

**1230f  ὦ παῖ:** cf. 234.

**ἐπὶ συμφοραῖσι** 'over the vicissitudes (of your life and his)':
συμφοραί are good accidents as well as bad.

**γεγηθὸς...δάκρυον** 'a tear of joy': the epithet being transferred
from μοι to δάκρυον.

### 1232–1287

The feelings aroused in the great Recognition-scene demand some
release less inhibited than is possible in the ordinary iambics. This is
provided by the following 'lyric between the actors' (μέλος ἀπὸ
σκηνῆς). As often in lyrical passages in which joy or triumph is
expressed, the metre relies largely on dochmiacs or cretics: we are
never far, however, from ordinary dialogue (witness the introduction
of ordinary iambics at 1235–6, 1238, 1243–4, 1251–2, and the corresponding lines of the antistrophe).

Since the meaning of a number of the following lines has been
disputed, it will be well to notice at the outset (as most of the dis-
putants have not noticed) that there is a very well-marked pattern
throughout the lyric. This pattern (providing as it does a context into
which any particular words must fit) will help us to decide (as they
would the audience) meanings which might otherwise be obscure.
The pattern is simply this: that Electra, overcome by joy at the
unexpected restoration of her brother to her, wishes to express that
oy to the uttermost, without consideration of consequences, or of the
time, the place or the circumstances in which she and Orestes are
placed. In these verses (the greatest dramatic height to which she
reaches in this play) she does, as it were, break loose from the whole
net of destiny, intrigue, and ready-made situation in which the plot
of the play set her (just as Clytaemnestra breaks loose from it, for a
brief moment, at 766–8 and 770–1). We have seen her cast throughout
the play as a *hater*; but this brief interlude (as well as the previous
scene) reveals her as a *lover*: cf. *Ant.* 523. But the converse of the pattern
is that Orestes, *not* forgetting his mission or his destiny and determined
to carry his plan through to the end of murdering his mother and
Aegisthus, *tries repeatedly to silence* Electra, to restrain her out-pouring
of emotion so as to subordinate it to the enterprise upon which he is
engaged. All his utterances can be shown to conform to this overall
pattern. And, since it is he who is urging sobriety and calm, it is no

accident that all the lines in iambics (this being the most prosaic metre, cf. 77n.) belong to him (except two, 1235 and 1256), and that throughout he speaks only in iambics.

**1232ff**  'Ah! birth – birth of a person to me most beloved – you came but this moment, you found out, you went, you saw those you desired to see!'

γοναί: it is the most psychologically telling word that Sophocles could have put into Electra's mouth at this moment. Starved of marriage and children (cf. 164f.), she sees her brother, whom she had herself nursed and fondled as a young child, practically as *her own child*, here reborn before her eyes! How much more prosaic to translate, with Jebb, 'son of the father whom I so loved'. I do not think that Agamemnon is concerned here, but that σωμάτων is the defining genitive, and = Orestes himself: cf. 1286 φιλτάταν ἔχων πρόσοψιν. γοναί...σωμάτων: the plural abstracts the object described, and, as it were, gives it a quality.

ἀρτίως = ἄρτι, cf. 347, 792.

ἐφηύρετ᾽, ἦλθετ᾽, εἴδεθ᾽ is the very effective rhetorical figure of the *tricolon* (cf. Quintilian 9. 3. 77), of which the best-known example is Caesar's *veni, vidi, vici*.

**1236**  Orestes' first command to *be quiet*.

πρόσμενε 'await' (events to come).

**1237**  'What is the matter?' (i.e. 'Why do you bid me be silent?'), cf. 921.

**1238**  A second, more specific request for silence.

μή: cf. 641n.

**1239**  Electra does not see why she should be silent, or conceal her joy, because she is *not afraid* of 'those within the house'. (Notice that she has no calculation, no stratagem, no δόλος. She is entirely taken up with feeling.)

τὰν ῎Αρτεμιν 'by Artemis' (cf. 1063n.). For ἅδμ cf. 707 etc.

ἀεί: the -ει is rendered short by the following vowel.

**1240f**  'I shall never deign to quail before *this* useless burden of womanhood that stays within forever.'

μέν: cf. 372n.

ἄχθος: cf. *Od.* 20. 379 ἄχθος ἀρούρης.

ἔνδον: with ὄν.

γυναικῶν: Clytaemnestra and Chrysothemis (and not forgetting Iphianassa? cf. 158). The normal role of Greek women was to stay at home within doors (cf. 312n.). For this attitude the masculine-spirited Electra has utter contempt.

**1243** 'Well! Yes, but (γε μὲν δή) beware that there is martial spirit even in women! You know that fully (ἐξ-) yourself, I should have thought (που), from bitter experience!' The 'bitter experience' is the active part which Clytaemnestra took in killing Agamemnon (though the words might also remind the audience that Electra herself had been willing to take up arms against Aegisthus, cf. 956).

ὅρα: cf. 580, 584.

**1245ff** 'Alas! Alas! You have called to mind a subject all clouded-over, never to be dispelled, and never to be forgotten, namely, the original nature (οἷον ἔφυ) of our misfortune!' The reference is not merely to the death of Agamemnon (which of course was irretrievable), but also, and above all, to the fact that it was the *mother* of Orestes and Electra who killed him. This is an evil that cannot ever be dispelled: that they are the children of a murderess. (Jebb explains that Electra alludes 'to her suffering at the hands of Clytaemnestra'. That seems a very narrow interpretation. And were Electra's own sufferings not expiable by the vengeance to come, on her own supposition that vengeance is an 'answer' to injury?)

**1246** ἀνέφελον: elsewhere this word means 'cloudless'; and so the Scholiast explains here: φανερόν, ἀνακεκαλυμμένον, i.e. not to be concealed or 'clouded-over'. But this would imply that the object concerned (the guilt of Clytaemnestra) was 'bright'; and it is not the habit of Greek imagery to represent *bad* things as bright (they are, rather, dark or cloudy: cf. the exx. of νέφος, νεφέλη given in Ellendt). I am therefore inclined to understand the ἀ- here as intensive (as, morphologically, it can be), not privative.

ἐνέβαλες: lit. 'you have thrown into' (conversation): cf. Plat. *Rep.* 1. 344d οἷον ἐμβαλὼν λόγον ἐν νῷ ἔχεις ἀπιέναι.

**1249** λησόμενον: Jebb translates (with Whitelaw) 'that never its own burden can forget'. But this seems highly artificial, and I should prefer to regard the middle form here as simply serving for a passive (though λήσομαι is not found elsewhere in this sense, and there is in fact no true passive form in use for λανθάνω in classical Greek), parallel to καταλύσιμον, which obviously has a passive sense. Middle and passive forms are fairly frequently interchangeable in poetry.

**1251f** The guide to understanding these difficult lines should be the context. Electra has said that 'our κακόν is indissoluble'. Orestes (misunderstanding) takes this to refer to her treatment at the hands of Clytaemnestra and Aegisthus. He replies then: 'I know fully *this also* (i.e. 'as well as knowing that Aegisthus and Clytaemnestra are evildoers who disgracefully murdered our father, I know that they have maltreated you'). But, when opportunity prompts us, *then* will be the time (χρεών sc. ἔσται) to remember these deeds.' (I.e. when the murderers *are dead* and we have freedom to speak, then will be the time to remember (i.e. *discuss*) their misdeeds. Now is not the time to do so!) So interpreted, the lines amount to a further (the third, cf. 1236 and 1238nn. and the general note to 1232ff.) request to Electra to be silent (a fourth such request is to follow at 1257, a fifth at 1259, and a sixth at 1271f.).

Jebb has a kind of intuitive perception of this interpretation but, rejecting initially the Scholiast's explanation that παρουσία here = καιρός, he opts for it to mean the presence of *Aegisthus and Clytaemnestra*, rendering, 'When their presence admonishes (φράζῃ) – gives the signal for action – then will be the time to recall their crimes': ἔργων τῶνδε μεμνῆσθαι would then mean, effectively, to *take notice* of Aegisthus' and Clytaemnestra's misdeeds, i.e. to be revenged upon them. Cf. A. A. Long, *C.R.* n.s. 14 (1964) 130–2; more recent commentators have similar explanations, e.g. H. Lloyd-Jones, *C.R.* n.s. 19 (1969) 35.

This view of παρουσία seems to me impossible. Consider: Clytaemnestra is already within the house; therefore she is *present already*. Aegisthus is, it is true, abroad (cf. 313); but Orestes does not know that. Nor can there be the slightest suspicion that he is waiting (in order to begin the vengeance) for Aegisthus to appear, because in the sequel he proceeds (without reckoning on Aegisthus) immediately to introduce himself into the palace and to kill Clytaemnestra (whom he knows to be there – παρεῖναι – all the time).

Since παρουσία cannot mean the presence of Aegisthus and

Clytaemnestra, we are left with the Scholiast's interpretation that it means καιρός. It is true that παρουσία is not found elsewhere in just this sense in classical Greek. But of course it is the context, and the plasticity of Greek, which moulds the word to this sense here. The vital elements are, first, Orestes' continued harping on 'time' and 'right time' in this play (cf. 75n. καιρός, 1259, 1292); second, Electra's ὁ πᾶς... παρών... χρόνος in the immediately following lines (1253f.): Electra picks up Orestes' παρουσία by παρών χρόνος (which jingles with it) and, by that phrase, shows that Orestes' παρουσία was to be understood within the sphere of χρόνος, i.e. to be = καιρός.

It is above all the jingle in παρών χρόνος that shows that παρουσία must be retained at 1251, and that the alternative reading of some later MSS, παρρησία (modified by Pearson in his Oxford Text to the form παρρησίᾳ – in which case understand τις as the subject ο φράζῃ, 'when we can all speak freely', cf. Pearson in *C.Q.* 23 (1929) 88), is to be rejected as a short-sighted emendation – made by someone, however, who saw the sense that is required.

Finally, we can make a cross-check upon our reasoning here about παρουσία. For Sophocles has a habit (as noted already, cf. the general note to 251 ff.) of re-stating (in a more precise form) in a following iambic passage, material which he has already expressed more allusively in a preceding lyric. Such a development of 1251–2 occurs at 1299–300 ὅταν γὰρ εὐτυχήσωμεν, τότε | χαίρειν παρέσται καὶ γελᾶν ἐλευθέρως. This clearly shows that Orestes meant by 1251–2 that Electra should wait till after the *murders were over* to express her exultation; and also that παρουσία at 1251 = παρουσία χρόνου ('time to do what we like'). (For further discussion cf. my article in *C.R.* n.s. 16 (1966) 255f.)

**1253ff** 'Any and every time, any and every, I say, would befit as an opportune time (to me) to declare these things rightfully.' Orestes has tried to repress Electra from 'discussing these deeds' (a vaguely allusive phrase). But for Electra τάδε = not merely her triumph over the murderers (now, she thinks, secure, because of the return of Orestes), but her pleasure and exultation at the return of her brother. This she has a 'right' (δίκᾳ) to declare. παρών is an *additional predicate*, the whole sentence standing for ὁ πᾶς χρόνος ἐμοὶ ἂν πρέποι (καὶ παρών ἐστιν) ἐννέπειν κτλ. Jebb's explanation of παρών ('"when present", i.e. "as it comes"') seems to make nothing of the word, and to obscure its intimate relation with Orestes' παρουσία at 1251. Notice the repetition of π's in this emotionally-charged utterance.

**1256** 'For it was with difficulty that I restrained as it is (sc. from the moment when I recognised you) my mouth which is used to speak the truth', i.e. I had difficulty in not letting out a great cry of 'Orestes is back, safe and well', which would have been heard within the palace. ἐλεύθερον is an attributive adjective and refers to the fact that Electra (as we know very well) is used to speaking her mind; and for ἔσχον= κατέσχον cf. 223n. For νῦν with a verb in the aorist of an action already begun and continued up to the time of speaking, cf. *Aj.* 995 (ὁδός) ἣν δὴ νῦν ἔβην. Editors usually make ἐλεύθερον predicative and ἔσχον 'I gained'. So Jebb: 'if she is overheard in the house, she may yet lose the newly-gained freedom', as if Electra had ever needed to gain 'freedom' (in that sense) or an ἐλεύθερον στόμα!

**1257** 'Yes! I agree. Therefore go on preserving this (conduct).' καί in κἀγώ is redundant. What Orestes agrees with Electra about is that their reunion has been a marvellous moment of happiness for them both, and that it represents a triumph for them over their enemies. '*Therefore* (says he) go on preserving this restraint.' (Otherwise, your enemies will detect you and you will give them the advantage over you, lose the triumph.) Editors, having misinterpreted ἔσχον ἐλεύθερον στόμα at 1256, as 'I achieved free speech', make σῷζου τόδε mean 'preserve *this freedom*', thus spoiling the symmetry of the dialogue in which everything said by Orestes means 'be quiet'.

**1259** 'Where it is not opportune, do not desire to speak at length.' The first μή is the generic μή (= 'in the kind of circumstances in which').

μακράν: ῥῆσιν can be understood; but it is not uncommon for Greek to form an adverb by simply using the feminine accusative of an adjective (no noun in agreement being supplied): cf. 1389.

**1260ff** 'Who then would thus (sc. as you bid me do) accept in exchange (μεταβάλοιτ') – *adequate* exchange (ἀντάξια) – for your appearance, silence of speech? Since, as it is, it was inconceivably and without expectation that I (at last) beheld you!'

ἀντάξι': neuter accusative plural used adverbially. Since Orestes'

return alive was such an unexpected event for Electra, she has now a
right to compensate for her previous despair by loud and triumphant
assertion of Orestes' presence.

**1264** Electra's last words might imply a reproach against Orestes
(cf. 168ff.) for not letting her know that he was coming. He replies
that he came when (*and only when*) the *gods* (θεοί emphatic) spurred
him on (ἐπώτρυναν) to come (and therefore she saw him then and
only then (τότ᾽ εἶδες). We do not know what particular set of circumstances led him in the first place to consult Delphi and it is not in the
style of Sophocles to fill in such details, when the action and the plot
do not require them.

After 1264 an iambic line, corresponding to 1252 of the strophe, has
accidentally been lost from the text. The kind of thing Orestes said
might have been, *exempli gratia*, 'without the gods aiding me I would
not have undertaken the task'.

**1265ff** 'You have revealed to me a still higher pleasure than the
previous one (that is, the pleasure of your unexpected appearance
and your revelation of yourself to me), if it was in fact a god that
conveyed you to our halls. I reckon it a heaven-sent event.' Electra
(not having heard hitherto of the oracular consultation of 32f.) has so
far only reckoned with Orestes' having turned up in the normal way
(i.e. by the law of blood-feud) as an avenger of his father's murder.
To know now that he was actually spurred on by a divine oracle
appears to her as a sort of bonus of joy and success.

ἐπόρισεν: as Jebb points out, πορίζω elsewhere means 'provide'.
But here he suggests that the context makes it equivalent to πορεύω
(cf. 801n.). This is another example of the plasticity of Sophocles'
language.

αὐτό, in so far as its meaning can be made precise, means 'your
appearing at this particular moment' (sc. when Electra was at the lowest
ebb of her resources). But, as so often throughout this lyric interlude,
the expression is deliberately vague, so that the words can take on
overtones of tragic irony. In this case the suggestion is perhaps that
the whole action from now on is a 'demonic' one, in which the nether
powers possess Orestes and Electra, in order to make of them instru-

ments through which to exact vengeance on Clytaemnestra and
Aegisthus.

**1271ff** 'On the one hand I hesitate to restrict you in your gladness,
but on the other hand I fear your giving way too much to indulgence',
i.e. I fear the consequences of your action (= a sixth suggestion that
Electra be quiet!). Orestes' iambics sound prosaic after Electra's lyric
outburst. The ἡδονή is the pleasure of emotional release.

**1273f** 'Ah! you who thought fit, after so long a time, to appear to
me thus on this gladdest of journeyings, do not, please, do to me,
seeing me thus full of suffering...'

φιλτάταν ὁδόν is a bold internal accusative with φανῆναι. For the
recurrent 'journey' motif, cf. 68, 1163, 1295, 1314. Electra is *afraid*
of Orestes' reasonableness, afraid that he will repress her feeling, and
so sink her further into misery. So she is timid and hesitant in her
prayer that she may be allowed to fondle his face. The hesitation is
conveyed by the τί (1275: used adverbially and indefinitely, the accent
being only a throw-back from the following enclitic με) and also by
the *antilabe* between the speakers which permits her to pause with her
sentence uncompleted, Orestes to break in with τί μὴ ποήσω; at
1276, and herself only to complete her thought with the rest of 1276-7.

**1276** 'Do not deprive me of the pleasure of your features, that I lose
it!'

μεθέσθαι is a redundant epexegetic infinitive, αὐτῆς (from τῶν
σῶν προσώπων ἀδονάν) being understood with it by zeugma.

Simultaneously with these words, Electra conveys by her gesture
that she wishes to take Orestes' face into her hands, to fondle it. But
she is afraid that, in his calculating caution, he will rebuff her.

**1279** 'Most assuredly I should be angry at any one else whom I saw
(trying to stop you)!'

κἂν ἄλλοισι: καί of a complementary action, redundant in
English: cf. 643.

Orestes is for the moment overcome by Electra's outburst of
emotion, and gives way to her.

**1280** 'You join me in approving' (sc. that I should embrace you)?
'Of course I do!'

ξυναινεῖς is still hesitant.

**1281ff** 'Ah! dear one, when I listened to your voice it was as to one that I should never (οὐδ' – lit. 'not even') have hoped again to hear. I restrained my temper so that it found no voice, and without outcry (οὐδὲ σὺν βοᾷ) – God save me! (ἁ τάλαινα), as I listened to your words. And now I have you! You have appeared to me, bearing the dearest countenance of all men – a countenance which I can never forget even in the midst of calamities.'

1232–87 have been difficult to follow partly because of the uncertainties of the text. But that uncertainty is due mainly to the nature of the passage. Such passages represent the very height of ancient tragic and choral composition. Meanings (clearly enough expressed by their counterparts in the iambic trimeters) are here treated briefly, allusively, and with the most poetic lyricism. The rhythms are complicated, and we must remember that the lyrical elements were accompanied by music and gestures now lost. It is no accident that passages such as this, in which the meaning and the emotion of many words are uncertain or difficult to deduce, are precisely those which have been most easily misunderstood, and have therefore suffered most corruption in our manuscripts.

Nevertheless, much of the feeling still communicates itself. We are aware that the scene represents a prolonged moral and psychological struggle in which the natural emotion of Electra is pitted against the cool, calculating rationalism of Orestes (who never loses sight of his overriding purpose to bring about the deaths of Clytaemnestra and Aegisthus). Electra's feelings are timeless, demanding 'any and every time' for their expression; Orestes' calculations depend upon time and *timing* (καιρός). Electra's outbursts represent her attempt to break away from circumstance; Orestes' admonitions to her are attempts to pin her down to it, to subdue her and her emotional nature. In the earlier part of the play, faced with those she hates (or loves only moderately) she has never allowed herself to be subdued, has always given her emotions full rein; now, faced with the man she loves, she does allow herself quite easily to be overcome, to accept destiny, circumstance and timely calculation as prescribed by him (even though he does appear to relax at 1279 and to give way to *her* emotions).

Finally, let us take full note of the terrible dramatic irony of 1287:

'I can never forget your face even amidst disasters.' Here is no preparation for a placid, Fury-less ending to the play. The 'disasters' forecast (although unconsciously on the part of Electra) are the murders of Clytaemnestra and Aegisthus.

### 1288-1300

The moment of emotional indulgence over, Orestes returns to his original character. We have already seen him in his first speech (23ff.) as the man of military discipline and precision, the man of fixed ideas, the ambitious man, a large part of whose aim is to recover his material prosperity intact, the man of action who distrusts argument and reflection, and prefers speed of decision and moral short-cuts. All these traits are once again mercilessly exposed in the following lines.

**1288ff** 'Spare me (ἄφες, lit. 'dispense with') the over-subtleties of justifications, and neither explain to me that our mother is an evil woman nor that Aegisthus is emptying out from our household our father's wealth – either simply wasting it, or sowing it abroad (sc. to make friends) purposelessly (sc. because I am going to end his usurpation). For you would find that (σοι = ethic dative) the telling would exclude the critical moment of time (sc. to accomplish the vengeance). But give me the word as to what will *square* with this time present here and now, namely, where we must show ourselves – or *hide* ourselves – so as to end through this present wayfaring of ours (sc. of Orestes and *Pylades*) our enemies who now exult over us. And mind that our mother does not become aware of you ('πιγνώσεται), by reason of your radiant countenance, now that we two have come against the house. No! rather go on making lament, as it were over the disaster, that has been described falsely (sc. the report of Orestes' own death). For when we succeed, then we shall have opportunity to rejoice and to exult (ourselves) with freedom.' For Orestes' use of the terms λόγοι, χρόνου καιρός, ἁρμόσει, σήμαιν', cf. the notes to 23f., 30f., 75f.

**1289** He does not need to be instructed that his mother is bad, because he has already made up his mind on the matter and intends to kill her.

**1290f** ἀντλεῖ 'bails out' (lit.): cf. 335n.

δόμων: cf. 78n. ἀντλεῖ is the general word; ἐκχεῖ and διασπείρει

describe particular instances of the general notion. We should therefore have expected ἀντλεῖ, τὰ μὲν ἐκχέων, τὰ δὲ διασπείρων. But
Sophocles has loosely constructed the sentence so that ἀντλεῖ (with
which understand μέν: cf. *Trach.* 117 στρέφει, τὸ δ’ αὔξει) is co-
ordinated with the other two verbs.

**1296**   οὕτως sc. πρᾶσσε.

**1299**   εὐτυχήσωμεν: a strange sort of εὐτυχία Orestes proposes.

**1301ff**   'Well, brother, just so (ὧδ’) as is agreeable to you, just in
this way will my part lie too. For I have won my pleasures having got
them from you, and not as my own. And I would not agree (δεξαίμην,
lit. 'accept') to gain for myself a large benefit, at the price of vexing
you even a tiny bit. For (if I were to do so), I should not be serving
fitly the good luck that now attends us.'

ὧδε...τῇδε: redundant repetition, like the καί's of καὶ σοὶ φίλον
κτλ.

**1304**   κοὐδ’ ἄν σε κτλ.: the intensive οὐδέ goes with βραχύ, the
words standing for καὶ οὐδὲ βραχὺ ἄν σε λυπήσασα δεξαίμην κτλ., in
'long' hyperbaton.

**1307**   ἀλλ’: changing the subject.
μέν without balancing δέ expressed.

**1308**   ὁθούνεκ’: cf. 1190n.

**1309**   ἐν οἴκοις by *variatio* from κατὰ στέγας at 1308.

**1309f**   ἥν: anticipatory accusative.
ὡς ὄψεται: usually a verb of fearing for the future takes μή with a
subjunctive. But ὡς or ὅπως with the fut. indic. is also found: cf. 581n.

**1311**   'A hatred of many years' standing has been ground into my
soul' (lit. has melted, fused into it).

**1313ff**   'For how could I leave off weeping, I who have beheld you
both dead and alive, through this one wayfaring?'

Her (naturally) loving nature is perverted already by excess of hate;
she was first cast into utter despair by the lying tale of Orestes' death,
then unnaturally overwrought by the joy of recognising him alive.
Now, her reason unhinged, she begins to be obsessed with the idea of

seeing her father walk the earth alive and well! In Aeschylus' *Choephori* it was *Orestes* who, possessed by the Furies arising from his mother's killing, went mad *after* that killing. In this play it is *Electra* who, possessed by the Furies arising from her father's murder by Clytaemnestra, goes mad *before* the killing of Clytaemnestra.

**1315** εἴργασαι δέ μ᾽ ἄσκοπα 'you have done to me unfathomable things' – a terrible phrase, significant of madness. For ἄσκοπος cf. 864n. In Aeschylus' *Choephori* Orestes (as he is possessed by the Furies arising from his mother's murder) feels a similar strangeness – as he puts it, 'like a charioteer riding outside the course' (*Cho.* 1021ff. ἀλλ᾽ ὡς ἂν εἰδῇτ᾽, οὐ γὰρ οἶδ᾽ ὅπῃ τελεῖ, | ὥσπερ ξὺν ἵπποις ἡνιοστροφῶ δρόμου | ἐξωτέρω). And he sees the Furies, where others cannot: οὐκ εἰσὶ δόξαι τῶνδε πημάτων ἐμοί· | σαφῶς γὰρ αἵδε μητρὸς ἔγκοτοι κύνες (1053f.). Similarly, Electra is now prepared to see her father, alive and well. And she *does* see him – in the shape of the Paedagogus! (1354f.).

**1316f** 'So that, if my father were to come to me alive, I should not now (lit. 'no longer') think it a monstrous vision, but should credit that I saw him.'

**1318ff** 'Since then you arrive for me at journey's end of such a wayfaring, rule me yourself as your desire takes you. For, left to myself, I should have achieved one of two things (lit. 'I should not have missed *both* of two things'); either I should have saved myself nobly, or I should have perished nobly.'

ὅτ᾽: cf. 38n.

τοιαύτην...ὁδόν: internal accusative.

ἡμίν: ethic dative.

ἐξήκεις: ἐξήκειν (lit. 'come out') is to 'end up', cf. 387 ἐξίκοιτο, *Trach.* 1157f. ἐξήκεις δ᾽ ἵνα | φανεῖς ὁποῖος ὢν ἀνὴρ ἐμὸς καλεῖ: 'arrive at the end of'.

**1319** αὐτός is in contrast to Agamemnon whom Electra is now *prepared* to see walking the earth but has not yet conceived that she does see.

**1319ff** ὡς ἐγὼ κτλ.: the thought is 'You cannot do to me any worse than I would have done to myself: for left to myself I should have risked my life honourably, to bring matters to an honourable conclusion' (sc. by trying to assassinate Aegisthus). For the form of expression as well as the thought, cf. Eur. *Or.* 1151f. ἑνὸς γὰρ οὐ σφαλέντες ἕξομεν κλέος, | καλῶς θανόντες ἢ καλῶς σεσωσμένοι. But in our context the doubled καλῶς acquires added ironic meaning from the *leit-motif* use of the word at 791 etc. (cf. 793n., 918n.).

## 1322-1338

Suddenly, from the palace doors a noise is heard, that of someone coming out. Orestes swiftly commands Electra to be silent (about what she has been discussing).

Like many mad people, she is hard-headed and cunning about achieving her ends. So here, she quickly takes up Orestes' warning that there may be hostile observers coming from the palace, and pretends that she is directing the 'Phocian strangers' towards the entrance. But the person who appears is no enemy, but the sinister Paedagogus. He is furious with Electra and Orestes for risking the success of the whole enterprise by what he regards as emotional dalliance, and he scolds them heartily.

**1322f** ἐπήνεσ': for the aorist cf. 388n.

ὡς κτλ.: 'Since I hear someone of those within going to come out.' At *Trach.* 531-2 (ἦμος, φίλαι, κατ' οἶκον ὁ ξένος θροεῖ | ταῖς αἰχμαλώ-τοις παισὶν ὡς ἐπ' ἐξόδῳ) ὡς goes with ἐπ' ἐξόδῳ (='as with the purpose of coming out'). Here the ὡς is needed to provide a connective with the preceding sentence (asyndeton here would be too abrupt, and un-Sophoclean in style). ἐπ' ἐξόδῳ must therefore mean 'to go out' (purposive) by itself.

ἔνδοθεν: for ἔνδον (ὄντων): cf. 1058 ἄνωθεν.

**1324f** 'particularly as you bear such objects as one could scarcely repel from the palace yet could scarcely rejoice at receiving' (sc. the supposed remains of Orestes). But the words in their oblique allusive-ness are deliberate irony. Aegisthus and Clytaemnestra can scarcely ward off what Orestes and Pylades bear (sc. the weapons that are to be used upon themselves), nor will they enjoy receiving them.

ἄλλως τε καί: the well-known idiom for emphasising a participle.

οὔτε...οὔτ': co-ordinating, but in this case expressing an anti-thesis.

**1326ff** ὦ πλεῖστα μῶροι κτλ. 'O most utterly stupid people, deprived of wits.' πλεῖστα: neuter plural used adverbially as a variant for μάλιστα.

πότερα παρ' οὐδὲν κτλ.: a mixture of two constructions: πότερα παρ' οὐδὲν ἔτι τίθεσθε τὸν βίον; and πότερα οὐδὲν ἔτι κήδεσθε τοῦ βίου;.

**1328** 'Or have you no innate intelligence in you?', i.e. Is it not that you have lost your wits, but that you never had them?

**1329f** 'that you do not perceive that you are, not *close to* (παρ') actual dangers, but *in the midst of* the greatest possible actual dangers!'

ὅτ' (despite the translation 'that' which comes naturally in English) is elided ὅτε (here explanatory, causative: 'I think you are mad since you –'). ὅτι does not elide.

**1331** ἀλλ' εἰ 'Why! if...'

σταθμοῖσι τοῖσδε 'at this doorway' (lit. 'doorposts'). For the dative cf. 312n.

**1332** φυλάσσων (used absolutely) = 'keeping guard'. The Paedagogus has made it his business to stay near the door, so as to prevent a chance encounter (before the real 'show-down') between the 'Phocian strangers' and Clytaemnestra's party within the palace.

**1332f** 'You would have had your doings in the house before your persons!' i.e. they would have known what you were up to before your bodies (and they would have been dead ones, because the inmates would have been quick to take action against you!) went into the house.

τὰ δρώμενα is (by a bold but lively sense-construction) treated as a concrete noun, and takes a possessive genitive ὑμῶν. The repetition ὑμῖν...ὑμῶν is admonitory, threatening.

**1334** 'But, as it was, *I* took care in advance in regard to these things.'

**1335ff** 'Even so now (i.e. in harmony with the attitude of careful calculation that I have shown) have done with lengthy speeches, and with this insatiable over-joyous outcry, and move forward to within the palace, since in such matters, *delay* is reprehensible, and it is the supreme moment to make an end' (sc. of the business). The characteristics that we have remarked in Orestes (his contempt for λόγοι, his dislike of emotionalism, his fondness for action, are almost more marked in the Paedagogus. Notice the repetition (which I have not tried to reproduce in English) ἀπαλλαχθέντε (1335), ἀπηλλάχθαι (1338): the first aorist passive and the first perfect passive used with a middle or intransitive meaning. Both have a heavy, harsh sound which seems to emphasise the Paedagogus' contempt for what he regards as the delaying tactics of Orestes and Electra. One sees again (cf. 14n.) from these lines who is the dominant figure behind the purpose to kill Clytaemnestra and Aegisthus. Thucydides' comment on the stasis at Corcyra, τόλμα μὲν γὰρ ἀλόγιστος ἀνδρεία φιλέταιρος ἐνομίσθη, μέλλησις δὲ προμηθὴς δειλία εὐπρεπής (3. 82. 4) seems apposite.

**1338**  ἀκμή cf. 22n.

## 1339-1345

These lines are heavily charged with dramatic irony. Orestes goes to kill his mother, cockily, almost cheerily, without reflection on the issues involved, just as if he were going off upon a military mission. Yet the words used suggest the pathos of the mother–son relationship and the spiritual peril of the matricide.

**1339**  'How then do I find things on their side when I go in?' He means of course, in *the military sense*. But we, the audience, think of the tragedy of the son at last crossing the divide which separates him from his mother, meeting her at last – and killing her! I think it better to take (with L.S.J.) τἀντεῦθεν here of place rather than (with Jebb) of time, though at 728 κἀντεῦθεν was used of time. For the attraction, cf. 1058n.

**1340**  'Well! For the foundation is laid that not a one will recognise you!' καλῶς: ironic *leit-motif*, cf. 793n.

**1342**  He means '*they* think you dead'. But the line has a grim *double entendre*: 'if you stay here, and kill your mother, you are as good as a dead man!'

**1343**  The whole plot of the Paedagogus depends upon obscuring the personal and moral issues. Orestes must not glimpse the reality of his mother. Above all, he must not know how her heart was wrung for his supposed death (770–1). But Orestes, at this moment, cannot avoid probing at the barrier which he knows subconsciously to exist. He wants to know how 'they' receive the news of his death. Are 'they' rejoicing? And what are 'they' talking about?

**1344f** 'I'd better tell you when things are being brought to a *conclusion*. As things are, matters are splendid on their side – even *those matters which are not splendid*!' So the Paedagogus enforces the barrier. As matters stand, things are 'fine', because Clytaemnestra within the palace is unsuspecting, off her guard. But she is off her guard *because she is grief-stricken for Orestes*. Matters are *not* well within the palace because the queen is horror-stricken and conscience-stricken at the death of her son. But from the point of view of the Paedagogus that 'not-wellness' is 'well', because it has distracted Clytaemnestra and will render her an easy victim. Jebb makes τὰ μὴ καλῶς mean 'Clytaemnestra's joy at the death of her son, and those insults which expressed her new sense of security'; and that is the usual version. It seems to me flat and mechanical, and to be out of keeping with the Clytaemnestra of 767ff., and of the sequel. (Is it conceivable that she could 'tend the urn' supposedly containing his ashes (1400f.), while rejoicing over him, insulting him?)

## 1346–1383

Orestes and the Paedagogus, in haste to murder Clytaemnestra, have reckoned without Electra, who now insists on inflicting upon them a period of delay during which she develops her illusion that the Paedagogus is in fact her father walking! The interlude is a curious one. But it is even more curious that critics and editors have made not the slightest attempt to explain it. Its significance appears when it is realised that Electra is showing signs of mounting madness.

**1347** οὐδέ γ' κτλ. 'No! Nor can I *conceive* (who he is)!' ἐς θυμὸν φέρειν is not found elsewhere; but its meaning is tolerably clear, and fits well the psychology of a person of disturbed mind, who has difficulty in conceiving reality (cf. Orestes' remark, *Cho.* 1023f. φέρουσι γὰρ νικώμενον | φρένες δύσαρκτοι – though φέρουσι there of course has quite a different meaning from φέρω here).

**1349f**  οὗ with χεροῖν, in circular hyperbaton.

**1353**  'This is the man! Do not cross-examine me with superfluous (lit. 'more' sc. than necessary) words.' Orestes dislikes ἐλέγχεσθαι, as do Socrates' interlocutors in the Platonic dialogues. The word is revealing.

**1354f**  But Electra is not to be denied. She insists on prostrating herself before the embarrassed Paedagogus.

ὦ φίλτατον φῶς, as at 1224.

σωτήρ (1354)...ἔσωσας (1356): dramatic irony, surely, that the Paedagogus should be hailed as the 'Saviour' of the house of Agamemnon.

**1357f**  'O dearest hands! O you who have the sweetest feet to do your errands (lit. 'the sweetest service of feet'), how was it that, all this while, though of our company (ξυνών), you eluded my notice and would not reveal to me (the truth of things), but made it your business to ruin me with words, though you had (in hand) deeds that are sweetness itself to me! Hail, father mine! For I seem to behold my father in you!' She fondles his hands and feet. The picture is grotesque, were it not for the sinister delusion that it embodies. Notice the imperfects ἔληθες (a poetic form of ἐλάνθανες), ἔφαινες, ἀπώλλυς, which denote continuing action, and should be translated as such.

**1360**  λόγοις: but words can kill, and drive mad!

**1361**  The delusion is manifest, the exaggeration apparent.

πατέρα: 'This is the only tragic trimeter in which the third foot is formed by a single word of three short syllables' (Jebb).

**1364ff**  'I think we have enough of that. As for words that stand in between us (sc. and our goal), many nights, and days to match, wheel upon earth's circling course, which will reveal these things to you in full clarity, Electra.' The Paedagogus' reply to Electra is (understandably) brusque. ταῦτα (1366) means, at the surface level, 'how I got here, why I kept silence'. But there is dramatic irony: there will be 'all the time in the world' to reflect upon the bloody deed of matricide.

τοὺς...λόγους κτλ.: the sentence is an anacoluthon, with τοὺς... λόγους loosely related to the following verbs as an accusative of respect. Jebb understands τοὺς ἐν μέσῳ λόγους as 'the story of the brother's and sister's experiences in the interval since Orestes left Mycenae'.

**κυκλοῦνται:** cf. *Trach.* 129f. ἀλλ' ἐπὶ πῆμα καὶ χαρὰ | πᾶσι κυκλοῦσιν, οἷον ἄρκ|του στροφάδες κέλευθοι.

**1367** 'But I really must (δ'...γε) advise you two who stand at the ready.'

**1368f** The inevitable 'καιρός'! 'Now Clytaemnestra is *alone*. Now there is no *man* within.' So it is two sturdy young men, trained as soldiers, against one woman who is the mother of one of them. We see now why Sophocles constructed his play as he did; it was in order to make the matricide *more odious*.

**1369ff** 'If you shall stay your hand now, reckon that you will have to contend with these people along with others more numerous and more cunning than these!' (sc. with Aegisthus and his followers). Clytaemnestra is *not* 'cunning', because she has let herself be distracted by the news of her son's supposed death.

**φροντίζεθ'** = φρονεῖτε.

**1372ff** 'It would seem that this undertaking of ours demands large speeches no longer (lit. 'is not any longer at all of large speeches'), but (we must now) march with all speed within the palace.' For 'logical' ἄν + optative cf. 245n.

**οὐδέν:** adverbial.

**ὅσον τάχος** (sc. ἐστί) = ὡς τάχιστα.

**χωρεῖν:** cf. 615n. The word has many nuances (depending upon tone, gesture, context) including the military sense 'march'. Since Orestes' language has throughout so many military overtones (cf. 23f., 73f., 1293f., 1495), I have understood his intensive use of χωρεῖν in this latter part of the play (here, 1491, 1495) in the military sense. For the understanding of δεῖ with χωρεῖν, cf. 466-7n.

**1374f** πατρῷα...ἕδη θεῶν = ἕδη ('statues') πατρῴων θεῶν: cf. 1177n.

**ὅσοιπερ κτλ.:** the gods who 'inhabit these portals' include the Apollo Προστατήριος to whom Clytaemnestra addresses her prayer at 637 and Electra hers at 1376, Zeus, and probably also Hermes, to whom the Chorus refer at 1396 (cf. Aesch. *Ag.* 509ff.).

Orestes and Pylades 'salute' (προσκύσαντε 1374) these gods, with the (implied) prayer that these will forward their mission.

**1376ff** Electra too wishes to be associated with the prayer. She (like Clytaemnestra at 634ff.) expects the gods to listen to her in recompense for favours received.

ἥ: circumstantial (cf. 596), 'since I'.

σε...προύστην 'addressed myself to you', 'stood before you' – the unlikely construction (προστῆναι governing an accusative) is vouched for by a single other instance, Soph. fr. 660 προστῆναι μέσην | τράπεζαν ἀμφὶ σῖτα καὶ καρχήσια.

πολλὰ δή 'many a time, for sure': cf. 603.

ἀφ' ὧν ἔχοιμι 'from what store I might have' (sc. at any particular time): indefinite optative.

λιπαρεῖ 'persevering', 'insistent' (the meaning supported by Ellendt (Lexicon) – 'generous' – seems perverse).

**1379** Λύκει': cf. 645n.

ἐξ οἵων 'on the basis of (i.e. 'at the price of') such possessions as I have': i.e. 'no longer with offerings – since none are at hand – but with heartfelt vows' (Jebb, and so the Schol.).

**1380f** πρόφρων...ἀρωγός 'a *willing* helper'.

**1382f** 'And show to men what kind of wages the gods bestow upon them for their wrong-doing': dramatically ironic words, for to kill one's mother is also δυσσεβές.

## 1384–1397

After 1383 Electra goes off, following Orestes and Pylades, into the Palace, leaving the Chorus alone to deliver the third Stasimon. But immediately after the Stasimon (at 1398) she re-emerges. Inheritors of the dark past of Aeschylean theology, the Chorus see the present vengeance as arising from the grave, the present avengers as the embodiment of the spirits of the dead who claim the blood of their slayers in compensation for their own blood. They voice their thoughts in a short passage of dochmiacs (with iambic lines interspersed) indicating their excitement.

**1384ff** 'See where Ares, heavily breathing that blood that breeds battles, spreads his domain. They are gone, this moment past, within the house, those inescapable hounds that speed on the tracks of evil misdeeds. So that the dream of my mind will not have to wait now (ἔτ') long suspended!' The spirit of vengeance, which works through Orestes and Pylades, is called 'Ares', because he is the god of all struggles and warfare.

προνέμεται: he extends his sphere of operations like a forest-fire 'grazing': cf. *Il.* 23. 177 ἐν δὲ πυρὸς μένος ἧκε (sc. upon the bodies of the Trojan captives slain over the body of Patroclus) σιδήρεον, ὄφρα νέμοιτο; Hdt. 5. 101. 2; Ps.-Longinus, *On the sublime* 12. 4.

δυσέριστον: the word appears to be *hapax legomenon*, and has been variously interpreted. I take it to mean that Ares brings with him 'ugly (δυσ-) strife': cf. the Schol., and *Il.* 5. 890f. ἔχθιστος δέ μοί ἐσσι θεῶν οἳ Ὄλυμπον ἔχουσιν· | αἰεὶ γάρ τοι ἔρις τε φίλη πόλεμοί τε μάχαι τε (spoken by Zeus to Ares).

φυσῶν: this word combines two notions: (1) this 'Ares' is a beast who breathes heavily (a sinister detail), (2) he 'breathes blood', because, being the embodiment of slaughter, he *oozes* blood: cf. *Ant.* 1238f. καὶ φυσιῶν ὀξεῖαν ἐκβάλλει ῥοήν (of the newly-slain body of Haemon).

δωμάτων: genitive of relation, with ὑπόστεγοι.

κακῶν πανουργημάτων: objective genitive after μετάδρομοι ('runners after').

μακράν: cf. 1259n.

**1391ff** 'For there is being led insidiously (παρ-) within the house the backer-up of the nether ones with his wily tread, into the mansion of the father with its ancient store of wealth, the backer-up having the new-whetted blood upon his hands. And Maia's son, Hermes, leads him upon the way, having concealed the guile in darkness, leads him to the goal itself – and no longer dallies.'

δολιόπους: because it is the *feet* of the tracking animal, stalking his prey, that must move silently, stealthily, cf. 490n.

ἀρωγός: because the power that exacts the vengeance belongs not only to the dead: it is that of the spirits of vengeance, which assert the dead's will, and of their living representatives, which aid, back up, that will.

**1393** As Sophocles is in so many ways the heir to Aeschylus' thought-processes, there seems here to be a brief reference to the superabundant wealth of the house of Atreus as being the source of its troubles, cf. Aesch. *Ag.* 772ff.

**1394** νεακόνητον: in this kind of highly allusive, succinct poetry, the meanings and the images are telescoped. As one word may include several meanings (like χαλκόπους at 491, δολιόπους at 1392), νεακόνητον αἷμα means both that the avenger has blood on his hands (the blood of Agamemnon, which has never been purged or purified by vengeance), and that this blood is 'new-whetted' (i.e. that it is equivalent to a *weapon*, newly-sharpened so that it may be used to exact vengeance from the murderers). (But the word is suspect, since, morphologically, the alpha should be long, but the metre requires a short. See *app. crit.*)

**1397** Notice the repetition (cf. 487n.) of ἀμμένει after ἀμμενεῖ at 1389.

### 1398–1421

I try to convey the feeling of this *kommos* (cf. the general note to 823ff.) by the following translation.

*El.* Dearest ladies, the men will be accomplishing the deed any moment now. Please stay silent.

*Cho.* Tell me now! What are they doing at this moment?

*El. She* is dressing the urn for burial, and they stand over her, near at hand.

*Cho.* And you – for what reason have you sped out of doors?

*El.* To guard lest Aegisthus enter without our knowledge.

*Clytaemnestra* ( *from within the palace, screams* ) Ah! house empty of friends! full of murderers!

*El.* Someone is crying out within! Do you not hear it, dear friends?

*Cho.* I heard a cry, alas! that should never have been heard, so that I shuddered at it!

*Clytaemnestra* Alas! God pity me! Where are you Aegisthus at all?

*El.* Listen, sure, again someone is crying.

*Clytaemnestra* O my child, my child, pity the mother that bore you!

*El.* But *he* was not judged worthy of pity by you, *or* the father that begot him!

*Cho.* Oh! city, oh! miserable family, now the sun of your daily lot sets, yes! sets.

*Clytaemnestra* A-a-ah! Stricken to the heart!

*El.* Strike her, if you have the strength, a double blow!

*Clytaemnestra* A-a-ah! Stricken again!

*El.* Yes! And would that it had been Aegisthus too!

*Cho.* The curses are doing their work! They walk, the ghostly dead!
Those who died of old are draining the blood – blood that flows in
recompense (παλίρρυτον) – from their killers!

**1399**  τελοῦσι: here future, cf. 971n.

σῖγα: an adverb.

πρόσμενε: addressing the Chorus-leader (*coryphaeus*) is a conventional way of addressing the whole Chorus; hence there is no effective
inconsistency between the singular here and φίλταται γυναῖκες at 1398.

**1400f**  The horror and ignominy of Orestes' murder of his mother is
enhanced by the detail that, at the moment that he stands over her,
waiting his chance to kill her, she is actually tending the urn which
she supposes to contain his ashes.

**1406**  τις: since Electra knows very well who is crying out, τις can
only be sarcastic: she is gloating over her mother's murder.

**1407f**  As is the habit of choruses, this one suddenly relinquishes the
role which it has been playing as an accomplice of the matricides,
takes on a disinterested, universal voice, and stands horror-stricken
at the terrible events of which it is the witness.

**1410f**  ἰδού of something heard, not seen: cf. *Aj.* 871f. ἰδοὺ ἰδού,
δοῦπον αὖ κλύω τινά.

τις: Electra repeats her sarcasm. The hissing *sigma* expresses
Electra's hatred of her mother and her desire to hurt her.

Clytaemnestra has now recognised Orestes, and makes the elemental
appeal to his pity. Cf. Aesch. *Cho.* 896f. ΚΛ. ἐπίσχες, ὦ παῖ, τόνδε δ᾽
αἴδεσαι, τέκνον, | μαστόν, πρὸς ᾧ σὺ πολλὰ δὴ βρίζων ἅμα | οὔλοισιν
ἐξήμελξας εὐτραφὲς γάλα.

**1411f**  You didn't pity him or his father: why should we pity you?
The doctrine of retribution, cf. Aesch. *Ag.* 1560ff. ὄνειδος ἥκει τόδ᾽
ἀντ᾽ ὀνείδους | δύσμαχα δ᾽ ἐστὶ κρῖναι. | φέρει φέροντ᾽, ἐκτίνει δ᾽ ὁ
καίνων. | μίμνει δὲ μίμνοντος ἐν θρόνῳ Διὸς | π α θ ε ῖ ν τ ὸ ν ἔ ρ ξ α ν τ α ·
θέσμιον γὰρ κτλ.

**1413f** I take the meaning to be that the house of Pelops has a 'daily' lot, which waxes in the morning, reaches its zenith at noon, and wanes in the evening. The 'days' are the periods or phases within which one generation or faction of the house's representatives hold power, having wrested it from the opposing faction (i.e. καθαμερία is metaphorical; therefore to be distinguished from the one other known example of the word, Eur. *Phoen.* 229, where it is used literally = 'daily'). Now, with the approaching end of Clytaemnestra, one of these phases is again coming to an end. But the picture suggested of *continuing* vicissitude does not augur well for the future of the present executants. A number of other interpretations have been offered, none of which seems to me plausible.

**1415f** ὤμοι πέπληγμαι... ὤμοι μάλ' αὖθις: cf. Aesch. *Ag.* 1343f. ὤμοι, πέπληγμαι καιρίαν πληγὴν ἔσω... | ὤμοι μάλ' αὖθις, δευτέραν πεπληγμένος.

παῖσον instead of the aorist of πλήσσω, which is not found in Attic.

εἰ σθένεις: Electra hates her mother so much that she imagines herself as having struck the blow. Then, it was struck with such vigour that she imagines she may not be able to muster sufficient strength for the second blow!

**1415** διπλῆν: at least one attempt has been made to tone down the sheer malice of παῖσον... διπλῆν. Ivan M. Linforth argues (*Electra's day in the tragedy of Sophocles* (1963) 109) that διπλῆν means a *matching*, a retaliating blow: the words then are addressed ironically to Clytaemnestra, not to Orestes, and mean 'Strike *back*, if you can.' But cf. *O.C.* 543f. δευτέραν | ἔπαισας ἐπὶ νόσῳ νόσον. And of course Clytaemnestra's ὤμοι μάλ' αὖθις does show that she has just been struck a second time.

**1419** γᾶς ὑπαί: ὑπαί (a form of ὑπό) in anastrophe.

**1420f** The dead 'drain' the blood (which 'flows in recompense': παλίρρυτον) from the living: for this vampire-like activity cf. 1384n., Aesch. *Eum.* 264ff.

### 1422–1441

And now the two murderers stride back through the palace doors on to the stage. Orestes holds his sword unsheathed, from which drips the blood of his mother.

**1422**  καὶ μήν 'Ah! now' (of a new occasion, a new appearance), cf. 78n.

**1423**  στάζει κτλ. 'drips with the sacrifice to Ares' (lit. of the sacrifice – partitive genitive).

οὐδ' ἔχω ψέγειν 'nor can I fault them', i.e. the scene is terrible, but I (the Chorus) cannot see that Orestes and Pylades were wrong to kill Clytaemnestra. The Chorus have now reverted to their role of allies and accomplices of Electra and Orestes. As Aristotle says (*Poet.* 1456a 25f.) καὶ τὸν χορὸν δὲ ἕνα δεῖ ὑπολαμβάνειν τῶν ὑποκριτῶν, καὶ μόριον εἶναι τοῦ ὅλου καὶ συναγωνίζεσθαι μὴ ὥσπερ Εὐριπίδῃ ἀλλ' ὥσπερ Σοφοκλεῖ. ψέγειν, Erfurdt's correction of the MSS' meaningless reading λέγειν, is a palmary emendation.

**1424f**  πῶς κυρεῖτε; = πῶς ἔχετε; 'how are you, how are things with you?'

τὰν δόμοισι μὲν κτλ. 'Things within the house are well – if Apollo oracled well!' But the renewed repetition of the *leit-motif* καλῶς makes the word heavily ironic, cf. 793n., 918n.

**1426f**  ἡ τάλαινα 'the wretch'.

μηκέτ' ἐκφοβοῦ κτλ. 'No longer fear that the haughty spirit of your mother will ever again dishonour you!' (But 'haughtiness' is a great over-simplification of the Clytaemnestra of this play. Thus again Orestes misreads the character of his mother.) ἐκφοβοῦ: for ἐκ- cf. 276n. For ὡς + fut. indic. cf. 1309n.

**1427ff**  From the fact that 1422–41 are evidently antistrophic to 1398–421, it would appear that three lines (corresponding to 1404–6) have been lost after 1427, that an iambic line (corresponding to 1409) has been lost after 1429, and that the latter half of the iambic line 1431 has been lost. The losses fortunately do not detract from the general sense; and it is clear, at 1428, that we have passed on to the second act of the vengeance, and the last of the drama.

**1430f**  'Back, lads!' sc. towards the palace, within which they will be hidden from the approaching Aegisthus.

ἄψορρον is adverbial (cf. 53), and the negative question amounts to a command.

εἰσορᾶτέ που: 'You see, I take it, the man (almost) upon us.' The exact construction of ἐφ' ἡμῖν is unclear, because of the lacuna. που: cf. 55.

**1432** 'There (οὗτος) he advances, overjoyed, from the city's outskirts.' Aegisthus is naturally delighted at the news of Orestes' death, since this event means the end of all threats to his life and his rule at Mycenae. Electra can see the joy in his face as he approaches, just as Oedipus sees, from a distance, the radiance on the face of Creon (*O.T.* 80–1).

ἐκ προαστίου : from the country, the fields, mentioned at 313.

**1433** Jebb suggests that βᾶτε κατ' ἀντιθύρων means 'make *for* the vestibule', but confesses that this use of κατά + genitive is unparalleled. If the text is sound I should be inclined rather to render '*Go down from* the vestibule', i.e. retire from the vestibule into the inward parts of the house – the vestibule being regarded as a 'high' (i.e. exposed) position.

**1434f** The words stand (by the use both of 'economy' and of hyperbaton) for ὡς τάδε πάλιν νῦν (εὖ θησόμενοι), τὰ πρὶν εὖ θέμενοι: 'as about to make a success of *these* matters again, having already made a success of the previous affair'.

θέμενοι: from the popular game of πεσσοί in which the player disposed his pieces to the best advantage according to the throw of dice: see Denniston's note to Eur. *El.* 639.

τελοῦμεν by *variatio* from εὖ θησόμεθα.

ᾗ virtually for οἷ: cf. *Ant.* 444.

ἔπειγε is used absolutely.

**1436** *Or.* Very well! I am gone. *El.* I believe *I* must see to matters here.

ἂν μέλοιτ': cf. 249n. The middle of μέλω can be used in poetry with the genitive in place of the more usual active in the sense 'be a concern to'.

**1437ff** δι' ὠτὸς ἂν κτλ.: as we say, to 'slip a word in his ear'. The first ὡς goes with ἠπίως and is redundant.

λαθραῖον κτλ. 'that he may rush upon a stealthy (treacherous) trial of justice', i.e. that he be lured, without his knowledge, into the trap (λαθραῖον being made predicative, or at least emphatic, by its prominent position in the sentence and its separation from ἀγῶνα).

## 1442–1465

Aegisthus enters in haste and addresses himself first to the Chorus and Electra, then particularly to Electra.

**1442** ποῦ ποθ᾿: cf. 823, 669n.

**1443f** 'to whom they say we owe the news that Orestes etc.' (lit. 'who they say have announced for us', ἡμῖν being the ethic dative: the announcement of Orestes' death affects, is of interest to, Aegisthus and Clytaemnestra).

    ναυαγίοις: cf. 730, 335n.

**1445ff** 'You I say, you it is I cross-examine. Yes, you! who used to have such a bold tongue in you! For I suppose you are most concerned and are most likely to give me the information from certain knowledge.' τοι is not here proverbial, but emphasises σέ. The repeated σέ conveys a rough, hectoring tone (cf. Ant. 441f. σὲ δή, σὲ τὴν νεύουσαν ἐς πέδον κάρα, | φής κτλ.).

**1448f** If the text is right it means, 'For (otherwise) why! (γε) I should be unaware of the fortune of my nearest and dearest' (sc. of Orestes). Jebb reads the variant τῆς φιλτάτης, translating 'of my mother, Clytaemnestra'. Then the whole phrase συμφορᾶς τῆς φιλτάτης has an 'inner' meaning – the *disaster* to my mother – 'which he (Aegisthus) cannot yet surmise'. I agree with Campbell (*Paralipomena Sophoclea* 153) that Electra would not 'speak of her mother as τῆς φιλτάτης in addressing Aegisthus'.

**1450** 'Where then *can* they be?'

    ἂν εἶεν: logical ἄν, with an overtone of impatience.

**1451** Here certainly is a deliberate *double entendre*. The surface-meaning is, 'for they have accomplished (their journey to the house) of a dear hostess' (as we say in English slang 'to make' a place, i.e. to arrive at it: for ἀνύειν in this sense cf. Aj. 607 ἀνύσειν ᾿Αϊδαν, O.C. 1562f. δόμον is easily understood). The 'hidden meaning' (Jebb) is, 'they have achieved *the murder of* their dear hostess'.

**1452** ἦ καί: 'Did they actually...?' cf. 314, 614n.

    ὡς ἐτητύμως with θανόντα: 'truly, actually *dead*'. For ὡς cf. 1437n.

**1453** 'Not (merely), but they actually displayed (the evidence), not just (told the story) in word alone.'

**1454** 'Is it possible then for *me* to make acquaintance with (this evidence) actually (καί) manifested?'

ἡμῖν=ἐμοί (since the context implies that Aegisthus has no attendants).

ὥστε is redundant after πάρεστι.

**1455** 'Certainly it is possible, though it be a right unenviable sight!' For πάρεστι picking up πάρεστι of 1454 cf. 390n.

**1456f** 'Assuredly you have bidden me greatly rejoice, in a manner unusual to you', i.e. you do not usually bring me good news. For ἤ cf. 1039n.

χαίροις ἄν: cf. 555n.

**1458ff** 'I order silence, and that the palace-gates be opened up for all the Mycenaeans and Argives to see, so that, if anyone of them was previously elated by empty hopes connected with this man, now, seeing his body, he may accept my bridle, and not have to experience me as a chastener, before under constraint he blossoms wisdom.'

σιγᾶν ἄνωγα κτλ.: lit. 'I order (sc. one – τινά) to be silent and open up.' As often in commands, the subject of the infinitive is indefinite and is left to be understood. But to whom are Aegisthus' commands actually addressed? σιγᾶν at least includes Electra, but probably applies to everyone else present as well (in effect the Chorus who may be supposed, for the occasion, to represent the Mycenaean populace): by a general silence Aegisthus wants the full effect of Orestes' death to be felt. ἀναδεικνύναι is addressed to Electra, since it is she who obeys the command (1464). As Jebb says, ἀναδεικνύναι πύλας is a pregnant way of saying 'open the doors and *open up* the palace'.

**1459** ὁρᾶν: a consecutive infinitive.

**1462f** στόμια: lit. 'my *bit*'.

μηδὲ πρὸς βίαν κτλ.: lit. 'only when he has met with me as a chastener...', the main emphasis being on the participial construction.

φύσῃ φρένας: cf. Aesch. *P.V.* 1of. ὡς ἂν διδαχθῇ τὴν Διὸς

τυραννίδα | στέργειν. Notice the harsh effect here of the alliteration φύσῃ φρένας.

**1464f** 'Well, indeed, my part of the instruction will be accomplished. For at long last I have acquired sense, so as to serve the interests of my superiors.' But τελεῖται can as well be present, if we imagine Electra to be opening up the doors, as she speaks. Jebb takes the (ostensible) meaning to be 'I, at least, am resolved to be loyal and docile', and detects a 'secret' meaning, 'My part in the vengeance is being accomplished.' This version is equally possible.

τἀπ' ἐμοῦ = τὰ ἀπ' ἐμοῦ (crasis).

τῷ χρόνῳ: cf. 1013n.

**1465** συμφέρειν τοῖς κρείσσοσιν: this phrase (complementary to 340 τῶν κρατούντων ἐστὶ πάντ' ἀκουστέα, 396 τοῖς κρατοῦσι δ' εἰκαθεῖν, and 1014 σθένουσα μηδὲν τοῖς κρατοῦσιν εἰκαθεῖν marks how *contemporary* Sophocles' *Electra* is. In Book 1 of Plato's *Republic*, Thrasymachus proposes that 'Justice' is nothing else but τὸ τοῦ κρείττονος συμφέρον (*Rep.* 1. 338c). In that case it would be 'right' in the case of subjects that they should συμφέρειν τοῖς κρείσσοσιν i.e. serve the interests of their superiors. Electra's συμφέρειν τοῖς κρείσσοσιν cannot, given the political atmosphere in which Sophocles wrote, be understood in any other sense than Thrasymachus' phrase is to be understood. But Jebb sees no connection with Thrasymachus, and makes συμφέρειν τοῖς κρείσσοσιν mean 'to agree with them, to live in accord with them'.

Electra has been accused throughout the play of lacking νοῦς or σοφία, not being able to 'be taught' (cf. 330f., 396, 1013f., 1015f.). 'Now', she says, 'I *have* learnt my lesson. I have adapted myself to the sophistic principle of recognising my physical superior for what he is, and submitting to his interest' (in other words, 'I have ceased trying to be καλὴ κἀγαθή at the cost of common sense', cf. 1087n.). Of course she is being ironical.

### 1466–1474

Electra obeys Aegisthus' command, goes up to the palace-doors and throws them wide open. From the dark interior Orestes and Pylades, still disguised as 'Phocian strangers', wheel out the *ekkyklema*. On it lies a body, swathed in cloths, which Aegisthus assumes to be that of

226 COMMENTARY: 1466–9

Orestes. Aegisthus regards it with awe from a distance, then approaches
and bends over the veiled figure.

**1466ff** 'Lord Zeus! I behold here an apparition that has fallen out,
true (μέν), not without some spite (on the part of the gods). But, in case
there is any ill-luck upon it, I say nothing (of it)! Undo all the wrapping
from the eyes, that blood of my blood, to be sure, may meet with due
laments even from me.'

ὦ Ζεῦ: Aegisthus, touched with awe at the sight of what he
believes to be Orestes' body, addresses the supreme deity, who dis-
penses disaster as well as triumph. φάσμα usually means an uncanny
sight. Aegisthus chooses the word because of the feeling of shock
which the veiled body conveys to him.

ἄνευ φθόνου κτλ.: Aegisthus means that Orestes must have
incurred some divine displeasure (cf. Jebb's note to *Phil.* 776),
probably because of his undutiful behaviour towards his mother
(cf. 793n.). This φθόνος has resulted in Orestes' supposed accident.
However, Aegisthus will not dwell on this side of things, in case there
might be a *nemesis* (same as φθόνος) on *himself*, for appearing to scold
or triumph (by saying 'I told you so!') over Orestes in his calamity.

πεπτωκός 'fallen out' (like a throw of dice). There is a change of
metaphor between φάσμα and πεπτωκός.

**1469** τὸ συγγενές: lit. 'that which is related to me', 'relationship'.
Then that abstract is itself understood as concrete ( = 'Orestes who is
my relation').

τοι: 'proverbial', i.e. it was a well-known motto, conventional,
that relative should mourn relative.

Jebb says of this speech: 'Aegisthus is not openly exulting here; he
veils his joy in specious language, for he is in public, and speaks before
hearers whom he mistrusts. He affects to think that the gods have
struck down his enemy'; and of 1467 he says, 'Aegisthus corrects
himself with hypocritical piety.' This seems to me to read into the
text what is not there. Aegisthus has spoken at 1466 as if he were taken
aback at the appearance of what he supposes to be Orestes' body. Nor
has he spoken at 1458 as if he cared in the least about what his hearers
may think of him. There is not the slightest reason to think that
Aegisthus does not express his true feelings at 1466f., any more than

there is to suspect Clytaemnestra's sincerity at 766–8 and 770–1. Indeed, Sophocles is in the process of doing to Aegisthus what he earlier did to Clytaemnestra: having depicted a villain, he goes on to show that the villain has decent, even generous emotions! Thus his dramatic world turns out to be, not a melodramatic one, but a complexity of issues too subtle to be solved by such simple formulae as 'an eye for an eye, and a tooth for a tooth'.

**1470f** βάσταζ' 'handle'. The irony continues. ' *You* are the relative', says Orestes, 'it is for you to look at, and pay your respects to the corpse.'

ταῦθ': what is contained in the wrappings.

**1472f** Aegisthus accepts the responsibility. But, as Clytaemnestra is an even nearer relative of Orestes, he proposes summoning her.

σὺ δέ: spoken to Electra, presumably.

**1474** Orestes' macabre sarcasm, as Aegisthus undoes the wrapping.

### 1475–1490

Aegisthus springs back in horror from what he now recognises to be the body of Clytaemnestra. His immediate reaction is to turn and stare, in deadly fear, at his interlocutors.

**1475** τίν' ἀγνοεῖς: since Aegisthus scans Orestes' face, trying to make out who he can be, and failing.

**1476f** 'Who can be the men into the midst of whose toils I have fallen, unlucky wretch that I am?'

ἐν μέσοις ἀρκυστάτοις: cf. Aesch. *Ag.* 1374f.

**1477f** 'Why (γάρ), do you not perceive that you have for some time now been addressing living men as though they were dead?' If the text is right, this, I think, is the meaning. By *thinking* of Orestes (who is alive) as 'dead' (i.e. as the dead body on the *ekkyklema*), Aegisthus had been treating him as if he were dead. True, Aegisthus has not specifically *addressed* the corpse as 'Orestes', but I do not think the word ἀνταυδᾷς should be pressed. The words of course are chosen for their dark allusiveness and riddling quality. Jebb translates 'thou

perversely (ἀντ-) speakest of the living as if they were dead'. But the
sense seems tamer, and the meaning assigned to ἀνταυδᾶν arbitrary.
(True, we might have expected a dative with ἀνταυδᾶν = 'address'.
But the word is *hapax legomenon*, and we cannot exclude the accusative
usage.)

The MSS do not read ζῶντας but ζῶν τοῖς and some scholars retain
this. So Lewis Campbell, translating, '"while yet in life, thou art
answering a dead man with accents of the dead", i.e. of one doomed
to die' (*Paralipomena Sophoclea* 155). If we knew ζῶν τοῖς to be the
reading, I should rather render it, 'you (the living) are *matching words*
with the dead' (i.e. you haven't really got a chance).

ἴσα: (adv.) cf. *O.T.* 1187f. ὡς ὑμᾶς ἴσα καὶ τὸ μη|δὲν ζώσας
ἐναριθμῶ.

**1479  ξυνῆκα τοὔπος:** i.e. I have read the riddle, cf. Aesch. *Cho.* 887f.

**1481  καί** *indignantis*, here taunting. The line obviously implies that
Aegisthus had some special qualifications in μαντική (cf. 1499). This
is part of the background story which appears to have been lost.
Perhaps the same detail induced Euripides to depict Aegisthus as
conducting a sacrifice, and inspecting the entrails for signs of the
future, when he was treacherously murdered by Orestes (Eur. *El.*
826f.).

**1483  κἂν σμικρόν** 'even if it be a little', 'just a few words'.
Aegisthus claims the right, jealously guarded in the Greek rudimentary
consciousness of international law, to speak a few words in his own
defence: for the implications of the claim and its refusal by Electra see
the Introduction 11 n. 1.

**1483f** 'Let him not speak further, in God's name, brother, or spin
out lengthy words.' Electra has now become as great a foe of 'long
words' as her brother and the Paedagogus.

**1485f** 'For when mortals are immeshed in troubles, what benefit can
he who is sure to die win from (allowance of) time?'

θνῄσκειν ὁ μέλλων = ὁ μέλλων θνῄσκειν. βροτῶν... μεμειγμένων
can be a partitive genitive with it, or a genitive absolute (as in my
translation).

τοῦ χρόνου: genitive of source: cf. 78n.

**ἄν...φέροι:** cf. 591n.

For the thought cf. *Aj.* 475f. τί γὰρ παρ' ἦμαρ ἡμέρα τέρπειν ἔχει, | προσθεῖσα κἀναθεῖσα τοῦ γε κατθανεῖν; We see here that the play's concern with *time* (cf. 22, 75n.) lasts to its conclusion. But I would see also dramatic irony in these lines. Aegisthus has 'no future'. But neither have Electra and Orestes. For vengeance is no solution to human troubles, nor is the condition of being a matricide a state of human happiness. Nor does βροτῶν σὺν κακοῖς μεμειγμένων apply only to Aegisthus; it includes also Orestes and Electra, cf. 1287.

**1487ff** 'No! kill him as quickly as may be, and having killed him expose him to such grave-diggers as this creature may expect to meet with, out of my sight. Since that is the only measure which could release me from the evils which have so long beset me.'

## 1491–1507

The finale of the play may be translated as follows:

*Or.* In with you – quickly! It's no trial of words now, but of your life!

*Aeg.* And why do you take me indoors? How is it, if this deed be honourable, that you need the dark, and are not ready to kill me now?

*Or.* Don't give orders! *March* – to where you killed our father, that you may die in the same place in which he did!

*Aeg.* Is it absolutely necessary that this house should see this day's griefs of Pelops' clan – ay! and tomorrow's?

*Or.* Well, yours anyway! I can prophesy you that with some accuracy!

*Aeg.* This is not a skill you can claim to have inherited from your father.

*Or.* You have a lot to say! But you're slackening the march! Get on with you!

*Aeg.* *You* lead the way.

*Or.* No! You're to go first.

*Aeg.* Afraid I shall give you the slip?

*Or.* No! Seeing to it that you don't die at ease! I have to see that you don't enjoy it!

This is the penalty that all should suffer without any shilly-shallying – anyone, that is (γε), who thinks of doing anything against the laws. *Kill them all!* You wouldn't have many rascals!

**1491**  χωροῖς ἄν: cf. 1372n. (spoken in another tone the expression can be polite: cf. *Phil.* 674).

**1492**  ἀγών (= ὁ ἀγών, by crasis). There is to be no 'trial' of words such as the debate between Clytaemnestra and Electra, 525ff., in the case of Aegisthus, but a 'struggle' or ordeal (ἀγών in its other sense) concerning the life of Aegisthus.

**1493**  Aegisthus leaves the stage, asking awkward questions. The first is, 'Why, if the deed is honourable, do you need *the dark* to do it in?'

**1495f**  Orestes knows only the letter of the law of retribution: Aegisthus must die *in the same place* as did Agamemnon.

**1497f**  Second awkwardness. Both Orestes and Aegisthus belong to the house of Pelops, and that house has been *accursed* since earlier generations (cf. 504n.), the curse expressing itself in a series of retributive killings to which there is no end, since one act of retribution demands another (cf. 582f.). So unless Orestes relents and breaks the series, the house of Pelops must 'see' not merely the present act of retribution but also that which will (in all expectation) follow it.

τά τ' ὄντα καὶ μέλλοντα: for τά τ' ὄντα καὶ τὰ μέλλοντα (the second τά being understood by 'economy' from the first: cf. 265n.).

**1499**  Orestes eludes the issue of the 'ills to come', but replies to Aegisthus with a sarcasm alluding to his interest in μαντική.

ἄκρος 'proficient', cf. Aesch. *Ag.* 628 ἔκυρσας ὥστε τοξότης ἄκρος σκοποῦ.

**1500f**  Aegisthus answers Orestes' sarcasm with another: 'Your father wasn't a good foreteller of the future, when he entered his house to get his death there.' Orestes has no answer to this (except to drive Aegisthus before him into the palace). So Aegisthus, physical victim though he is of Orestes' *coup*, has the last word.

Campbell comments on this line (*Paralipomena Sophoclea* 155): 'Compare the end of the *Trachiniae*, where the spectators are aware of "the glory that is to follow", though it is hidden from Hyllus and the rest.' But we have *nothing but* the surviving *Trachiniae* and *Electra* to tell us what Sophocles thought about the actions depicted in either play. We ought not to add suppositions not implicit in the actual plays.

ἀλλ' οὐ πατρῴαν κτλ.: lit. 'you have boasted of the skill not as being one derived from your father' (πατρῴαν predicative).

**1503f** (Is your action) 'lest I escape you?'

μή final: cf. 641n.

μὴ μὲν οὖν κτλ.: cf. 459.

φυλάξαι δεῖ με κτλ. 'I must save this for you ('see to it that it is') painful.' No refinement of vindictive savagery is to be spared.

**1505ff** I imagine these lines to be spoken as a sort of *envoi* to the audience. *Whoever* does anything 'against the laws' is to be killed. (Not judicially tried, mark: εὐθύς excludes that.) Then you wouldn't have 'many rascals'. For Orestes' last words, see Introduction 12.

**1508ff** 'O seed of Atreus, how, having suffered much, you have at long last made your way to liberty, having been made perfect through this present onset!'

σπέρμ' = Orestes.

δι' ἐλευθερίας...ἐξῆλθες: lit. 'have come *out* (of trouble) *in* a state of freedom'. For ἐξ- cf. 387, 1318n.

μόλις: lit. 'only just'.

The play ends (like so many Greek tragedies) with a short perfunctory address (in anapaests) by the Chorus. After the brutal realism of the final scene, this taglike ending cannot tell us anything about the play's meaning. Indeed, it is difficult not to detect irony in it. τελεωθέν may remind us too uncomfortably of τέλειος used of beasts ripe for sacrifice! (Cf. Clytaemnestra's sinister *double-entendre* in Aeschylus, *Ag.* 972f. ἀνδρὸς τελείου δῶμ' ἐπιστρωφωμένου. | Ζεῦ Ζεῦ τέλειε, τὰς ἐμὰς εὐχὰς τέλει.)

# APPENDIX 1

## THE LYRIC METRES

Greek lyric metre is a difficult subject for the beginner and the uninitiated; and it is not absolutely necessary to understand its details in order to appreciate Greek drama. This is why I have contented myself in the commentary with merely referring to some of the characteristic rhythms of the lyrics. But the more the metre is understood, the more the sense (and the understanding) of the poetry is enriched. For those, therefore, who seek more precise knowledge, I append the following metrical analysis of the lyrics of the *Electra*. It rests upon the analysis made by the late Miss A. M. Dale, and I am grateful to Professor E. W. Handley (Director of the London Institute of Classical Studies, acting in this case on behalf of Professor T. B. L. Webster, Miss Dale's husband) for permission to print it. In a few minor details, where matters seemed to me conjectural in any case, I have slightly modified the original script in the direction of what I thought simpler or clearer. I am very grateful to Miss M. L. Cunningham (herself a pupil of Miss Dale's) for checking the final draft and assisting me with her expert knowledge.

In the scheme, $\frown$ = two short syllables standing for a long; $=$ = a long standing for two shorts; $\smile$ = a short standing (at the end of a cadence or clausula) for a long (*brevis in longo*); $\parallel$ = a cadence or clausula. See p. 239n. for syllables contracted by *synizesis*. For further information (and explanation of the technical descriptive terms used of the various metrical units) the reader is referred to A. M. Dale, *Greek lyric metre*[2] (Cambridge University Press 1968), and D. S. Raven, *Greek metre – an introduction* (Faber & Faber 1962). The London Institute of Classical Studies is shortly to publish a collective analysis by Miss Dale of the various lyrical passages in Greek Tragedy.

## 121–250

### 121–36 (strophe) = 137–52 (antistrophe)

| | |
|---|---|
| – – – – – ∪ ∪ – | choriambic dimeter |
| – – – – – ∪ ∪ – – – | choriambic dimeter plus spondee |
| – ∪ ∪ – ∪ – – – | choriambic dimeter with dragged close |
| – ∪ ∪ – ∪ ∪ – ∪ ∪ – ∪ ∪ | dactylic tetrameter |
| – ∪ ∪ – ∪ ∪ – ∪ ∪ – ∪ ∪ | dactylic tetrameter |
| ∪ – ∪ ⏝ – ⏝⏝ ∪ – ∪ ∪ ∪ ∪ – | iambic trimeter |
| ∪ – – – ∪ – ∪ – – | syncopated iambic trimeter catalectic |
| – ∪ ∪ – – – – | dactylic trimeter pendant |
| – ∪ ∪ – ∪ ∪ – ∪ ∪ – ∪ ∪ | dactylic tetrameter |
| – ∪ ∪ – ∪ ∪ – ∪ ∪ – ∪ ∪ | dactylic tetrameter |
| – ∪ ∪ – ∪ ∪ – ∪ ∪ – ∪ ∪ | dactylic tetrameter |
| – ∪ ∪ – ∪ ∪ – ∪ ∪ – ∪ ∪ | dactylic tetrameter |
| – – – – – ∪ ∪ – ∪ ∪ – ∪ ∪ – ∪ ∪ | dactylic dimeter plus tetrameter |
| ⊻ – ∪ – ∪ – – | iambic dimeter catalectic |
| – – ∪ – – | iambic penthemimer |

### 153–72 (2nd strophe) = 173–92 (2nd antistrophe)

| | |
|---|---|
| – ⸬ – ⸬ – | contracted hemiepes |
| ⌒ ∪ ⌒ ∪ – ∪ – | lecythion |
| ⊻ ⌒ ∪ – – ∪ – ∪ – – | syncopated iambic trimeter catalectic |
| – ⌒ ∪ – – ∪ – ∪ – ⌣ ‖ | syncopated iambic trimeter catalectic |
| – – – ⏝⏝ – ⏝⏝ – ⏝⏝ – ∪ ∪ – – | dactylic hexameter |
| ⊽ – ∪ – ∪ – – ‖ | iambic dimeter catalectic |
| – ⌒ ∪ – – – | contracted iambic dimeter |
| – ⌒ ∪ – – – | contracted iambic dimeter |
| – ∪ ∪ – ∪ ∪ – ∪ ∪ – ∪ ∪ | dactylic tetrameter |
| – ⌒ ∪ ⏝ ∪ – ∪ ⏝ ∪ – – | iambic trimeter catalectic |
| – ⌒ ∪ ⌒ ∪ ⏝ ∪ – ∪ – – | iambic trimeter catalectic |
| ∪ ⏝ ∪ – – ∪ – ∪ – – | syncopated iambic trimeter catalectic |
| – ∪ ∪ – ∪ ∪ – ∪ ∪ – ∪ ∪ | dactylic tetrameter |

| | |
|---|---|
| – ∪∪ – ∪∪ – ∪∪ – ∪∪ | dactylic tetrameter |
| – ∪∪ – ∪∪ – ∪∪ – ∪∪ | dactylic tetrameter |
| – ∪∪ – ∪∪ – ∪∪ – ∪∪ | dactylic tetrameter |
| ∪ – – – ∪ – | syncopated iambic dimeter |
| ∪ – – – ∪ – ∪ – – | syncopated iambic trimeter catalectic |

### 193–212 (3rd strophe) = 213–32 (3rd antistrophe)

| | |
|---|---|
| – – – – – – | paroemiac |
| – – – – – – – | anapaestic dimeter |
| ∪∪ – – – – – – | anapaestic dimeter |
| ⏔ – – – – – | paroemiac |
| ∪∪ – ∪∪ – ∪∪ – – – | anapaestic dimeter |
| – – – – ⏔ – – – | anapaestic dimeter |
| – – ⏕ – ∪∪ – ∪∪ – | anapaestic dimeter |
| – ∪ – ∪ – – | ithyphallic |
| – – – – – ⏔ – ⏔ | anapaestic dimeter |
| – – – – – – | paroemiac |
| – – – – – – – | anapaestic dimeter |
| – – – – | anapaestic monometer |
| – ⏒⏒∪ – | dochmiac |
| ∪∪ – ⏕ – ∪∪ – ⏕ – | anapaestic dimeter |
| – ⏒∪ – – ∪ – | syncopated iambic dimeter |
| ⏒∪ – ∪ – ∪ – | lecythion |
| ⏓⏒∪⏒∪ – ∪ – | iambic dimeter |
| ⏓⏒∪⏒∪ – ∪ – | iambic dimeter |
| – ∪∪ – ∪∪ – ∪∪ – ∪∪ | dactylic tetrameter |
| ⏓⏒∪ – ∪ – ⌣ | iambic dimeter catalectic |

### 233–50 (epode)

| | |
|---|---|
| – – – – – – | paroemiac |
| – – – – – – | paroemiac |
| – – – – – – | paroemiac |
| – ∪∪ – ∪∪ – ∪∪ – ∪∪ | dactylic tetrameter |
| – ∪∪ – ∪∪ – ∪∪ – ∪∪ | dactylic tetrameter |
| – ∪∪ – – – – – | dactylic tetrameter |
| – – – – – – – | anapaestic dimeter |
| – – – – – – – | anapaestic dimeter |

| | |
|---|---|
| – – – – – – ∪ ∪ – | anapaestic dimeter |
| – – – – – – ∪ ∪ ⏑ ‖ | anapaestic dimeter |
| – ⌒ – ∪ – | dochmiac |
| – ⌒ – ∪ – – ⌒ – ∪ – | double dochmiac |
| – ∪ – ∪ – | hypodochmius |
| – ∪ – ∪ – | hypodochmius |
| – – – ∪ ∪ – ∪ – | glyconic |
| – – ∪ – – | iambic penthemimer |
| ∪ – – – ∪ – ∪ – – | syncopated iambic trimeter catalectic |

## 472–515

### 472–87 (strophe) = 488–503 (antistrophe)

| | |
|---|---|
| – – – ∪ ∪ – – ∪ ∪ – | choriambic decasyllable |
| – – – – ∪ ∪ – – ∪ – | choriambic enneasyllable |
| – ∪ – ∪ – – | ithyphallic |
| ∪ – ∪ – ∪ ⌒ ∪ – ∪ – ∪ – | iambic trimeter |
| ∪ – ∪ – – ∪ – ∪ – | syncopated iambic trimeter |
| ∪ – ∪ – – ⏑ ‖ | contracted iambic dimeter |
| – ∪ ∪ – ∪ – ⏑ ‖ | aristophanean |
| – ∪ – ∪ – ∪ – | lecythion |
| – – ∪ – – – ∪ – | iambic dimeter |
| – – – – ∪ – | syncopated iambic dimeter |
| – – ∪ – – – ∪ – | iambic dimeter |
| ⊻ – – – ∪ ⏑ ‖ | syncopated iambic dimeter |
| – – ∪ ∪ – ∪ – ⏑ | choriambic enoplian |
| – ∪ – – – | syncopated contracted iambic dimeter |

## 504–15 (epode)

| | |
|---|---|
| – ⌒ ∪ – – – | iambo-dochmiac colarion |
| ∪ ⌒ ∪ – – – | iambo-dochmiac colarion |
| – ⌒ ∪ – – – | iambo-dochmiac colarion |
| – ∪ – | cretic |
| – ⌒ ∪ – – – | iambo-dochmiac colarion |
| – ⌒ ∪ – – – | iambo-dochmiac colarion |

| | |
|---|---|
| – – – ∪ – | dochmiac |
| – – – – – – | double molossus |
| – – ∪ – – – | iambo-dochmiac colarion |
| – ∪ – | cretic |
| ∪⌢ – – – – | iambo-dochmiac colarion |
| ∪⌢∪ – – – | iambo-dochmiac colarion |

### 823–70

#### 823–36 (strophe) = 837–48 (antistrophe)

| | |
|---|---|
| – ⌢∪ – – ∪∪ – – | iambic penthemimer plus ionic monometer |
| ∪∪ – – ∪∪ – – ∪∪ – – | plus ionic trimeter |
| – – ∪∪ – – ‖ | ionic colarion |
| ∪∪ – – | ionic monometer |
| – – ∪∪ – – | ionic colarion |
| – – – ∪∪ – ⌣ ‖ | ionic dimeter |
| ∪∪ – – | ionic monometer |
| – – ∪∪ – – ∪∪ – – | seven major ionic metra ending |
| ∪∪ – – ∪∪ – – | with molossus as cadence? |
| ∪∪ – – ∪∪ – – ∪∪ – – – | (cf. *Greek Lyric Metre*[2] 122; *ibid.* 155 for a different explanation) |

#### 849–58 (2nd strophe) = 859–70 (2nd antistrophe)

| | |
|---|---|
| – ∪ – – ∪ – ∪ – | cretic plus hypodochmius |
| – – – – – ∪∪ – – | melic anapaestic dimeter |
| – – – – – – – – | melic anapaestic dimeter |
| – – – – – – ∪ ‖ | paroemiac |
| – ∪∪ – ∪ – | dochmiac |
| – ∪ – – ⌢ | hypodochmius with dragged close |
| ⌢∪ – ∪ – ∪ – | lecythion |
| ∪ – ∪ – ∪ – ∪∪ – ∪∪ – | iambelegus |
| – ∪∪ – ∪ – – | aristophanean |

### 1058–97

#### 1058–69 (strophe) = 1070–81 (antistrophe)

| | |
|---|---|
| ∪ – ∪ – – ∪∪ – ∪ – ∪ – | iambo-choriambic trimeter plus |
| – ∪∪ – ∪ – ∪ – | choriambic dimeter |

| | |
|---|---|
| – ⏑ ⏑ – ⏑ – ⏑ – | choriambic dimeter plus |
| – ⏑ ⏑ – ⏑ – ⏑ – | choriambic dimeter plus |
| – ⏑ ⏑ – ⏑ ⏑ – ⏑ – ⏓ ‖ | alcaic decasyllable |
| – – – ⏑ ⏑ – ⏑ – | glyconic |
| – – – ⏑ ⏑ – ⏑ – | glyconic |
| – ⏓ – ⏑ ⏑ – – ‖ | pherecratean |
| – ⏑ ⏑ – ⏑ – ⏑ – | choriambic dimeter plus |
| – ⏑ ⏑ – ⏑ – ⏑ – | choriambic dimeter plus |
| – ⏑ ⏑ – ⏑ – ⏑ – | choriambic dimeter plus |
| – ⏑ ⏑ – ⏑ ⏑ – ⏑ – – | alcaic decasyllable |

**1082–9 (2nd strophe) = 1090–7 (2nd antistrophe)**

| | |
|---|---|
| – – – ⏑ ⏑ – – | pherecratean |
| ⏑ – – – ⏑ – – – ⏑ – | syncopated iambic trimeter |
| – ⏑ ⏑ – – – | dodrans |
| ⏒ – ⏑ – – ⏑ – | syncopated iambic dimeter |
| – ⏑ – ⏑ – – | ithyphallic |
| ⏑ – ⏑ ⏔ ⏑ – ⏑ – | iambic dimeter |
| ⏑ ⏖ ⏑ – ⏑ ⏖ ⏑ – | iambic dimeter |
| ⏑ – ⏑ – – ⏑ – ⏑ – – | syncopated iambic trimeter catalectic |

**1232–87**

**1232–52 (strophe) = 1253–72 (antistrophe)**

| | |
|---|---|
| ⏑ – ⏑ – | iambic monometer |
| ⏑ – – ⏑ – ⏑ – – ⏑ – | double dochmiac |
| ⏑ ⏖ – ⏑ – | dochmiac |
| (1235–6, 1256–7 | 2 iambic trimeters) |
| ⏑ – ⏒ ‖ | bacchiac |
| (1238, 1259 | iambic trimeter) |
| ⏒ – – – ⏑ – | molossus [bacchiac] plus cretic |
| – ⏖ – ⏒ – | dochmiac |
| ⏑ ⏖ – ⏑ – ⏑ – – ⏑ – | double dochmiac |
| ⏑ – ⏑ – ⏑ – – | iambic dimeter catalectic |
| ⏑ – – ⏑ – – | double bacchiac |
| (1243–4, 1264 + lost line | 2 iambic trimeters) |
| – ⏑ ⏔ – ⏑ – | double cretic |

| | |
|---|---|
| ⊻⌒⌒∪⌒ \| –⌒⌒∪⌒ | double dochmiac |
| –∪⌒–∪⌒–∪⌒ | triple cretic |
| –⌒–∪⌣ \|\| | dochmiac |
| (1251–2, 1271–2 | 2 iambic trimeters) |

## 1273–87 (epode)

| | |
|---|---|
| ∪–∪– | iambic monometer |
| ∪––∪–∪⌒–∪– | double dochmiac plus |
| ––∪–∪–– | iambic dimeter catalectic |
| –⌒∪⌒∪–∪– | iambic dimeter |
| ∪–∪–––∪–∪–– | iambic trimeter catalectic |
| ––∪–––∪–∪–– | iambic trimeter catalectic |
| ––∪–––∪–––∪– | iambic trimeter |
| ∪––∪– | double bacchiac |
| –∪⌒∪–∪–∪–∪–– | trochaic trimeter |
| –∪––∪–∪ | syncopated trochaic dimeter |
| –∪–∪–∪––∪–∪ | syncopated trochaic trimeter |
| –∪–∪–∪–∪ | trochaic dimeter |
| –∪–∪–∪–∪ | trochaic dimeter |
| –∪–∪–∪–∪–– | contracted trochaic trimeter |

## 1384–441

### 1384–90 (strophe) = 1391–7 (antistrophe)

| | |
|---|---|
| ⌒∪–⌒∪– | double cretic |
| ∪⌒–∪–∪––∪– | double dochmiac |
| ⊻–∪–∪–∪–∪–∪– | iambic trimeter |
| ∪⌒–∪–∪––∪– | double dochmiac |
| ∪––∪– | dochmiac |
| ––∪–∪–∪– | iambic dimeter |
| ––∪–∪–∪–⊽–∪– | iambic trimeter |

### 1398–1421 (2nd strophe) = 1422–41 (2nd antistrophe)

| | |
|---|---|
| (1398–1403, 1422–7 | 6 iambic trimeters) |
| ∪⌒–∪– [line lost] | dochmiac |
| (1405–6, 2 lines lost | 2 iambic trimeters) |
| ––∪––∪– | syncopated iambic dimeter plus |
| –∪–∪–– | ithyphallic |
| (1409–12, lost line + 1430–2 | 4 iambic trimeters) |
| (some words lost) | |

| | |
|---|---|
| $-\cup\cup-\cup\cup-\cup-\cup-\overline{\cup}$ | encomiologus |
| $-\cup\cup-\cup\cup-\cup-\cup-$ | encomiologus catalectic |
| (1415–16, 1435–6 | 2 iambic trimeters) |
| $\cup-\cup--\cup-$ | syncopated iambic dimeter |
| $-\cup--\cup-$ | syncopated iambic dimeter |
| $\cup-\cup-\cup-\cup-\overline{\cup}-\cup-$ | iambic trimeter |
| $\cup---\cup-\cup-\smile$ | syncopated iambic trimeter catalectic |

*Note*. In the following places adjacent vowels are pronounced together to give a single long syllable (*synizesis*): 133 μὴ οὐ, 159 ἀχέων, 179 θεός, 838 Ἀμφιάρεων, 1281 ἐγὼ οὐδ', 1287 ἐγὼ οὐδ'.

# APPENDIX 2

## EXCURSUS ON 1087–97

The words of this passage are to be seen against the great conflict of values in the late fifth century. The conflict is between two polarities: on the one side that which is morally good (variously described as ἀγαθόν, δίκαιον, καλόν, εὐκλεές and so on), on the other side that which is expedient (variously described as σοφόν, χρήσιμον, συμφέρον etc.). Characters who represent the older ideals of aristocratic society tend to choose the 'good' principle of action in preference to the 'expedient' (where the two conflict): the situation may be illustrated from the lavish use of καλόν by Electra in her early exchanges with Chrysothemis and Clytaemnestra in this play (cf. 345f.). For Electra either absolute καλόν is itself σοφόν, or (if σοφία is something else) then σοφία is to be rejected.

It was still possible for the remnants of the Athenian aristocracy to preserve such attitudes at the end of the fifth century, and Sophocles' aristocrats are far too vivid and urgent creations not to represent in some degree people he knew from the actual life of his times. But ordinary people had recognised that the pressures of the age rendered such ideals impracticable or indeed disastrous (as they proved for the people of Melos, who tried to hold out in pursuit of an ideal of independence against the Athenian empire, and were ruthlessly suppressed, the men being massacred and the women and children sold into slavery: Thuc. 5. 87ff.).

In such circumstances, it became common-sense to 'by-pass' (cf. 338n.) the καλόν issue, and to adhere in practice to what was συμφέρον. In cases where one was subject to government based upon naked force (as in the case of the *de facto* government of Mycenae by Aegisthus and Clytaemnestra), it became practical prudence to submit to the authority of the despots (though not of course to acquiesce in it). Hence the principle of σοφία (= νοῦς = εὖ φρονεῖν) which Chrysothemis more than once declares (and the Chorus, being ordinary Mycenaeans, support her in this, cf. 219–20 and 1014–18).

So much for the two points of view – the moral and the amoral, the noble and the ignoble, the idealistic and the common-sense – which are opposed to one another throughout the *Electra*. There sprang up however a third, truly sinister, point of view during the late fifth century. The 'ordinary' citizens (Chrysothemis and the Chorus) certainly repudiate heroic idealism throughout the play, but they do so somewhat shamefacedly; what they do *not* do is to try, cynically, to claim that the policy which they advocate is not merely 'expedient' but 'good' as well. They do not try to get the best of two possible worlds (though it is true that Chrysothemis does say at 398 καλόν γε μέντοι μὴ 'ξ ἀβουλίας πεσεῖν). But, since hardly anyone likes to go on feeling 'not good' all the time, there must have been a great temptation to do that: and we read in Thucydides (2. 53) that, under the stress of the Plague at Athens, standards became so confused that τὸ μὲν προσταλαιπωρεῖν τῷ δόξαντι καλῷ οὐδεὶς πρόθυμος ἦν...ὅτι δὲ ἤδη τε ἡδὺ πανταχόθεν τε ἐς αὐτὸ κερδαλέον, τοῦτο καὶ καλὸν καὶ χρήσιμον κατέστη. The person who showed the way to identifying συμφέρον with καλόν was the sophist Protagoras (cf. 466n.); and as a teacher of juristic eloquence he taught his pupils how to present an ἄδικος λόγος in court and make it victorious over the δίκαιος λόγος (Aristophanes, *Clouds* 882ff.). The ἄδικος λόγος did not of course (outside Comedy) actually *say* that it was ἄδικος; it said, no doubt, that it was in fact δίκαιος – not in the ordinary, approved sense, but in its own special relative sense.

This teaching led, at the close of the century, and not much later (if at all) than the composition of Sophocles' *Electra*, to the moral nihilism of Antiphon the Sophist, Thrasymachus who features in Plato, *Rep.* 1 (with his 'Justice is the expediency of the stronger'), and Critias the leader of the illegal and tyrannous government of the Thirty. It was embraced by at least some of the aristocratic minds at Athens. The most illuminating instance of the application of such thinking to politics is provided by the character of Odysseus in *Philoctetes*. Odysseus represents to Neoptolemus the political *expediency* of getting Philoctetes' bow away from him, and using him and it in accordance with Helenus' prophecy to bring the war against Troy to a successful conclusion. But this involves tricking Philoctetes and lying to him. Neoptolemus, who represents the old, true type of aristocratic thinking, objects because telling lies is 'wrong' (cf. 108

οὐκ αἰσχρὸν ἡγῇ δῆτα τὰ ψευδῆ λέγειν;) – wrong, that is, in the absolute sense, in Antigone's or Electra's sense. Odysseus replies at first (111) ὅταν τι δρᾷς ἐς κέρδος, οὐκ ὀκνεῖν πρέπει 'you must not admit moral scruple when you do anything likely to benefit you', i.e. κερδαλέον is preferable to δίκαιον: the parallel to *Electra* 61 is exact, and should warn us that it is the same moral ground that we are treading, but he ends up with 'Do it', ὡς τοῦτό γ' ἔρξας δύο φέρῃ δωρήματα (118), which he explains by σοφός τ' ἂν αὐτὸς κἀγαθὸς κεκλῇ' ἅμα i.e. if you do it, you will get the best of two possible worlds; you would have, *being one and the same person*, the name of being *both* 'wise' and 'good' (Odysseus plays here, of course, on the two senses of ἀγαθός = both 'aristocratic' ( = καλὸς κἀγαθός) and 'successful' (in this case successful at bringing the Trojan War to a successful conclusion); for this sense of ἀγαθός cf. Adkins, *Merit and responsibility* 30ff.). The parallelism of the *Philoctetes* and the *Electra* passages is so exact (δύο φέρειν = δύο φέρῃ δωρήματα, ἐν ἑνὶ λόγῳ = αὐτός. . .ἅμα, σοφά τ' ἄριστα τε = σοφός τε. . .κἀγαθός, κεκλῆσθαι = ἂν κεκλῇ'; and cf. *Phil.* 84f. κᾆτα τὸν λοιπὸν χρόνον | κέκλησο πάντων εὐσεβέστατος βροτῶν – εὐσεβέστατος = a variant of δικαιότατος, ἄριστος) that, coupled with the logic which has led us to emend τὸ μὴ καλὸν καθοπλίσασα, it must in fact be the key to the thought.

And this leads us to the following conclusion. The Chorus in our passage is complimenting Electra precisely on *not* doing what Odysseus signally does (or recommends Neoptolemus to do) in *Philoctetes*. Odysseus' 'goodness' consists in doing what is expedient and *calling* it good (earning therefore the right in the process to be called both 'wise' and 'good'), Electra's consists in adhering to 'goodness' (her own, absolute 'goodness'), even at the price of parting company with 'wisdom'. She has *resisted the temptation* to cultivate a relative, compromising kind of 'goodness' (*à la* Protagoras, *à la* Odysseus) because that is to cultivate the art of the ἄδικος λόγος and to 'give arms to' τὰ μὴ καλά ( = what is not good according to Electra's own absolute standard of 'goodness'). There could not be a better description of the Protagorean ethic and the Protagorean technique than to call it 'giving arms to τὰ μὴ καλά'.

# APPENDIX 3

## THE TRANSMISSION OF
## THE TEXT[1]

Sophocles was a highly successful playwright in his own time: he won more victories[2] than any other known tragedian, and he remained an undisputed classic throughout antiquity. To a large extent he must have owed his great prestige to the actual performances of his plays; although plays were performed only once at the City Dionysia during the fifth century it is very likely that admired pieces were put on again at the dramatic festivals in the demes of Attica, the Rural Dionysia,[3] and we know that in the fourth century revivals were very common at these festivals. After 386 B.C. an old play was a regular part of the programme of the City Dionysia, and Sophocles was certainly one of the authors whose plays were revived,[4] though he was not as outstandingly popular as Euripides. Even so, we cannot account satisfactorily for the many allusions to his work in the fifth and fourth centuries and for its survival in bulk into the Hellenistic period without assuming that written texts of the plays circulated freely more or less from the start. It is hardly possible that these texts were all faithful reproductions of what Sophocles wrote, especially since for the first two centuries the plays must have been transmitted without any defence against corruption and interpolation. There was no 'standard' scholarly edition to exert a stabilising influence (Aristotle and his followers, though much interested in tragedy, do not

---

[1] For a general survey of the background see L. D. Reynolds and N. G. Wilson, *Scribes and scholars* (1968).

[2] About two-thirds of his 123 plays must have been successful: he won eighteen victories at the Dionysia = seventy-two plays, and probably six at the Lenaea, where the number of plays submitted by each dramatist is not known for certain. Cf. A. Dain, *Sophocle* tome I (1955) viii–x.

[3] A. W. Pickard-Cambridge, *The dramatic festivals of Athens²* (1968) 52 and 99.

[4] Revivals: *Antigone* (Dem. 19. 246–7), a popular favourite; *Oenomaus* (at Kollytos, Dem. 18. 180); *Tyro* (Menander, *Ep.* 108ff.).

seem to have concerned themselves with recension of the text),[1] and in a period when the plays were still performed they were at risk from the interpolations and alterations of the actors. Our extant Sophocles, it is true, shows far fewer traces of histrionic meddling[2] than Euripides, but Sophocles was included in the well-known decree of Lycurgus (c. 338–326 B.C.),[3] which provided that an official copy of the plays of all three great tragedians be kept in the public archives and the actors compelled to keep to this text, and the implication must be that his work too was thought to need protection. Scholars have doubted whether the decree had any lasting effect, but it is possible that the official Athenian copy found its way to Alexandria in the reign of Ptolemy III (246–221 B.C.) and was used by the Alexandrian editors, so that it may have exerted some long-term influence.[4]

The work of these editors was crucially important. Through their threefold activity of classification, recension, and exegesis they imposed order on the mass of material salvaged from the past and established texts which had a remarkable influence on the future. The key figure for Sophocles is Aristophanes of Byzantium (c. 257–c. 180 B.C.), who seems to have concerned himself at any rate with classification and recension. In the *Life* of Sophocles, which is preserved in many of our MSS, Aristophanes is quoted as the authority for the number and genuineness of the plays; it is interesting that as many as seven plays attributed to Sophocles were regarded as spurious by the third century B.C.[5] Our evidence for Aristophanes' recension of the text is rather fragmentary but on the whole convincing; variant readings are ascribed to him in some of the papyri,[6] and there is one

[1] For a general discussion of Peripatetic literary studies see A. J. Podlecki, *Phoenix* 23 (1969) 114–37. A few traces of the work on Sophocles of these early scholars are preserved in the *Life* and in the scholion on *O.C.* 900.

[2] D. L. Page, *Actors' interpolations in Greek tragedy* (1934) 91.

[3] [Plutarch], *Decem oratorum vitae* 7, 841 F.

[4] R. Pfeiffer, *History of classical scholarship* (1968) 82, warns against overestimating the critical value of this copy.

[5] *Vita Soph.* 18: ἔχει δὲ δράματα, ὥς φησιν Ἀριστοφάνης, ρλ΄. τούτων δὲ νενόθευται ζ΄. (reading ζ΄ with G against ιζ΄ in A: this squares with the total number of genuine plays given by the Suda). According to Pfeiffer (287, cf. 133), Aristophanes probably made this statement in his supplement to the *Pinakes*, Callimachus' great critical inventory of Greek literature.

[6] Variant readings are ascribed to Αρν, Αρ, and Αριν in P.Oxy. 9 (1912) 1174 (*Ichneutae*), to Αρ in P.Oxy. 15 (1922) 1805 (*Trach.*), and to Αρι in

reference to him by name in the scholia.[1] We can also be reasonably certain that he was the first to divide the lyrics into cola (previously they had been written out like prose) and that he composed brief introductions, ὑποθέσεις, to the plays: the extant *Hypothesis I* to *Antigone* is ascribed to him in the MSS, and his introductions were probably the basis for the *Hypotheses* of some of the other plays. There is no evidence that he also wrote commentaries, but it is very likely that he interpreted Sophocles orally, and not impossible that his pupil Callistratus published his lecture notes.[2] But it may have been Aristarchus (c. 216–c. 144 B.C.) who was responsible for the first thoroughgoing set of commentaries (ὑπομνήματα); here again we are reduced to guessing from fragmentary evidence.[3] At all events we can be certain that *some* fundamental work of exegesis went on at Alexandria, because the extant scholia are known to derive ultimately from the work of Didymus in the second half of the first century B.C., and Didymus habitually based his commentaries on earlier authorities. The scholia in fact contain several explicit references to 'the commentators', who must be Didymus' predecessors.

The type of information (though not always the critical judgments) offered by these earliest commentators was comparatively sophisticated: they discussed textual problems, grammar and usage, and points of antiquarian or mythological interest, but as time went on readers of Sophocles needed more elementary help, such as paraphrases of difficult expressions, and the old commentaries were adapted and new ones composed to suit contemporary needs. The scholia as we have them are the product of a long process of excerpting and re-working;[4] it is perhaps not surprising that their content ranges from the profoundly learned to the preposterously naïve. They appear in our medieval MSS as marginal commentaries, but this was not the original arrangement: to begin with the ὑπομνήματα from which they

P.Oxy. 27 (1962) 2452 (*Theseus*, if correctly ascribed to Sophocles: see H. Lloyd-Jones, *Gnomon* 35 (1963) 434–6), but the editor of this fragment, E. G. Turner, is not certain that the letters could not be read as an abbreviation for Aristarchus (Αρχ).                    [1] On *Ajax* 746.

[2] Pfeiffer 210, cf. W. S. Barrett, *Euripides, Hippolytos* (1964) 47 n. 1.

[3] Pfeiffer 222–3.

[4] Sallustius (fourth century A.D.) seems to have been one of the most influential revisers of the scholia. On the history of the scholia see V. De Marco, *Scholia in Sophoclis Oedipum Coloneum* (1952) xvi–xxvii.

were compiled were issued as separate works, physically independent of the texts on which they commented. These had a quite separate transmission for a long period,[1] with the important result that the scholia sometimes preserve readings which have disappeared from the text of all our MSS, e.g. *Phil.* 954, where all the MSS read αὖ θανοῦμαι, but the scholion in L offers the correct αὐανοῦμαι as a variant.

The importance of the Alexandrians is beyond question; but we cannot tell to what extent their work altered the text of Sophocles or how quickly it standardised the tradition, because there is no pre-Alexandrian papyrus of any of the seven extant plays and therefore we cannot compare the state of the text before and after the time of Aristophanes. Probably we ought to consider 'the Alexandrian edition' as the beginning of a process that went on developing for several generations: for instance, Theon, a scholar of the first century A.D., is quoted repeatedly in the papyrus of the *Ichneutae* as a source of variant readings, and it is quite likely that he produced a recension of his own. As Pfeiffer has pointed out (189), 'there was a continuous and lively scholarly activity in the field of drama throughout the later centuries which has obscured its beginnings in Alexandria'.

The papyri do, however, provide some useful information: they reinforce the impression made by quotations and references in Roman and later Greek authors that a wide range of Sophocles' plays was still being read in the second century A.D. There are no papyri written after about the middle of the third century which have been certainly identified as belonging to the lost plays; this is what we should expect, judging by the way in which direct quotations of Sophocles in other authors tend about this date to concentrate on our seven extant plays. But there are not enough papyri of Sophocles to throw light on the question of why these seven survived and not others. The orthodox view since Wilamowitz has been that someone in the late second century made a selection from each of the three great dramatists for

---

[1] How long is still disputed: see N. G. Wilson, *C.Q.* 17 (1967) 244–56, Barrett, *Hippolytos* 49. We can be sure that the commentaries were transmitted independently of the text for at least three centuries, and possibly much longer, since the regular use of margins for full-scale commentaries cannot have started until the codex had replaced the roll as the standard book form (between the second and the fourth century A.D.). E. G. Turner (*Greek papyri* (1968) 121–3) argues convincingly for a gradual process of transition.

use in schools; this so imposed itself on the reading public that the rest of the plays gradually lost their influence and thereby their chance of survival. However, it has recently been shown for Euripides[1] that the 'select' plays were already more widely read from the Alexandrian period onwards, so that the selection may perhaps be seen as a symptom of a well-established trend[2] rather than as a new departure, since the non-select plays were in any case losing ground. For Sophocles we can trace no such clear pattern, because none of the papyri of the extant plays antedates the second century A.D.

Whatever may be the true historical background to the making (or evolution) of the selection, Wilamowitz was certainly right to stress the importance of its use in schools; it cannot be an exaggeration to say that Sophocles survived to the extent that he did because the plays, or some of them, were 'set books'. Even in periods of considerable cultural decay *some* school texts are still wanted, and it looks from the evidence as though some of Sophocles' plays, *Ajax* in particular, were used as standard text books in schools not only in late antiquity but for most of the Byzantine Middle Ages. For Greek literature there is nothing strictly comparable to the Dark Ages of the medieval West; pagan literature, or a minute selection of it, was a standard element in Byzantine education, and there were even periods in the history of the Greek East when scholarly study of pagan texts was a highly respectable intellectual activity. Our latest Sophoclean fragment from antiquity belongs to the late sixth or early seventh century[3] and our earliest medieval MS probably to the late tenth,[4] but there is evidence that during the intervening period, or at any rate the part of it from the mid-ninth century onwards, Sophocles was an author familiar to every educated inhabitant of Constantinople.[5]

[1] By Barrett (*Hippolytos* 51–3) and C. H. Roberts (*Mus. Helv.* 10 (1953) 270).

[2] Barrett suggests (*a*) that a play's popularity may have depended on whether or not a commentary was available, and (*b*) that the selection may have become permanent when the codex superseded the roll as the standard book form, and seven plays were conveniently accommodated by a single codex.

[3] P.Ant. 2. 72 (parchment): fragment of *Electra*.          [4] L: see below.

[5] Arethas in a letter mentions *Ajax* as the play every schoolboy knew (S. B. Kougeas, ὁ Καισαρείας Ἀρέθας καὶ τὸ ἔργον αὐτοῦ (1913) 142, 122) The Suda, which was compiled about A.D. 1000, quotes frequently from *Aj.*, *El.*, *O.T.*, and *O.C.*

It is true that from about the sixth to the mid-ninth century there can
have been almost no interest in Greek tragedy beyond the limited
needs of the schools, and that the Iconoclasts, who were in the
ascendant in the eighth century, were actively hostile to pagan
literature, so that a great many works known to late antiquity had
vanished by the time of the δεύτερος ἑλληνισμός, the great resurgence
of interest in the ancient world which took place in the ninth century.
This was a period of crucial importance for the survival of classical
texts. A new type of script, minuscule, had recently been developed as
a book-hand to replace the uncial which had been standard from
antiquity, and old texts now had to be laboriously transliterated into
the new characters. Many works which survived into the ninth
century must have been lost because no one was interested enough to
have them transliterated, but once a text had been copied into
minuscules its chances of survival were very good, since the learned
men of the ninth century greatly reinvigorated the intellectual
climate, and classical literature was never seriously challenged for the
rest of the Middle Ages. These scholars seem to have been more
interested in prose writers than in poets, but our extant MSS prove
that at any rate in the tenth and eleventh centuries there was a lively
demand for poetic texts, and for the twelfth century we know of two
scholars, Tzetzes and Eustathius, who took some interest in tragedy
though they did not produce recensions of the plays. Eustathius
(fl. c. 1160–92) is quite important for the text of Sophocles because of
his many quotations (he has preserved a line of *Antigone* (1167) which
is missing from all our MSS), but we have to wait until the end of the
thirteenth century, the so-called Palaeologan Renaissance, before
we find evidence of large-scale scholarly work on the tragedians.

This period, from about 1290 until about 1320, was one of intense
activity in classical studies. Now more systematically than at any time
since the Alexandrian period individual scholars set about producing
new recensions of the texts of ancient authors and new scholia to go
with them, with results that were sometimes beneficial but often
merely compounded corruption.[1] The man who seems to have given
this movement its first main impetus was the monk Maximus Planudes
(c. 1255–1305). We do not know whether he produced a full-scale

---

[1] On the Sophoclean recensions of this period see A. Turyn, *T.A.Ph.A.* 80
(1949) 94–173.

recension of any play of Sophocles, but he at any rate wrote scholia on the 'Byzantine triad' (*Ajax*, *Electra* and *Oedipus Tyrannus*), which appear in a group of MSS alongside the scholia of his pupil Manuel Moschopulus. Moschopulus' recension of the three plays (*c.* 1290) was one of the major events in the history of the text: it became widely popular,[1] it stimulated further work on Sophocles, and indirectly (through the manuscript A) it exerted an influence which is still strongly felt. It was soon followed by the edition of Thomas Magister, who was perhaps fired with the ambition to outdo Moschopulus. His commentaries (on the triad and *Antigone*) contain polemic against his predecessor, and it is possible that he established a text of all seven plays, but his scholarship is markedly inferior. The best known of the scholars of this generation is Demetrius Triclinius, who drew heavily on Moschopulus and Thomas in his texts and commentaries, but has the distinction of being the first critic since antiquity to take an intelligent interest in lyric metre. His recension was extremely influential: Turnebus used it as a basis for his text of 1553 which dominated Sophoclean studies until Brunck's edition appeared in 1786. The Byzantine editors have been criticised for treating their texts in too cavalier a fashion on the basis of too little knowledge, and it is true that they were far more like modern scholars than like the Alexandrian editors in their fondness for emendation, but they deserve some credit for having stimulated a vigorous interest in Sophocles, and for having occasionally recovered genuine readings for us, whether by conjecture, or by collating old MSS lost to later generations.[2]

It was in the Byzantine world centred on Constantinople that Greek civilisation survived until the end of the Middle Ages, but by the greatest good fortune a new market for Greek texts was opened up in the West about half a century before the Turks virtually put an end to Byzantine culture in 1453. Through their study of the Latin authors of antiquity the Italian humanists were inspired with the desire to recover the Greek classics: they invited scholars from Constantinople to teach in Italy, organised book-collecting missions to the East, and hired Greek scribes to make copies. As a result there was a steady flow

---

[1] More than seventy Moschopulean MSS are still extant.

[2] On the use of old MSS by scholars in the thirteenth and fourteenth centuries see R. Browning, *B.I.C.S.* 7 (1960) 11–19.

of Greek books into Italy in the early fifteenth century, among them the manuscript L of Sophocles, which was acquired in Constantinople by Giovanni Aurispa in the course of one of his ambitious expeditions in search of texts (1421–3) and sent to his friend Niccolo de' Niccoli. Greek authors were slower to find their way into print than Latin, and it was not until the last decade of the century that the first systematic attempts were made to print the Greek classics. In 1502 the seven plays of Sophocles were printed at Venice by Aldus Manutius, seven years after four plays of Euripides and sixteen years before Aeschylus, an order which fairly represents Sophocles' standing from the fourth century B.C. onwards. Ever since the time of the *editio princeps* his survival has been assured, at least for as long as Western civilisation survives.[1]

## THE MANUSCRIPTS

Alexander Turyn's fundamental study of the MSS of Sophocles appeared in 1952;[2] much detailed investigation remains to be done, but his work has greatly clarified the nature of the tradition and defined the questions that still have to be answered. Turyn began by identifying the recensions of Moschopulus, Thomas Magister, and Triclinius, and separating off the very numerous copies of these editions from the so-called 'old' MSS, i.e. those copies (of whatever date) that offer a more or less uncontaminated and unedited version of the text of antiquity. Following the lead given by V. De Marco in his work on the scholia, Turyn distinguished two families in the old tradition, which are now generally called Laurentian and Roman after an important representative of each class. The Laurentian family consists of L (Laur. 32, 9, probably late tenth century), and the Leiden palimpsest Λ or P (B.P.G. 60 A, of the same date as L), which was first brought to light by J. Vürtheim in 1926 and found to be a close though fragmentary relative of L. There is no doubt that these two MSS should be classed as 'old',[3] but some scholars have

---

[1] For the history of the printed text see U. von Wilamowitz-Moellendorff, *Einleitung in die griechische Tragödie* (1907) ch. 4; R. C. Jebb, *Sophocles, the text of the seven plays* (1897) xxxi–xliv.

[2] *Studies in the manuscript tradition of the tragedies of Sophocles, Illinois studies in language and literature*, 36, 1–2 (1952).

[3] Though of course it would be surprising if they were quite untouched by emendation, cf. e.g. *Aj.* 1205.

been reluctant to give the same status to the Roman family, which comprises G (Laur.Conv.Soppr. 152, dated 1282, widely used by editors since the time of Dindorf), R (Vat.Gr. 2291, fifteenth century), Q (Par.Suppl.Gr. 109, sixteenth century), and M (Mut.Est.α.T.9.4, fifteenth century, containing scholia only). Further investigation of these and other MSS, particularly of the group which Turyn calls *deteriores*, could well alter the details of the picture, but provisionally it may be said that the Roman family is a class independent of the Laurentian and free enough from interpolation to be taken seriously as a witness to the old tradition.[1]

The most controversial theory advanced by Turyn concerns the famous manuscript A (Par.Gr. 2712), which has enjoyed great prestige ever since it was used by Brunck; it has also been influential in an indirect way, first because one of its close relatives was used as the basis of the Aldine edition, and secondly because its scribe introduced a large number of corrections into the text of L, which until recently were not recognised as deriving from A. Turyn maintained that A is essentially an edited text, the work of some Byzantine scholar who relied mainly on Moschopulus in the triad and based his text of the remaining four plays on the Laurentian and Roman families with many interpolations of his own. It is now beyond question that A is not the representative of an uncontaminated tradition: its closeness to Moschopulus in the triad and its general concern for metrical correctness (in iambics)[2] mark it out as quite different in character from an 'old' MS. But what is by no means settled yet is whether the editor responsible for A (and its relatives) had access to old sources now lost: for example, did he, as Dain has suggested,[3] transliterate and emend an uncial MS found in the thirteenth century, or did he at any rate collate an old text and incorporate some of its readings in his recension? Turyn believes that there is nothing in A that derives from an old tradition independent of the Laurentian and Roman families: in his view the unique readings of A are Byzantine emendations. It may well never be possible to answer these questions defini-

---

[1] For collations of G, R, and Q see *C.Q.* 17 (1967) 52–79 (*Ajax*) and *C.Q.* 19 (1969) 57–85 (*Philoctetes*).

[2] The results are not always happy: e.g. *Phil.* 933. John Jackson made this point in 1912 (*C.Q.* 6 (1912) 152–3).

[3] *Sophocle* tome 1 (1955) xlvi.

tively, but further collations of other MSS[1] and further study of A's readings may reduce the area of controversy.[2] The issue is complicated by the fact that A's precise date is not known; traditionally it has been assigned to the thirteenth century, but Turyn has argued for a somewhat later date, which would fit the chronology of the Byzantine recensions more satisfactorily.[3]

In the present state of our knowledge we cannot determine the date of the common source of our medieval MSS; there is one fact, however, which commands attention: the striking homogeneity of the MS tradition. It is only very rarely that the MSS diverge at all widely, and in almost every major crux they all essentially share the corruption; the papyri, too, are on the whole very closely in accord with the medieval MSS. Thus we no doubt have the means of reconstructing with tolerable accuracy the vulgate current in late antiquity, but between that and the autograph of Sophocles there is a long gap, which can be bridged only by the skill of the textual critic.

The text of A. C. Pearson used in this edition is an eclectic one based on a large number of MSS, with L and A as leading witnesses. The manuscript G is quoted from time to time (symbol Γ); of the *recentiores* the most frequently cited is T, representing the Triclinian recension. The Suda ('Suidas') is an important secondary witness for the text of *Electra*.

---

[1] In particular the Byzantine recensions and Turyn's *deteriores*.

[2] Recent discussion of A: R. M. Rattenbury, *C.R.* 4 (1954) 104–5; J. C. Kamerbeek, *Mnemosyne* 11 (1958) 25–31; P. E. Easterling, *C.Q.* 10 (1960) 51–64; H. P. Dietz, *Thomas Magistros' recension of the Sophoclean plays O.C., Trach., Phil.* (Diss. Illinois 1965) 201–22; R. D. Dawe, *P.C.Ph.S.* 14 (1968) 5–7.

[3] Cf. Dietz, 58–65.

# INDEXES

(Numerals in square brackets refer to pages of the Introduction, other numerals to lines of the play.)

## 1. *Greek words*

## 2. General

## 3. *Deviations from the Oxford Classical Text*

## DATE DUE

| | | | |
|---|---|---|---|
| OCT - 4 1998 | | | |
| | | | |
| | | | |
| | | | |
| | | | |
| | | | |
| | | | |
| | | | |
| | | | |
| | | | |
| | | | |
| | | | |
| | | | |
| | | | |
| | | | |
| | | | |
| | 261-2500 | | Printed in USA |